THREE PERSPECTIVES ON ETHNICITY

Blacks, Chicanos, and Native Americans

Three Perspectives on Ethnicity

BLACKS, CHICANOS, AND NATIVE AMERICANS

BY

Carlos E. Cortés, Arlin I. Ginsburg,
Alan W. F. Green, James A. Joseph

G. P. PUTNAM'S SONS, NEW YORK

Capricorn Books, New York

SBN: 399-11485-8

Library of Congress Cataloging in Publication Data
Main entry under title:

Three perspectives on ethnicity--Blacks, Chicanos, and Native Americans.

Includes bibliographical references.

1. Afro-Americans--Addresses, essays, lectures. 2. Mexican Americans--Addresses, essays, lectures. 3. Indians of North America--Addresses, essays, lectures. I. Cortes, Carlos.

E185.T47 1975 301.45'1'0420973 75-29178

PRINTED IN THE UNITED STATES OF AMERICA

Contents

THREE PERSPECTIVES ON ETHNICITY

Blacks, Chicanos, and Native Americans

Introduction

"With Liberty and Justice for All" . . . "All Men Are Created Equal" . . . "Land of the Free" . . . "Secure the Blessings of Liberty to Ourselves and Our Posterity." So go some of the basic refrains of our nation's past. They express the promise of America, the hopes and goals to which the United States has dedicated and rededicated itself.

But historical realities have not lived up to this glowing promise. And as the United States reaches its bicentennial year celebration, a serious inspection of the contemporary scene reveals how far short of these hopes and goals the nation has fallen. This gap has been particularly evident in the case of ethnic minorities, for whom the United States has too often meant conquest and repression, discrimination and exploitation, suffering and frustration.

This anthology looks at the experiences of three United States ethnic minorities—Blacks, Chicanos, and Native Americans. Our decision to limit the scope of the book to three groups in no way implies that they are the only ones who have suffered and struggled against discrimination in the nation's history. Chinese Americans, Japanese Americans, Puerto Ricans, Hawaiians, Eskimos, some white ethnic groups, certain religious minorities, and women, for example, have each encountered various problems trying to achieve the promise of America. To expand further the number of groups covered, however, would have made the book unwieldly. Moreover, it would have severely impeded the achievement of the basic intent of the book—to illuminate some of the significant themes of ethnic minority history in the United States while providing sufficient depth on each included group, making its particular experience comprehensible both as to uniqueness and as to comparability with experiences of other ethnic minorities. Therefore, we decided to focus on only three groups in our analysis.

The anthology is divided into six sections which cover, in a thematic manner, United States history from its colonial origins to the present. Chapter One deals with the colonial and early national period of the country. It emphasizes the origins and institutionalization in America of English and Anglo-American attitudes toward Spaniards, Blacks, Native Americans, and Mexicans. Alternatively, it indicates the image of Anglo-Americans as they came to be seen by Blacks, Mexicans, and Native Americans.

Chapter Two focuses on nineteenth-century wars engaged in by the United States involving current and future ethnic minorities and the aftermath of these conflicts. The chapter first looks at the thorny question of United States ideals, as expressed in official documents arising from these wars. In contrast to these ideals stand the realities of post-war experience. The chapter examines these realities in terms of both destruction of ethnic minority power and responses by ethnic minorities.

Chapter Three examines the impact of an urbanizing society on ethnic minorities. Each of the groups studied in this book has had a special relationship to the land; each has been affected by urbanization; and each has had its unique patterns of migration, with resulting physical and psychic dislocation. But for all, the city, once the embodiment of dreams of a better future for ethnic minorities, turned out for many to be a nightmare of suffering.

Chapter Four looks at the impact of United States institutions on ethnic minorities during the twentieth century. Three institutions are singled out for examination—government and the law, the military, and the educational system. The articles in this section reflect the variety of relationships which have developed between these institutions and ethnic minorities. As the articles reveal, ethnic peoples have viewed such institutions as a source of hope, but have often found them a source of deep frustration and disappointment.

Chapter Five focuses on the development of ethnic self-affirmation. The chapter looks at efforts made by ethnic minorities to strengthen their own group self-image and their concomitant efforts to challenge stereotypes which others have tried to impose upon them.

Chapter Six dramatizes the post-World II response of ethnic minorities to societal repression. The first section reflects the ongoing debate among members of ethnic minority groups over the goals that should be sought, either as individuals or as groups. The rest of the chapter illustrates the variety of strategies and tactics which ethnic minorities have adopted in the struggle for their many goals.

And the struggle has not yet ended, as the goals have not been reached. For the nation's ethnic minorities, America has fallen far short of its stirring promises. But as the nation celebrates the completion of its 200th year, the hope still exists that America's third century will bring what its first two have failed to produce—the fulfillment of those promises and the realization of the dream of equality, justice, peace, understanding, and happiness for all.

I. Colonial Heritage and Early National Period

When English colonists settled permanently in the Western Hemisphere in 1607, they brought with them more than material goods. They carried also the values, attitudes, and prejudices of the mother country. Among these were particular views—some as yet only vaguely articulated—of Spaniards, Africans, and Native Americans.

The origins of many of these views can be found in the reign of Elizabeth I (1558-1603), the period of England's first significant contact with the world outside Europe. Following the lead of Portugal and Spain, adventuresome sea captains like John Hawkins, Francis Drake, Martin Frobisher, and Walter Raleigh cruised the Atlantic; some even moved into the Pacific in search of riches and a way to the Orient. The commercial promise of the lands they encountered was immediately apparent.

In 1562 Hawkins carried his first cargo of slaves from West Africa to Hispaniola. Soon, with tacit royal approval, English adventurers began to prey on Spanish treasure ships carrying gold and silver from America to Europe. At the same time collections of travel narratives by Richard Hakluyt, Samuel Purchas, and others proliferated, presenting tales of strange lands and bizarre peoples oceans removed. Such exotic figures as Othello, the black Moor, and Caliban, the New World savage, entered the mainstream of English literature. Philosophers throughout England and the Continent speculated on the scientific and metaphysical implications of lands, peoples, religions, and customs so foreign to their own.

England's overseas expansion was complicated by tensions generated by European religious and national rivalries. The accession of Elizabeth brought ultimately a Protestant triumph in England's domestic religious turmoil. As defender of the Roman Catholic faith and smarting from English incursions into his nation's monopoly in the Caribbean, Phillip II of Spain burned with desire to drive Elizabeth from the throne and her "sea dogs" from the Spanish Main. A similar antagonism existed in France, where Protestantism had been on the defensive since the St. Bartholomew's Day killing of thousands of Huguenots in 1572. Fearing that a Catholic victory in France would increase Spanish influence in Paris, the English aided the beleaguered Huguenots.

Confronted, they believed, by enemies of God as much as of themselves and buoyed by a common pride in English overseas exploits and domestic achievements, Englishmen drew together as a nation during Elizabeth's reign. In the process of defining their nationality they established their own English characteristics as standards against which the rest of humanity would be evaluated. The customs, institutions, and physical appearances of others were judged either good or bad, civilized or savage, according to how closely they resembled or how widely they varied from the way the English perceived themselves.

In the Western Hemisphere English settlers encountered persons of other societies—Indians already inhabiting the land, black Africans imported to the colonies as a labor supply, and Spaniards in the Caribbean and along the southern frontier. English relations with these groups were in part determined by the opinions they had brought with them to America. In turn those opinions were affected by day-to-day relations with non-English groups.

The first two sections of Chapter I describe early English attitudes toward Spaniards, Mexicans, Blacks, and Native Americans, and trace the development and institutionalization of those attitudes from the colonial period into the nineteenth century. The third section reveals the thoughts of Blacks, Mexicans, and Indians about Anglo America during the same period.

A. ENGLISH ATTITUDES TOWARD SPANISH CATHOLICS, AFRICANS, AND THE NEW WORLD INHABITANTS

This section presents early English attitudes toward Spaniards, Africans, and Native Americans. We are concerned here with English attitudes because England produced the dominant cultural heritage of what was to become the United States of America.

Bartolomé de Las Casas, the great Spanish reformer-priest who cried out against Spanish cruelty toward natives of the West Indies, was a favorite of the English avid for news of Spanish depradations. They used Las Casas' writings to support their belief that Catholicism combined with innate depravity to produce the Spanish character. This belief, nurtured through generations of tension and war between England and Spain, grew into the so-called Black Legend of Spain—that set of unquestioned negative stereotypes employed by Englishmen and other non-Hispanic Europeans to describe all Spanish-speaking peoples. The introduction to the first English edition of Las Casas' *The Tears of the Indians . . .* reveals the nature of English prejudice against Spaniards.

Winthrop D. Jordan has examined the travel narratives, philosophical writings, and belles lettres of the sixteenth century to describe the complex mosaic of English impressions and speculations about black Africans. Such attitudes and impressions—and similar ones formed as the number of Africans increased in the colonies—became important factors in the debasement of Blacks in early America. The Jordan selection describes Elizabethan attitudes and shows the predisposition of the English to view Blacks unfavorably.

Roy Harvey Pearce's article, like the preceding two, is a study of the English responses to "different" people. Puritan attitudes toward the American Indian, expressed in the word "savage," were formed as much by the English desire for Indian land as by native manners and appearance. Here for the first time we see the pattern for America's later western expansion—the resolute acquisition of land and the destruction of indigenous cultures in the name of civilization, divine election, Christian destiny, and the salvation of the savage.

1. INTRODUCTION TO BARTOLOMÉ DE LAS CASAS'

*The Tears of the Indians . . .**

TO ALL TRUE ENGLISH-MEN

Never had we so just cause to exclaim, in the words of the Prophet Jeremiah; O that our heads were waters, and our eyes fountains of tears, that we might weep for the Effusion of so much Innocent Blood which provok'd these, sad Relations of devout CASAUS, by reason of the cruel Slaughters and Butcheries of the Jesuitical Spaniards, perpetrated upon so many Millions of poor innocent Heathens, who having only the light of Nature, not knowing their Saviour Jesus Christ, were sacrificed to the Politick Interest and Avarice of the wicked Spaniards.

The blood of Ireland, spilt by the same Faction, in comparison of these Massacres, was but as a Drop to the Ocean. It was the Saying of Christ himself, the Son of Mercy, and Redeemer of the World, That we ought not to cast the Childrens Bread to dogs: But what would he have judg'd of those, that not onely cast the Bread, but the Blood; and not onely the Blood, but the Innocent Blood of men, women and children, to satisfie the contemptible

*Bartolomé de Las Casas, *The Tears of the Indians* . . . First English edition. (London, 1656), Reprinted by permission of the Henry E. Huntington Library, San Marino, California.

hunger of their Hounds? The intention of these men was Murder; and they kill'd up the poor Indians, not as if they had been their Fellow-Mortals, but like Death itself; and invaded their Land, not like Men, but like the Pestilence, whose destruction is Epidemical.

When our own Case had a small Resemblance of this, how sensible the People were, and how they mourned at the burning of a poor Village; the usual Accidents, or rather, things to be expected, in a tedious and necessitated War: but, had you been Eyewitnesses of the transcending Massacres here related; had you been one of those that lately saw a pleasant Country, now swarming with multitudes of People, but immediately all depopulated, and drown'd in a Deluge of Bloud: had you been one of those that saw great Cities of Nations and Countries in this moment flourishing with Inhabitants, but in the next, totally ruin'd with such a general desolation, as left neither Person living, nor House remaining: had you seen the poor innocent Heathens shaming and upbraiding, with the ghastliness of their Wounds, the devilish Cruelties of those that called themselves Christians: had you seen the poor creatures torn from the peace and quiet of their own Habitations, where God had planted them, to labour in a Tormenting Captivity, by many degrees worse then that of Algier, or the Turkish Galleys; your Compassion must of necessity have turn'd into Astonishment: the tears of Men can hardly suffice; these are Enormities to make the Angels mourn and bewail the loss of so many departed souls, as might have been converted and redeemed to their eternal Mansions.

We read of old, of the Ten Persecutions wherein the Primitive Christians were destroy'd by the Cruelties of the Heathen Emperors: but we now read of Christians, the Professors of a Religion grounded upon Love and Charity, massacring, where there was no case of Antipathy, but their own obstinate Barbarism; as if because their Wickedness had so far transform'd them into Devils, they were resolved to deface the image of God, so innocently conversing among them. The Turks and Scythians shall be now no more the Adagies of Cruelty among us; for here is a Christian Nation which hath taken off that Envie from them, and entayl'd it upon themselves.

And now, O men of England, let me ask you but this Question; Whether you, that for these many years have had the Honour to be the Patrons of Religion; whose Charity hath still relieved, and whose Power hath still defended the Cause of the Oppressed at home and abroad; whether you can withdraw your Assistance from this Great Work, and deprive your selves of that Birth-right which you seem to have among the Nations, God still continuing the Management of his Justice in the hands of our most fortunate and Lawful Magistrate, whom he hath rais'd up, as his Great Instrument, to revenge the Blood of that innocent People.

Consider this, moreover, That you are not now to fight against your Country-men, but against your Old and Constant Enemies, the SPANIARDS, a Proud, Deceitful, Cruel, and Treacherous Nation, whose chiefest Aim hath been the Conquest of this Land, and to enslave the People of this Nation; witness those Invasions in the days of Queen ELIZABETH; whose Leagues of Amity we had more reason to repent of, then to rejoyce at, as being destructive to the Nation, and made with those that onely sought the Advantages of Peace, that they might be more safe to do us Mischief: and so little they car'd for Peace with us, that they never sought it, but when meer Urgencies of State requir'd; and never kept their Articles, when they had the least hope of Profit to themselves: Of which we need not look for ancient Examples; they are fresh in Memory, and have been too sadly and undeservedly sustain'd, both nearer home, and of late years in the West-Indies also, as appears by that Pious and Prudent DECLARATION set forth by his Highness the LORD PROTECTOR; as if Providence has so ordain'd it, that by the Wrongs of our Country-men in those Parts, we should be interested in the Quarrel of those Innocent Nations.

Neither need we to fear the Vaunts of the Spanish Monarch, whose Government stands not on those strong Foundations that some imagine; Blood and Tyrannie being the chief Pillars of his Greatness, or rather, his Arcana Imperii; and his Empire being onely strong in this, That the Weaknesses thereof have not yet been well look'd into. Should we chase him from his Indian Treasures, he would soon retire to his Shell, like a Snail tapt upon the horns. And perhaps it would not a little avail to the General Peace of Europe, whereby we should be strengthened against the Common Enemy of Christianitie. For doubtless it hath been the Satanical Scope of this Tyrant, To set all the European Princes at Variance, and to keep them busie at home, that they might not have leasure to bend their Forces against his Golden Regions. But he pretends a Right to them, though upon very slender Grounds: for that the English may better claim them himself; it being first discovered, as is well known, and tendered to Henry the Seventh, by Sebastian Cabot, one of his own Captains. Which brings to minde the Poor Spirits of our English Kings, who would not regard such an Advantage, so highly importing the Honour of the Nation, so far as to be almost guilty of the Bloud shed in those parts, through their neglect. But for farther satisfaction concerning the Right of the English to the West Indies, I shall refer you to a further Treatise, which I may ere long put forth.

And now, honoured Country-men, seeing that by Divine Providence the Cruelties and Barbarous Massacres of the Spaniards have been so apparently presented to you, I cannot but be confident of your Endeavours, as you tender the Good and Welfare of your Native Country, to acquit your selves in so just a Cause, which God hath put into the Heart and Hands of our Supreme Magistrate, who is so Vigilant to embrace all Opportunities for the Good of the Nation.

2. WINTHROP D. JORDAN

First Impressions: The Initial English Confrontation with Africans*

When the Atlantic nations of Europe began expanding overseas in the sixteenth century, Portugal led the way in Africa and to the east while Spain founded a great empire in America. It was not until the reign of Elizabeth that Englishmen came to realize that overseas exploration and plantations could bring home wealth, power, glory, and fascinating information. . . .

English voyagers did not touch upon the shores of West Africa until after 1550, nearly a century after Prince Henry the Navigator had mounted the sustained Portuguese thrust southward for a water passage to the Orient. Usually Englishmen came to Africa to trade goods *with* the natives; the principal hazards of these ventures proved to be climate, disease, and the jealous opposition of the "Portingals" who had long since entrenched themselves in forts along the coast. The earliest English descriptions of West Africa were written by adventurous traders, men who had no special interest in converting the natives or, except for the famous Hawkins voyages, in otherwise laying hands on them. Extensive English participation in the slave trade did not develop until well into the seventeenth century. The first permanent English settlement on the African coast was at Kormantin in 1631, and the Royal African Company was not chartered for another forty years. Initially, therefore, English contact with Africans did not take place primarily in a context which prejudged the Negro as a slave, at least not as a slave of Englishmen. Rather, Englishmen met Negroes merely as another sort of men.

*Winthrop D. Jordan, *White Over Black: American Attitudes Toward the Negro, 1550-1815* (Chapel Hill, University of North Carolina Press, 1968), pp. 3-9, 24-28, 40-43. Published for the Institute of Early American History and Culture, Williamsburg, Virginia. Reprinted by permission of the University of North Carolina Press.

Englishmen found the natives of Africa very different from themselves. Negroes looked different; their religion was un-Christian, their manner of living was anything but English; they seemed to be a particularly libidinous sort of people. All these clusters of perceptions were related to each other, though they may be spread apart for inspection, and they were related also to circumstances of contact in Africa, to previously accumulated traditions concerning that strange and distant continent, and to certain special qualities of English society on the eve of its expansion into the New World.

THE BLACKNESS WITHOUT

The most arresting characteristic of the newly discovered African was his color. Travelers rarely failed to comment upon it indeed when describing Negroes they frequently began with complexion and then moved on to dress (or rather lack of it) and manners. . . .

Englishmen actually described Negroes as *black*—an exaggerated term which in itself suggests that the Negro's complexion had powerful impact upon their perceptions. Even the peoples of northern Africa seemed so dark that Englishmen tended to call them "black" and let further refinements go by the board. Blackness became so generally associated with Africa that every African seemed a black man. In Shakespeare's day, the Moors, including Othello, were commonly portrayed as pitchy black and the terms *Moor* and *Negro* used almost interchangeably. With curious inconsistency, however, Englishmen recognized that Africans south of the Sahara were not at all the same people as the much more familiar Moors. Sometimes they referred to Negroes as "black Moors" to distinguish them from the peoples of North Africa. During the seventeenth century the distinction became more firmly established and indeed writers came to stress the difference in color, partly because thes delightem in correcting their predecessors and partly because Negroes were being taken up as slaves and Moors, increasingly, were not. In the more detailed and accurate reports about West Africa of the seventeenth century, moreover, Negroes in different regions were described as varying considerably in complexion. In England, however, the initial impression of Negroes was not appreciably modified: the firmest fact about the Negro was that he was "black."

The powerful impact which the Negro's color made upon Englishmen must have been partly owing to suddenness of contact. Though the Bible as well as the arts and literature of antiquity and the Middle Ages offered some slight introduction to the "Ethiope," England's immediate acquaintance with black-skinned peoples came with relative rapidity. While the virtual monopoly held by Venetian ships in England's foreign trade prior to the sixteenth century meant that people much darker than Englishmen were not entirely unfamiliar, really black men were virtually unknown except as vaguely referred to in the hazy literature about the sub-Sahara which had filtered down from antiquity. Native West Africans probably first appeared in London in 1554; in that year five "Negroes," as the legitimate trader William Towrson reported, were taken to England, "kept till they could speake the language," and then brought back again "to be a helpe to Englishmen" who were engaged in trade with Negroes on the coast. Hakluyt's later discussion of these Negroes, who he said "could wel agree with our meates and drinkes" though "the colde and moyst aire doth somewhat offend them," suggests that these "black Moores" were a novelty to Englishmen. In this respect the English experience was markedly different from that of the Spanish and Portuguese who for centuries had been in close contact with North Africa and had actually been invaded and subjected by people both darker and more highly civilized than themselves. The impact of the Negro's color was the more powerful upon Englishmen, moreover, because England's principal contact with Africans came in West Africa and the Congo where men were not merely dark but almost literally black: one of the fairest-skinned nations suddenly came face to face with one of the darkest peoples on earth. . . .

In England perhaps more than in southern Europe, the concept of blackness was loaded with intense meaning. Long before they found that some men were black, Englishmen found in the idea of blackness a way of expressing some of their most ingrained values. No other color except white conveyed so much emotional impact. As described by the *Oxford English Dictionary*, the meaning of *black* before the sixteenth century included, "Deeply stained with dirt; soiled, dirty, foul. . . . Having dark or deadly purposes, malignant; pertaining to or involving death, deadly, baneful, disastrous, sinister. . . . Foul, iniquitous, atrocious, horrible, wicked. . . . Indicating disgrace, censure, liability to punishment, etc." Black was an emotionally partisan color, the handmaid and symbol of baseness and evil, a sign of danger and repulsion.

Embedded in the concept of blackness was its direct opposite—whiteness. No other colors so clearly implied opposition, "beinge coloures utterlye contrary"; no others were so frequently used to denote polarization:

> Everye white will have its blacke,
> And everye sweete its sowre.

White and black connoted purity and filthiness, virginity and sin, virtue and baseness, beauty and ugliness, beneficence and evil, God and the devil.

Whiteness, moreover, carried a special significance for Elizabethan Englishmen: it was, particularly when complemented by red, the color of perfect human beauty, especially *female* beauty. This ideal was already centuries old in Elizabeth's time, and their fair Queen was its very embodiment: her cheeks were "roses in a bed of lillies." (Elizabeth was naturally pale but like many ladies then and since she freshened her "lillies" at the cosmetic table.) An adoring nation knew precisely what a beautiful Queen looked like.

Her cheeke, her chinne, her neck, her nose,
This was a lillye, that was a rose;
Her hande so white as whales bone,
Her finger tipt with Cassidone;
Her bosome, sleeke as Paris plaster,
Held upp twoo bowles of Alabaster.

Shakespeare himself found the lily and the rose a compelling natural coalition.

'Tis beauty truly blent, whose red and white
Nature's own sweet and cunning hand laid on.

By contrast, the Negro was ugly, by reason of his color and also his "horrid Curles" and "disfigured" lips and nose. As Shakespeare wrote apologetically of his black mistress.

My mistress' eyes are nothing like the sun;
Coral is far more red than her lips' red:
If snow be white, why then her breasts are dun;
If hairs be wires, black wires grow on her head.
I have seen roses damask'd, red and white,
But no such roses see I in her cheeks.

Some Elizabethans found blackness an ugly mask, superficial but always demanding attention.

Is *Byrrha* browne? Who doth the question aske?
Her face is pure as Ebonie jeat blacke,

It's hard to know her face from her faire maske,
Beautie in her seemes beautie still to lacke.
Nay, she's snow-white, but for that russet skin,
Which like a vaile doth keep her whitenes in,

A century later blackness still required apology and mitigation: one of the earliest attempts to delineate the West African Negro as a heroic character, Aphra Behn's popular story *Oroonoko* (1688), presented Negroes as capable of blushing and turning pale. It was important, if incalculably so, that English discovery of black Africans came at a time when the accepted standard of ideal beauty was a fair complexion of rose and white. Negroes not only failed to fit this ideal but seemed the very picture of perverse negation. . . .

SAVAGE BEHAVIOR

The condition of savagery—the failure to be civilized—set Negroes apart from Englishmen in an ill-defined but crucial fashion. Africans were *different* from Englishmen in so many ways: in their clothing, huts, farming, warfare, language, government, morals, and (not least important) in their table manners. Englishmen were fully aware that Negroes living at different parts of the coast were not all alike; it was not merely different reactions in the observers which led one to describe a town as "marveilous artificially builded with muddle walles . . . and kept very cleane as well in their streetes as in their houses" and another to relate how "they doe eate" each other "alive" in some places but dead in others "as we wolde befe or mutton." No matter how great the actual and observed differences among Negroes, though, none of these black men seemed to live like Englishmen.

To judge from the comments of voyagers, Englishmen had an unquenchable thirst for the details of savage life. Partly their curiosity was a matter of scientific interest in the "natural productions" of the newly opened world overseas. To the public at large, the details of savage behavior appealed to an interest which was not radically different from the scientist's; an appetite for the "wonderful" seems to have been built into Western culture. It is scarcely surprising that civilized Englishmen should have taken an interest in reports about cosmetic mutilation, polygamy, infanticide, ritual murder and the like—of course *English* men did not really *do* any of these things themselves. Finally, reports about savages began arriving at a time when Englishmen very much needed to be able to translate their apprehensive interest in an uncontrollable world out of medieval, religious terms. The discovery of savages overseas enabled them to make this translation easily, to move from miracles to verifiable monstrosities, from heaven to earth.

As with skin color, English reporting of African customs constituted an exercise in self-inspection by means of comparison. The necessity of continuously measuring African practices with an English yardstick of course tended to emphasize the differences between the two groups, but it also made for heightened sensitivity to instances of similarity. Thus the Englishman's ethnocentrism tended to distort his perception of African culture in two opposite directions. While it led him to emphasize differences and to condemn deviations from the English norm, it led him also to seek out similarities (where perhaps none existed) and to applaud every instance of conformity to the appropriate standard. Though African clothing and personal etiquette were regarded as absurd, equivalents to European practices were at times detected in other aspects of African culture. Particularly, Englishmen were inclined to see the structures of African societies as analogous to their own, complete with kings, counselors, gentlemen, and the baser sort. Here especially they found Africans like themselves, partly because they knew no other way to describe a society and partly because there was actually good basis for such a view in the social organization of West African communities.

Most English commentators seem to have felt that Negroes would behave better under improved circumstances; a minority thought the Africans naturally wicked, but even these observers often used "natural" only to mean "ingrained." (English accounts of West Africa did not emphasize ingrained stupidity in the natives, defect of "Reason" was seen as a function of savagery.) Until well into the eighteenth century there was no debate as to whether the Negro's non-physical characteristics were inborn and unalterable; such a question was never posed with anything like sufficient clarity for men to debate it. There was no precise meaning in such statements about the Africans as, "Another (as it were) innate quality they have [is] to Steal any thing they lay hands of, especially from Foreigners . . . this vicious humor [runs] through the whole race of *Blacks,*" or in another comment, that "it would be very surprizing if upon a scrutiny into their Lives we should find any of them whose perverse Nature would not break out sometimes; for they indeed seem to be born and bred Villains: All sorts of Baseness having got such sure-footing in them, that 'tis impossible to lye concealed." These two vague suggestions concerning innate qualities in the Negro were among the most precise in all the English accounts of West Africa. It was sufficient to depict and describe. There might be disagreement as to the exact measure of tenacity with which the African clung to his present savage character, but this problem would yield to time and accurate description.

Despite the fascination and self-instruction Englishmen derived from expatiating upon the savage behavior of Africans, they never felt that savagery was as important a quality in Africans as it was in the American Indians. Two sets of circumstances made for this distinction in the minds of Englishmen. As was the case with heathenism, contrasting social contexts played an important role in shaping the English response to savagery in the two peoples. Inevitably, the savagery of the Indians assumed a special significance in the minds of those actively engaged in a program of bringing civilization into the American wilderness. The case with the African was different: the English errand into Africa was not a new or a perfect community but a business trip. No hope was entertained for civilizing the Negro's steaming continent, and Englishmen lacked compelling reason to develop a program for remodeling the African natives. The most compelling necessity was that of pressing forward the business of buying Negroes from other Negroes. It was not until the slave trade came to require justification, in the eighteenth century, that some Englishmen found special reason to lay emphasis on the Negro's savagery.

From the beginning, also, the importance of the Negro's savagery was muted by the Negro's color. Englishmen could go a long way toward expressing their sense of being different from Negroes merely by calling them black. By contrast, the aboriginals in America did not have the appearance of being radically distinct from Europeans except in religion and savage behavior. English voyagers placed much less emphasis upon the Indian's color than upon the Negro's, and they never permitted the Indian's physiognomy to distract their attention from what they regarded as his essential quality, his savagery. Even in the eighteenth century, when the savages of the world were being promoted to "nobility" by Europeans as an aid to self-scrutiny and reform at home, the Negro was not customarily thought of as embodying all the qualities of the noble savage. Certainly he never attained the status of the Indian's primitive nobility. It was not merely that Negroes had by then become pre-eminently the slaves of Europeans in the Americas. The Negro's appearance remained a barrier to acceptance as the noble type. In one of the earliest attempts to dramatize the nobility of the primitive man (1688), Aphra Behn described her hero Oroonoko in terms which made clear the conditions under which the Negro could be admitted as a candidate for admiration:

> The most famous Statuary could not form the Figure of a Man more admirably turn'd from Head to Foot. His Face was not of that brown rusty Black which most of that Nation are, but a perfect Ebony, or polished Jet. His Eyes were the most aweful that could be seen, and very piercing; the White of 'em being like Snow, as were his Teeth. His nose was rising and *Roman* instead of *African* and flat: His Mouth the finest shaped that could be seen; far from those great turn'd Lips, which are so natural to the rest of the Negroes. The whole Proportion and Air of his Face was so nobly and exactly form'd, that bating his Colour there could be nothing in Nature more beautiful, agreeable and handsome.

As this description makes clear, the Negro might attain savage nobility only by approximating (as best he could) the appearance of a white man.

It would be a mistake, however, to slight the importance of the Negro's savagery, since it fascinated Englishmen from the very first. English observers in West Africa were sometimes so profoundly impressed by the Negro's deviant behavior that they resorted to a powerful metaphor with which to express their own sense of difference from him. They knew perfectly well that Negroes were men, yet they frequently described the Africans as "brutish" or "bestial" or "beastly." The hideous tortures, the cannibalism, the rapacious warfare, the revolting diet (and so forth page after page) seemed somehow to place the Negro among the beasts. The circumstances of the Englishman's confrontation with the Negro served to strengthen this feeling. Slave traders in Africa handled Negroes the same way men in England handled beasts, herding and examining and buying. The Guinea Company instructed Bartholomew Haward in 1651 "to buy and put aboard you so many negers as yo'r ship can cary, and for what shalbe wanting to supply with Cattel, as also to furnish you with victualls and provisions for the said negers and Cattel." Africa, moreover, teemed with strange and wonderful animals, and men that killed like tigers, ate like vultures, and grunted like hogs seemed indeed to merit comparison with beasts. In making this instinctive analogy, Englishmen unwittingly demonstrated how powerfully the African's different culture—for Englishmen, his "savagery"—operated to make Negroes seem to Englishmen a radically different kind of men.

THE BLACKNESS WITHIN

The Protestant Reformation in England was a complex development, but certainly it may be said that during the century between Henry VIII and Oliver Cromwell the content and tone of English Christianity were altered in the direction of Biblicism, personal piety, individual judgment, and more intense self-scrutiny and internalized control. Many pious Englishmen, not all of them "Puritans," came to approach life as if conducting an examination and to approach Scripture as if peering in a mirror. As a result, their inner energies were brought unusually close to the surface, more frequently into the almost-rational world of legend, myth, and literature. The taut Puritan and the bawdy Elizabethan were not enemies but partners in this adventure which we usually think of in terms of great literature—of Milton and Shakespeare—and social conflict—of Saints and Cavaliers. The age was driven by the twin spirits of adventure and control, and while "adventurous Elizabethans" embarked upon voyages of discovery overseas, many others embarked upon inward voyages of discovery. Some men, like William Bradford and John Winthrop, were to do both.

Given this charged atmosphere of (self-) discovery, it is scarcely surprising that Englishmen should have used peoples overseas as social mirrors and that they were especially inclined to discover attributes in savages which they found first but could not speak of in themselves.

Nowhere is the way in which certain of these cultural attributes came to bear upon Negroes more clearly illustrated than in a passage by George Best, an Elizabethan adventurer who sailed with Martin Frobisher in 1577 in search of the Northwest Passage. In his discourse demonstrating the habitability of all parts of the world, Best veered off to the problem of the color of Negroes. The cause of their blackness, he decided, was explained in Scripture. Noah and his sons and their wives were "white" and "by course of nature should have begotten . . . white children. But the envie of our great and continuall enemie the wicked Spirite is such, that as hee coulde not suffer our olde father Adam to live in the felicite and Angelike state wherein he was first created, . . . so againe, finding at this flood none but a father and three sons living, hee so caused one of them to disobey his fathers commandment, that after him all his posteritie should bee accursed." The "fact" of this "disobedience," Best continued, was this: Noah "commanded" his sons and their wives to behold God "with reverence and feare," and that "while they remained in the Arke, they should use continencie, and abstaine from carnall copulation with their wives: . . . which good instructions and exhortations notwithstanding his wicked sonne Cham disobeyed, and being perswaded that the first childe borne after the flood . . . should inherite . . . all the dominions of the earth, hee . . . used company with his wife, and craftily went about thereby to dis-inherite the off-spring of his other two brethren.'' To punish this ''wicked and detestable fact,'' God willed that ''a sonne should bee born whose name was Chus, who not onely it selfe, but all his posteritie after him should bee so blacke and lothsome, that it might remain a spectacle of disobedience to all the worlde. And of this blacke and cursed Chus came all these blacke Moores which are in Africa.''

The inner themes running throughout this extraordinary exegesis testify eloquently to the completeness with which English perceptions could integrate sexuality with blackness, the devil, and the judgment of a God who had originally created man not only ''Angelike'' but ''white.'' These running equations lay embedded at a deep and almost inaccessible level of Elizabethan culture; only occasionally do they appear in complete clarity, as when evil dreams.

> . . . hale me from my sleepe like forked Devils,
> Midnight, thou Aethiope, Empresse of Black Soules, Thou general
> Bawde to the whole world.

But what is still more arresting about George Best's discourse is the shaft of light it throws upon the dark mood of strain and control in Elizabethan culture. In an important sense, Best's remarks are not about Negroes; rather they play upon a theme of external discipline exercised upon the man who fails to discipline himself. The linkages he established—''disobedience'' with ''carnall copulation'' with something ''black and lothsome''—were not his alone; the term *dirt* first began to acquire its meaning of moral impurity, of smuttiness, at the very end of the sixteenth century. Perhaps the key term, though, is ''disobedience''—to God and parents—and perhaps, therefore, the passage echoes one of the central concerns of Englishmen of the sixteenth and early seventeenth centuries. Tudor England was undergoing social ferment, generated by an increasingly commercialized economy and reflected in such legislative monuments as the Statute of Apprentices and the Elizabethan vagrancy and poor laws. Overseas mercantile expansion brought profits and adventure but also a sense, in some men, of disquietude. One commentator declared that the merchants, ''whose number is so increased in these our daies,'' had ''in times past'' traded chiefly with European countries but ''now in these daies, as men not contented with these journies, they have sought out the east and west Indies, and made now and then suspicious voiages.''Literate Englishmen generally (again not merely the Puritans) were concerned with the apparent disintegration of social and moral controls at home; they fretted endlessly over the ''masterless men'' who had once had a proper place in the social order but who were now wandering about, begging, robbing, raping. They fretted also about the absence of a spirit of due subordination—of children to parents and servants to masters. They assailed what seemed a burgeoning spirit of avariciousness, a spirit which one social critic described revealingly as "a barbarous or slavish desire to turne the penie." They decried the laborers who demanded too high wages, the masters who would squeeze their servants, and the landed gentlemen who valued sheep more than men—in short, the spirit of George Best's Cham, who aimed to have his son "inherite and possesse all the dominions of the earth."

It was the case with English confrontation with Negroes, then, that a society in a state of rapid flux, undergoing important changes in religious values, and comprised of men who were energetically on the make and acutely and often uncomfortably self-conscious of being so, came upon a people less technologically advanced, markedly different in appearance and culture. From the first, Englishmen tended to set Negroes over against themselves, to stress what they conceived to be radically contrasting qualities of color, religion, and style of life, as well as animality and a peculiarly potent sexuality. What Englishmen did not at first fully realize was that Negroes were potentially subjects for a special kind of obedience and subordination which was to arise as adventurous Englishmen sought to possess for themselves and their children one of the most bountiful dominions of the earth. When they came to plant themselves in the New World, they were to find that they had not entirely left behind the spirit of avarice and insubordination. Nor does it appear, in light of attitudes which developed during their first two centuries in America, that they left behind all the impressions initially gathered of the *Negro* before he became preeminently the *slave*.

3. Roy Harvey Pearce

The "Ruines of Mankind": The Indian and the Puritan Mind*

The Indian whom colonial Americans everywhere encountered was, above all, an obstacle to civilization. And he was an obstacle not only to overcome, but also to understand and then perhaps to civilize in the over-

*Roy Harvey Pearce, "The 'Ruines of Mankind': The Indian and the Puritan Mind," *Journal of the History of Ideas,* Vol. XIII (1952), pp. 200-15. Reprinted by permission of the *Journal of the History of Ideas.*

coming. For in his very nature, in what was taken to be his essential humanity, the Indian seemed to be capable of that civil state which the colonizers had achieved, yet seemed somehow not to be inclined toward the state. The problem for those Americans who wanted to understand him was to define the nature of his savage society—what in the eighteenth century came to be called his ''savagism''—in such a way as to relate it to the nature of the high civilization which they were bringing to the new world. Thus, in the perspective of our cultural history a colonial understanding of savagism is really a colonial understanding of civilization—of the good life as the Indian did and did not share in it. And colonial definitions of savage life are really re-definitions of civilized life, apologia for that life, expressions and applications of theories of civilization.

So it is that we may comprehend our colonial civilization concretely and particularly as it realizes itself in working out its ideas of the savage. So it is that the New England Puritan obsession with the savage is a significant aspect of the New England Puritan obsession with the civilized. This essay, then, is offered as a study in the history of colonial New England civilization—a history in terms of the Puritan idea of the savage, as that idea came to be worked out in the context of Puritan experience with the Indian and his society.

1

For the Englishman going to New England in the 1620's and 30's the destiny of the Indians could be understood only as it related to the destiny of the whole colonial enterprise. In Plymouth the Pilgrim rejoiced to find that it had pleased God so to possess the Indians with a fear and love of the English that they would forthwith submit themselves as loyal and dutiful subjects. Moreover, it was to be observed that God had lately sent a ''wonderful plague'' among the savages and had so destroyed them and left most of their lands free for civilized occupation. The Indians whom the Pilgrims found were amenable enough; watched closely, dealt with fairly, punished occasionally, they gave little trouble. But then, God had already shown them the way with His plague.

For Puritans in the Massachusetts Bay Colony and what came to be Connecticut, matters were somewhat more difficult. Although in 1634 John Winthrop could write to an English friend, ''[the natives] are neere all dead of the small Poxe, so as the Lord hathe cleared our title to what we possess,'' yet Indians to the south and north, who were plagued mainly by the English themselves, were relatively strong and independent. Twice in the century formal frontier war was waged: in 1637, against the Pequots, who were easily slaughtered at Mystic by Mason's expedition; and in 1675-1676, against the Wampanoags and their leader King Philip, who were destroyed in their turn, though not quite so easily as had been the Pequots. And continually there was trouble on a small scale; the problem was to keep various tribal groups split up and thus weak in striking power, to protect frontier settlements from marauding bands of Indians, somehow to combat papist French influence on the northern Indians, and gradually to take over lands as the proper time came. Steadily, as the colonies developed in holdings and in power, the English moved further inland from their coastal settlements and took over more Indian land. Warfare resulted. But this too was part of God's Way with New England.

For, and Puritans took this as the meaning of their own history, God had meant the savage Indians' land for the civilized English, and, moreover, had meant the savage state itself as a sign of Satan's power and savage warfare as a sign of earthly struggle and sin. The colonial enterprise was in all ways a religious enterprise. Demonstrating land tenure from theology had been simple even for Pilgrim precursors of the Puritans. Robert Cushman, if it was he who in 1622 contributed the concluding section to the Pilgrim *Mourt's Relation*, argued merely that the Indians were heathens and thus in need of conversion; that Indians' lands were empty, English lands full, and the English therefore bound to go to the Indians and fill their lands:

> Their land is spacious and void, and there are few, and do but run over the grass, as do also the foxes and the wild beasts. They are not industrious, neither have art, science, skill or faculty to use either the land or the commodities of it; but all spoils, rots, and is marred for want of manuring, gathering, ordering, &c. As the ancient patriarchs, therefore, removed from straiter places into more roomy, where the land lay idle and waste, and none used it, though there dwelt inhabitants by them, as Gen. xiii, 6, 11, 12, and xxxiv, 21, and xli, 20, so it is lawful now to take a land which none useth, and make use of it.

This argument was at the center of the New England understanding of the Indian in the seventeenth century as, in fact, it was in some version to be at the center of American understanding of the Indian until the middle of the nineteenth century. For the Pilgrim as for the Puritan, religion and empire, christianization and civilization, divine order and natural order, were known to be one. So Cushman concluded,

> Yea, and as the enterprise is weighty and difficult, so the honor is more

worthy, to plant a rude wilderness, to enlarge the honor and fame of our dread sovereign, but chiefly to display the efficacy and power of the Gospel, both in zealous preaching, professing, and wise walking under it, before the faces of these poor blind infidels.

Such statements on this problem of land tenure as came some seven years later from Massachusetts authorities were characteristically more legal in tone and concern than Cushman's but were pointed towards the same conclusions. Indian lands were to be bought if local savages should pretend to ownership, but to be bought only as a means of keeping peace with those savages. For, in truth, the Indians possessed their lands only as a natural right, since that possession existed anterior to and outside of a properly civilized state and since that possession was not in accordance with God's commandment to men to occupy the earth, increase, and multiply; what followed, then, was that the land was technically *vacuum domicilium*, and that the English, who would farm the land and make it fructify, who would give it order, were obliged to take over. If the Indians were ever to be civilized, if they were ever to know the true God, they would be obliged to let God's chosen people lead them to God's chosen civilization; specifically, the way to God was through His chosen civilization. This is perhaps essentially what we call the Protestant-capitalistic ethic; but it is also, and more particularly, a late Renaissance ethic—a solemn and brave, even desperate, determination to hold on to the idea of a received, assured order which would give meaning and direction to all life. For John Winthrop, in 1629, it was a matter of such divine logic:

. . . the whole earth is the Lord's garden, and he hath given it to the sons of Adam to be tilled and improved by them. Why then should we stand starving here for the places of habitation, (many men spending as much labor and cost to recover or keep sometimes an acre or two of lands as would procure him many many hundreds of acres, as good or better, in another place), and in the mean time suffer whole countries, as profitable for the use of man, to lie waste without any improvement.

2

Convinced thus of his divine right to Indian lands, the Puritan discovered in the Indians themselves evidence of a satanic opposition to the very principle of divinity. In a world in which the divine plan was so clear, in a world through which the Bible would guide all men in all things, in a world in which civilization and the divinely illuminated human reason had to count for everything, the Indian might well be a terrifying anomaly, at best a symbol of what men might become if they lived far from God's Word. Yet these savages were essentially men; and so they had to be brought to manhood and the civilized responsibilities of manhood. And this was to be achieved through bringing them eventually to God. As the wild lands of New England were to be improved, so were the wild men. For the Puritan there could be no half-way measures in his own life or in the lives of the savages about him. It was never a question of understanding the savage as he was, of knowing him in his low state. Rather it was a question—a driving necessity, really—first, of finding the savage's place in a Puritan world, and then, of making the savage over into a Puritan. If one looked closely at the savage, it was to look closely at a similitude to God's Way with the world—as one would look closely at a storm, or an illness, or a death, or a birth, or a quarrel among one's children—and so to discover evidence of that Way.

Wherever the Indian opposed the Puritan, there Satan opposed God. Satan had possessed the Indian until he had become virtually a beast. Indian worship was devil worship. . . . Satanism, it was abundantly evident, was at the very core of savage life. And it was not hard to associate with his spiritual state; hence, everywhere one might see in the flesh what it meant to be a devil-worshipper. So racial and cultural tension mounted throughout the century, until, in the 1690's, the very presence of evil Indian devil-worshippers was taken as part of the evidence of that great visitation of witches to New England, which we call the Witchcraft Craze. Indian witch doctors clearly were sharing diabolically in the wonders of the invisible world. At the end of the century, when Cotton Mather interpreted the continuing (now French-inspired) Indian skirmishes after King Philip's War as the direct result of God's harrowing sinful and weakening New England through Satan, he too was sure that New England witchcraft and Indian witchcraft were all of a piece:

> The Story of the Prodigious War, made by the Spirits of the Invisible World upon the People of New-England, in the year, 1692, hath Entertain'd a great part of the English World, with a just Astonishment: and I have met with some Strange Things, not here to be mentioned, which have made me often think, that this inexplicable War might have some of its Original among the Indians, whose chief Sagamores are well known unto some of our Captives, to have been horrid Sorcerers, and hellish Conjurers and such as conversed with Daemons.

Practical experience seemed to bear all this out. Fighting to hold on to their lands and their culture, the Indians would properly be savage. Inevitably New Englanders living on the frontier settlements suffered raids, destruction, sometimes captivity, and inevitably they interpreted each as God's warning to New England through Satan.

In the frontier settlements to the west and south and to the north in Maine, it was destroy or be destroyed. And it seemed everywhere continuingly evident that this frontier fight for survival was but another skirmish in man's Holy War against Satan, now on a new-world battlefield. When, as late as 1703, Solomon Stoddard recommended to Governor Joseph Dudley that troublesome Indians be hunted down with dogs, he was arguing as John Underhill (second in command to Mason at the proceedings at Mystic) had argued some sixty-five years before in defense of the massacre of the Pequots:

> It may be demanded, Why should you be so furious? (as some have said). Should not Christians have more mercy and compassion? But I would refer you to David's war. When a people is grown to such a height of blood, and sin against God and man, and all confederates in the action, then he hath no respect to persons, but harrows them, and saws them, and puts them to the sword, and the most terribelest death that may be. Sometimes the Scripture declareth women and children must perish with their parents. Sometimes the case alters; but we will not dispute it now. We had sufficient light from the Word of God for our proceedings.

Thus it was that the whole history of the relations with the Indians, which was part of the whole history of the Puritan enterprise, was read in light from the Word of God. Edward Johnson's *Wonder-Working Providence of Sion's Saviour in New England* (1654) deals characteristically with that history. Now, Johnson's account is generally concerned with the whole history of New England seen properly *sub specie aeternitatis*; as a result, he is able to find the right place and the right amount of space for each of the important events in the course of colonial relations with the Indians. Devoting large parts of some seven of his eighty-three chapters to the discussion of Indian affairs, he tells how God had sent a plague in 1619 (the correct date is, of course, 1616-1617) to clear the way for the settlers at Plymouth and how the Indians had been thus disposed to receive those settlers peacefully; he tells how a plague among the Massachusetts Indians likewise saved the Bay Colony in 1631 ("Thus did the Lord allay their quarrelsome spirits, and made roome for the following part of his army."); he recounts the history of the Pequot War in some detail, pointing out, as had many another, how this war and the Antinomian troubles of the 1630's were equally Satanic trials for men establishing a Holy Commonwealth; he recounts further God's intervention in a possible Indian war in 1645; and finally, he insists that by the 1650's missionary work to the Satanic heathen is going well. In every event he can find evidence that God, through Satan, has been showing the colonists at once their own sinfulness and the promise of their great undertaking.

Later Puritan historians deal more specifically with Indian troubles, and, of course, they recount later troubles—King Philip's War and the continuing skirmishes in the northeast throughout the seventeenth century and into the eighteenth. Yet in tone and orientation their work simply duplicates Johnson's *Wonder-Working Providence* and reflects equally the integrative orthodoxy of Puritan culture. Often writing more in detail and from broader and more immediate experience than does Johnson, they emphasize even more than he the brutish, diabolical quality of the Indian enemy. To this end, Captain John Mason appends to his *Brief History of the Pequot War* (at first printed separately in 1736) a list of "special providences" by means of which the English have won their victory. In his three-part report (1675-1676) of King Philip's War, Nathaniel Saltonstall insists that however heavily the hand of the Lord lies upon his Puritan sinners, still He "hath Commission to the Sword" to destroy the crafty, bestial diabolical creatures who oppose those sinners. William Hubbard, in his *Narrative of the Indian Wars in New England* (1677), is sure that King Philip's War in particular is nothing less than a Satanic plot against God's Chosen People: The war could not possibly have occurred because of anything the English have done to the Indians.

> What can be imagined, therefore, [he says] besides the instigation of Satan, that envied at the prosperity of the church of God here seated, or else fearing lest the power of the Lord Jesus, that had overthrown his kingdom in other parts of the world, should do the like here, and so the stone taken out of the mountain without hands, should become a great mountain itself, and fill the whole earth: no cause of provocation being given by the English.

Thus through the century and beyond, the Puritans wrote down their history and discovered and rediscovered the Indians' place in that history. History was everywhere cosmically and eternally meaningful. A Satanic principle was part of that meaningfulness; and the New England Indians somehow embodied that principle. The Indian was significant precisely as history was significant.

3

Out of such an understanding of the nature and destiny of civilized man in New England, there rose the Puritan understanding of the nature and destiny of savage man. There was, at the outset, no difficulty in accounting for the origin and genesis of the savage: Universally it was agreed that the Indians were of the race of men—descendants, in order, of Adam, Noah, and those Asiatic Tartars who had come to America by a land-bridge from northern Asia. This was orthodox seventeenth-century opinion. And it allowed Puritans to account simply for the savage, heathenish state of the Indian. Was he not perhaps the farthest of all God's human creatures from God Himself? Descended from wanderers, had he not lost his sense of civilization and law and order? Had he not lost—except for a dim recollection—God Himself? And wasn't he, as a direct result of this loss, in the power of Satan? Seen thus—and only thus—as one item in a God-centered course of experience, the Indian took on an awful meaning for the Puritan mind.

The Puritan writer on the Indian was, therefore, less interested in the Indian's culture than in the Indian's fallen spiritual condition as it was to be seen everywhere about him. Such early accounts of the Indians as those contained in Edward Winslow's *Good Newes from New England* (1624), Francis Higginson's *New-England's Plantation* (1630), and William Wood's *New England's Prospect* (1634) describe the appearance, social organization, and customs of the local Indians sketchily and, considering the tone of later accounts, somewhat optimistically: The heathen Indians, almost wiped out by the plague, living without the benefits of civilization, fearing their enemies, will certainly welcome the English; and it will be, presumably, no great task to civilize them and so to bring them to Christianity. But as the century wore on, as more distant Indians became better known, and as all the Indians seemed more and more to be setting themselves against civilization and Christianity, as disputes and warfare broke out, it seemed clearer and clearer that all Indians were inextricably involved in their low state and so not worth discussing in great detail. By the 1680's even Daniel Gookin, in charge of Christian Indian settlements for the United Colonies and so known to be soft toward the savages, could give only a despairing account of Indian culture. His account of the Indians in his "Of the Language, Customs, Manners, and Religion of the Indians" is straightforward and gloomy. The Indians have been and continue to be—with a few Christianized exceptions—brutish and barbarous; they indulge in polygamy; they are revengeful; the men only hunt and fish and fight while the women cook and do a little planting; they are all thieves and liars and by now they have virtually all become drunkards. True enough they are hospitable and have some faintly systematic way of government. Yet their worship of the sun, moon, and the earth and of both a supreme doer of good and a supreme doer of evil and their submitting to their powwows, who are nothing hut witches and wizards holding familiarity with Satan, damn them forever. Gookin might have held out a hope for missionary efforts with the Indians; but his evidence is not far from that which caused William Hubbard, in 1677, fiercely to denounce an Englishman who had turned Indian during King Philip's War, married a squaw, "renounced his religion, nation, and natural parents, all at once fighting against them." Captured, this man had been examined and condemned to die. And Hubbard had been obliged to comment:

> As to his religion he was found as ignorant as a heathen, which no doubt caused the fewer tears to be shed at his funeral, by, being unwilling to lavish pity upon him that had divested himself of nature itself, as well as religion, in a time when so much pity was needed elsewhere.

Savage life, then, could be only a life against nature and against religion.

What mattered, therefore, was not the intrinsic character of the New England Indians, but rather the meaning that that character might have for the whole of New England life.

4

From the first, the Puritans, like most other seventeenth-century colonizers; firmly intended to convert the heathen. This was an essential part of their mission on earth as they understood it. They were justified in taking Indian lands because they could use those lands as God had intended them to be used; yet God had also intended that His colonizers give civil and spiritual form to aboriginal dwellers in those lands. Practically, then, Indians were to be made into Puritans. Now, this was to be merely the peculiarly Puritan form of the Renaissance obsession with order and rationality; the Puritan mind, however, was to be so intense, so very fierce in its seizing upon ultimately supernaturalistic and absolutistic sanctions for a particular and local notion of order and rationality, that, unable to face the fact of cultural change and human variance, it was virtually blind to such alien forms of order and rationality as existed in aboriginal New England cultures. Equally, there is little evidence that Puritan order and Puritan reason, with their special scriptural ground, ever meant very much to the New England aborigines who were to be saved by that order and that reason. . . .

Yet for all their faith in themselves, their society, and savage potentialities for civilization and God, the few missionaries who worked with the Indians were bound to fail. The Indian wars of the 1630's and 70's, the expansion of New England, the very clash of civilized and primitive cultures—these spelled the doom of the New England Indian, in spite of the effort of a "sprinkling" of missionaries; for, as we know now, the missionaries themselves carried an alien and destructive culture to the Indians. Actually, by the end of the seventeenth century, it seemed very clear to all concerned that the New England missionary enterprise was likely to fail. The trials of King Philip's War had hardened Puritan hearts; even the Christian Indians, well on the way to salvation, were mistreated. A list drawn up in 1698 gives 2500 as the number of converts in the Indian towns, and points out that most of these are dying off rapidly. For this Cotton Mather blamed not the citizens of the Holy Commonwealth but the English traders who were bringing liquor and vice to the Indians. His father, seeing the Puritan faith weakening everywhere about him went further and instanced both the failure of the missions and the successes of the corrupt traders as partial proof of that weakening. Instead of being converted, he sermonized, the Indians are being perverted; for there are no more goodly Eliots among us; and now God has sent disease among the Indians as a final warning to us to mend our ways before he withdraws his Glory from us as he has from the Jews and from the Spanish and even from those in old England. Indian drunkenness, which had been sadly remarked before, came regularly to be denounced in a kind of ritualistic Puritan breastbeating. Yet we can see that the cause of failure went deeper than the introduction of disease and drunkenness and vice. It stemmed from the very quality of Puritan understanding of the Indian, necessarily from high Puritanism itself—from the desperate need of those who had settled New England to hold on to their special beliefs about the nature and destiny of man if they were to hold on to their God-ordained way of life. They had to assume that the Indian's nature; for the very integrative orthodoxy of their society demanded such an absolute. Herein they might very well fool themselves. Or so a Royal Commission noted in 1665—reporting first that in Rhode Island "is the greatest number of Indians yet they never had any thing allowed towards the civilizing and converting of the Indians," and then that in Massachusetts:

> They convert Indians by hiring them to come & heare Sermons: by teaching them not to obey their Heathen Sachims, & by appointing Rulers amongst them over tenns, twenties, fifties, &c. The lives, Manners, & habits of those, whom they say are converted, cannot be distinguished

> from those who are not, except it be by being hyred to heare Sermons, which the more generous natives scorne.

This is perhaps unfair, certainly antagonistic. Yet it points, however obliquely, to the essential fact: that the seventeenth-century Puritan, in trying to recover for the Indian a civil and religious purity which he was sure he had already recovered for himself, was simply defining one reality in terms of another, the primitive in terms of the civilized, the Indian in terms of the Puritan. And, in the nature of things, he was bound to be wrong—and so to fail in his holy enterprise. . . .

Always deriving its meaning from the Puritan view of man and his nature, inevitably the Puritan understanding of the Indian issued, towards the middle of the eighteenth century, into a particular form of the revivalism and anti-rationalism into which the Puritan view in general had issued. And so, this final Puritan understanding of the Indian is to be comprehended essentially as it relates to the Edwardean neo-Calvinism of the Great Awakening. Always the Puritan mind had worked from the inside out, from God and Scripture and reason to man and nature. Whatever he saw outside, the Puritan had somehow already seen inside. Understanding the Indian as he was related to man and nature, the Puritan thus succeeded—if he did succeed—only in knowing a little more about God and Scripture and reason, and in understanding himself. There is a simple explanation, perhaps: In order to make his new society in a new world, the Puritan could not afford to understand anyone but himself.

B. INSTITUTIONALIZATION OF ATTITUDES FOLLOWING ANGLO-AMERICAN CONQUEST

By the early nineteenth century, original Anglo-American attitudes toward Africans, Indians, and Spanish-speaking peoples had hardened into even stronger prejudices, which affected the legal and social status of those groups in America. The selections in this section illuminate that process and suggest reasons why it occurred.

Winthrop D. Jordan describes the development of the institution of Negro slavery in the American colonies, treating as well the evolution of historical thinking on the subject. Uncertainty remains both about the original status of the first Africans brought to America and about the actual causes of Negro debasement, but most agree that the Anglo-American belief in Blacks as different and inherently inferior was one important factor.

Thomas Jefferson, in *Notes on the State of Virginia*, outlines commonplace white attitudes toward Indians and Negroes in late eighteenth-century America. In the case of the Indians he tries to correct prevailing misconceptions about them and their culture. He is less charitable with regard to Blacks. Convinced of their innate inferiority and potential for dragging down white civilization, Jefferson doubts that Negro slaves could ever be successfully emancipated and absorbed into American society as equals. In *Notes on the State of Virginia* we have a catalogue of generalizations by which most Americans came to "understand" and "explain" the black and red strangers in their midst.

Next Reginald Horsman examines early national policy toward the Indians of the Old Northwest, the region between the Ohio and Mississippi rivers. The primary objective of United States policy was the acquisition of lands controlled by the Indians. The quest was justified by the claim that Indians were uncivilized and would be better off adopting the values and life-style of white society. Even Jefferson, who had some appreciation for the merits of Indian civilization, believed that Indians should abandon their land and customs—or be persuaded to abandon them—and become "civilized." We must ask, however, if this method of acquiring new lands was peculiar to America or whether it falls within the nature of all powerful, expanding nations obstructed by militarily weaker neighbors.

The same question may be asked in regard to American relations with Mexico in the 1830s and 1840s. The two concluding selections describe American opinions of the Spanish-speaking inhabitants of California and New Mexico on the eve of the Mexican-American War (1846-48). Thomas J. Farnham, a New England-born and educated lawyer, traveled through California in the early 1840s. His impressions, published in 1844, reflect the spirit of Manifest Destiny and in turn may have helped to fuel that spirit by calling the Californios an inferior race who deserved to be conquered. Josiah Gregg moved to Santa Fe in 1831 and spent most of the next nine years in New Mexico. His journal, first published in 1844, contains an unflattering view of New Mexicans, which, like Farnham's work, reflects a well-developed prejudice against Mexicans.

1. WINTHROP D. JORDAN

Modern Tensions and the Origins of American Slavery*

Thanks to John Smith we know that Negroes first came to the British continental colonies in 1619. What we do not know is exactly when Negroes were first enslaved there. This question has been debated by historians for the past seventy years, the critical point being whether Negroes were enslaved almost from their first importation or whether they were at first simply servants and only later reduced to the status of slaves. The long duration and vigor of the controversy suggest that more than a simple question of dating has been involved. In fact certain current tensions in American society have complicated the historical problem and greatly heightened its significance. Dating the origins of slavery has taken on a striking modern relevance.

During the nineteenth century historians assumed almost universally that the first Negroes came to Virginia as slaves. So close was their acquaintance with the problem of racial slavery that it did not occur to them that Negroes could ever have been anything but slaves. Philip A. Bruce, the first man to probe with some thoroughness into the early years of American slavery adopted this view in 1896, although he emphasized that the original difference in treatment between white servants and Negroes was merely that Negroes served for life. Just six years later, however, came a challenge from a younger, professionally trained historian, James C. Ballagh. His *A History of Slavery in Virginia* appeared in the *Johns Hopkins University Studies in Historical and Political Science*, an aptly named series which was to usher in the new era of scholarly detachment in the writing of institutional history. Ballagh offered a new and different interpretation; he took the position that the first Negroes served merely as servants and that enslavement did not begin until around 1660, when statutes bearing on slavery were passed for the first time.

There has since been agreement on dating the statutory establishment of slavery, and differences of opinion have centered on when enslavement began in actual practice. Fortunately there has also been general agreement on slavery's distinguishing characteristics: service for life and inheritance of like obligation by any offspring. Writing on the free Negro in Virginia for

*Winthrop D. Jordan, "Modern Tensions and the Origins of American Slavery." *Journal of Southern History,* Vol. XXVIII (1962), pp. 18-30. Reprinted by permission of the *Journal of Southern History.* A modified and much more complete description of the origin of American slavery is in Winthrop D. Jordan, *White Over Black: American Attitudes Toward the Negro, 1550-1812* (Chapel Hill, University of North Carolina Press 1968).

the Johns Hopkins series, John H. Russell in 1813 tackled the central question and showed that some Negroes were indeed servants but concluded that "between 1640 and 1660 slavery was fast becoming an established fact. In this twenty years the colored population was divided, part being servants and part being slaves, and some who were servants defended themselves with increasing difficulty from the encroachments of slavery." Ulrich B. Phillips, though little interested in the matter, in 1918 accepted Russell's conclusion of early servitude and transition toward slavery after 1640. Helen T. Catterall took much the same position in 1926. On the other hand, in 1921 James M. Wright, discussing the free Negro in Maryland, implied that Negroes were slaves almost from the beginning, and in 1940 Susie M. Ames reviewed several cases in Virginia which seemed to indicate that genuine slavery had existed well before Ballagh's date of 1660.

All this was a very small academic gale, well insulated from the outside world. Yet despite disagreement on dating enslavement, the earlier writers—Bruce, Ballagh, and Russell—shared a common assumption which, though at the time seemingly irrelevant to the main question, has since proved of considerable importance. They assumed that prejudice against the Negro was natural and almost innate in the white man. It would be surprising if they had felt otherwise in this period of segregation statutes, overseas imperialism, immigration restriction, and full-throated Anglo-Saxonism. By the 1920's, however, with the easing of these tensions, the assumption of natural prejudice was dropped unnoticed. Yet only one historian explicitly contradicted that assumption: Ulrich Phillips of Georgia, impressed with the geniality of both slavery and twentieth-century race relations, found no natural prejudice in the white man and expressed his "conviction that Southern racial asperities are mainly superficial, and that the two great elements are fundamentally in accord."

Only when tensions over race relations intensified once more did the older assumption of natural prejudice crop up again. After World War II American Negroes found themselves beneficiaries of New Deal politics and reforms, wartime need for manpower, world-wide repulsion at racist excesses in Nazi Germany, and growing successful colored anticolonialism. With new militancy Negroes mounted an attack on the citadel of separate but equal, and soon it became clear that America was in for a period of self-conscious reappraisal of its racial arrangements. Writing in this period of heightened tension (1949) a practiced and careful scholar, Wesley F. Craven, raised the old question of the Negro's original status, suggesting that Negroes had been enslaved at an early date. Craven also cautiously resuscitated the idea that white men may have had natural distaste for the Negro, an idea which fitted neatly with the suggestion of early enslavement. Original antipathy would mean rapid debasement.

In the next year (1950) came a sophisticated counterstatement, which contradicted both Craven's dating and implicitly any suggestion of early prejudice. Oscar and Mary F. Handlin in "Origins of the Southern Labor System" offered a case for late enslavement, with servitude as the status of Negroes before about 1660. Originally the status of both Negroes and white servants was far short of freedom, the Handlins maintained, but Negroes failed to benefit from increased freedom for servants in mid-century and became less free rather than more. Embedded in this description of diverging status were broader implications: Late and gradual enslavement undercut the possibility of natural, deep-seated antipathy toward Negroes. On the contrary, *if whites and Negroes could share the same status of half freedom for forty years in the seventeenth century, why could they not share full freedom in the twentieth?*

The same implications were rendered more explicit by Kenneth M. Stampp in a major reassessment of Southern slavery published two years after the Supreme Court's 1954 school decision. Reading physiology with the eye of faith, Stampp frankly stated his assumption "that innately Negroes *are*, after all, only white men with black skins, nothing more, nothing less." Closely following the Handlins' article on the origins of slavery itself, he almost directly denied any pattern of early and inherent racial antipathy: ". . . Negro and white servants of the seventeenth century seemed to be remarkably unconcerned about their visible physical differences." As for "the trend toward special treatment" of the Negro, "physical and cultural differences provided handy excuses to justify it." Distaste for the Negro, then, was in the beginning scarcely more than an appurtenance of slavery.

These views squared nicely with the hopes of those even more directly concerned with the problem of contemporary race relations, sociologists and social psychologists. Liberal on the race question almost to a man, they tended to see slavery as the initial cause of the Negro's current degradation. The modern Negro was the unhappy victim of long association with base status. Sociologists, though uninterested in tired questions of historical evidence, could not easily assume a natural prejudice in the white man as the cause of slavery. Natural or innate prejudice would not only violate their basic assumptions concerning the dominance of culture but would undermine the power of their new Baconian science. For if prejudice was natural there would be little one could do to wipe it out. Prejudice must have followed enslavement, not vice versa, else any liberal program of action would be badly compromised. One prominent social scientist suggested in a UNESCO pamphlet that racial prejudice in the United States commenced with the cotton gin!

Just how closely the question of dating had become tied to the practical matter of action against racial prejudice was made apparent by the suggestions of still another historian. Carl N. Degler grappled with the dating problem in an article frankly entitled "Slavery and the Genesis of American Race Prejudice." The article appeared in 1959, a time when Southern resistance to school desegregation seemed more adamant than ever and the North's hands none too clean, a period of discouragement for those hoping to end racial discrimination. Prejudice against the Negro now appeared firm and deep-seated, less easily eradicated than had been supposed in, say, 1954. It was Degler's view that enslavement began early, as a result of white settlers' prejudice or antipathy toward the first Negroes. Thus not only were the sociologists contradicted but the dating problem was now overtly and consciously tied to the broader question of whether slavery caused prejudice or prejudice caused slavery. A new self-consciousness over the American racial dilemma had snatched an arid historical controversy from the hands of an unsuspecting earlier generation and had tossed it into the arena of current debate.

Ironically there might have been no historical controversy at all if every historian dealing with the subject had exercised greater care with facts and greater restraint in interpretation. Too often the debate entered the realm of inference and assumption. For the crucial early years after 1619 there is simply not enough evidence to indicate with any certainty whether Negroes were treated like white servants or not. No historian has found anything resembling proof one way or the other. The first Negroes were sold to the English settlers, yet so were other Englishmen. It can be said, however, that Negroes were set apart from white men by the word *Negroes*, and a distinct name is not attached to a group unless it is seen as different. The earliest Virginia census reports plainly distinguished Negroes from white men, sometimes giving Negroes no personal name; and in 1629 every commander of the several plantations was ordered to "take a generall muster of all the inhabitants men woemen and Children as well *Englishe* as Negroes." Difference, however, might or might not involve inferiority.

The first evidence as to the actual status of Negroes does not appear until about 1640. Then it becomes clear that *some* Negroes were serving for life and some children inheriting the same obligation. Here it is necessary to suggest with some candor that the Handlins' statement to the contrary rests on unsatisfactory documentation. That some Negroes were held as slaves after about 1640 is no indication, however, that American slavery popped into the world fully developed at that time. Many historians, most cogently the Handlins, have shown slavery to have been a gradual development, a process not completed until the eighteenth century. The complete deprivation of civil and personal rights, the legal conversion of the Negro into a chattel, in short slavery as Americans came to know it, was not accomplished overnight. Yet these developments practically and logically depended on the practice of hereditary lifetime service, and it is certainly possible to find in the 1640's and 1650's traces of slavery's most essential feature.

The first definite trace appears in 1640 when the Virginia General Court pronounced sentence on three servants who had been retaken after running away to Maryland. Two of them, a Dutchman and a Scot, were ordered to serve their masters for one additional year and then the colony for three more, but "the third being a negro named John Punch shall serve his said master or his assigns for the time of his natural life here or else where." No white servant in America, so far as is known, ever received a like sentence. Later the same month a Negro was again singled out from a group of recaptured runaways; six of the seven were assigned additional time while the Negro was given none, presumably because he was already serving for life. After 1640, too, county court records began to mention Negroes, in part because there were more of them than previously—about two per cent of the Virginia population in 1649. Sales for life, often including any future progeny, were recorded in unmistakable language. In 1646 Francis Pott sold a Negro woman and boy to Stephen Charlton "to the use of him . . . forever." Similarly, six years later William Whittington sold to John Pott "one Negro girle named Jowan; aged about Ten yeares and with her Issue and produce duringe her (or either of them) for their Life tyme. And their Successors forever"; and a Maryland man in 1649 deeded two Negro men and a woman "and all their issue both male and Female." The executors of a York County estate in 1647 disposed of eight Negroes—four men, two women, and two children—to Captain John Chisman "to have hold occupy posesse and inioy and every one of the afforementioned Negroes forever[.]" The will of Rowland Burnham of "Rapahanocke," made in 1657, dispensed his considerable number of Negroes and white servants in language which clearly differentiated between the two by specifying that the whites were to serve for their "full terme of tyme" and the Negroes "for ever." Nor did anything in the will indicate that this distinction was exceptional or novel.

In addition to these clear indications that some Negroes were owned for life, there were cases of Negroes held for terms far longer than the normal five or seven years. On the other hand, some Negroes served only the term usual for white servants, and others were completely free. One Negro freeman, Anthony Johnson, himself owned a Negro. Obviously the enslavement of some Negroes did not mean the immediate enslavement of all.

Further evidence of Negroes serving for life lies in the prices paid for them. In many instances the valuations placed on Negroes (in estate inventories and bills of sale)) were far higher than for white servants, even those servants with full terms yet to serve. Since there was ordinarily no preference for Negroes as such, higher prices must have meant that Negroes were more highly valued because of their greater length of service. Negro women may have been especially prized, moreover, because their progeny could also be held perpetually. In 1645, for example, two Negro women and a boy were sold for 5,500 pounds of tobacco. Two years earlier William Burdett's inventory listed eight servants (with the time each had still to serve) at valuations ranging from 400 to 1,100 pounds, while a "very anntient" Negro was valued at 3,000 and an eight-year-old Negro girl at 2,000 pounds, with no time-remaining indicated for either. In the late 1650's an inventory of Thomas Ludlow's large estate evaluated a white servant with six years to serve at less than an elderly Negro man and only one half of a Negro woman. The labor owned by James Stone in 1648 was evaluated as follows:

	lb tobo
Thomas Groves, 4 yeares to serve	1300
Francis Bomley for 6 yeares	1500
John Thackstone for 3 yeares	1300
Susan Davis for 3 yeares	1000
Emaniell a Negro man	2000
Roger Stone 3 yeares	1300
Mingo a Negro man	2000

Besides setting a higher value on the two Negroes, Stone's inventory, like Burdett's, failed to indicate the number of years they had still to serve. It would seem safe to assume that the time remaining was omitted in this and similar documents simply because the Negroes were regarded as serving for an unlimited time.

The situation in Maryland was apparently the same. In 1643 Governor Leonard Calvert agreed with John Skinner, "mariner," to exchange certain estates for seventeen sound Negro "slaves," fourteen men and three women between sixteen and twenty-six years old. The total value of these was placed at 24,000 pounds of tobacco, which would work out to 1,000 pounds for the women and 1,500 for the men, prices considerably higher than those paid for white servants at the time.

Wherever Negro women were involved, however, higher valuations may have reflected the fact that they could be used for field work while white women generally were not. This discrimination between Negro and white women, of course, fell short of actual enslavement. It meant merely that Negroes were set apart in a way clearly not to their advantage. Yet this is not the only evidence that Negroes were subjected to degrading distinctions not directly related to slavery. In several ways Negroes were singled out for special treatment which suggested a generalized debasing of Negroes as a group. Significantly, the first indications of debasement appeared at about the same time as the first indications of actual enslavement.

The distinction concerning field work is a case in point. It first appeared on the written record in 1643, when Virginia pointedly recognized it in her taxation policy. Previously tithable persons had been defined (1629) as "all those that worke in the ground of what qualitie or condition soever." Now the law stated that all adult men and *Negro* women were to be tithable, and this distinction was made twice again before 1660. Maryland followed a similar course, beginning in 1654. John Hammond, in a 1656 tract defending the tobacco colonies, wrote that servant women were not put to work in the fields but in domestic employments, "yet som wenches that are nasty, and beastly and not fit to be so imployed are put into the ground." Since all Negro women were taxed as working in the fields, it would seem logical to conclude that Virginians found them "nasty" and "beastly." The essentially racial nature of this discrimination was bared by a 1668 law at the time slavery was crystallizing on the statute books:

> Whereas some doubts, have arisen whether negro women set free were still to be accompted tithable according to a former act, *It is declared by this grand assembly* that negro women, though permitted to enjoy their freedome yet ought not in all respects to be admitted to a full fruition of the exemptions and impunities of the English, and are still lyable to payment of taxes.

Virginia law set Negroes apart in a second way by denying them the important right and obligation to bear arms. Few restraints could indicate more clearly the denial to Negroes of membership in the white community. This action, in a sense the first foreshadowing of the slave codes, came in

1640, at just the time when other indications first appear that Negroes were subject to special treatment.

Finally, an even more compelling sense of the separateness of Negroes was revealed in early distress concerning sexual union between the races. In 1630 a Virginia court pronounced a now famous sentence: "Hugh Davis to be soundly whipped, before an assembly of Negroes and others for abusing himself to the dishonor of God and shame of Christians, by defiling his body in lying with a negro." While there were other instances of punishment for interracial union in the ensuing years, fornication rather than miscegenation may well have been the primary offense, though in 1651 a Maryland man sued someone who he claimed had said "that he had a black bastard in Virginia." There may have been nothing racial about the 1640 case by which Robert Sweet was compelled "to do penance in church according to laws of England, for getting a negroe woman with child and the woman whipt." About 1650 a white man and a Negro woman were required to stand clad in white sheets before a congregation in Lower Norfolk County for having had relations, but this punishment was sometimes used in ordinary cases of fornication between two whites.

It is certain, however, that in the early 1660's when slavery was gaining statutory recognition, the colonial assemblies legislated with feeling against miscegenation. Nor was this merely a matter of avoiding confusion of status, as was suggested by the Handlins. In 1662 Virginia declared that "if any christian shall committ fornication with a negro man or woman, hee or shee soe offending" should pay double the usual fine. Two years later Maryland prohibited interracial marriages:

> forasmuch as divers freeborne English women forgettfull of their free Condicõn and to the disgrace of our Nation doe intermarry with Negro Slaves by which alsoe divers suites may arise touching the Issue of such woemen and a great damage doth befall the Masters of such Negros for prevention whereof for deterring such freeborne women from such shamefull Matches . . .,

strong language indeed if the problem had only been confusion of status. A Maryland act of 1681 described marriages of white women with Negroes as, among other things, "always to the Satisfaccõn of theire Lascivious & Lustfull desires, & to the disgrace not only of the English butt allso of many other Christian Nations." When Virginia finally prohibited all interracial liaisons in 1691, the assembly vigorously denounced miscegenation and its fruits as "that abominable mixture and spurious issue."

One is confronted, then, with the fact that the first evidences of enslavement and of other forms of debasement appeared at about the same time. Such coincidence comports poorly with both views on the causation of prejudice and slavery. If slavery caused prejudice, then invidious distinctions concerning working in the fields, bearing arms, and sexual union should have appeared only after slavery's firm establishment. If prejudice caused slavery, then one would expect to find such lesser discriminations preceding the greater discrimination of outright enslavement.

Perhaps a third explanation of the relationship between slavery and prejudice may be offered, one that might fit the pattern of events as revealed by existing evidence. Both current views share a common starting point: They predicate two factors, prejudice and slavery, and demand a distinct order of causality. No matter how qualified by recognition that the effect may in turn react upon the cause, each approach inevitably tends to deny the validity of its opposite. But what if one were to regard both slavery and prejudice as species of a general debasement of the Negro? *Both may have been equally cause and effect,* constantly reacting upon each other, dynamically joining hands to hustle the Negro down the road to complete degradation. Mutual causation is, of course, a highly useful concept for describing social situations in the modern world. Indeed it has been widely applied in only slightly altered fashion to the current racial situation: Racial prejudice and the Negro's lowly position are widely accepted as constantly reinforcing each other.

This way of looking at the facts might well fit better with what we know of slavery itself. Slavery was an organized pattern of human relationships. No matter what the law might say, it was of different character than cattle ownership. No matter how degrading, slavery involved human beings. No one seriously pretended otherwise. Slavery was not an isolated economic or institutional phenomenon; it was the practical facet of a general debasement without which slavery could have no rationality. (Prejudice, too, was a form of debasement, a kind of slavery in the mind.) Certainly the urgent need for labor in a virgin country guided the direction which debasement took, molded it, in fact, into an institutional framework. That economic practicalities shaped the external form of debasement should not tempt one to forget, however, that slavery was at bottom a social arrangement, a way of society's ordering its members in its own mind.

2. THOMAS JEFFERSON

Notes on the State of Virginia*

(INDIANS)

The Indian of North America being more within our reach, I can speak of him somewhat from my own knowledge, but more from the information of others better acquainted with him, and on whose truth and judgment I can rely. From these sources I am able to say, in contradiction to this representation, that he is neither more defective in ardor, nor more impotent with his female, than the white reduced to the same diet and exercise; that he is brave, when an enterprise depends on bravery; education with him making the point of honor consist in the destruction of an enemy by stratagem, and in the preservation of his own person free from injury; or, perhaps, this is nature, while it is education which teaches us to honor force more than finesse; that he wils defend himmelf against a host of enemies, always choosing to be killed, rather than to surrender, though it be to the whites, who he knows will treat him well; that in other situations, also, he meets death with more deliberation, and endures tortures with a firmness unknown almost to religious enthusiasm with us; that he is affectionate to his children, careful of them, and indulgent in the extreme; that his affections comprehend his other connections, weakening, as with us, from circle to circle, as they recede from the centre; that his friendships are strong and faithful to the uttermost extremity; that his sensibility is keen, even the warriors weeping most bitterly on the loss of their children, though in general they endeavor to appear superior to human events; that his vivacity and activity of mind is equal to ours in the same situation; hence his eagerness for hunting, and for games of chance. The women are submitted to unjust drudgery. This I believe is the case with every barbarous people. With such, force is law. The stronger sex imposes on the weaker. It is civilization alone which replaces women in the enjoyment of their natural equality. That first teaches us to subdue the selfish passions, and to respect those rights in others which we value in ourselves. Were we in equal barbarism, our females would be equal drudges. The man with them is less strong than with us, but their women stronger than ours; and both or the same obvious reason; because our man

*Thomas Jefferson, *Notes on the State of Virginia* in *The Writings of Thomas Jefferson*, H.A. Washington, ed., Vol.VIII (New York, Riker, Thorne & Co., 1854), pp. 304-307, 431-34, 380-87.

and their woman is habituated to labor, and formed by it. With both races the sex which is indulged with ease is the least athletic. An Indian man is small in the hand and wrist, for the same reason for which a sailor is large and strong in the arms and shoulders, and a porter in the legs and thighs. They raise fewer children than we do. The causes of this are to be found, not in a difference of nature, but of circumstance. The women very frequently attending the men in their parties of war and of hunting, child-bearing becomes extremely inconvenient to them. It is said, therefore, that they have learned the practice of procuring abortion by the use of some vegetable; and that it even extends to prevent conception for a considerable time after. During these parties they are exposed to numerous hazards, to excessive exertions, to the greatest extremities of hunger. Even at their homes the nation depends for food, through a certain part of every year, on the gleanings of the forest; that is, they experience a famine once in every year. With all animals, if the female be badly fed, or not fed at all, her young perish; and if both male and female be reduced to like want, generation becomes less active, less productive. To the obstacles, then, of want and hazard, which nature has opposed to the multiplication of wild animals, for the purpose of restraining their numbers within certain bounds, those of labor and of voluntary abortion are added with the Indian. No wonder, then, if they multiply less than we do. Where food is regularly supplied, a single farm will show more of cattle, than a whole country of forests can of buffaloes. The same Indian women, when married to white traders, who feed them and their children plentifully and regularly, who exempt them from excessive drudgery, who keep them stationary and unexposed to accident, produce and raise as many children as the white women. Instances are known, under these circumstances, of their rearing a dozen children. An inhuman practice once prevailed in this country, of making slaves of the Indians. It is a fact well known with us, that the Indian women so enslaved produced and raised as numerous families as either the whites or blacks among whom they lived. It has been said that Indians have less hair than the whites, except on the head. But this is a fact of which fair proof can scarcely be had. With them it is disgraceful to be hairy on the body. They say it likens them to hogs. They therefore pluck the hair as fast as it appears. But the traders who marry their women, and prevail on them to discontinue this practice, say, that nature is the same with them as with the whites. Nor, if the fact be true, is the consequence necessary which has been drawn from it. Negroes have notoriously less hair than the whites; yet they are more ardent. But if cold and moisture be the agents of nature for diminishing the races of animals, how comes she all at once to suspend their operation as to the physical man of the new world, whom the Count acknowledges to be "à peu près de même stature que l'homme de notre monde," and to let loose their influence on his moral faculties? How has this "combination of the elements and other physical causes, so contrary to the enlargement of animal nature in this new world, these obstacles to the development and formation of great germs," been arrested and suspended, so as to permit the human body to acquire its just dimensions, and by what inconceivable process has their action been directed on his mind alone? To judge of the truth of this, to form a just estimate of their genius and mental powers, more facts are wanting, and great allowance to be made for those circumstances of their situation which call for a display of particular talents only. This done, we shall probably find that they are formed in mind as well as in body, on the same module with the "Homo sapiens Europoeus." . . .

Monsieur Buffon has indeed given an afflicting picture of human nature in his description of the man of America. But sure I am there never was a picture more unlike the original. He grants indeed that his stature is the same as that of the man of Europe. He might have admitted, that the Iroquois were larger, and the Lenopi, or Delawares, taller than people in Europe generally are. But he says their organs of generation are smaller and weaker than those of Europeans. Is this a fact? I believe not; at least it is an observation I never heard before.—"They have no beard." Had he known the pains and trouble it costs the men to pluck out by the roots the hair that grows on their faces, he would have seen that nature had not been deficient in that respect. Every nation has its customs. I have seen an Indian beau, with a looking-glass in his hand, examining his face for hours together, and plucking out by the roots every hair he could discover, with a kind of tweezer made of a piece of fine brass wire, that had been twisted round a stick, and which he used with great dexterity.—"They have no ardor for their females." It is true they do not indulge those excesses, nor discover that fondness which is customary in Europe; but this is not owing to a defect in nature but to manners. Their soul is wholly bent upon war. This is what procures them glory among the men, and makes them the admiration of the women. To this they are educated from their earliest youth. When they pursue game with ardor, when they bear the fatigues of the chase, when they sustain and suffer patiently hunger and cold; it is not so much for the sake of the game they pursue, as to convince their parents and the council of the nation that they are fit to be enrolled in the number of the warriors. The songs of the women, the dance of the warriors, the sage counsel of the chiefs, the tales of the old, the triumphal entry of the warriors returning with success from battle, and the respect paid to those who distinguish themselves in war, and in subduing their enemies;

in short, everything they see or hear tends to inspire them with an ardent desire for military fame. If a young man were to discover a fondness for women before he has been to war, he would become the contempt of the men, and the scorn and ridicule of the women. Or were he to indulge himself with a captive taken in war, and much more were he to offer violence in order to gratify his lust, he would incur indelible disgrace. The seeming frigidity of the men, therefore, is the effect of manners, and not a defect of nature. Besides, a celebrated warrior is oftener courted by the females, than he has occasion to court; and this is a point of honor which the men aim at. Instances similar to that of Ruth and Boaz are not uncommon among them. For though the women are modest and diffident, and so bashful that they seldom lift up their eyes, and scarce ever look a man full in the face, yet, being brought up in great subjection, custom and manners reconcile them to modes of acting, which, judged of by Europeans, would be deemed inconsistent with the rules of female decorum and propriety. I once saw a young widow, whose husband, a warrior, had died about eight days before, hastening to finish her grief, and who, by tearing her hair, beating her breast, and drinking spirits, made the tears flow in great abundance, in order that she might grieve much in a short space of time, and be married that evening to another young warrior. The manner in which this was viewed by the men and women of the tribe, who stood round, silent and solemn spectators of the scene, and the indifference with which they answered my question respecting it, convinced me that it was no unusual custom. I have known men advanced in years, whose wives were old and past child-bearing, take young wives, and have children, though the practice of polygamy is not common. Does this savor of frigidity, or want of ardor for the female? Neither do they seem to be deficient in natural affection. I have seen both fathers and mothers in the deepest affliction, when their children have been dangerously ill; though I believe the affection is stronger in the descending than the ascending scale, and though custom forbids a father to grieve immoderately for a son slain in battle. "That they are timorous and cowardly," is a character with which there is little reason to charge them, when we recollect the manner in which the Iroquois met Monsieur———, who marched into their country; in which the old men, who scorned to fly, or to survive the capture of their town, braved death, like the old Romans in the time of the Gauls, and in which they soon after revenged themselves by sacking and destroying Montreal. But above all, the unshaken fortitude with which they bear the most excruciating tortures and death when taken prisoners, ought to exempt them from that character. Much less are they to be characterized as a people of no vivacity, and who are excited to action or motion only by the calls of hunger and thirst. Their dances in which they so much delight, and which to an European would be the most severe exercise, fully contradict this, not to mention their fatiguing marches, and the toil they voluntarily and cheerfully undergo in their military expeditions. It is true, that when at home, they do not employ themselves in labor or the culture of the soil; but this again is the effect of customs and manners, which have assigned that to the province of the women. But it is said, they are averse to society and a social life. Can anything be more inapplicable than this to a people who always live in towns or clans? Or can they be said to have no "republic," who conduct all their affairs in national councils, who pride themselves in their national character, who consider an insult or injury done to an individual by a stranger as done to the whole, and resent it accordingly? In short, this picture is not applicable to any nation of Indians I have ever known or heard of in North America. . . .

(NEGROES)

. . . It will probably be asked, Why not retain and incorporate the blacks into the State, and thus save the expense of supplying by importation of white settlers, the vacancies they will leave? Deep-rooted prejudices entertained by the whites; ten thousand recollections, by the blacks, of the injuries they have sustained; new provocations; the real distinctions which nature has made; and many other circumstances, will divide us into parties, and produce convulsions, which will probably never end but in the extermination of the one or the other race. To these objections, which are political, may be added others, which are physical and moral. The first difference which strikes us is that of color. Whether the black of the negro resides in the reticular membrane between the skin and scarf-skin, or in the scarf-skin itself; whether it proceeds from the color of the blood, the color of the bile, or from that of some other secretion, the difference is fixed in nature, and is as real as if its seat and cause were better known to us. And is this difference of no importance? Is it not the foundation of a greater or less share of beauty in the two races? Are not the fine mixtures of red and white, the expressions of every passion by greater or less suffusions of color in the one, preferable to that eternal monotony, which reigns in the countenances, that immovable veil of black which covers the emotions of the other race? Add to these, flowing hair, a more elegant symmetry of form, their own judgment in favor of the whites, declared by their preference of them, as uniformly as is the preference of the Oranootan for the black woman over those of his own species. The circumstance of superior beauty, is thought worthy attention in the propagation of our horses, dogs, and other domestic animals; why not in that of man? Besides those of color, figure, and hair, there are other physical distinctions proving a difference of race. They have less hair on the face and body. They secrete less by the kidneys, and more by the glands of the skin, which gives them a very strong and disagreeable odor. This greater degree of transpiration, renders them more tolerant of heat, and less so of cold than the whites, Perhaps, too, a difference of structure in the pulminary apparatus, which a late ingenious experimentalist has discovered to be the principal regulator of animal heat, may have disabled them from extricating, in the act of inspiration, so much of that fluid from the outer air, or obliged them in expiration, to part with more ot it. They seem to require less sleep. A black after hard labor through the day, will be induced by the slightest amusements to sit up till midnight, or later, though knowing he must be out with the first dawn of the morning. They are at least as brave, and more adventuresome. But this may perhaps proceed from a want of forethought, which prevents their seeing a danger till it be present. When present, they do not go through it with more coolness or steadiness than the whites. They are more ardent after their female; but love seems with them to be more an eager desire, than a tender delicate mixture of sentiment and sensation. Their griefs are transient. Those numberless afflictions, which render it doubtful whether heaven has given life to us in mercy or in wrath, are less felt, and sooner forgotten with them. In general, their existence appears to participate more of sensation than reflection. To this must be ascribed their disposition to sleep when abstracted from their diversions, and unemployed in labor. An animal whose body is at rest, and who does not reflect, must be disposed to sleep of course. Comparing them by their faculties of memory, reason, and imagination, it appears to me that in memory they are equal to the whites; in reason much inferior, as I think one could scarcely be found capable of tracing and comprehending the investigations of Euclid; and that in imagination they are dull, tasteless, and anomalous. It would be unfair to follow them to Africa for this investigation. We will consider them here, on the same stage with the whites, and where the facts are not apochryphal on which a judgment is to be formed. It will be right to make great allowances for the difference of condition, of education, of conversation, of the sphere in which they move. Many millions of them have been brought to, and born in America. Most of them, indeed, have been confined to tillage, to their own homes, and their own society; yet many have been so situated, that they might have availed themselves of the conversation of their masters; many have been brought up to the handicraft arts, and from that circumstance have always been associated with the whites. Some have been liberally educated, and all have lived in countries where the arts and sciences are cultivated to a considerable degree, and all have had before their eyes samples of the best works from abroad. The Indians, with no advantages of this kind, will often carve figures on their pipes not destitute of design and merit. They will crayon out an animal, a plant, or a country, so as to prove the existence of a germ in their minds which only wants cultivation. They astonish you with strokes of the most sublime oratory; such as prove their reason and sentiment strong, their imagination glowing and elevated. But never yet could I find that a black had uttered a thought above the level of plain narration; never saw even an elementary trait of painting or sculpture. In music they are more generally gifted than the whites with accurate ears for tune and time, and they have been found capable of imagining a small catch. Whether they will be equal to the composition of a more extensive run of melody, or of complicated harmony, is yet to be proved. Misery is often the parent of the most affecting touches in poetry. Among the blacks is misery enough, God knows, but no poetry. Love is the peculiar oestrum of the poet. Their love is ardent, but it kindles the senses only, not the imagination. Religion, indeed, has produced a Phyllis Whately; but it could not produce a poet. The compositions published under her name are below the dignity of criticism. The heroes of the Dunciad are to her, as Hercules to the author of that poem. Ignatius Sancho has approached nearer to merit in composition; yet his letters do more honor to the heart than the head. They breathe the purest effusions of friendship and general philanthropy, and show how great a degree of the latter may be compounded with strong religious zeal. He is often happy in the turn of his compliments, and his style is easy and familiar, except when he affects a Shandean fabrication of words. But his imagination is wild and extravagant, escapes incessantly from every restraint of reason and taste, and, in the course of its vagaries, leaves a tract of thought as incoherent and eccentric, as is the course of a meteor through the sky. His subjects should often have led him to a process of sober reasoning; yet we find him always substituting sentiment for demonstration. Upon the whole, though we admit him to the first place among those of his own color who have presented themselves to the public judgment, yet when we compare him with the writers of the race among whom he lived and particularly with the epistolary class in which he has taken his own stand, we are compelled to enrol him at the bottom of the column. This criticism supposes the letters published under his name to be genuine, and to have received amendment from no other hand; points which would not be of easy investigation. The improvement of the blacks in body and mind, in the first instance of their mixture with the whites, has been observed by every one, and proves that their inferiority is not the effect merely of their condition of life. We know that among the Romans, about the Augustan age especially, the condition of their slaves was much more deplorable than that of the blacks on the continent of America. The two sexes were confined in separate apartments, because to raise a child cost the master more than to buy one. Cato, for a very restricted indulgence to his slaves in this particular, took from them a certain price. But in this country the slaves multiply as fast as the free inhabitants. Their situation and manners place the commerce between the two sexes almost without restraint. The same Cato, on a principle of economy, always sold his sick and superannuated slaves. He gives it as a standing precept to a master visiting his farm, to sell his old oxen, old wagons, old tools, old and diseased servants, and everything else become useless. . . . The American slaves cannot enumerate this among the injuries and insults they receive. It was the common practice to expose in the island Aesculapius, in the Tyber, diseased slaves whose cure was like to become tedious. The emperor Claudius, by an edict, gave freedom to such of them as should recover, and first declared that if any person chose to kill rather than to expose them, it should not be deemed homicide. The exposing them is a crime of which no instance has existed with us; and were it to be followed by death, it would be punished capitally. We are told of a certain Vedius Pollio, who, in the presence of Augustus, would have given a slave as food to his fish, for having broken a glass. With the Romans, the regular method of taking the evidence of their slaves was under torture. Here it has been thought better never to resort to their evidence. When a master was murdered, all his slaves, in the same house, or within hearing, were condemned to death. Here punishment falls on the guilty only, and as precise proof is required against him as against a freeman. Yet notwithstanding these and other discouraging circumstances among the Romans, their slaves were often their rarest artists. They excelled too in science, insomuch as to be usually employed as tutors to their master's children. Epictetus, Terence, and Phaedrus, were slaves. But they were of the race of whites. It is not their condition then, but nature, which has produced the distinction. Whether further observation will or will not verify the conjecture, that nature has been less bountiful to them in the endowments of the head, I believe that in those of the heart she will be found to have done them justice. That disposition to theft with which they have been branded, must be ascribed to their situation, and not to any depravity of the moral sense. The man in whose favor no laws of property exist, probably feels himself less bound to respect those made in favor of others. When arguing for ourselves, we lay it down as a fundamental, that laws, to be just, must give a reciprocation of right; that, without this, they are mere arbitrary rules of conduct, founded in force, and not in conscience; and it is a problem which I give to the master to solve, whether the religious precepts against the violation of property were not framed for him as well as his slave? And whether the slave may not as justifiably take a little from one who has taken all from him, as he may slay one who would slay him? That a change in the relations in which a man is placed should change his ideas of moral right or wrong, is neither new, nor peculiar to the color of the blacks. Homer tells us it was so two thousand six hundred years ago.

> Jove fix'd it certain, that whatever day
> Makes man a slave, takes half his worth away.

But the slaves of which Homer speaks were whites. Notwithstanding these considerations which must weaken their respect for the laws of property, we find among them numerous instances of the most rigid integrity, and as many as among their better instructed masters, of benevolence, gratitude, and unshaken fidelity. The opinion that they are inferior in the faculties of reason and imagination, must be hazarded with great diffidence. To justify a general conclusion, requires many observations, even where the subject may be submitted to the anatomical knife, to optical glasses, to analysis by fire or by solvents. How much more then where it is a faculty, not a substance, we are examining; where it eludes the research of all the senses; where the conditions of its existence are various and variously combined; where the effects of those which are present or absent bid defiance to calculation; let me add too, as a circumstance of great tenderness, where our conclusion would degrade a whole race of men from the rank in the scale of beings which their Creater may perhaps have given them. To our reproach it must be said, that though for a century and a half we have had under our eyes the races of black and of red men, they have never yet been viewed by us as subjects of natural history. I advance it, therefore, as a suspicion only, that the blacks, whether originally a distinct race, or made distinct by time and circumstances, are inferior to the whites in the endowments both of body and mind. It is not against experience to suppose that different species of the same genus, or varieties of the same species, may possess different qualifications. Will not a lover of natural history then, one who views the gradations in all the races of animals with the eye of philosophy, excuse an effort to keep those in the department of man as distinct as nature has formed them? This unfortunate difference of color, and perhaps of faculty, is a powerful obstacle to the emancipation of these people. Many of their advocates, while they wish to vindicate the liberty of human nature, are anxious also to preserve its dignity and beauty. Some of these, embarrassed by the question, "What further is to be done with them?" join themselves in opposition with those who are actuated by sordid avarice only. Among the Romans emancipation required but one effort. The slave, when made free, might mix with, without staining the blood of his master. But with us a second is necessary, unknown to history. When freed, he is to be removed beyond the reach of mixture. . . .

3. REGINALD HORSMAN

American Indian Policy in the Old Northwest, 1783-1812*

In the years from 1783 to 1812 the one consistent element in American Indian policy in the Old Northwest was the desire to acquire the land between the Ohio and the Mississippi. The host of subsidiary objectives were all subordinated to this end. In theory, its attainment was simply a matter of telling the Indian inhabitants of the region that England had ceded it to the United States in 1783 and that the Indians could live only on lands allotted to them by the American government. In practice, it soon became apparent that the Indians were not prepared to acknowledge the English right to give away Indian land; the Americans were obliged to obtain their objective in other ways. Between 1783 and 1812 the American government developed a policy that would secure land in the simplest and least expensive manner. Not only did it thus secure land, it also succeeded in convincing itself that what it was doing was in the best interests of the Indians. What had started out in 1783 as naked desire for land had, by 1812, been transmuted into lofty moral purpose. By 1812 American leaders were not only trying to convince others, but apparently had also convinced themselves that they were working for the ultimate benefit of the Indian. The manner in which national interest and moral purpose became entangled is a key to the history of nineteenth-century expansion.

The first phase of post-Revolutionary American Indian policy in the Old Northwest lasted from 1783 to 1787. In the Treaty of Paris which ended the Revolution the British ignored their Indian allies. The Indians were left to make their own peace with the Americans, and their position was compli-

*Reginald Horsman, "American Indian Policy in the Old Northwest, 1783-1812," *William and Mary Quarterly*, third series, Vol. XVIII (1961), pp. 35-53. Reprinted by permission of Reginald Horsman.

cated by the fact that the Americans desired more than the cessation of hostilities in the Northwest. American frontiersmen had long since pushed into western Pennsylvania and down the Ohio to Kentucky. They were now anxious to settle the rich lands northwest of the Ohio. Moreover, the government of the Confederation had a financial interest in the movement of settlers into that region. By the sale of lands the Confederation hoped to solve its acute financial problems. It had already been agreed that the states with claims north of the Ohio would cede them to the central government, and by 1786 these cessions were accomplished. On October 10, 1780, Congress had promised that lands ceded to the United States would be disposed of for the common good, "and be settled and formed into distinct republican states." Thus, in establishing peace with the Indians of the Northwest, the Confederation wished to begin the process of acquiring the lands between the Ohio and the Mississippi.

The document on which the Confederation based its Northwestern Indian policy from 1783 to 1787 was the report presented to Congress by James Duane, chairman of the committee on Indian affairs, on October 15, 1783. This resolved that a convention should be held with the Indians to make peace and establish boundary lines. The Indians were to be told that the land on which they lived had been ceded by Great Britain in the Treaty of Paris, and that as they had fought on the side of the British during the Revolution, they could justly be expelled to the north of the Great Lakes along with their allies. However, it was argued that America was prepared to forgive what was past and to draw a boundary line between the Americans and the Indians. As the United States needed land, both for her expanding population and for extinguishing her national debt, the Indians would have to cede a portion of their territory. This was justified as reparations for Indian hostility during the war. A boundary line was suggested that would have given most of the modern state of Ohio to the United States. Though these suggestions were to be modified in detail, they formed the basis of policy until 1787.

The reasoning behind this report can best be understood by a consideration of letters sent to the committee on Indian affairs during the previous summer. The suggestions that most obviously influenced the committee were those made by George Washington and by General Philip Schuyler. Washington had twice written to express his views. In June 1783 he had supported the plan for establishing settlements of ex-soldiers in the west, arguing that the appearance of such formidable settlements in the vicinity of the Indian towns "would be the most likely means to enable us to purchase upon equitable terms of the Aborigines their right of preoccupancy; and to induce them to relinquish our Territories; and to remove into the illimitable regions of the West.'' A far more comprehensive plan was submitted by Schuyler on July 29. He argued that America would be ill-advised to continue the war with the Indians to expel them from the country—it would cost a great deal, and the Indians would return if the force that expelled them should retire. Moreover, if driven to reside in British territory, the Indians would add strength to Great Britain. Even if America could expel the Indians at moderate cost, Schuyler argued, it would not be worth while. America should merely take the land she needed for present purposes: ''It will be little or no obstacle to our in future improving the very country they may retain, whenever we shall want it. For as our settlements approach their country, they must from the scarcity of game, which that approach will induce to, retire farther back, and dispose of their lands, unless they dwindle comparatively to nothing, as all savages have done, who gain their sustenance by the chace, when compelled to live in the vicinity of civilized people, and thus leave us the country without the expence of a purchase, trifling as that will probably be.''

Schuyler's ideas had influential support. On September 7, 1783, Washington wrote to Duane telling him that his sentiments exactly coincided with those expressed by Schuyler in his letter of July 29, and making further suggestions for the guidance of the committee. The Indians should be informed of the British cessions, and told that because of their hostility in the Revolution they might well be expelled beyond the Great Lakes. The United States, however, was prepared to be generous, and would draw a boundary line between the Americans and the Indians. Washington thought that America should not grasp too much, and that if the Indians were dissatisfied with the boundary they should be given compensation. Also, settlers should be restrained from crossing the boundary line. This would keep the peace and would make possible further land acquisitions. ''The Indians as have been observed under General Schuylers Letter,'' wrote Washington, ''will ever retreat as our Settlements advance upon them and they will ever be ready to sell, as we are to buy; That is the cheapest as well as the least distressing way of dealing with them.'' And he left little doubt of his own view of the Indians: ''the gradual extension of our Settlements will as certainly cause the Savage as the Wolf to retire; both being beasts of prey tho' they differ in shape.''

The committee on Indian affairs thus paid close attention to the advice of Washington and Schuyler in its report of October 15, 1783, though needless to say the report did not mention that the drawing of a boundary line was intended as the prelude to the gradual extermination or expulsion of the Indians. In carrying out this policy in the following years, the Confederation stressed the idea that the Northwest had been ceded by the British, but it paid little attention to Washington's suggestion that the Indians should be conciliated in order to facilitate future land acquisitions. Between 1783 and 1786 land northwest of the Ohio was acquired by three treaties—Fort Stanwix in 1784, Fort McIntosh in 1785, and Fort Finney in 1786. They were all dictated treaties. Though the extent of the lands treated for was not as large as that envisioned by Congress originally, these negotiations resulted in the cession to the United States of what is now eastern and southern Ohio. . . .

Despite its apparent success, the Indian policy from 1783 to 1786 was disastrous. The United States not only proceeded on the assumption that the Indians should cede some of their land as retribution for their part in the Revolution, but also assumed that the territorial sovereignty granted by England in 1783 completely eliminated any Indian right to the soil of the Northwest. The Indians who inhabited the region naturally would not accept this interpretation of the Treaty of Paris. They could not conceive that the lands upon which they lived and hunted were not their own, and, moreover, during the colonial period they had become accustomed to the idea that the whites would purchase the Indian right to the soil in formal treaty. The American post-Revolutionary policy quickly produced Indian opposition. By 1786 hostilities were breaking out on the Northwest frontier, and the Indians were ready to fight to prevent American settlement northwest of the Ohio. The Shawnee almost immediately disavowed Fort Finney, and the Mohawk Joseph Brant was, with British assistance, striving to unite the Northwestern tribes. America had treaties to show her ownership of lands northwest of the Ohio, but in her straitened financial position she could not occupy and defend them.

An indication that force might soon be tempered by diplomacy came in the famous Northwest Ordinance of July 13, 1787. In regard to the intended acquisition of land from the Ohio to the Mississippi, the ordinance was perfectly in accord with previous policy. It laid down the system by which the land between those two rivers would come into the Union, and provided for not less than three nor more than five states in that area. This plan of course included the land allotted to the Indians between 1783 and 1786, in addition to Indian lands farther to the west. It was Article Three that foreshadowed a change in American thinking. "The utmost good faith shall always be observed towards the Indians," it stated; "their lands and property shall never be taken from them without their consent; and in their property, rights and liberty, they never shall be invaded or disturbed, unless in just and lawful wars authorised by Congress; but laws founded in justice and humanity shall from time to time be made, for preventing wrongs being done to them, and for preserving peace and friendship with them."

Though the language of the ordinance seems so incongruous in view of what had gone before, the United States was in fact changing her policy in the summer of 1787. The objective of land acquisition remained the same, but the methods were to be modified. The change had been forced upon the United States by the extent of Indian resistance. On July 10, 1787, Secretary of War Henry Knox reported to Congress that there was neither sufficient money nor an adequate army to carry on an Indian war. Peace was essential. Within two weeks Knox again told Congress of the precarious position and argued that it was better to spend a small sum on the purchase of land than to fight an expensive Indian war. Knox's report was referred to a congressional committee on Indian affairs, headed by Nathan Dane. The committee reported on August 9, 1787, recommending changes in American Indian policy. It argued that American desires could be obtained more simply than by war. Rather than acting from a position of superiority, the United States should treat with the Indians on a basis of equality and "convince them of the Justice and humanity as well as the power of the United States and of their disposition to promote the happiness of the Indians." Would it not be better, it was asked, to proceed on the principle of fairly purchasing lands rather than of giving lands to the Indians as though the land were already American?

In accord with the suggestions of Knox and the committee, the United States moved toward a more diplomatic policy. On October 5 Congress acted on the committee report and recommended a general treaty. Later in the month it appropriated twenty thousand dollars for holding Indian treaties wherever Congress thought it necessary. This sum was added to in the following years, and the United States attempted to follow a policy of purchase rather than conquest. However, the object of acquiring all the land to the Mississippi had not been abandoned—far from it. The instructions sent at the end of October 1787 to the governor of the Northwest Territory, Arthur St. Clair, told him: "You will not neglect any opportunity that may offer of extinguishing the Indian rights to the westward as far as the river Mississippi."

The general treaty with the Indians, which was suggested as desirable in the summer of 1787, took a long time to accomplish. Neither the Confederation nor the Indians were noted for speed in negotiation, and it was not until the close of 1788 that Governor St. Clair met with the Indians at Fort Harmar on the Ohio in an attempt to bring peace to the Northwest. The council lasted into January 1789, and eventually St. Clair accomplished two treaties—one with the Six Nations and the other with the Wyandots, Delawares, Ottawas, and Chippewas. It was found impossible to obtain the boundaries suggested in St. Clair's instructions, but at least the new American policy was partially put into effect. In essence, St. Clair told the Indians that though the United States claimed the land by conquest she was prepared to pay for it as well. He obtained confirmation of the treaties of Fort Stanwix and Fort McIntosh by large payments to the Indians. Though he did not fully concede the Indian right to the land of the Northwest, he did reintroduce the principle of purchase. The treaty with the Wyandots and the other western tribes attempted to keep the peace by deceiving them as to America's future intentions. The Wyandot treaty stated that the Fort McIntosh line was confirmed "to the end that the same may remain as a division line between the lands of the United States of America, and the lands of said nations forever." This was nothing but a meaningless formula.

Thus in the spring of 1789, when the Federal government came to power, American policy was already changing in regard to the manner of acquiring lands. This change was to be accentuated by the new government. An immediate problem, however, was that the heavy-handed policy since 1783 had produced a crisis in the Northwest. The Fort Harmar treaty pleased the Indians no more than the treaties of Stanwix and McIntosh had done. It did nothing to solve the basic Indian dissatisfaction at losing their lands. Encouraged by the British, the Northwestern tribes were ready to insist once again upon an Ohio River boundary. They demanded that American settlers advance no farther.

Henry Knox, who continued as Secretary of War, now made a determined effort to develop the new tendencies in American Indian policy. From this time forward the element of national honor played an increasingly important part in determining the methods of land acquisition. In a report of June 15, 1789, Knox urged negotiation rather than war. Even if the necessary force were available, he argued, it was debatable from the point of view of justice whether it would be wise to use it. In addition, he maintained that America did not have sufficient money to expel the Indians. Justice and expediency made negotiation essential. Knox estimated that to attach the Indians north and south of the Ohio to the United States for the next fifty years might cost $15,000 annually, whereas to coerce them would not only cost more money, but would also stain the character of the nation "beyond all pecuniary calculation." After these praiseworthy sentiments a rather more realistic calculation, reminiscent of Philip Schuyler's suggestion of July 29, 1783, entered into Knox's report: "As the settlements of the whites shall approach near to the Indian boundaries established by treaties, the game will be diminished, and the lands being valuable to the Indians only as hunting grounds, they will be willing to sell further tracts for small considerations. By the expiration, therefore, of the above period [fifty years], it is more probable that the Indians will, by the invariable operation of the causes which have hitherto existed in their intercourse with the whites, be reduced to a very small number."

Several weeks later, in a report mainly concerned with the southern Indians, Knox moved a step further in suggesting an acceptable Indian policy. He pointed out that in time there would probably be no Indians east of the Mississippi and he asked whether, instead of extermination, there should not be civilization of the Indians. He suggested the possibility of the use of missionaries and argued that even if this did not fully civilize the Indians, it would at least attach them to the American interest. To accomplish this, he also urged fair purchase from the Indians, the recognition of the Indian right of soil, the treatment of the Indian tribes as foreign nations, and the regulation of white emigration. Knox was moving toward the idea that the acquisition of Indian land could be accomplished more easily, and with fewer pangs of conscience, if accompanied by a spreading of American civilization among the Indians and the protection of the Indians from brazen insult.

In the following years America was to pass various laws designed to protect the Indians from overt acts of violence and from exploitation. Regulations concerning the mode of white settlement, the encroachment on Indian land, the selling of liquor, and fair trading practices toward the Indians were all put into effect. These often did not work, owing to the problem of controlling the frontiersmen, but the American government was sincere in its effort to make them work. Everything possible was to be done to keep the Indians at peace. If fixed boundaries were established and peace were maintained, the land of the Northwest would eventually be absorbed by the American government at a small cost. Moreover, it would be asborbed in a manner that, it was presumed, would cast least discredit on the government.

The irony of the situation was that the United States, though moving rapidly in 1789 toward a policy of peace and absorption, found it necessary to wage a five-year Indian war for which she had not the slightest desire. The Indians by 1789 were actively resisting the American advance—they did not want to yield any land beyond the Ohio either by war or purchase, and America would have to wage a successful campaign before she could put her desired policy into effect. General Josiah Harmar's defeat in 1790 made another campaign essential, and in 1791 St. Clair was sent into the Indian country. Secretary of State Thomas Jefferson expressed the position clearly in April 1791 when he said before St. Clair's expedition that "I hope we shall drub the Indians well this summer & then change our plan from war to bribery." Unfortunately for the United States it was St. Clair who was drubbed, and this necessitated another three years of crisis before Anthony Wayne defeated the Indians at Fallen Timbers in August 1794. While these hostilities were proceeding, the American government advanced its plans to avoid such conflicts in the future.

In his messages to Congress, Washington advocated fair dealing with the Indians, impartial justice, reasonable trading practices, and strict regulation of the manner in which Indian lands might be obtained. He also moved further in desiring the Americanization of the Indian. By 1792 the idea of teaching the Indians how to farm, to keep domesticated animals, and to build comfortable homes was entering into the instructions of American envoys to the Northwest. In May of that year Knox wrote to Rufus Putnam, who was being sent in an effort to attain peace with the Wabash tribes, that "The United States are highly desirous of imparting to all the Indian tribes the blessings of civilization, as the only means of perpetuating them on the earth." The American government, particularly Knox, was becoming most concerned with the effect of its Indian policy on the national honor. Knox wrote to Anthony Wayne on January 5, 1793, that "If our modes of population and War destroy the tribes the disinterested part of mankind and posterity will be apt to class the effects of our Conduct and that of the Spaniards in Mexico and Peru together." In fact, while America fought her bitter battle in the Northwest from 1789 to 1794, the late Confederation policy of fair purchase was transmuted into the idea of just treatment of the Indians in all matters *except* the vital one of their lands. For the land problem there was no real solution. The rapidly expanding American population could no more be expected to ignore the rich, sparsely settled lands to the west than could the Indians be expected to yield them without a struggle. The American government could make the process less painful, but it could not solve the basic dilemma. When Knox retired from office at the end of 1794, he issued final words of advice regarding American Indian policy. Once again he spoke of the necessity for fair dealing with the Indians, of bringing them the advantages of civilized life, and he warned that "a future historian may mark the causes of this destruction of the human race in sable colors." Yet, as earnestly as Knox advised justice, there would be no lasting peace while land remained the object of American Indian policy.

The military victory of Anthony Wayne in August 1794 allowed the government to put into effect its desired Indian policy. Already, in April

1794, instructions in regard to the peace had been sent to Wayne. He was to obtain the boundaries of the Treaty of Fort Harmar and could confirm to the Indians their right of soil in the remainder of the Northwest. However, and this was vital, the United States must have the right of pre-emption. According to the prevalent theories, the Indians would inevitably want to sell more lands, and all the United States needed was the exclusive right to purchase them. This had been a *sine qua non* of peace with the Northwest Indians since the start of the new national government in 1789. Given the right of pre-emption, America would inevitably advance to the Mississippi.

When, in the spring of 1795, Wayne was near to the conclusion of a treaty with the Northwestern Indians, the new Secretary of War, Timothy Pickering, sent additional instructions for his guidance. Pickering explicitly renounced the policy pursued by the Confederation government in the post-1783 period—that is, the policy of claiming the Northwest by conquest—and said that the land belonged to the Indians. He stressed that peace and the satisfaction of the Indians were the most important considerations in the treaty. As a result the United States would claim little more land than had been obtained in 1789 at Fort Harmar. This seems most reasonable unless another statement made by Pickering to Wayne is taken into consideration. "When a peace shall once be established," he wrote, "and we also take possession of the posts now held by the British, we can obtain every thing we shall want with a tenth part of the trouble and difficulty which you would now have to encounter." He was paying his respects to the now well-established idea that if a boundary and peace were established Indian lands would soon fall into the hands of the Americans. Ten years before, Pickering had urged caution in the acquisition of more land at that time: "The purchase will be as easily made at any future period as at this time. Indians having no ideas of wealth, and their numbers always lessening in the neighbourhood of our Settlements, their claims for compensation will likewise be diminished; and besides that, fewer will remain to be gratified, the game will be greatly reduced, and lands destitute of game will, by hunters, be lightly esteemed." Pickering, like Washington, Knox, and Schuyler, saw that war was not the easiest method of removing the Indians from the land of the Northwest.

The resounding phrases of the famous Treaty of Greenville thus meant very little. Though only eastern and southern Ohio, together with a strip of what is now southeastern Indiana, were granted to the United States, and though the United States relinquished her claims to all lands beyond these boundaries, it was quite evident to the American government that this was not a permanent division. Article Five gave the right of pre-emption in the remaining land of the Northwest to the United States—it was put in because it was quite obvious that it was going to be used. Moreover, by the treaty, the United States was given sixteen reservations of land on the Indian side of the boundary line to use as posts and was also granted free communication between them. Indians throughout the Northwest were to have the contact with white civilization that would result in their withdrawal or diminution in numbers. The Indians thought the Greenville line was to last forever; the Americans knew better. The territorial organization of the Northwest proceeded in spite of the Greenville line; in 1796 Wayne County was organized, stretching westward to Lake Michigan, and in 1800 the organization of the Indiana Territory also ignored the division made at Greenville. The peace that reigned after Greenville allowed American settlers to pour into the ceded areas.

The period of calm lasted little longer than the administration of John Adams, for American settlers soon looked beyond the land ceded at Greenville. From 1801 to 1809 President Thomas Jefferson sought the land between the Ohio and the Mississippi rivers with all the eagerness of the Confederation. With the ambivalence that is so characteristic of Jefferson, he was able to combine an apparent genuine interest in the welfare of the Indian with a voracious appetite for Indian land. In his public utterances Jefferson viewed the harsh realities of American-Indian relations through a roseate mist. His first annual message, December 1801, expressed happiness that the Indians were becoming "more and more sensible" of the advantages of farming and "the household arts" over hunting and fishing. The wish was apparently father to the thought. In the following month he told a visiting delegation of Miamis, Potawatomis, and Weas that the United States would "with great pleasure see your people become disposed to cultivate the earth, to raise hea os of the useful animals and to spin and weave, for their food and clothing, these resources are certain, they will never disappoint you while those of hunting may fail, and expose your women and children to the miseries of hunger and cold." This became the rallying call of Jefferson throughout his presidency. He was convinced that the United States should take every opportunity to persuade the Indians to abandon their old modes of life. His motives were not entirely altruistic.

In January 1803 Jefferson submitted a message to Congress recommending the continuance of the system of American trading factories among the Indians. He went on to comment upon American-Indian relations and told Congress that the Indian tribes had been growing increasingly uneasy at the diminution of their land, and that the policy of refusing to contract any further sales had been growing among them. To counteract this policy, "and to provide an extension of territory which the rapid increase of our numbers will call for," Jefferson recommended two measures. The first suggestion was to encourage the Indian tribes to abandon hunting and to engage instead in stock raising, agriculture, and domestic manufacture. He argued that it would be possible to show the Indians that by following this new way of life they could live better with less land and less labor. Their extensive forests would thus become useless to them, and they would see the advantage of exchanging these lands for the means of improving their farms and increasing their domestic comforts. His second suggestion was to multiply trading-houses among the Indians, "and place within their reach those things which will contribute more to their domestic comfort than the possession of extensive but uncultivated wilds." These measures would, he argued, prepare the Indians to share ultimately in the benefits of American government and civilization. "I trust and believe," stated Jefferson, "we are acting for their greatest good."

The intimate connection of these plans with Jefferson's desire for land in the Northwest can plainly be seen from his letter to Governor William Henry Harrison of the Indiana Territory in the following month. Already in 1802, acting on the suggestion of the American government, Harrison had prepared the way for a large cession in Indiana by "defining" the Vincennes tract, which had been granted to the United States at Greenville, and now Jefferson urged him to continue the appropriation of land to the Mississippi. The President informed him on February 17, 1803, that as the Spanish had ceded Louisiana to the French the Indians would become reluctant to make further land cessions. Harrison was told, therefore, that "whatever can now be obtained, must be obtained quickly." Earlier in this letter Jefferson had stated that he wanted perpetual peace with the Indians (though his desire for lands would, of course, make this impossible) and had told Harrison of his plans to encourage agriculture, spinning, and weaving among the Indians. They would then need little land, and would exchange it for other necessaries. Jefferson urged the extension of trading-houses among the Indians, and stated that he would be glad to see influential Indians run into debt. When the debts were more than they could pay, he argued, they would be willing to settle them by a cession of land. The President added that he would like to see the purchase of all the country east of the Mississippi. Needless to say, he wanted the letter to be kept a secret from the Indians.

The transformation of the Indian into an American farmer, and the resulting surplus of land that would be happily yielded to the United States, was a vision which beset Jefferson throughout his two terms as president. Time and time again he told visiting delegations of Indians that the United States wanted them to abandon the difficulties of the chase and engage in the pleasures of farming. As game became increasingly scarce, he warned them, their families would starve. Jefferson did not merely want the Indians to live in the American manner; eventually he wanted them to be absorbed into the American population. He spoke of the ultimate point of rest and happiness for the Indians as being when the two races would become one people and when the Indians would become American citizens. The Indians would throw off their own traditions and would assume those of the United States. The original aim of appropriating Indian land was now becoming inextricably entwined with the moralistic aim of bringing civilization to the Indians.

Thus Jefferson conjured up a dreamland in which the Indians would agree that the white man's civilization was superior and would be eager to yield their surplus lands to the expanding Americans. The fact is, of course, that Governor Harrison of Indiana, acting on instructions from Jefferson, pressed the Indians into selling a goodly portion of the modern states of Indiana and Illinois between 1802 and 1809. Jefferson's letter of February 1803, which urged the purchase of land westward to the Mississippi, produced immediate action by Harrison. The treaties that were signed between 1803 and 1805 not only extended American control over southern Indiana, but also encompassed lands far to the west. Harrison rode roughshod over Indian opposition. Though the Indians were most reluctant to confirm the Vincennes cession of the previous September, their uneasy acquiescence was secured by Harrison at the treaty of Fort Wayne in June 1803. Encouraged by this success, he treated for much of southern Indiana by the close of 1805. Meanwhile, giant strides carried the United States to the Mississippi. In August 1803 at Vincennes the remnant of the Kaskaskias ceded much of what is now southern Illinois to the United States, and this large foothold on the Mississippi was greatly enlarged in 1804 when Harrison journeyed to St. Louis. On November 3, 1804, the Sac and Fox ceded a vast area in what is now northwestern Illinois, northern Missouri, and southern Wisconsin. Jefferson's aim of purchasing all the land east of the Mississippi was near to realization.

While Jefferson spoke in his messages to Congress as though all this met with the approbation of the Northwestern Indians, the intensity of their resistance was becoming increasingly obvious in the years after 1802. Rather than rushing forward to sell their surplus lands to taste the delights of agriculture, spinning, and weaving, the Indians were in these years becoming infuriated at the flouting of promises made at Greenville. By 1805 Tecumseh and the Prophet were beginning to organize resistance in the Northwest, and by the time Jefferson left office in 1809 the area was on the verge of war. In spite of this, Harrison in September 1809 secured yet another tract of land in Indiana. . . .

Meanwhile Jefferson continued his policy of peace, civilization, and land appropriation. For a time, after the purchase of Louisiana in 1803, he toyed with the possibility of removal west of the Mississippi as a solution to the Indian problem, but his interest in this project soon faded. To the end of his second term, his desire for land, and the linked desire of civilizing the Indians, continued unassuaged. In his annual message in December 1805, the year the Prophet began his activities at Greenville, he was able to say: "Our Indian neighbors are advancing, many of them with spirit, and others beginning to engage in the pursuits of agriculture and household manufacture. They are becoming sensible that the earth yields subsistence with less labor and more certainty than the forest, and find it their interest from time to time to dispose of parts of their surplus and waste lands for the means of improving those they occupy and of subsisting their families while they are preparing their farms." For a man of Jefferson's brilliance this was a remarkably nonsensical statement.

In December 1808 he told the Miami chief, Little Turtle, of the advantage of agriculture over hunting, and then continued by saying that "I have therefore always believed it an act of friendship to our red brethren whenever they wished to sell a portion of their lands, to be ready to buy whether we wanted them or not—because the price enables them to improve the lands they retain and turning their industry from hunting to agriculture the same exertions will support them more plentifully." It would seem that Jefferson had come to believe that not only was the civilization of the Indian convenient for acquisition of land, but that he was also acquiring land in order to civilize the Indian.

Shortly before he left office he spoke with conviction, and with an eloquent peroration, when he told an assembled gathering of Northwestern Indians: "I repeat that we will never do an unjust act towards you—On the contrary we wish you to live in peace, to increase in numbers, to learn to labor as we do and furnish food for your ever encreasing numbers, when the game shall have left you. We wish to see you possessed of property and protecting it by regular laws. In time you will be as we are: you will become one people with us: your blood will mix with ours: and will spread with ours over this great island. Hold fast then my children, the chain of friendship which binds us together: and join us in keeping it forever bright and unbroken."

It was magnificent, but it was not realistic. Jefferson bequeathed to James

Madison a host of Indian problems in the Northwest, stemming directly out of the cession of lands beyond the Greenville line in the years after 1795. Madison had no time to develop an Indian policy for the Northwest—his administration was soon to be plunged into war, both with the Indians and with England. Yet, following the tradition of Jefferson, Madison assured Congress in December 1810 that "With the Indian tribes also the peace and friendship of the United States are found to be so eligible that the general disposition to preserve both continues to gain strength." This was only a few weeks after Tecumseh had visited the British at Amherstburg to tell them he was ready for war.

American Indian policy in the Northwest during these hectic years revolved around the problem of the acquisition of land. The Confederation government first tried the simple methods of force, and discovered there was no surer way of producing Indian war. Anxious to avoid war, from financial as well as humanitarian motives, the Confederation turned to a policy of purchase, which involved the recognition of Indian rights to land beyond certain boundary lines. Recognition of this right did not mean that America expected any difficulty in acquiring further areas of land. The government acted on the assumption that the pressure of white population up to the demarcation line would produce a diminution in game, a reduction in the Indian population, and a desire to sell land cheaply. The new federal government inherited this policy from the Confederation and added to it. The most important addition was a more acute awareness that the national honor was involved. An attempt was made to give the Indians as much justice as was compatible with the wholesale acquisition of land. In fact, the government was prepared to defend the Indian against everyone except itself. In the 1790's there was a growing governmental interest in the possibility of bringing civilization to the Indian—that is, in transforming him into an American farmer. There seems to have been little realization that the Indian might not consider this an advantage. From the American point of view it was an ideal solution, for the Indian would cede his vast lands, and what was left of the Indian population would be absorbed into American civilization. This concept received far greater development after 1800 during the presidency of Thomas Jefferson. Though comparatively little progress was made in this direction, Jefferson acted as if the whole program was taking tremendous strides and proceeded to support William Henry Harrison in the acquisition of considerable areas of land. He never seemed to realize the wide discrepancy between the lofty nature of his aims and the rather sordid land-grabbing that was taking place in the Northwest. . . .

4. THOMAS J. FARNHAM

"The Indolent, Mixed Race of California"*

Their character is quite peculiar. The half-breed, as might be expected, exhibits much of the Indian character; the dull suspicious countenance, the small twinkling piercing eye, the laziness and filth of a free brute, using freedom as the mere means of animal enjoyment. This class of Californians usually compose the soldiery of the Presidios, and the herdsmen of the Ranches or plantations, and in these capacities perhaps perform their duties as well as their white relatives do theirs. However, it should here be stated that as soldiers it makes no kind of difference in the exhibition of their bravery, whether their guns have either lock, stock, or barrel; for never, in a single instance, since the country was settled, have the Californian troops been so wanting in courage as to fire at an enemy, unless he were in a helpless condition, nor so wanting in discretion as to wait to be fired at, when there was a chance to run away in safety.

The intelligence of these meztizos, as they are called, is quite limited; and what little they do possess, is of very doubtful utility. For it seems to be used chiefly in directing their choice of shade trees, under which they shall spend the day in sloth, or in stealing a bullock's hide on which to throw their lazy carcasses at night. Their dress, when they chance to have any, is composed of neat's hide tanned and stamped like certain species of saddle-leather. This is made into short roundabouts, which are buttoned up tightly in front. Of the same material they make loose pantaloons, leaving the outer seam open to the knee, and at intervals higher up, for the purpose, as it seemed, from what I daily saw, of enabling them with greater facility to kill their fleas and lice. On their feet they wear sandals of raw bull's hide; their heads are generally without any other covering than their long dark hair, usually in anything but a cleanly condition. In some instances, however, they don an ancient sombrero, long ago worn out in the service of some ragged cavallero. These people generally speak both the Indian and Spanish tongues, and are equally familiar with the ignorance accompanying the one, and the arrogance and self-conceit inherent in the other. . . .

That part of the population which by courtesy are called white, are the descendants of the free settlers from Mexico and the soldiers of the garrisons and Missions, who were permitted by his most Catholic Majesty to take

*Thomas J. Farnham, *Travels in the Californias and Scenes in the Pacific Ocean* (New York, Saxton & Miles, 1844), pp. 356-57, 358-59, 363, and 413.

wives. Their complexion is a light clear bronze; not white, as they themselves quite erroneously imagine; and, withal, not a very seemly color; not remarkably pure in any way; a lazy color. . . .

The speaking gait, the bland gesture of complaisant regard, the smile, that ray of the soul, all seemed civilized—truly Castilian. The wide-brimmed and conical-crowned sombrero also, with its rope-like silver cord band, well betasseled, shoes and shoe-buckles, pantaloons well opened at the side seams, showing the snow-white flaunting drawers, the snugly-fitted roundabout, with its spherical silver buttons, and the largely proportioned vest, swinging loosely to the wind, the keen Spanish knife sitting snugly in its sheath along the calf of the leg, all would indicate to the sojourner of a day among them, that these Castilianos Californios were accustomed to be men fulfilling some of the important ends of existence, in a worthy and gentlemanly way. And so they do, as understood in the Californias. They rise in the morning, that is to say, before noon-day, from their couches of blankets or bulls' hides, and breakfast upon broiled or boiled beef and fried beans. After breakfast, they muster a tinder-box from the pocket, strike fire, light cigars made of tobacco rolled up in little slips of paper, till the ignited weed burns and discolors their thumb and fore-finger aristocratically, and then betake themselves to their napping again. Thus stands or lies their humanity till the dinner hour. Roast beef, *frijoles*, and chocolate, brandy and wine, if, indeed, Señor Poverty own a corkscrew and its appendages, make up the *matériel* of this event. And having eaten and drunken liberally, Señor crosses himself reverently over his gastric apparatus, lays himself carefully upon his couch, and gives himself and his digestion to his guitar, till chocolate comes at sunset, to bedew his inner man for the slumbers of the night. Thus we have a glance at *los hombres Californios.*

Whenever want or a revulsion of nature long unused, drives these people to corporeal exercise, they, true to their laziness, make the horse perform the greater part of it. Indeed, a Californian is never the half of himself unless he be on horseback. And to go abroad for any purpose without a saddle under him would, in his opinion, be as ridiculous as to breakfast without beans, or be a Christian without praying to the Saints. They are excellent horsemen; the very best in North America; and, I am inclined to believe, the best on the continent. . . .

Thus much for the Spanish population of the Californias; in every way a poor apology of European extraction; as a general thing, incapable of reading or writing, and knowing nothing of science or literature, nothing of government but its brutal force, nothing of virtue but the sanction of the Church, nothing of religion but ceremonies of the national ritual. Destitute of industry themselves, they compel the poor Indian to labor for them, affording him a bare savage existence for his toil, upon their plantations and the fields of the Missions. In a word, the Californians are an imbecile, pusillanimous, race of men, and unfit to control the destinies of that beautiful country. . . .

No one acquainted with the idolent, mixed race of California, will ever believe that they will populate, much less, for any length of time, govern the country. The law of Nature which curses the mulatto here with a constitution less robust than that of either race from which he sprang, lays a similar penalty upon the mingling of the Indian and white races in California and Mexico. They must fade away; while the mixing of different branches of the Caucasian family in the States will continue to produce a race of men, who will enlarge from period to period the field of their industry and civil domination, until not only the Northern States of Mexico, but the Californias also, will open their glebe to the pressure of its unconquered arm. The old Saxon blood must stride the continent, must command all its northern shores, must here press the grape and the olive, here eat the orange and fig, and in their own unaided might, erect the altar of civil and religious freedom on the plains of the Californias.

5. JOSIAH GREGG

The General Character of New Mexicans*

The New Mexicans appear to have inherited much of the cruelty and intolerance of their ancestors, and no small portion of their bigotry and fanaticism. Being of a highly imaginative temperament and of rather accommodating moral principles—cunning, loquacious, quick of perception and sycophantic, their conversation frequently exhibits a degree of tact—a false glare of talent, eminently calculated to mislead and impose. They have no stability except in artifice; no profundity except for intrigue: qualities for which they have acquired an unenviable celebrity. Systematically cringing and subservient while out of power, as soon as the august mantle of authority falls upon their shoulders, there are but little bounds to their arrogance and vindictiveness of spirit. While such are the general features of the character

*Josiah Gregg, *Commerce of the Praries: or, the Journal of a Santa Fe Trader,* 2d ed. (New York, J. & H.G. Langley, 1845), Vol. I, p. 219.

of the Northern Mexicans, however, I am fain to believe and acknowledge, that there are to be found among them numerous instances of uncompromising virtue, good faith and religious forbearance.

C. COUNTER-IMAGE AND COUNTER-RESPONSE: THE ANGLO-AMERICAN THROUGH INDIAN, BLACK, AND MEXICAN EYES

Just as the first English settlers in America and their descendants developed stereotyped opinions of Indians, Africans, and Spanish-speaking peoples, those groups, too, formed opinions of and reacted to Anglo-Americans. This section illustrates minority attitudes and responses to Anglo America during the colonial period and the first half of the nineteenth century.

Nancy Oestereich Lurie points out that from the beginning of their contact with the English the Indians of Virginia never thought very highly of whites or European civilization. Though some selective borrowing did occur, the most the English could offer the Virginia natives were some of the products of advanced technology and occasional political alliances for leverage in intertribal disputes. Preferring their own ways, the majority of the Indian civilizations steadfastly resisted white culture until crushed by the pressure of English expansion.

Blacks, too, had strong opinions about whites. Those few who had the chance to express themselves in print often bitterly indicted American society, although they did not always agree on what to do about it. David Walker and Frederick Douglass both denounced the oppressions of Blacks in America but proposed different methods of dealing with the problem. Walker, writing in 1829, believed that the United States would never allow Blacks to be free and called for slave resistance to white tyranny as the only solution. Douglass, perhaps because of his own experience—escape from slavery, self-education, and in the end honor and high diplomatic office—retained a belief in eventual Negro equality and acceptance. Blacks, he declared, had the same abilities as whites and would rise if given legal equality and the right to live without interference.

The response of Mexicans to United States westward expansion was, according to Gene M. Brack, determined in large part by their opinion of Americans. Having observed the harsh treatment of Negroes and Indians to the north and the tendency of Americans to regard alien cultures as inferior, Mexicans preferred to fight in 1846 rather than submit passively to what they believed would be their inevitable cultural extinction at the hands of the racist-minded, expansionist Yanquis.

1. NANCY OESTEREICH LURIE

Indian Cultural Adjustment to European Civilization*

In 1907, on the 300th anniversary of the beginning of English colonization in America, James Mooney made the brief observation that the Jamestown settlers "landed among a people who already knew and hated whites." In effect, this remark summed up the accepted anthropological explanation for the Indians' unpredictable behavior; it indicated why they alternated elaborate expressions and actions of good will with apparent treachery. Mooney implied that the Indians' attitudes and behavior were more than justified by the demonstrated greed and aggressiveness of the whites.

Little work was done in the succeeding years to explore the complete significance of Mooney's remark or to probe more deeply into underlying motivations for the Indians' actions. This neglect was inevitable, since attention had to be devoted to a more fundamental problem. Before achieving an understanding of Indian reaction to the effects of contact with Europeans, it was necessary to establish a valid and cohesive picture of aboriginal culture. Thanks to the labors of such scholars as Mooney, Frank G. Speck, David I. Bushnell, John R. Swanton, Maurice A. Mook, and others, the fragmentary data relating to native life have been gathered into comprehensive and analytical accounts concerned with such problems as Indian demography, the cultural and linguistic identity of given tribes, tribal locations, and the prehistoric diffusion and changes in Indian cultures. . . .

Turning to Mooney's contention, there is evidence that the Virginia Indians had several opportunities to form opinions about Europeans both in terms of direct experience and of information communicated to them. Direct knowledge of Europeans may have occurred as early as the first quarter of the sixteenth century, when Giovanni de Verrazano and Estevan Gomez are believed to have made observations in the Chesapeake Bay region. Of

*Nancy Oestereich Lurie, "Indian Cultural Adjustment to European Civilization," in *Seventeenth-Century America,* James Morton Smith, ed. (Chapel Hill, University of North Carolina Press, 1959), pp. 33-60. Published for the Institute of Early American History and Culture, Williamsburg, Virginia. Reprinted by permission of the University of North Carolina Press.

somewhat greater significance is the alleged founding of a Spanish Jesuit mission on the York River in 1570. According to this theory, the missionaries were killed by Indians under the leadership of a native known as Don Luis de Velasco, who had lived in Spain, where he was educated and converted to Christianity. The Spaniards had hoped that he would act as guide and model in the proselytizing of his people, but it appears that the effects of his early life negated his later training. In 1572 a punitive expedition under Pedro Menendez de Aviles attacked and defeated the Indians responsible for the destruction of the mission; in succeeding years Menendez made other forays into the region. A recent study insists that this area must have been along the Virginia coast.

Whether or not the case for a sixteenth-century mission in Virginia has been proved is problematical. Many details are uncertain: the precise location of the mission on the York River, the tribal affiliations of Don Luis, the extent of his leadership, his age at the time he lived in Spain, and his possible genealogical affiliations with the ruling hierarchy of the Virginia Indians of the seventeenth century. However, historical investigation leaves no doubt of Spanish activity at this time, and these ventures must have occurred between St. Augustine and the Potomac River. The natives of Virginia, who borrowed cultural traits from neighboring tribes along the coast and further inland, could have received news of European explorations to the south and west by the same routes that carried purely native ideas. Generalized impressions of Europeans were doubtless prevalent in the Virginia area long before 1607.

The Spaniards came to America primarily as adventurers and fortune seekers. Although they attempted to found settlements their efforts usually met with failure. They plundered Indian villages but did not remain long in any one region; they were frequently routed by angry Indians or by their own inability to subsist in a strange terrain. After 1520, raids were conducted along the Gulf and southern Atlantic coast to obtain slaves for shipment to the West Indies. News of these incursions may have reached Virginia via the various coast tribes, and similarly Virginia natives may have heard of De Soto's helpless wanderings to the south and west. Even though the Spaniards later achieved success in colonization in Florida through the use of missionaries, the first hostile impressions had been made.

The French entered the scene to the south of Virginia in 1562. Because of lack of supplies and Spanish aggression, they failed in their attempts to establish a foothold in the region. However, the interests of France as well as of Britain were served by unknown numbers of piratical freebooters from the Caribbean area who touched along the coast of the Carolinas and intrigued with the Indians. Even then, Spanish dominion remained precarious, although the Spanish Franciscans continued to extend their missions up the coast. Finally, in 1597, a general uprising among the Carolina tribes destroyed these religious outposts and forced Spain again to concentrate most of her forces in Florida.

Thus, during much of the sixteenth century Europeans were active in regions immediately adjacent to Virginia and possibly in Virginia itself. Their activity was often associated with violence, and there was sufficient time for rumors concerning them to have reached the Virginia natives before any direct contacts were made. By the time the English attempted to found colonies on the east coast toward the close of the sixteenth century, they encountered difficulties which may have been more than the simple result of European inexperience in developing techniques for survival in the New World. Raleigh's enterprise, for example, may have been singularly ill-timed. A general unrest in Indian-white relationships marked the period from 1577 to 1597 in the Carolina region where Raleigh's followers chose to remain. Pemisipan, a Secotan chief who attempted to organize opposition to the British in 1585, could hardly have been blamed if he saw a curious similarity to accounts he may have heard concerning the Spanish when, for the trifling matter of the theft of a silver cup, the English burned the corn and destroyed the buildings at his village of Aquascogoc.

The later events at Cape Henry, the first landfall of the Jamestown colonists, suggest that the immediate hostility expressed by the Indians was inspired by fear of reprisals for the fate of Raleigh's colony. The Indians who attacked the English belonged to the Chesapeake tribe, immediately adjacent to the tribes with whom Pemisipan conspired. It is also possible, as Mooney implies, that by 1607 the Virginia Indians evaluated any sudden appearance of Europeans as evil and took immediate measures to repel them. However, this view oversimplifies several important factors. Long before any Europeans arrived at Jamestown, the Indians had been fighting over matters of principle important to them, such as possession of land and tribal leadership. If they were aware of the fate of other Indians at the hands of Europeans, there was no reason for them to assume that their fate would be similar; they were not necessarily allied with the beleaguered tribes, nor did they share a sense of racial kinship. Sharp cultural differences and even sharper linguistic differences separated the various Indian societies. While there was reason to fear and hate the Europeans as invaders who made indiscriminate war on all Indians, the fear was only that of being taken unawares and the hate could be modified if the tribes which had fallen victim thus far were strangers or even enemies. If the Indians of Virginia had any knowledge of Europeans, they must have been aware that the white men were fundamentally outnumbered, frequently unable to support themselves in an environment which the Indians found eminently satisfactory, and that European settlements were usually short lived. The appearance of the English was probably far less alarming than 350 years of hindsight indicate ought to have been the case.

This is demonstrated by the fact that the Virginia Indians under the leadership of Powhatan seem to have made their first adjustments to Europeans in terms of existing native conditions. Primary among these conditions were Powhatan's efforts to gain firmer control over his subject tribes and to fight tribes traditionally at enmity with his followers. It was expedient to help the settlers stay alive, for they could be useful allies in his established plans; but at the same time he could not allow them to gain ascendancy. The situation was complicated by factionalism in Powhatan's ranks and lack of accord among the settlers. However, recognition of the fundamental aboriginal situation makes the early events at Jamestown understandable on a rational basis. It offers a logical foundation for subsequent developments in Indian-white relationships and Indian adjustments to European civilization as the result of something more than barbaric cupidity and a thirst for the white man's blood.

Certainly a wary sensitivity to any sign of hostility or treachery characterized the behavior of both whites and Indians at the outset of settlement at Jamestown. The Europeans were still seriously concerned about the probable fate of Raleigh's colony and they had already been attacked by the Indians at Cape Henry. The Indians, in turn, may well have possessed information concerning the alarmingly retributive temperament of Europeans, at least in terms of the incident at nearby Aquascogoc, if not through generalized opinions derived from the long history of intermittent European contact along the east coast.

Nevertheless, the party of Europeans that set out on exploration of the country about Jamestown encountered a welcome at the various Indian villages different from the greetings offered at Cape Henry. Except for one cold but not overtly hostile reception in the Weanoc country, the white men were feted, fed, and flattered. At the same time a suggestion of the uncertainty of the next years occurred before the exploring party had even returned to their headquarters—at Jamestown the remaining colonists were attacked by a party of local Indians. Events of this nature as well as the general observations recorded during the first two years at Jamestown are particularly instructive in any attempt to understand Indian motivations and policy regarding the British.

The narratives are difficult to follow because of the variety of orthographies employed for Indian words. Certain features remain speculative because initial communication between whites and Indians was limited to the use of signs and the few native words that could be learned readily. However, it is possible to see native culture in terms of regularities and consistencies which were not obvious to the colonists. Likewise, the apparent inconsistencies on the part of the natives, recounted by the settlers as innate savage treachery, indicate that the aboriginal culture was in a process of growth, elaboration, and internal change. These phases of culture, which included both extensive tendencies of intertribal confederation and divisive reactions expressed by individual tribes, were interrupted and redirected but not initiated by the arrival of Europeans in 1607.

From the viewpoint of the twentieth century, it is difficult to realize that the material differences between the Indians and the European colonists, who lived before the full development of the industrial revolution, were equalled if not outweighed by the similarities of culture. This was especially true in Virginia, where a local florescence of culture and a demonstrated ability to prevail over other tribes gave the Indians a sense of strength which blinded them to the enormity of the threat posed by the presence of Europeans. There was actually little in the Europeans' imported bag of tricks which the Indians could not syncretize with their own experience. Metal was not unknown to them: they used native copper, brought in from the West, for decorative purposes. Metal weapons and domestic utensils were simply new and effective forms of familiar objects to accomplish familiar tasks. Even guns were readily mastered after the noise, which evoked astonishment at first, was understood as necessary to their operation. Likewise, fabrics and articles of personal adornment were part of Indian technology. Many utilitarian objects such as nets, weirs, and gardening implements were very similar in both Indian and European culture. European ships were simply larger and different, as was fitting for a people interested in traveling greater distances by open water than the Indians had ever cared to do.

Expansive accounts of the size and permanence of the great European cities could easily have been likened by the natives to the impressive aboriginal developments in the lower Mississippi Valley; archeological evidence suggests that knowledge of this cultural complex was widespread. Even if these Indian models of nascent urbanization are discounted, the statements made by Europeans about their country and king may well have sounded like the exaggerations of outnumbered strangers endeavoring to buttress their weaknesses with talk of powerful but distant brothers. This explanation is admittedly conjectural, although we find ample documentation of the Indians' disinclination to admit any significant superiority in white culture at a somewhat later period. During the early nineteenth century, when the industrial revolution was underway and the eastern United States was heavily populated by whites, Indian visitors were brought from the West in the hope that they would be cowed by the white man's power and cease resistance to the forces of civilization. The Indians remained singularly unimpressed. Furthermore, at the time Jamestown was founded in the seventeenth century, the only knowledge Indians possessed concerning Europeans indicated that Indians were well able to oppose white settlement. Raleigh's ill-fated colony was a clear reminder of the Europeans' mortality.

Although the early accounts tend to take a patronizing view of the Indians, the points on which the Europeans felt superior had little meaning for the aborigines: literacy, different sexual mores, ideas of modesty, good taste in dress and personal adornment, and Christian religious beliefs. The argument of technological superiority at that time was a weak one; despite guns and large ships the Europeans could not wrest a living from a terrain which, by Indian standards, supported an exceptionally large population. Scientific knowledge of generally predictable group reactions thus suggests that the degree of ethnocentrism was probably equal on both sides of the contact between Indians and Europeans in Virginia. Recognition of the Indians' self-appraisal is necessary for a clear understanding of their basis of motivation and consequent behavior in relation to Europeans.

Moreover, it was evident to the colonists that they were dealing with a fairly complex society, exhibiting many characteristics of leadership, social classes, occupational specialization, social control, and economic concepts that were eminently comprehensible in European terms. If the exploring parties overstated the case when they translated *weroance* as "king" and likened tribal territories to European kingdoms, they at least had a truer understanding of the nature of things than did the democratic Jefferson, who first designated the Virginia tribes as the "Powhatan Confederacy." Since the term "Confederacy" is so firmly entrenched in the literature, it will be retained here as a matter of convenience, but, in reality, Powhatan was in the process of building something that approximated an empire. By 1607 it was not an accomplished fact, but the outlines were apparent and the process was sufficiently advanced to allow a geographical description of the extent of Powhatan's domain.

Powhatan's influence, if not his undisputed control, extended over some thirty Algonkian-speaking tribes along the entire length of the present Virginia coast, including the Accohannoc and Accomac of the Eastern

Shore. The nucleus of this domain consisted of six tribes which were centrally located in the region drained by the James, Pamunkey, and Mattaponi rivers. These tribes were the Powhatan, Arrohattoc, Pamunkey, Youghtanund, Appomattoc, and Mattaponi, with Powhatan's own tribe, the Pamunkey, consistently referred to in the early narratives as the largest and most powerful. The Confederacy was bounded to the north and south by other Algonkian tribes. Except on the basis of their declared political allegiance, the uniformity of language and culture in the region makes it difficult to differentiate between the tribes within the Confederacy and even between the Confederacy and neighboring Maryland and Carolina groups. . . .

Powhatan inherited the six central tribes as an already unified intertribal organization and extended his domain by conquest from the south bank of the Potomac to the Norfolk region. The Chesapeake Indians are included in the Confederacy, but this southernmost group was not fully under Powhatan's control at the time the settlers arrived. Their attack on the colonists at Cape Henry gave Powhatan the opportunity to gain favor with the English by swiftly avenging the hostile action. Although some historians have implied that Powhatan destroyed the entire tribe, it is far more likely that he simply killed the leaders and placed trusted kinsmen in these positions.

Powhatan's method of fighting and his policy of expanding political control combined a reasoned plan of action with quick ferocity and a minimum of bloodshed. Indian warfare was generally limited to surprise attacks and sniping from cover. Constant replacements of fighting men kept the enemy occupied and wore down their resistance, while actual casualties were relatively limited in number. Accounts of Powhatan's conquests and the occurrences observed after 1607 point to a carefully devised method of establishing his control over a wide territory. Entire communities might be killed if they proved exceptionally obstinate in rendering homage and paying tribute, but in most cases Powhatan simply defeated groups of questionable loyalty and upon their surrender moved them to areas where he could keep better watch over them. Trusted members of the Confederacy were then sent to occupy the vacated regions, while Powhatan's relatives were distributed throughout the tribes in positions of leadership. Mook's studies indicate that the degree of Powhatan's leadership decreased in almost direct proportion to the increase in geographical distance between the Pamunkey and the location of a given tribe. Throughout the entire region, however, the combination of ample sustenance, effective techniques of production, provident habits of food storage, and distribution of supplies through exchange offset shortcomings in the political framework connecting the tribes and helped to cement social ties and produce a commonality of culture. Despite certain internal dissensions the Confederacy can be seen as a unified bloc, distinct from neighboring tribes. To the north were numerous small Algonkian-speaking tribes, either friendly or representing no serious danger to Powhatan. They tended to shade off in cultural characteristics toward the more northern Algonkian types to be found along the coast into New England. . . .

The western border, formed by the fall line and paralleling the coast, was characterized by greater cultural and linguistic differences than those observed to the north and south of the Confederacy; it also represented a definite danger area for Powhatan. Virtually all Indian occupation ended somewhat east of the falls, however, allowing a strip of land a mile to ten or twelve miles wide as a safe margin between the Powhatan tribes and their nearest neighbors, who were also their deadliest enemies, the tribes of the Virginia piedmont region. These peoples have long been designated as Siouan-speaking but a recent study casts doubt on this identification. It is now suggested that these groups spoke a highly divergent and extremely old dialect of the basic Algonkian language stock. Except for linguistic distinctiveness little is known about these piedmont people. This is most unfortunate, since they appear to figure as a key to much of Powhatan's policy toward the English and helped to influence the course of Indian adjustment to European settlement. A few of these tribes are known by name, but they are usually considered as having comprised two major confederacies, comparable in some measure to the groupings associated with Powhatan. These were the Manahoac on the upper Rappahannock and surrounding region, and the Monacan along the upper James and its tributary streams. Both were aggressive groups, and their incursions were a constant threat to the tidelands Indians. Powhatan's desire to subdue these westerly tribes as a matter of protection was underscored by another consideration: copper, highly prized by the Virginia Confederacy, came from the West, and the enemy tribes formed an obstacle to trade for that commodity.

Thus, at the outset of colonization in 1607 Powhatan's policies can best be understood in relation to circumstances antedating the arrival of the Jamestown settlers. Powhatan saw the whites in his territory as potential allies and as a source of new and deadly weapons to be used in furthering his own plans for maintaining control over his Confederacy and protecting the Confederacy as a whole against the threat posed by the alien tribes of the piedmont region. Likewise, existing concepts of intertribal trade in foodstuffs and other commodities were extended to include trade with the newly arrived whites. It is worth noting that European novelties, apart from weapons, were of far less interest to Powhatan than the fact that the British possessed copper, an object vested with traditional native values and heretofore obtained with great difficulty.

In the initial stages of contact between the Indians and the whites, therefore, it is hardly surprising that Powhatan and his people felt at least equal to the English. The chieftain could appreciate the foreigners as allies in the familiar business of warfare and trade, but in general there seemed little to emulate in European culture and much to dislike about the white men. However, even in the most difficult phases of their early relationship, Powhatan did not indulge in a full-scale attack against the settlers. At that time he was still engaged in strengthening his Confederacy and perhaps he could not risk extensive Indian defection to the side of the whites. But there is an equal likelihood that Powhatan's primary motivation was the desire to control and use the whites for his own purposes rather than to annihilate them.

At the time Jamestown was founded, native civilization was enjoying a period of expansion, and Powhatan had ample reason for sometimes considering the English as more an annoyance than a serious danger. The unusually rich natural environment and the security offered by the Confederacy stimulated the growth of social institutions and cultural refinements. In addition, the Virginia Indians were exceptionally powerful and, by aboriginal standards, their population was large: the entire Confederacy numbered some 8,500 to 9,000 people, or a density of approximately one person to every square mile. The Indians lived according to a well-ordered and impressively complex system of government. They dwelled in secure villages, had substantial houses and extensive gardens, and had a notable assemblage of artifacts for utilitarian, religious, and decorative purposes.

The Indians won the grudging respect of the colonists for their advanced technology, but the Europeans were contemptuous of their seemingly hopeless commitment to superstition, while their ceremonialism appeared to the whites a ridiculous presumption of dignity. A typical bias of communication between Europeans and Indians is seen in Smith's account of the Quiyoughcohannock chief who begged the settlers to pray to the Christian God for rain because their own deities had not fulfilled the Indians' requests. Smith asserted that the Indians appealed to the whites because they believed the Europeans' God superior to their own, just as the Europeans' guns were superior to bows and arrows. Yet Smith notes with some wonder that the Quiyoughcohannock chief, despite his cordiality and interest in the Christian deity, could not be prevailed upon to "forsake his false Gods." Actually this chief of one of the lesser tribes of the Confederacy illustrated the common logic of polytheistic people who often have no objection to adding foreign deities to their pantheon if it seems to assure more efficient control of the natural universe. The chief was not interested in changing his religious customs in emulation of the Europeans; he merely wished to improve his own culture by judicious borrowing—a gun at one time, a supernatural being at another.

Nor would the chief have dared respond to a new religion in its entirety, even if such an unlikely idea had occurred to him. The whole structure of tribal life relied upon controlling the mysterious aspects of the world by a traditional body of beliefs which required the use of religious functionaries, temples, idols, and rituals. These were awesome arrangements and not to be treated lightly, although improvement by minor innovations might be permitted.

The geopolitical sophistication of the Virginia tribes is reflected in the secular hierarchy of leadership which extended in orderly and expanding fashion from the villages, through the separate tribes, up to Powhatan as head of the entire Confederacy. A gauge of the complexity of government is the fact that the Confederacy shared with the Europeans such niceties of civilization as capital punishment. In small societies having a precarious economy, indemnities in goods or services are usually preferred to taking the life of a culprit even in crimes as serious as murder. However, where the life of the offender or one of his kinsmen is exacted for the life of the victim, punishment is the concern of the particular families involved; the rest of the group merely signifies approval of the process as a means of restoring social equilibrium after an offense is committed. Powhatan's government, however, was much closer to that of the English than it was to many of the tribes of North America. Punishment was meted out by a designated executioner for an offense against the society as the society was symbolized in the person of the leader.

Nevertheless, despite its elaborate civil structure, the Confederacy exhibited a universal rule of any society: a complex theory of government does not necessarily assure complete success in application. Powhatan not only had unruly subjects to deal with, but entire tribes in his domain could not be trusted. Relations between whites and Indians therefore were always uncertain, largely because of political developments within the Confederacy. When the colonists were supported by Powhatan, they were in mortal danger from those dissatisfied tribes of the Confederacy which had the foresight to realize that the English might one day assist Powhatan to enforce his authority. When Powhatan and his closest associates turned upon the settlers, the less dependable tribes became friendly to the whites.

In view of this morass of political allegiances, it is little wonder that early accounts of the settlers are replete with material which seems to prove the innate treachery of the Indians. Yet the militant phases of Indian activity, as illustrated by the initial attack on Jamestown and Powhatan's vengeance on the offending Chesapeake tribe, must be seen as part of a larger policy involving alternative methods of settling inter-group differences. Although the settlers knew that dissatisfaction among Powhatan's followers offered a means of preventing a coordinated Indian attack, they also discovered that established mechanisms of diplomacy existed among the Indians that could be employed for their benefit. For example, the Jamestown settlement was located in the territory of the Paspehegh tribe, and relations with this tribe frequently became strained. The Powhatan forces represented by the leaders of the Pamunkey, Arrohattoc, Youghtanund, and Mattaponi offered to act as intermediaries in negotiating peace with the Paspehegh and other hostile tribes or, if necessary, to join forces with the settlers in an armed assault on mutual enemies.

If the Europeans found it difficult to live among the Indians, the Europeans seemed equally unpredictable to the Indians. Early in his relationship with the English, Powhatan was promised five hundred men and supplies for a march on the Monacan and Manahoac; but instead of finding wholehearted support among his allies for this campaign, Powhatan discovered that the whites were helpless to support themselves in the New World. As time wore on and they became increasingly desperate for food, the Europeans were less careful in the difficult business of trying to distinguish friends from enemies. They extorted supplies promiscuously, driving hard bargains by the expedient of burning villages and canoes.

It is problematical whether, as Smith implies, Powhatan was actually unable to destroy the handful of English because he could not organize his tribes for a full-scale offensive or whether he was biding his time in the hope of eventually establishing a clear-cut power structure in which the colonists would be allowed to survive but remain subservient to his designs in native warfare. At any rate, after two years of English occupation at Jamestown, Powhatan moved from his traditional home on the Pamunkey River some fifteen miles from the Europeans and settled in a more remote village upstream on the Chickahominy River. Violence flared periodically during these early years: colonists were frequently killed and often captured. Sometimes, being far from united in their allegiance, they fled to the Indian villages, where they were usually well treated. Captives and runaways were exchanged as hostages when one side or the other found it convenient. However, if Powhatan was willing to take advantage of dissident feeling among the whites, he was no fool and he finally put to death two colonists who seemed to be traitors to both sides at the same time. The execution was much to Smith's satisfaction, for it saved him from performing the task and assured a far more brutal punishment than he would have been able to inflict upon the renegades.

Throughout the period from 1607 to 1609, the chronicles include a complexity of half-told tales involving alliances and enmities and mutual suspicions, of Indians living among settlers and settlers living among Indians. Although this interaction was of an individual nature, the two groups learned something of each other; yet each side maintained its own values and traditions as a social entity. The Indians were primarily concerned with obtaining new material goods. By theft, trade, and the occupation of European artisans in their villages, they increased their supply of armaments and metal work. With the use of Indian guides and informants, the settlers became familiar with the geography of the region, and they also learned the secrets of exploiting their new environment through techniques of native gardening. For the most part, however, conscious efforts to bridge the cultural gap were unavailing. There was one amusing attempt to syncretize concepts of Indian and European monarchy and thereby bring about closer communication, when Powhatan was treated to an elaborate "coronation." The chief *weroance* was only made more vain by the ceremonies; he was by no means transformed into a loyal subject of the English sovereign, as the white settlers had intended.

An increasing number of settlers arrived in Virginia and, with the help of Indians who by this time had ample reason to let the whites perish, managed to weather the hazards of the "starving time." As the whites became more firmly established, competition between Europeans and Indians took on the familiar form of a struggle for land. Armed clashes occurred frequently, but there were no organized hostilities, and the Indians continued to trade with the English. A peace which was formally established in 1614 and lasted until 1622 is often attributed to a refinement of Powhatan's sensibilities because of the marriage of Pocahontas and John Rolfe. Although Pocahontas was indeed the favorite child of Powhatan, it is likely that the chieftain's interest in her marriage was not entirely paternal. This strengthening of the social bond between Indians and Europeans helped solidify Powhatan's power and prestige among the confederated tribes, as he was thus enduringly allied with the whites.

Continuation of harmony between Indians and whites for a period of eight years was doubtless rendered possible because enough land still remained in Virginia for both settlers and Indians to live according to their accustomed habits. The seriousness of the loss of Indian land along the James River was lessened by the existence of a strip of virtually unoccupied territory just east of the fall line which ran the length of the Confederacy's holdings. If properly armed and not disturbed by internal dissensions and skirmishes with the English, the Powhatan tribes could afford to settle at the doorstep of their piedmont neighbors and even hope to expand into enemy territory. Hostilities require weapons, and peaceful trade with the English meant easier access to arms which the Confederacy could turn against the Monacan and Manahoac. It is also possible that by this time Powhatan realized the vast strength of the English across the sea and was persuaded to keep the settlers as friends. Knowledge of Europe would have been available to the chieftain through such Indians as Machumps, described by William Strachey as having spent "somtym in England" as well as moving "to and fro amongst us as he dares and as Powhatan gives him leave."

Whatever were Powhatan's reasons for accepting the peace, it appears that he utilized the lull in hostilities to unify the Confederacy and deal with his traditional enemies. We have no direct evidence of activities against the piedmont tribes, for there is little historical data regarding the western area at this time. However, by the time the fur trade became important in the West the Monacan and Manahoac had lost the power which had once inspired fear among the tribes of the Confederacy. In view of Powhatan's years of scheming and the probable closer proximity of the Confederacy to the piedmont region after 1614, it may be conjectured that the Virginia chieftain and his people took some part in the downfall of the Monacan and Manahoac.

When Powhatan died in 1618, his brother Opechancanough succeeded him as leader of the Confederacy. Opechancanough continued to observe Powhatan's policy of peace for four years, although relations between Indians and Europeans were again degenerating. The Indians' natural resources were threatened as the increasing tobacco crops encroached on land where berries had grown in abundance and game had once been hunted. In the face of European advance, the Indians became restive and complained of the settlers' activities; but these signs went unnoticed by the colonists. Opechancanough was aware that the real danger to the Confederacy arose from neither internal dissensions nor traditional Indian enemies but from the inexorable growth of European society in Virginia. He was apparently able to convince all the member tribes of this fact, if they had not already drawn their own conclusions. The subsequent uprising of 1622 was a well-planned shock to the English; it was alarming not so much for the destruction wrought, since by that time the Europeans could sustain the loss of several hundred people, but for the fact that the Confederacy could now operate as a unified fighting organization. This was a solidarity which Powhatan either had been unable or was disinclined to achieve.

Doubtless Opechancanough expected reprisals, but he was totally unprepared for the unprecedented and utter devastation of his lands and the wholesale slaughter of his people. The tribes were scattered, some far beyond the traditional boundaries of their lands, and several of the smaller groups simply ceased to exist as definable entities. Gradually as the fury of revenge died down, the remnants of the Confederacy regrouped and began to return to their homelands. However, the settlers were no longer complacent about their Indian neighbors. In addition to campaigning against the natives, they erected a string of fortifications between Chesiac and Jamestown, and they tended to settle Virginia in the south rather than toward the north and west. In effect, therefore, Opechancanough accomplished a limited objective; a line was established between Indians and Europeans, but the line was only temporary and the Indians paid a terrible price.

Morever, the cultural gap widened during the ensuing years. Following the period of reprisals the Indians were left to make a living and manage their affairs as best they could. Many old grievances seemed to be forgotten, and the natives gave the appearance of accepting their defeat for all time. Opechancanough, who had eluded capture immediately after the attack of 1622, remained at large, but the Europeans attempted to win tribes away from his influence rather than hunt him down at the risk of inflaming his followers. Finally, white settlement once more began to spread beyond the safety of concentrated colonial population. Tensions were re-created on the frontier, and there were minor skirmishes; the Indians complained to the English, but they also continued their trading activities. Thus matters continued for more than twenty years until large-scale hostilities again broke out.

The uprising of 1644 was surprisingly effective. It is generally known that in both the 1622 and the 1644 uprisings the percentage of Indians killed in relation to the total Indian population was far greater than the percentage of settlers killed in relation to the total white population. Yet with far fewer Indians to do the fighting, Opechancanough managed to kill at least as many Europeans in the second attack as he had in the first. The uprising is another proof that the Indians' method of adjusting to changes wrought by the Europeans continued to be an attempt to prevail over or remove the source of anxiety—the settlers—rather than to adapt themselves to the foreign culture. Certainly the Indians never felt that their difficulties would be resolved by assimilation among the whites, a solution which the colonists at times hoped to effect through the adoption of Indian children, intermarriage, and Indian servitude.

Hopeless though the uprising appears in retrospect, it was entirely logical within Opechancanough's own cultural frame of reasoning. It is impossible to determine whether the Indians were aware of the futility of their action, nor do we know enough about the psychology of these people to ascribe to them such a grim fatalism that they would prefer a quick and honorable death to the indignities of living in subjection to the whites. But there is something impressive about Opechancanough, an old and enfeebled man, being carried on a litter to the scene of battle. Whatever the outcome his days were numbered. His young warriors, however, knew of the horrible reprisals of 1622 and they understood the cost of being defeated by the white man. Yet they too were willing to risk an all-out attack.

There is little doubt that Opechancanough realized the danger inherent in rebellion. He was a shrewd strategist and a respected leader. It is entirely possible that he hoped for assistance from forces outside the Confederacy. Tension had existed between the whites of Virginia and Maryland for a number of years, and in one instance the Virginians had hoped to incite the Confederacy against their neighbors. Maryland had been settled only ten years before the second uprising, and although hostile incidents between whites and Indians had occurred, her Indian policy had been more just and humane than Virginia's. If Opechancanough did expect military assistance from whites for his uprising against whites, he had historical precedent to inspire him. Powhatan had exploited factionalism among the Jamestown settlers, and it may be that the tension between Virginia and Maryland suggested an extension of his policy to Opechancanough. Whatever the motivations behind Opechancanough's design for rebellion, the second uprising attested to the strength of the old Confederacy and indicated clearly the stubborn resistance of the Indians to cultural annihilation.

Although the usual revenge followed the attack of 1644, Virginia's Indian policy was beginning to change. The Powhatan tribes were too seriously reduced in numbers to benefit greatly by the progress, but their treatment at the hands of the colonists following the uprising marked a new development in Indian-white relations, one which eventually culminated in the modern reservation system. In 1646 a formal treaty was signed with the Powhatan Confederacy establishing a line between Indian and white lands and promising the Indians certain rights and protection in their holdings. While their movements were to be strictly regulated, the natives were guaranteed recognition for redress of wrongs before the law. There were two particularly important features of the treaty. First, the Indians were to act as scouts and allies against the possibility of outside tribes' invading the colony; this policy was in contrast to the earlier device of attempting to win the friendship of peripheral tribes to enforce order among the local Indians. Second, and consistent with the growing importance of the fur trade in colonial economics, the Indians were to pay a tribute each year in beaver skins. . . .

The condition of the Indians toward the end of the seventeenth century is illustrated in many contemporary documents. A letter from the Reverend Mr. Clayton provides a detailed and well-organized summary. It is worth special attention for its factual data and as an illustration that both whites and Indians continued to view each other from their own culture's frame of logic, without any real understanding. Describing the populational degeneration which had resulted largely from disease, deprivation, and malnutrition, the letter states:

> This is very certain that the Indian inhabitants of Virginia are now very inconsiderable as to their numbers and seem insensibly to decay though they live under the Engltsh proteciion and have no violeoce offered them. They are undoubtedly no great breeders.

Clayton, like many white observers imbued with Christian concepts of proselytization, appeared surprised that one of the most striking retentions of native patterns was the cultural aspect of religion. He noted that special structures were still set aside for temples and that the shaman or *wichiost* enjoyed a degree of prestige which was secondary only to that accorded to their "King and to their great War Captain." The retention of this prestige illustrates secular authority distinguished from the sacred sway of the *wichiost* and shows a continuity of concepts regarding homage and tribute in the form of personal services performed by other members of the tribe. Apparently the ruling position was still hereditary within a line of descent recognized as that of the chief family. . . .

The role of the ordinary Indian woman generally receives little notice in accultural descriptions by untrained observers, and the Clayton letter is no exception. A brief sentence notes gardening, cooking, pottery making, and the weaving of mats. The domestic phase of Indian life was easily overlooked although it changed less than other aspects. Actually, the domesticity of the whites and Indians differed only slightly. Kingdoms might rise and fall but housekeeping, child care, cooking, and garment making had to be regularly performed in both cultures. Like many European observers, Clayton describes hunting, a principal occupation of the Indian male, as "Exercise." This error probably contributed to an early and persistent stereotype of the Indian: the industrious, overburdened woman, the slothful, pleasure-seeking man. Like all stereotypes, it is worthy of examination and it is an especially interesting example of adjustment to change. The traditional division of labor was approximately equal, the men hunting, the women gardening. These two activities supplied the principal subsistence. The English depended on the hunt in the early stages of settlement, but as soon as it ceased to have great economic importance they reverted to the European tradition of categorizing it as sport. The Indians also had their tradition: both men and women considered agriculture to be an unmanly task. When game diminished and gardening became the primary productive activity, they found it extremely difficult to make appropriate changes in the socio-economic role of the male.

Clayton's references to the material culture of the Indians may be augmented from many sources, as this was the most easily discerned aspect of Indian life. The natives frequently observed traditional habits of dress. They continued to use indigenous material such as deerskin for clothing, but they prized European textiles, being especially fond of linen goods and a heavy woolen cloth, called a "matchcoat," which they often used instead of fur or feather mantles. Certain changes in style, if not modesty, may be noted in the matter of dress. When the Queen of Appomattoc greeted the Europeans in 1607, she wore only a skirt and a great amount of jewelry, but "all ells was naked"; but the Queen of Pamunkey was clad in Indian finery from neck to ankles for an occasion of state in 1677.

Although the blue and white shell beads known as "wampum" probably originated as a currency through the trade with the New England tribes, they were manufactured in great quantities by Europeans for use in the fur trade and by 1687 figured as a quasi currency as far south as Virginia. The Indian shaman who also acted in the capacity of physician was paid by the natives in wampum as well as in skins and other commodities. When he treated English settlers, the *wichiost* usually received his remuneration in matchcoats or rum. Further details from Clayton's letter reveal that metal armaments, tools, and utensils were in common usage by the end of the century, although the bow and arrow and native pottery continued to be available.

From Clayton's observations and comparable data it is evident that Indian adjustment to European civilization in the late seventeenth century continued to take the form of resistance whenever there remained any possibility of retaining essential elements of the old culture. Specific items were accepted, as they fitted into existing patterns and represented elaboration or improvement of familiar features. In-group recognition of the danger posed for their traditional ways is illustrated in a fragment of folklore included in

Clayton's account. There was supposedly an ancient prophecy, made long before the Europeans arrived, that "bearded men . . . should come and take away their country and that there should none of the original Indians be left within a certain number of years, I think it was an hundred and fifty." This rationalization of history is a recurrent myth found among many Indian groups. It helps to preserve a degree of dignity and pride by saying in effect, "We knew it all along, but we put up an admirable fight anyway."

The cultural disorganization noted in 1687 was to be a continuing process. The prophecy of destruction has now been fulfilled, to the extent that the Indians have ceased to exist as a culturally definable entity, although remnant groups maintain their social identities and tribal names. Throughout the seventeenth and eighteenth centuries the tribes which had temporarily resided with the Pamunkey wandered back to their original territories, leaving only the Pamunkey and part of the Mattaponi on lands secured to them by colonial treaties and guaranteed today by the state of Virginia. Traditional habits were generally abandoned as it became ever more difficult to exist in the white man's world. Eventually, the only effective economic system was that practiced by the surrounding Europeans; the Indians who were not located on reservations tended to settle in neighborhoods and acquire land on an individual basis. The destruction of the native social and religious mores, almost a predictable consequence of the disastrous wars and scattering of tribes, was virtually accomplished. A civil and religious structure which had been designed to accommodate the needs and activities of thirty tribes, almost nine thousand people, was impossibly cumbersome when the population had dwindled to one thousand people who were not in regular communication with one another and who were at any rate overwhelmingly occupied with the problem of sheer physical survival. The Indians in time found social and religious satisfaction in the traditions of their white neighbors; but they remained socially distinct from them. . . .

Although the Virginia Indians were utterly defeated by the close of the seventeenth century, the experience of that period laid the foundations for modern adjustment to the white man's culture. As a result of stubborn opposition to amalgamation, some tribes have survived into the mid-twentieth century as populational entities, although they have been unable to retain a distinctive culture. Their primary technique of adjustment to European civilization, at least as documented in the Virginia tidelands region, was, with few exceptions, one of rigid resistance to alien ways which held no particular attractions, except for disparate items. Their culture simply disintegrated under the strain of continued pressure placed upon it. In contrast, the tribes further inland, by their more flexible adaptation to Europeans, achieved a social and cultural continuity which is still impressive despite many material innovations from European and American civilization.

2. DAVID WALKER

Walker's Appeal . . . to the Coloured Citizens of the World*

Now I appeal to heaven and to earth, and particularly to the American people themselves, who cease not to declare that our condition is not *hard*, and that we are comparatively satisfied to rest in wretchedness and misery, under them and their children. Not, indeed, to show me a coloured President, a Governor, a Legislator, a Senator, a Mayor, or an Attorney at the Bar.—But to show me a man of colour, who holds the low office of a Constable, or one who sits in a Juror Box, even on a case of one of his wretched brethren, throughout this great Republic! !—But let us pass Joseph the son of Israel a little farther in review, as he existed with that heathen nation.

"And Pharaoh called Joseph's name Zaphnathpaaneah; and he gave him to wife Asenath the daughter of Potipherah priest of On. And Joseph went out over all the land of Egypt."

Compare the above, with the American institutions. Do they not institute laws to prohibit us from marrying among the whites? I would wish, candidly, however, before the Lord, to be understood, that I would not give a *pinch of snuff* to be married to any white person I ever saw in all the days of my life. And I do say it, that the black man, or man of colour, who will leave his own colour (provided he can get one, who is good for any thing) and marry a white woman, to be a double slave to her, just because she is *white*, ought to be treated by her as he surely will be, viz: as a NIGGER! ! ! ! It is not, indeed, what I care about inter-marriages with the whites, which induced me to pass this subject in review; for the Lord knows, that there is a day coming when they will be glad enough to get into the company of the blacks, notwithstanding, we are, in this generation, levelled by them, almost on a level with the brute creation: and some of us they treat even worse than they do the brutes that perish. I only made this extract to show how much lower we are held, and how much more cruel we are treated by the Americans, than were the children of Jacob, by the Egyptians.—We will notice the sufferings

*From *David Walker's Appeal*, in four articles, (3rd ed., Boston, 1830) pp10-15, 17-20, 22, 24-27, 33, 35, 41, 74.

of Israel some further, under *heathen Pharaoh,* compared with ours under the *enlightened Christians of America.*

"And Pharaoh spoke unto Joseph, saying, thy father and thy brethren are come unto thee:

"The land of Egypt is before thee: in the best of the land make thy father and brethren to dwell; in the land of Goshen let them dwell: and if thou knowest any men of activity among them, then make them rulers over my cattle."

I ask those people who treat us so *well,* Oh! I ask them, where is the most barren spot of land which they have given unto us? Israel had the most fertile land in all Egypt. Need I mention the very notorious fact, that I have known a poor man of colour, who laboured night and day, to acquire a little money, and having acquired it, he vested it in a small piece of land, and got him a house erected thereon, and having paid for the whole, he moved his family into it, where he was suffered to remain but nine months, when he was cheated out of his property by a white man, and driven out of door! And is not this the case generally? Can a man of colour buy a piece of land and keep it peaceably? Will not some white man try to get it from him, even if it is in a *mud hole?* I need not comment any farther on a subject, which all, both black and white, will readily admit. But I must, really, observe that in this very city, when a man of colour dies, if he owned any real estate it most generally falls into the hands of some white person. The wife and children of the deceased may weep and lament if they please, but the estate will be kept snug enough by its white possessor.

But to prove farther that the condition of the Israelites was better under the Egyptians than ours is under the whites. I call upon the professing Christians, I call upon the philanthropist, I call upon the very tyrant himself, to show me a page of history, either sacred or profane, on which a verse can be found, which maintains, that the Egyptians heaped the *insupportable insult* upon the children of Israel, by telling them that they were not of the *human family.* Can the whites deny this charge? Have they not, after having reduced us to the deplorable condition of slaves under their feet, held us up as descending originally from the tribes of *Monkeys* or *Orang-Outangs?* O! my God! I appeal to every man of feeling—is not this insupportable? Is it not heaping the most gross insult upon our miseries, because they have got us under their feet and we cannot help ourselves? Oh! pity us we pray thee, Lord Jesus, Master.—Has not Mr. Jefferson declared to the world, that we are inferior to the whites, both in the endowments of our bodies and our minds? It is indeed surprising, that a man of such great learning, combined with such excellent natural parts, should speak so of a set of men in chains. I do not know what to compare it to, unless, like putting one wild deer in an iron cage, where it will be secured, and hold another by the side of the same, then let it go, and expect the one in the cage to run as fast as the one at liberty. So far, my brethren, were the Egyptians from heaping these insults upon their slaves, that Pharaoh's daughter took Moses, a son of Israel for her own. . . .

In all probability, Moses would have become Prince Regent to the throne, and no doubt, in process of time but he would have been seated on the throne of Egypt. But he had rather suffer shame, with the people of God, than to enjoy pleasures with that wicked people for a season. O! that the coloured people were long since of Moses' excellent disposition, instead of courting favour with, and telling news and lies to our *natural enemies*, against each other—aiding them to keep their hellish chains of slavery upon us. Would we not long before this time, have been respectable men, instead of such wretched victims of oppression as we are? Would they be able to drag our mothers, our fathers, our wives, our children and ourselves, around the world in chains and hand-cuffs as they do, to dig up gold and silver for them and theirs? This question, my brethren, I leave for you to digest; and may God Almighty force it home to your hearts. . . . Let our enemies go on with their butcheries, and at once fill up their cup. Never make an attempt to gain our freedom or *natural right,* from under our cruel oppressors and murderers, until you see your way clear—when that hour arrives and you move, be not afraid or dismayed; for be you assured that Jesus Christ the King of heaven and of earth who is the God of justice and of armies, will surely go before you. And those enemies who have for hundreds of years stolen our *rights,* and kept us ignorant of Him and His divine worship, he will remove. . . . They think because they hold us in their infernal chains of slavery, that we wish to be white, or of their color—but they are dreadfully deceived—we wish to be just as it pleased our Creator to have made us, and no avaricious and unmerciful wretches, have any business to make slaves of, and hold them in cruel slavery, and murder them as they do us?—But is Mr. Jefferson's assertion true? viz. "that it is unfortunate for us that our Creator has been pleased to make us *black.*" We will not take his say so, for the fact. The world will have an opportunity to see whether it is unfortunate for us, that our Creator *has made us* darker than the *whites.*

Fear not the number and education of our *enemies*, against whom we shall have to contend for our lawful right; guaranteed to us by our Maker; for why should we be afraid, when God is, and will continue, (if we continue humble) to be on our side?

The man who would not fight under our Lord and Master Jesus Christ, in the glorious and heavenly cause of freedom and of God—to be delivered from the most wretched, abject and servile slavery, that ever a people was afflicted with since the foundation of the world, to the present day—ought to be kept with all of his children or family, in slavery, or in chains, to be butchered by his *cruel enemies*. . . .

Mr. Jefferson's very severe remarks on us have been so extensively argued upon by men whose attainments in literature, I shall never be able to reach, that I would not have meddled with it, were it not to solicit each of my brethren, who has the spirit of a man, to buy a copy of Mr. Jefferson's "Notes on Virginia," and put it in the hand of his son. For let no one of us suppose that the refutations which have been written by our white friends are enough—they are *whites*—we are *blacks*. We, and the world wish to see the charges of Mr. Jefferson refuted by the blacks *themselves*, according to their chance; for we must remember that what the whites have written respecting this subject, is other men's labours, and did not emanate from the blacks. I know well, that there are some talents and learning among the coloured people of this country, which we have not a chance to develope, in consequence of oppression; but our oppression ought not to hinder us from acquiring all we can. For we will have a chance to develope them by and by. God will not suffer us, always to be oppressed. Our sufferings will come to an *end*, in spite of all the Americans this side of *eternity*. Then we will want all the learning and talents among ourselves, and perhaps more, to govern ourselves.—"Every dog must have its day," the American's is coming to an end. . . .

Are we MEN! !—I ask you, O my brethren! are we MEN? Did our Creator make us to be slaves to dust and ashes like ourselves? Are they not dying worms as well as we? Have they not to make their appearance before the tribunal of Heaven, to answer for the deeds done in the body, as well as we? Have we any other Master but Jesus Christ alone? Is He not their Master as well as ours?—What right then, have we to obey and call any other Master, but Himself? How we could be so *submissive* to a gang of men, whom we cannot tell whether they are *as good* as ourselves or not, I never could conceive. However, this is shut up with the Lord, and we cannot precisely tell—but I declare, we judge men by their works.

The whites have always been an unjust, jealous, unmerciful, avaricious and blood-thirsty set of beings, always seeking after power and authority.—We view them all over the confederacy of Greece, where they were first known to be any thing, (in consequence of education) we see them there, cutting each other's throats—trying to subject each other to wretchedness and misery—to effect which, they used all kinds of deceitful, unfair, and unmerciful means. We view them next in Rome, where the spirit of tyranny and deceit raged still higher. We view them in Gaul, Spain, and in Britain.—In fine, we view them all over Europe, together with what were scattered about in Asia and Africa, as heathens, and we see them acting more like devils than accountable men. But some may ask, did not the blacks of Africa, and the mulattoes of Asia, go on in the same way as did the whites of Europe. I answer, no—they never were half so avaricious, deceitful and unmerciful as the whites, according to their knowledge.

But we will leave the whites or Europeans as heathens, and take a view of them as Christians, in which capacity we see them as cruel, if not more so than ever. In fact, take them as a body, they are ten times more cruel, avaricious and unmerciful than ever they were; for while they were heathens, they were bad enough it is true, but it is positively a fact that they were not quite so audacious as to go and take vessel loads of men, women and children, and in cold blood, and through devilishness, throw them into the sea, and murder them in all kind of ways. While they were heathens, they were too ignorant for such barbarity. But being Christians, enlightened and sensible, they are completely prepared for such hellish cruelties. . . .

Ignorance, my brethren, is a mist, low down into the very dark and almost impenetrable abyss in which, our fathers for many centuries have been plunged. The Christians, and enlightened of Europe, and some of Asia, seeing the ignorance and consequent degradation of our fathers, instead of trying to enlighten them, by teaching them that religion and light with which God had blessed them, they have plunged them into wretchedness ten thousand times more intolerable, than if they had left them entirely to the Lord. . . .

Ignorance, as it now exists among us, produces a state of things, Oh my Lord! too horrible to present to the world. Any man who is curious to see the full force of ignorance developed among the coloured people of the United States of America, has only to go into the southern and western states of this confederacy, where, if he is not a tyrant, but has the feelings of a human being, who can feel for a fellow creature, he may see enough to make his very heart bleed! He may see there, a son take his mother, who bore almost the pains of death to give him birth, and by the command of a tyrant, strip her as naked as she came into the world, and apply the cow-hide to her, until she falls a victim to death in the road! He may see a husband take his dear wife, not unfrequently in a pregnant state, and perhaps far advanced, and beat her for an unmerciful wretch, until his infant falls a lifeless lump at her feet! Can the Americans escape God Almighty? If they do, can he be to us a God of

Justice? God is just, and I know it—for he has convinced me to my satisfaction—I cannot doubt him. My observer may see fathers beating their sons, mothers their daughters, and children their parents, all to pacify the passions of unrelenting tyrants. He may also, see them telling news and lies, making mischief one upon another. These are some of the productions of ignorance, which he will see practised among my dear who are held in unjust slavery and wretchedness, by avaricious and unmerciful tyrants, to whom, and their hellish deeds, I would suffer my life to be taken before I would submit. And when my curious observer comes to take notice of those who are said to be free, (which assertion I deny) and who are making some frivolous pretentions to common sense, he will see that branch of ignorance among the slaves assuming a more cunning and deceitful course of procedure.—He may see some of my brethren in league with tyrants, selling their own brethren into *hell upon earth*, not dissimilar to the exhibitions in Africa, but in a more secret, servile and abject manner. Oh Heaven! I am full! ! ! ! ! I can hardly move my pen! ! ! ! and as I expect some will try to put me to death, to strike terror into others, and to obliterate from their minds the notion of freedom, so as to keep my brethren the more secure in wretchedness, where they will be permitted to stay but a short time (whether tyrants believe it or not)—I shall give the world a development of facts, which are already witnessed in the courts of heaven. My observer may see some of those ignorant and treacherous creatures (coloured people) sneaking about in the large cities, endeavouring to find out all strange coloured people, where they work and where they reside, asking them questions, and trying to ascertain whether they are runaways or not, telling them, at the same time, that they always have been, are, and always will be, friends to their brethren; and, perhaps, that they themselves are absconders, and a thousand such treacherous lies to get the better information of the more ignorant! ! ! There have been and are at this day in Boston, New-York, Philadelphia, and Baltimore, coloured men, who are in league with tyrants, and who receive a great portion of their daily bread, of the moneys which they acquire from the blood and tears of their more miserable brethren, whom they scandalously delivered into the hands of our *natural enemies*! ! ! ! ! ! . . . .

Men of colour, who are also of sense, for you particularly is my APPEAL designed. Our more ignorant brethren are not able to penetrate its value. I call upon you therefore to cast your eyes upon the wretchedness of your brethren, and to do your utmost to enlighten them—*go to work and enlighten your brethren!*—Let the Lord see you doing what you can to rescue them and yourselves from degradation. . . .

There is a great work for you to do, as trifling as some of you may think of it. You have to prove to the Americans and the world, that we are men, and not *brutes*, as we have been represented, and by millions treated. Remember, to let the aim of your labours among your brethren, and particularly the youths, be the dissemination of education and religion. It is lamentable, that many of our children go to school, from four until they are eight or ten, and sometimes fifteen years of age, and leave school knowing but a little more about the grammar of their language than a horse does about handling a musket—and not a few of them are really so ignorant, that they are unable to answer a person correctly, general questions in geography, and to hear them read, would only be to disgust a man who has a taste for reading. . . .

It is a notorious fact, that the major part of the white Americans, have, ever since we have been among them, tried to keep us ignorant, and make us believe that God made us and our children to be slaves to them and theirs. *Oh! my God, have mercy on Christian Americans*! ! ! . . .

Will any of us leave our homes and go to Africa? I hope not. Let them commence their attack upon us as they did on our brethren in Ohio, driving and beating us from our country, and my soul for theirs, they will have enough of it. Let no man of us budge one step, and let slave-holders come to beat us from our country. America is more our country, than it is the whites—we have enriched it with our *blood and tears*. The greatest riches in all America have arisen from our blood and tears:—and will they drive us from our property and homes, which we have earned with our *blood*? They must look sharp or this very thing will bring swift destruction upon them. The Americans have got so fat on our blood and groans, that they have almost forgotten the God of armies. . . .

3. FREDERICK DOUGLASS

What the Black Man Wants: Speech at the Annual Meeting of the Massachusetts Anti-Slavery Society at Boston (April, 1865)*

Mr. President. . . .

I do not know, from what has been said, that there is any difference of opinion as to the duty of abolitionists, at the present moment. How can we

*From *The Equality of All Men Before the Law Claimed and Defended; in Speeches by Hon. William D. Kelley, Wendell Phillips, and Frederick Douglass* . . . (Boston, 1865), pp. 36-39.

get up any difference at this point, or at any point, where we are so united, so agreed? I went especially, however, with that word of Mr. Phillips, which is the criticism of Gen. Banks and Gen. Banks's policy. I hold that that policy is our chief danger at the present moment; that it practically enslaves the negro, and makes the Proclamation of 1863 a mockery and delusion. What is freedom? It is the right to choose one's own employment. Certainly it means that, if it means anything; and when any individual or combination of individuals, undertakes to decide for any man when he shall work, where he shall work, at what he shall work, and for what he shall work, he or they practically reduce him to slavery. (Applause.) He is a slave. That I understand Gen. Banks to do—to determine for the so-called freedman, when, and where, and at what, and for how much he shall work, when he shall be punished, and by whom punished. It is absolute slavery. It defeats the beneficent intentions of the Government, if it has beneficent intentions, in regard to the freedom of our people.

I have had but one idea for the last three years, to present to the American people, and the phraseology in which I clothe it is the old abolition phraseology. I am for the "immediate, unconditional, and universal" enfranchisement of the black man, in every State in the Union. (Loud applause.) Without this, his liberty is a mockery; without this, you might as well almost retain the old name of slavery for his condition; for, in fact, if he is not the slave of the individual master, he is the slave of society, and holds his liberty as a privilege, not as a right. He is at the mercy of the mob, and has no means of protecting himself.

It may be objected, however, that this pressing of the negro's right to suffrage is premature. Let us have slavery abolished, it may be said, let us have labor organized, and then, in the natural course of events, the right of suffrage will be extended to the negro. I do not agree with this. The constitution of the human mind is such, that if it once disregards the conviction forced upon it by a revelation of truth, it requires the exercise of a higher power to produce the same conviction afterwards. The American people are now in tears. The Shenandoah has run blood—the best blood of the North. All around Richmond, the blood of New England and of the North has been shed—of your sons, your brothers and your fathers. We all feel, in the existence of this Rebellion, that judgments terrible, wide-spread, far-reaching, overwhelming, are abroad in the land; and we feel, in view of these judgments, just now, a disposition to learn righteousness. This is the hour. Our streets are in mourning, tears are falling at every fireside, and under the chastisement of this Rebellion we have almost come up to the point of conceding this great, this all-important right of suffrage. I fear that if we fail to do it now, if abolitionists fail to press it now, we may not see, for centuries to come, the same disposition that exists at this moment. (Applause.) Hence, I say, now is the time to press this right.

It may be asked, "Why do you want it? Some men have got along very well without it. Women have not this right." Shall we justify one wrong by another? That is a sufficient answer. Shall we at this moment justify the deprivation of the negro of the right to vote, because some one else is deprived of that privilege? I hold that women, as well as men, have the right to vote (applause), and my heart and my voice go with the movement to extend suffrage to woman; but that question rests upon another basis than that on which our right rests. We may be asked, I say, why we want it. I will tell you why we want it. We want it because it is our *right*, first of all. (Applause.) No class of men can, without insulting their own nature, be content with any deprivation of their rights. We want it, again, as a means for educating our race. Men are so constituted that they derive their conviction of their own possibilities largely from the estimate formed of them by others. If nothing is expected of a people, that people will find it difficult to contradict that expectation. By depriving us of suffrage, you affirm our incapacity to form an intelligent judgment respecting public men and public measures; you declare before the world that we are unfit to exercise the elective franchise, and by this means lead us to undervalue ourselves, to put a low estimate upon ourselves, and to feel that we have no possibilities like other men. Again, I want the elective franchise, for one, as a colored man, because ours is a peculiar government, based upon a peculiar idea, and that idea is universal suffrage. . . . Here, where universal suffrage is the rule, where that is the fundamental idea of the Government, to rule us out is to make us an exception, to brand us with the stigma of inferiority, and to invite to our heads the missiles of those about us; therefore, I want the franchise for the black man.

There are, however, other reasons. . . . I believe that when the tall heads of this Rebellion shall have been swept down, as they will be swept down, when the Davises and Toombses and Stephensons, and others who are leading in this Rebellion shall have been blotted out, there will be this rank undergrowth of treason, to which reference has been made, growing up there, and interfering with, and thwarting the quiet operation of the Federal Government in those States. You will see those traitors handing down, from sire to son, the same malignant spirit which they have manifested, and which they are now exhibiting, with malicious hearts, broad blades, and bloody hands in the field, against our sons and brothers. That spirit will still remain; and whoever sees the Federal Government extended over those Southern

States will see that Government in a strange land, and not only in a strange land, but in an enemy's land. A post-master of the United States in the South will find himself surrounded by a hostile spirit; a collector in a Southern port will find himself surrounded by a hostile spirit; a United States marshal or United States judge will be surrounded there by a hostile element. That enmity will not die out in a year, will not die out in an age. The Federal Government will be looked upon in those States precisely as the Governments of Austria and France are looked upon in Italy at the present moment. They will endeavor to circumvent, they will endeavor to destroy, the peaceful operation of this Government. Now, where will you find the strength to counterbalance this spirit, if you do not find it in the negroes of the South? They are your friends, and have always been your friends. They were your friends even when the Government did not regard them as such. They comprehended the genius of this war before you did. It is a significant fact, it is a marvellous fact, it seems almost to imply a direct interposition of Providence, that this war, which began in the interest of slavery on both sides, bids fair to end in the interest of liberty on both sides. (Applause.) It was begun, I say, in the interest of slavery on both sides. The South was fighting to take slavery out of the Union, and the North fighting to keep it in the Union; the South fighting to get it beyond the limits of the United-States Constitution, and the North fighting to retain it within those limits; the South fighting for new guarantees;—both despising the negro, both insulting the negro. Yet, the negro, apparently endowed with wisdom from on high, saw more clearly the end from the beginning than we did. . . . They are our only friends in the South, and we should be true to them in this their trial hour, and see to it that they have the elective franchise.

I know that we are inferior to you in some things—virtually inferior. We walk about among you like dwarfs among giants. Our heads are scarcely seen above the great sea of humanity. The Germans are superior to us; the Irish are superior to us; the Yankees are superior to us (laughter); they can do what we cannot, that is, what we have not hitherto been allowed to do. But while I make this admission, I utterly deny that we are originally, or naturally, or practically, or in any way, or in any important sense, inferior to anybody on this globe. (Loud applause.) This charge of inferiority is an old dodge. It has been made available for oppression on many occasions. It is only about six centuries since the blue-eyed and fair-haired Anglo-Saxon were considered inferior by the haughty Normans, who once trampled upon them. If you read the history of the Norman Conquest, you will find that this proud Anglo-Saxon was once looked upon as of coarser clay than his Norman master, and might be found in the highways and byways of old

England laboring with a brass collar on his neck, and the name of his master marked upon it. *You* were down then! (Laughter and applause.) You are up now. I am glad you are up, and I want you to be glad to help us up also. (Applause.)

The story of our inferiority is an old dodge, as I have said, for wherever men oppress their fellows, wherever they enslave them, they will endeavor to find the needed apology for such enslavement and oppression in the character of the people oppressed and enslaved. When we wanted, a few years ago, a slice of Mexico, it was hinted that the Mexicans were an inferior race, that the old Castilian blood had become so weak that it would scarcely run down hill, and that Mexico needed the long, strong and beneficent arm of the Anglo-Saxon care extended over it. We said that it was necessary to its salvation, and a part of the "manifest destiny" of this Republic, to extend our arm over that dilapidated government. So, too, when Russia wanted to take possession of a part of the Ottoman Empire, the Turks were "an inferior race." So, too, when England wants to set the heel of her power more firmly in the quivering heart of old Ireland, the Celts are an "inferior race." So, too, the negro, when he is to be robbed of any right which is justly his, is an "inferior man." It is said that we are ignorant; I admit it. But if we know enough to be hung, we know enough to vote. If the negro knows enough to pay taxes to support the government, he knows enough to vote; taxation and representation should go together. If he knows enough to shoulder a musket and fight for the flag, fight for the government, he knows enough to vote. If he knows as much when he is sober as an Irishman knows when drunk, he knows enough to vote, on good American principles. (Laughter and applause.)

But I was saying that you needed a counterpoise in the persons of the slaves to the enmity that would exist at the South after the Rebellion is put down. I hold that the American people are bound, not only in self-defence, to extend this right to the freedmen of the South, but they are bound by their love of country, and by all their regard for the future safety of those Southern States, to do this—to do it as a measure essential to the preservation of peace there. But I will not dwell upon this. I put it to the American sense of honor. The honor of a nation is an important thing. It is said in the Scriptures, "What doth it profit a man if he gain the whole world, and lose his own soul?" It may be said, also, What doth it profit a nation if it gain the whole world, but lose its honor? I hold that the American government has taken upon itself a solemn obligation of honor, to see that this war—let it be long or let it be short, let it cost much or let it cost little—that this war shall not cease until every freedman at the South has the right to vote. (Applause.) It has bound itself to it. What have you asked the black men of the South, the black men of the whole country, to do? Why, you have asked them to incur the deadly enmity of their masters, in order to befriend you and to befriend this Government. You have asked us to call down, not only upon ourselves, but upon our children's children, the deadly hate of the entire Southern people. You have called upon us to turn our backs upon our masters, to abandon their cause and espouse yours; to turn against the South and in favor of the North; to shoot down the Confederacy and uphold the flag—the American flag. You have called upon us to expose ourselves to all the subtle machinations of their malignity for all time. And now, what do you propose to do when you come to make peace? To reward your enemies, and trample in the dust your friends? Do you intend to sacrifice the very men who have come to the rescue of your banner in the South, and incurred the lasting displeasure of their masters thereby? Do you intend to sacrifice them and reward your enemies? Do you mean to give your enemies the right to vote, and take it away from your friends? . . . When this nation was in trouble, in its early struggles, it looked upon the negro as a citizen. In 1776 he was a citizen. At the time of the formation of the Constitution the negro had the right to vote in eleven States out of the old thirteen. In your trouble you have made us citizens. In 1812 Gen. Jackson addressed us as citizens—"fellow-citizens." He wanted us to fight. We were citizens then! And now, when you come to frame a conscription bill, the negro is a citizen again. He has been a citizen just three times in the history of this government, and it has always been in time of trouble. In time of trouble we are citizens. Shall we be citizens in war, and aliens in peace? Would that be just? . . .

What I ask for the negro is not benevolence, not pity, not sympathy, but simply *justice.* (Applause.) The American people have always been anxious to know what they shall do with us. .en. Banks was distressed with solicitude as to what he should do with the negro. Everybody has asked the question, and they learned to ask it early of the abolitionists, "What shall we do with the negro?" I have had but one answer from the beginning. Do nothing with us! Your doing with us has already played the mischief with us. Do nothing with us! If the apples will not remain on the tree of their own strength, if they are worm-eaten at the core, if they are early ripe and disposed to fall, let them fall! I am not for tying or fastening them on the tree in any way, except by nature's plan, and if they will not stay there, let them fall. And if the negro cannot stand on his own legs, let him fall also. All I ask is give him a chance to stand on his own legs! Let him alone! If you see him on his way to school, let him alone,—don't disturb him! If you see him going to the dinner-table at a hotel, let him go! If you see him going to the ballot-box, let him alone,—don't disturb him! (Applause.) If you see him going into a work-shop, just let him alone,—your interference is doing him a positive injury. Gen Banks's "preparation" is of a piece with this attempt to prop up the negro. Let him fall if he cannot stand alone! If the negro cannot live by the line of eternal justice, so beautifully pictured to you in the illustration used by Mr. Phillips, the fault will not be yours, it will be his who made the negro, and established that line for his government. (Applause.) Let him live or die by that. If you will only untie his hands, and give him a chance, I think he will live. . . .

4. GENE M. BRACK

Mexican Opinion, American Racism, and the War of 1846*

When Mexican forces attacked a detachment of General Zachary Taylor's army on the east bank of the Rio Grande in April 1846, President James K. Polk justified a declaration of war against Mexico with the charge that "American blood" had been shed upon "American soil." The clash culminated two decades of abrasive relations between the United States and Mexico. By 1846 the most palpable cause of contention was the rapid expansion of the United States toward the borderlands of Mexico. The Polk administration appeared determined to carry forward a program of expansion which would ultimately embrace much of northern Mexico. The Mexican government seemed equally determined to avoid losing any part of her national domain. For nine years Mexico had refused to recognize Texas independence and more recently had rejected Polk's offer to purchase upper California. Failing to gain concessions by peaceful means, Polk then made a show of force: it did not fit the purpose of the president's war message to acknowledge that the boundary between the United States and Mexico was undetermined, the area between the Nueces and Rio Grande rivers being disputed territory rather than "American soil"; that for weeks the mouth of the Rio Grande had lain under an American blockade; that an American squadron hovered near Vera Cruz; or that an American "exploratory" expedition had entered upper California.

Merely to cite American provocations does not wholly explain Mexico's reaction. Her decision to fight rather then surrender territory by any means

*Gene M. Brack, "Mexican Opinion, American Racism, and the War of 1846," *Western Historical Quarterly*, Vol. I (1970), pp. 161-74. Reprinted by permission of Gene M. Brack and the Western History Association.

was a momentous one for both countries, yet since the publication in 1919 of Justin H. Smith's *The War With Mexico,* American writers have given scant attention to the factors that may have influenced Mexico's course of action. Smith explained that the decision was in large measure based upon Mexican confidence in their military superiority; believing their army larger and more powerful, Mexicans also remembered that the United States had demonstrated martial ineptitude during the War of 1812. Thus, according to Smith, Mexicans sought war, for, "vain and superficial, they did not realize their weakness."

But for years Mexico had vowed to respond to American annexation of Texas with an immediate declaration of war against the United States. Therefore, if she sought war, why did Mexico not launch it in 1845 when Texas joined the American Union? It was the administration of José Joaquín de Herrera, who had become president in December 1844, that determined Mexico's response to annexation. Herrera's alternatives were to preserve peace by simply recognizing the irrevocable loss of Texas, or to act upon the threats of previous administrations and to declare war. The president appeared obligated to pursue the latter course, not only because of Mexico's previously announced position, but also because the revolution that brought Herrera to power had as an important purpose the creation of a government that would take a firm stand against the United States.

Herrera nevertheless wished to avoid war. He explained his position in a pamphlet which declared that it served the true interests of the country to preserve peace, that there was no longer any hope of recovering Texas, and that war, in Mexico's present circumstances, would lead to disaster. In accordance with Herrera's conciliatory policy, the government agreed in October of 1845 to admit an American envoy. Such a measure required support from outside the administration, however, and in November 1845 the foreign secretary sent a circular letter to local officials throughout Mexico soliciting their cooperation. The secretary agreed that Mexico had ample justification for declaring war, but he realized also that the country lacked the means to support an army hundreds of miles away on the distant frontier. The northern divisions could scarcely maintain their garrisons, let alone take the offensive. The secretary informed the local officials that Mexico could depend upon neither military nor financial support from other nations, and that in such circumstances the administration believed it expedient to avoid disaster by peacefully ceding an underpopulated part of Mexico's immense territory.

Thwarted by the combined opposition of the press, an aroused public, and rival political factions, Herrera's appeals went unheeded. When the American envoy arrived late in 1845 he was refused recognition, nominally because his credentials were improper, actually because Herrera could not afford further to offend public opinion by negotiating with a representative of the United States. The concession failed to save Herrera. He had assumed a moderate position when Mexicans would accept no course but a militant one. In December 1845 he was overthrown by General Mariano Paredes y Arrillaga. But the new president was also unable to breathe energy into a bankrupt and divided people.

When Paredes seized power he was aware of the nation's impotence. During the summer of 1845 while commanding a large body of the Mexican army at San Luis Potosí, Paredes himself had predicted that a clash with the United States would disgrace his nation before the eyes of the world. And correspondents from the capitol had informed Paredes that, for lack of funds, the army could not be strengthened.

During the summer and fall of 1845 Paredes had received frequent communications from General Mariano Arista, commanding Mexican forces on the northern frontier, informing him of Mexican weakness along the Rio Grande. In July Arista wrote that the army was in a state of "dreadful misery"; an advance upon Texas was out of the question, because the army lacked the means of bare subsistence. To Arista the frontier appeared threatened, and he wrote that he would do what he could to protect it, but that it was impossible to defend the nation with "hungry and naked" troops. He felt that he would weaken his army even more by sending a brigade to protect the department of Coahuila; to guard the entire line of the Rio Grande appeared impossible. Arista informed Paredes that he was convinced that the United States intended to attack and that Mexico would be defeated and then "dominated by Americans."

In October Arista wrote that he was desperate, his troops were hungry and that "the situation was very sad." Apparently preparing to advance upon Matamoros, the gringos had seized all of the passages across the Nueces, and Arista could do nothing to prevent it. The autumn weather was frigid, his men had neither coats nor blankets. They were perishing from cold and hunger, and yet the "public writers" had declared war.

Thus Arista, who would be ordered in the spring of 1846 to initiate hostilities, appeared more apprehensive than bellicose. And Paredes, regardless of his intentions when he entered the presidency, knew that Mexico was vulnerable and did not order an attack until seriously provoked by the United States. Arista's lament that the public writers had declared war clearly underscores the role of the press and of public opinion in creating the paradoxical situation confronted successively by the administrations of

Herrera and Paredes. And within the tangled web of events that led to war it is particularly significant that American officials were aware of the paradox.

Prior to the termination of official diplomatic relations in the spring of 1845, the American minister at Mexico had informed his government that Mexican opinion was so decidedly hostile to the United States that Mexican leaders were considered traitorous unless they appeared to cater to that opinion. In one of his last despatches from Mexico, the American minister reported that the Mexicans who realized war would be "ruinous" and "disastrous" were compelled "to join the public clamor, in order to maintain their positions."

When formal relations were terminated, the Polk administration continued to receive despatches from its consul and from William Parrott, its "confidential agent" in Mexico City. Both repeatedly informed their government that Mexican opinion favored war, but that Mexican officials, realizing their army was weak and the treasury empty, would stop short of fighting. In the summer of 1845 the American consul reported that the present Mexican government had no intention of declaring war. Nor did he think the opposition, should it come to power, would "ever seriously think of entering into a war (in earnest) with the United States." Parrott informed the Polk administration of Arista's weakness when he reported in September that the Mexican general had no more than three thousand men to defend a line of "about 140 leagues," and thus could have no hope of success even if he did not intend to launch an attack.

From such reports the Polk administration must have known that Mexican officials sought to avoid war if possible; it also must have known that public opinion in Mexico limited the options of Mexican leaders. But by ordering General Taylor to the Rio Grande and by taking other hostile measures during the winter and and spring of 1845-1846, was not the Polk administration further inflaming Mexican opinion and restricting the freedom of action of the Mexican government? It might be argued that the Slidell mission offered peace to Mexico, but Paredes logically defended his dismissal of Slidell by stating that the presence of an American army on the Rio Grande and of an American fleet in Mexican waters prohibited negotiations. To the Mexican president it appeared that by intimidating Mexico the United States hoped to acquire territory for the asking. Paredes was trapped by forces beyond his control: his countrymen demanded war, and the actions of the United States apparently left him no room for manuevering. The only alternative was to surrender territory to the Americans, and that was clearly unacceptable.

The historian must approach public opinion with great care. Modern devices measure it none too accurately, and when one is dealing with scattered fragments of the past, the difficulties are enormously increased. But if the foregoing is a reasonably accurate reconstruction of the circumstances leading to the Mexican War, it becomes important to devote more than passing attention to the factors that created a climate of opinion so rigidly hostile toward the United States that it led Mexico into a war for which she was dubiously prepared. In other words, it becomes important to know why the alternative—ceding territory to the United States—was so abhorrent to Mexicans.

At least a partial explanation may be that some Mexicans, like many Americans of that period, discerned a relationship between American expansion and racist elements within the United States. They were aware that many Americans looked upon Mexicans as inferior beings; the implications, when combined with the American desire for Mexican soil, were frightening. Americans apparently had no respect for the culture of those whom they considered inferior. They had been merciless in their treatment of the Indian. The Negro, also deemed inferior, had been reduced to a brutal form of servitude. Similar treatment probably awaited Mexicans should their northern departments fall under American control. The American failed to respect his agreements with the Indian; he could hardly be relied upon to be trustworthy when dealing with Mexicans. Perhaps this is what many Mexicans had in mind when they insisted that should Texas and California be lost, other Mexican territory would soon follow.

During the two decades prior to the war, Mexicans often criticized the United States for proclaiming humanitarian principles while driving the Indian from his land and condoning slavery. The degree to which the United States was prepared officially to defend slavery became apparent to Mexicans in the 1820s when Joel Poinsett, the first American minister to Mexico, introduced the subject while negotiating a treaty of limits between the two countries. Mexicans questioned a clause in the treaty providing for the detention of escaped slaves. They maintained that public opinion in Mexico would be outraged by the proposed clause. Poinsett reasoned that the border ought to be settled by a law-abiding population and suggested that slave-owners were an especially orderly and desirable class. The treaty was eventually ratified without the offending clause, but Poinsett's arguments in its defense revealed to Mexico the ardor with which the United States would support the rights of its citizens to own human property.

Accounts of Poinsett's activities, as well as of other matters pertaining to the United States, were disseminated in newspapers throughout Mexico. Each important faction in Mexican politics usually had one or more newspapers to articulate its position, and these newspapers were widely distributed. In *tertulias*—informal discussions, often held in taverns—a literate Mexican might read aloud to his non-reading friends; all would then discuss the topics of the day. The United States was among the topics. Much of the information in Mexican newspapers was likely to be doctored and misleading, but they did place the subject of the United States frequently before the public.

Typical of the kind of information that began appearing in the Mexican press during the 1820s was an anecdote describing a tyrannical Virginia slaveholder who ordered an old black man to hit a recaptured slave three hundred times, whereupon the old man fatally stabbed first the owner and then himself. At this time Mexicans also began to reveal an interest in American treatment of the Indian. The important conservative newspaper *El Sol* printed a letter written by John C. Calhoun in which the American cabinet official recommended sending Indians to uninhabited western regions. The Mexican editor urged his countrymen to take note of the matter not only because it seemed to reflect the American attitude toward Indians, but also because it portended future danger to the frontier of Mexico. The same newspaper later printed a letter written by an unidentified American citizen who criticized his government's Indian policy for being too lenient. Making treaties and compensating Indians for their lost land, he thought, only created needless expense. Instead of negotiating with the Indian, the United States should simply force the Indian to submit. It was absurd to purchase land from those who failed to cultivate it, for in this way the savages became the "depositories of the wealth that resulted from the progress and industry of the white population." The Mexican editor declared the letter typical of the American attitude toward the Indians. In 1840 *El Mosquito Mexicano* told its readers that Branch Archer of the Texas government favored the conquest of all Mexico and was known to have said that Mexicans, like the Indians, should give way to the energetic force of the Anglo-Americans.

El Amigo del Pueblo was a liberal organ whose editors were friendly toward the United States, but it too expressed concern at the systematic demoralization of the Indian by Americans. It reported in 1828 that it was the objective of the United States to expand to the Pacific. The process would eventually threaten Mexican territory, but presently the chief victim was the Indian. He was first deprived of his lands by a combination of deceit and force, and then his institutions were shattered. In this way a noble, brave, fiercely independent soul was reduced to a state of utter degradation. And Spaniards also had been insulted, cheated and robbed by the United States in the course of acquiring Florida. Therefore Mexicans should be concerned at the rapid approach of Americans toward the frontier.

Mexicans expressed alarm with increasing frequency at the threat of American expansion and at the growing realization that American condescension toward others included Mexicans. As early as 1822 the first Mexican minister at Washington warned his government that the Americans were an arrogant people who thought of Mexicans as inferiors. *El Sol* reported in 1826 that John Randolph in a senate speech insisted that his countrymen ought not to associate as equals with the people of Latin America, some of whom had descended from Africans. The Mexican editor believed that Randolph's view was typical of the "fanatical intolerance" that prevailed in the United States.

An article in *La Aguila Mexicana* stressed American contempt for the civilization and culture of Indians, who were called savages because their customs were different from those of the Anglo-Saxons. The writer was certain that Americans viewed Mexicans in the same way. An anonymous Mexican who claimed to have resided for a time in New Orleans reported in the newspaper *El Correo* that Americans seemed totally disinterested in understanding Mexicans; the American press gave more attention to "Persians and to Asian Tartars" than to Mexicans, and any notice accorded their southern neighbors was invariably insulting. Shortly before the Texas revolution *El Mosquito Mexicano* declared that the "refined egoism" of the white race caused Americans to treat persons of color with utter contempt and to assume the right to oppress them. The paper warned that Mexicans had much to fear from a people capable of such cruelty.

Manuel Eduardo de Gorostiza, Mexican minister to the United States during the Texas revolution, was the leading man of letters in Mexico and an experienced diplomat. Arriving in Washington in 1836 he was shocked to hear widespread statements of hatred and contempt for Mexico. Treated rudely by the Jackson administration, Gorostiza returned to Mexico and published a pamphlet criticizing Americans for their complicity in the Texas revolution and for their condescending attitude toward Mexicans. In 1840 Gorostiza urged the Mexican government not to surrender its claim to Texas. For Gorostiza there was a clear link between the expansionism of the United States and racism. He thought that Mexicans should make every sacrifice to retain Texas because they stood in danger of losing not only that territory, religion, of language, and of customs. . . ."

The struggle to halt American expansion was a "war of race, of religion, of language, and of customs. . . ."

The church also seemed threatened. A pamphlet published in Puebla following the Texas revolution warned that when the United States acquired Mexican territory "the Catholic religion will disappear from Mexican soil." Mexicans, like the Indians in the United States, would be deprived of the last traces of their civilization. *El Mosquito Mexicano* declared that the American advance toward Mexico involved more than the mere loss of Mexican territory; it threatened "the safety of the Catholic religion." A newspaper published in northern Mexico stated that it was essential to prevent American encroachments because a new religion would be established upon Mexican soil. Mexican citizens would be "sold as beasts" since "their color was not as white as that of their conquerors." *El Mosquito Mexicano* editors believed that the Catholic Church in Mexico faced the same danger from the United States as that of "the English under Henry VIII, the Irish under William, and Quebec under Wolfe."

Mexican editors often supported their allegations of American condescension with evidence drawn from newspapers published in the United States. The official gazette of the department of Tamaulipas reported in 1836 that a New Orleans newspaper had declared the Texas revolution to be one of the most notable events of modern times. The American paper had gone on to say that greater events would follow because "the superiority of the Anglo-American over the primitive inhabitants" of Mexico was so clearly manifest that it "presaged the conquest of Mexico itself." *El Diario* alleged that certain American newspapers had proclaimed that within ten years an "Anglo-Saxon" would be president of Mexico because Mexicans were incapable of governing themselves. A New York newspaper had said that fighting Mexicans was similar to "coon hunting." *El Siglo Diez y Nueve* expressed shock at the patronizing attitude of American journalists who believed that Mexico deserved to be conquered by those who were more industrious and efficient than her present inhabitants. Both *El Diario* and *El Mosquito Mexicano* reprinted an unidentified Texan's speech that encouraged his fellow Texans to support the conquest of Mexico. He was reported to have said cowardly Mexican troops would abandon the population and "immense wealth" might be seized from Mexican churches and from contributions imposed upon a "vagrant, corrupt, and lascivious clergy"; that such a conquest would undoubtedly expand the limits of slavery was said to be an additional advantage.

If any Mexican newspaper could be termed pro-American during these years, it would be the influential *El Siglo Diez y Nueve*, but in analyzing the differences separating the two countries, *El Siglo* also recognized the element of racism. The new world, it said, was divided between two distinct races, the Spanish and the English. Each had won its independence from colonial powers and had established almost identical institutions, but the two peoples had become strangers, if not enemies. Their laws, ideas, religion and customs were different: one was Catholic, generous, warlike and impetuous; the other Protestant, calculating, businesslike, astute. That the two should struggle when they made contact, as in Texas, was not strange. *El Siglo* found it particularly annoying that Americans should judge Mexico so unsympathetically. Mexico's history made it difficult for her to advance as rapidly as the United States, yet Americans assumed that her slow progress was a mark of inferiority. American newspapers spoke of Mexicans as "savage, barbaric, immoral and corrupt." These words might describe an individual criminal but not an entire community. *El Siglo* hoped that Americans would recognize that the generality of Mexicans was no more lawless than the people of New York, for example, which though highly civilized also harbored immoral and corrupt individuals.

Despite their moderation the editors of *El Siglo* nonetheless felt that Mexico must not surrender its claim to Texas. The fact that Americans in Texas owned slaves and professed opinions about the inferiority of all men "not of their race" made their defeat necessary. And by 1844 *El Siglo* had lent its voice to those who warned that the United States threatened the very existence of Mexico. Lacking respect for other civilizations, the United States, according to *El Siglo*, conquered only to acquire land, giving no thought to improving the condition of the conquered. Some American politicians had declared themselves in favor of exterminating the "odious Spanish race" along with their religion. These Americans shared eccentric beliefs and professed the most contradictory doctrines. They could be terrorized by the predictions of insane religious fanatics, and they proclaimed liberty for all and yet had virtually annihilated the Indian. Given the chance, they would do the same to Mexicans. Americans would not be content with merely acquiring Mexican territory; they would only be satisfied when they had destroyed the "Mexican Race."

The question before Mexico was obvious: "To be or not to be?" Americans recognized neither the rights of the Indians they had destroyed, nor of the Negroes, nor of Mexicans, whose territory they clearly intended to seize. Every action taken by the United States in relation to Texas was covered in the Mexican press. Readers were persistently reminded that the loss of Texas would lead to even greater losses in the future. Much of the diplomatic correspondence between the two nations was printed, and in almost every instance the Mexican editors pointed to the apparent relationship between American slavery and expansionism.

A pamphlet of 1845, urging Mexicans to fight for Texas, declared that

Americans were energetic and ruthless in pursuing their objectives. They had displayed remarkable efficiency in eradicating their Indians and could be relied upon to treat Mexicans in the same way. *El Estandarte Nacional* perhaps best summarized the Mexican attitude in April of 1845: to make territorial concessions would open the door to the "triumph of the Anglo-Saxon race," the enslavement of the Mexican people, the destruction of their language and customs, to the loss of what was most "dear and precious, their nationality."

The cumulative effect of these and similar observations contributed to the creation of a public opinion that by the spring of 1846 was so rigidly opposed to American expansion that it forced Mexico into a war that she was not likely to win. Many of the pronouncements demanding war in order to "defend the national honor" (pronouncements often quoted by American writers who blame Mexico for the war) may be dismissed as chauvinistic appeals of demagogic politicians, ambitious soldiers, or irresponsible journalists, or as attempts to pursue private ends by exploiting anti-Americanism. But these demands struck a responsive chord among Mexicans who, rightly or wrongly, from their knowledge of the racist nature of American society, had come to fear the extinction of Mexican civilization should the United States acquire dominion in Mexico.

II. Nineteenth-Century Wars and Their Aftermath

In one way or another, directly or indirectly, Indians, Mexicans, and Blacks, were involved in nineteenth-century American wars. Indians fought an almost countless series of battles against settler and soldier as land-hungry whites pushed into the "empty" west. Mexicans stood as physical and cultural barriers to American expansion to the southwest. Blacks were the subject of the debate over slavery and its expansion, a debate that finally exploded in secession and civil war.

From the point of view of most white Americans these wars invariably were fought for high ideals and lofty purposes. Upon the conclusion of hostilities, therefore, the United States made treaties, laws, and constitutional amendments at least superficially consistent with those ideals and purposes. The Treaty of Greenville (1795), signed after the defeat of an Indian confederation by General Anthony Wayne, promised the Indian nations of the Old Northwest that a line of demarcation would exist perpetually between Indian land and the area of white settlement in the region. The Treaty of Guadalupe Hidalgo (1848) ended the Mexican-American War and guaranteed that the inhabitants of the lands ceded by Mexico to the United States would be secure in their property, religion, and traditional rights. The Thirteenth, Fourteenth, and Fifteenth Amendments to the United States Constitution outlawed slavery, made Blacks citizens, and extended the protection of the constitution to all Black Americans. The Civil Rights Act of 1875 specifically required equal treatment of Blacks in all places of public accommodation.

In reality, however, idealistic declarations and hopes for a better future were nullified by the official and unofficial practices of the victors. The Treaty of Greenville proved to be little more than the first step toward the U. S. seizure of the entire Northwest. Significant protections of the original Treaty of Guadalupe Hidalgo were abrogated by President Polk and the United States Senate, and Mexicans in the ceded territories were abandoned to unfamiliar United States law and its less scrupulous practitioners. The short experiment of post-Civil War Reconstruction soon collapsed before the tide of white supremacy and political expediency.

If by mid-century white opinions and reactions to minorities had taken form in well-defined patterns of prejudice and mistreatment, so too had ethnic perceptions and responses followed predictable contours. One reason for this, or course, was that problems faced by ethnic groups had not changed essentially over the years. For Indians the main problem continued to be how to retain their land in the face of white expansion. For Blacks the principal challenge of the nineteenth century, as always, was gaining freedom to be what they wanted to be in a society determined to tolerate them only as strangers. As Mexicans struggled for social, economic, and cultural survival, their dominant concern, like that of Native Americans, remained Anglo expansion.

Most ethnic leaders were realists who knew they had to devise some satisfactory means of survival for their people. But because they perceived their problems differently, survival meant different things to them. Some Blacks, like the eminent and successful Booker T. Washington, still trusting in America, believed in the progressive advance toward that equality promised and then withdrawn after the Civil War. Chief Young Joseph of the Nez Percé Indians preferred peaceful accommodation with the white man, but in the end was forced to give up his lands, then take up arms in a desperate attempt to save his people from enforced exile to the Southwest. Many Chicanos, who had had their fill of American perfidy, recognized that submission to the Anglos would bring not peace, prosperity, and a better life, but agony and humiliation. Juan Cortina symbolized the decision of some Chicanos to take up arms rather than surrender without a struggle.

A. THE IDEAL: COMMITMENTS OF THE UNITED STATES GOVERNMENT

The documents in this section illustrate the high moral tone and assurances of peace that characterized official United States policy toward Indians, Mexicans, and Blacks following nineteenth-century conflicts involving those groups. While some of these documents reflect an honest idealism, it must be remembered that the congressional deliberations that produced them were also marked by a hard pragmatism, if not cynicism, which in the end proved to be the more powerful determinant. Congress never appropriated funds sufficient to enforce these laws and agreements properly. This omission left matters to the voluntary compliance of individual citizens, which meant little or no compliance at all.

During the early 1790s the Indian nations residing north of the Ohio River resisted Anglo advances westward, fearing the loss of their ancestral lands to whites streaming into the Ohio Territory. Their resistance ended in defeat at Fallen Timbers in 1794. In the Treaty of Greenville (1795), the Indians surrendered most of the present state of Ohio, a portion of southeastern Indiana, and a number of strategic outposts within the remaining Indian territory. In return the United States promised material compensation to the Indians and relinquished all claims to the remaining land north of the Ohio and east of the Mississippi. On its face the treaty established peace in the Old Northwest and secured perpetual boundaries for the Indians of the region.

During the 1830s and 1840s trouble also brewed in northern Mexico. First was the loss of Texas to Yanqui settlers there in 1836. Then came the question of boundaries, which in 1846 escalated into war between Mexico and the United States when the latter invaded territory claimed by Mexico. The war ended two years later in Mexican defeat. By the terms of the Treaty of Guadalupe Hidalgo (1848) the United States received almost one third of the territory of Mexico—extending from New Mexico to the shores of California—in return for which the United States promised peace, monetary compensation, guarantees to holders of Spanish and Mexican land grants, and security for the Catholic Church in the conquered territory. Mexicans residing in the annexed lands were assured that their traditional rights would be protected.

Forthright guarantees of basic rights also came in the aftermath of the American Civil War, as the United States eliminated the blight of human slavery and racial inequality by legislating freedom for its Black population. Slavery was abolished and Blacks were admitted to citizenship with full legal and civil rights. It was hoped by many that Blacks, no longer bound in servitude would, with the help of the government, be able to take their place as equal members of society.

However, as the Senate draft of the Treaty of Guadalupe Hidalgo in this section shows—and as Section II-B following further illustrates—reality soon intruded on these and similar declarations of goodwill. The potential for genuine peace and harmony following each conflict could not withstand the combined pressure of Anglo land-hunger and racial prejudice.

1. The Treaty of Greenville (August 3, 1795)*

A treaty of peace between the United States of America and the Tribes of Indians, called the Wyandots, Delawares, Shawanoes, Ottawas, Chipewas, Putawatimes, Miamis, Eel-river, Weea's, Kickapoos, Piankashaws, and Kaskaskias.

To put an end to a destructive war, to settle all controversies, and to restore harmony and a friendly intercourse between the said United States, and Indian tribes; Anthony Wayne, major-general, commanding the army of the United States, and sole commissioner for the good purposes above-mentioned, and the said tribes of Indians, by their Sachems, chiefs, and warriors, met together at Greeneville, the head quarters of the said army, have agreed on the following articles, which, when ratified by the President, with the advice and consent of the Senate of the United States, shall be binding on them and the said Indian tribes.

ARTICLE I.

Henceforth all hostilities shall cease; peace is hereby established, and shall be perpetual; and a friendly intercourse shall take place, between the said United States and Indian tribes.

ARTICLE II.

All prisoners shall on both sides be restored. The Indians, prisoners to the United States, shall be immediately set at liberty. The people of the United States, still remaining prisoners among the Indians, shall be delivered up in ninety days from the date hereof, to the general or commanding officer at Greeneville, Fort Wayne or Fort Defiance; and ten chiefs of the said tribes shall remain at Greeneville as hostages, until the delivery of the prisoners shall be effected.

ARTICLE III.

The general boundary line between the lands of the United States, and the lands of the said Indian tribes, shall begin at the mouth of Cayahoga river, and run thence up the same to the portage between that and the Tuscarawas

**Indian Affairs, Laws and Treaties,* Charles J. Kappler, ed. (Washington, D.C., Government Printing Office, 1904), Vol. II, pp. 39-44.

branch of the Muskingum; thence down that branch to the crossing place above Fort Lawrence; thence westerly to a fork of that branch of the great Miami river running into the Ohio, at or near which fork stood Loromie's store, and where commences the portage between the Miami, of the Ohio, and St. Mary's river, which is a branch of the Miami which runs into Lake Erie; thence a westerly course to Fort Recovery, which stands on a branch of the Wabash; then south-westerly in a direct line to the Ohio, so as to intersect that river opposite the mouth of Kentucke or Cuttawa river. And in consideration of the peace now established; of the goods formerly received from the United States; of those now to be delivered, and of the yearly delivery of goods now stipulated to be made hereafter, and to indemnify the United States for the injuries and expenses they have sustained during the war; the said Indians tribes do hereby cede and relinquish forever, all thei. claims to the lands nying eastwardly and southwardly of the general boundary line now described; and these lands, or any part of them, shall never hereafter be made a cause or pretence, on the part of the said tribes or any of them, of war or injury to the United States, or any of fhe people thereof.

And for the same considerations, and as an evidence of the returning friendship of the said Indian tribes, of their confidence in the United States, and desire to provide for their accommodation, and for that convenient intercourse which will be beneficial to both parties, the said Indian tribes do also cede to the United States the following pieces of land; to-wit. (1.) One piece of land six miles square at or near Loromie's store before mentioned. (2.) One piece two miles square at the head of the navigable water or landing on the St. Mary's river, near Girty's town. (3.) One piece six miles square at the head of the navigable water of the Au-Glaize river. (4.) One piece six miles square at the confluence of the Au-Glaize and Miami rivers, where Fort Defiance now stands. (5.) One piece six miles square at or near the confluence of the rivers St. Mary's and St. Joseph's, where Fort Wayne now stands, or near it. (6.) One piece two miles square on the Wabash river at the end of the portage from the Miami of the lake, and about eight miles westward from Fort Wayne. (7.) One piece six miles square at the Ouatanon or old Weea towns on the Wabash river. (8.) One piece twelve miles square at the British fort on the Miami of the lake at the foot of the rapids. (9.) One piece six miles square at the mouth of the said river where it empties into the Lake. (10.) One piece six miles square upon Sandusky lake, where a fort formerly stood. (11.) One piece two miles square at the lower rapids of Sandusky river. (12.) The post of Detroit and all the land to the north, the west and the south of it, of which the Indian title has been extinguished by gifts or grants to the French or English governments; and so much more land to be annexed to the district of Detroit as shall be comprehended between the river Rosine on the south, lake St. Clair on the north, and a line, the general course whereof shall be six miles distant from the west end of lake Erie, and Detroit river. (13.) The post of Michillimackinac, and all the land on the island, on which that post stands, and the main land adjacent, of which the Indian title has been extinguished by gifts or grants to the French or English governments; and a piece of land on the main to the north of the island, to measure six miles on lake Huron, or the strait between lakes Huron and Michigan, and to extend three miles back from the water of the lake or strait, and also the island De Bois Blanc, being an extra and voluntary gift of the Chipewa nation. (14.) One piece of land six miles square at the mouth of Chikago river, emptying into the south-west end of Lake Michigan, where a fort formerly stood. (15.) One piece twelve miles square at or near the mouth of the Illinois river, emptying into the Mississippi. (16.) One piece six miles square at the old Piorias fort and village, near the south end of the Illinois lake on said Illinois river: And whenever the United States shall think proper to survey and mark the boundaries of the lands hereby ceded to them, they shall give timely notice thereof to the said tribes of Indians, that they may appoint some of their wise chiefs to attend and see that the lines are run according to the terms of this treaty.

And the said Indian tribes will allow to the people of the United States a free passage by land and by water, as one and the other shall be found convenient, through their country, along the chain of posts herein before mentioned; . . .

And the said Indian tribes will also allow to the people of the United States the free use of the harbors and mouths of rivers along the lakes adjoining the Indian lands, for sheltering vessels and boats, and liberty to land their cargoes where necessary for their safety.

ARTICLE IV.

In consideration of the peace now established and of the cessions and relinquishments of lands made in the preceding article by the said tribes of Indians, and to manifest the liberality of the United States, as the great means of rendering this peace strong and perpetual; the United States relinquish their claims to all other Indian lands northward of the river Ohio, eastward of the Mississippi, and westward and southward of the Great Lakes and the waters uniting them, according to the boundary line agreed on by the United States, and the king of Great-Britain, in the treaty of peace made between them in the year 1783. But from this relinquishment by the the

United States, the following tracts of land, are explicitly excepted. 1st. The tract of one hundred and fifty thousand acres near the rapids of the river Ohio, which has been assigned to General Clark, for the use of himself and his warriors. 2d. The post of St. Vincennes on the river Wabash, and the lands adjacent, of which the Indian title has been extinguished. 3d. The lands at all other places in possession of the French people and other white settlers among them, of which the Indian title has been extinguished as mentioned in the 3d article; and 4th. The post of fort Massac towards the mouth of the Ohio. To which several parcels of land so excepted, the said tribes relinquish all the title and claim which they or any of them may have.

And for the same considerations and with the same views as above mentioned, the United States now deliver to the said Indian tribes a quantity of goods to the value of twenty thousand dollars, the receipt whereof they do hereby acknowledge; and henceforward every year forever the United States will deliver at some convenient place northward of the river Ohio, like useful goods, suited to the circumstances of the Indians, of the value of nine thousand five hundred dollars; reckoning that value at the first cost of the goods in the city or place in the United States, where they shall be procured. . . .

Provided, That if either of the said tribes shall hereafter at an annual delivery of their share of the goods aforesaid, desire that a part of their annuity should be furnished in domestic animals, implements of husbandry, and other utensils convenient for them, and in compensation to useful artificers who may reside with or near them, and be employed for their benefit, the same shall at the subsequent annual deliveries be furnished accordingly.

ARTICLE V.

To prevent any misunderstanding about the Indian lands relinquished by the United States in the fourth article, it is now explicitly declared, that the meaning of that relinquishment is this: The Indian tribes who have a right to those lands, are quietly to enjoy them, hunting, planting, and dwelling thereon so long as they please, without any molestation from the United States; but when those tribes, or any of them, shall be disposed to sell their lands, or any part of them, they are to be sold only to the United States; and until such sale, the United States will protect all the said Indian tribes in the quiet enjoyment of their lands against all citizens of the United States, and against all other white persons who intrude upon the same. And the said

Indian tribes again acknowledge themselves to be under the protection of the said United States and no other power whatever.

ARTICLE VI

If any citizen of the United States, or any other white person or persons, shall presume to settle upon the lands now relinquished by the United States, such citizen or other person shall be out of the protection of the United States; and the Indian tribe, on whose land the settlement shall be made, may drive off the settler, or punish him in such manner as they shall think fit; and because such settlements made without the consent of the United States, will be injurious to them as well as to the Indians, the United States shall be at liberty to break them up, and remove and punish the settlers as they shall think proper, and so effect that protection of the Indian lands herein before stipulated.

ARTICLE VII.

The said tribes of Indians, parties to treaty, shall be at liberty to hunt within the territory and lands which they have now ceded to the United States, without hindrance or molestation, so long as they demean themselves peaceably, and offer no injury to the people of the United States.

ARTICLE VIII.

Trade shall be opened with the said Indian tribes; and they do hereby respectively engage to afford protection to such persons, with their property, as shall be duly licensed to reside among them for the purpose of trade, and to their agents and servants; but no person shall be permitted to reside at any of their towns or hunting camps as a trader, who is not furnished with a license for that purpose, under the hand and seal of the superintendent of the department north-west of the Ohio, or such other person as the President of the United States shall authorize to grant such licenses; to the end, that the said Indians may not be imposed on in their trade. And if any licensed trader shall abuse his privilege by unfair dealing, upon complaint and proof thereof, his license shall be taken from him, and he shall be further punished according to the laws of the United States. And if any person shall intrude himself as a trader, without such license, the said Indians shall take and bring him before the superintendent or his deputy, to be dealt with according to law. And to prevent impositions by forged licenses, the said Indians shall at least once a year give information to the superintendent or his deputies, of the names of the traders residing among them.

ARTICLE IX.

Lest the firm peace and friendship now established should be interrupted by the misconduct of individuals, the United States, and the said Indian tribes agree, that for injuries done by individuals on either side, no private revenge or retaliation shall take place; but instead thereof, complaint shall be made by the party injured, to the other: By the said Indian tribes, or any of them, to the President of the United States, or the superintendent by him appointed; and by the superintendent or other person appointed by the President, to the principal chiefs of the said Indian tribes, or of the tribe to which the offender belongs; and such prudent measures shall then be pursued as shall be necessary to preserve the said peace and friendship unbroken, until the Legislature (or Great Council) of the United States, shall make other equitable provision in the case, to the satisfaction of both parties. Should any Indian tribes meditate a war against the United States or either of them, and the same shall come to the knowledge of the before-mentioned tribes, or either of them, they do hereby engage to give immediate notice thereof to the general or officer commanding the troops of the United States, at the nearest post. And should any tribe, with hostile intentions against the United States, or either of them, attempt to pass through their country, they will endeavor to prevent the same, and in like manner give information of such attempt, to the general or officer commanding, as soon as possible, that all causes of mistrust and suspicion may be avoided between them and the United States. In like manner the United States shall give notice to the said Indian tribes of any harm that may be meditated against them, or either of them, that shall come to their knowledge; and do all in their power to hinder and prevent the same, that the friendship between them may be uninterrupted.

ARTICLE X.

All other treaties heretofore made between the United States and the said Indian tribes, or any of them, since the treaty of 1783, between the United States and Great Britain, that come within the purview of this treaty, shall henceforth cease and become void.

In testimony whereof, the said Anthony Wayne, and the sachems and war chiefs of the beforementioned nations and tribes of Indians, have hereunto set their hands and affixed their seals.

Done at Greenville, in the territory of the United States northwest of the river Ohio, on the third day of August, one thousand seven hundred and ninety-five.

2. The Treaty of Guadalupe Hidalgo (February 2, 1848)*

ARTICLE VIII

Mexicans now established in territories previously belonging to Mexico and which remain for the future within the limits of the United States as defined by the present limit of the United States, as defined by the present treaty, shall be free to continue where they now reside, or to remove at any time to the Mexican republic retaining the property which they possess in the said territories, or disposing thereof, and removing the proceeds wherever they please, without their being subjected, on this account, to any contribution, tax, or charge whatever.

Those who shall prefer to remain in the said territories, may either retain the title and rights of Mexican citizens, or acquire those of citizens of the United States. But they shall be under obligation to make their election within one year from the date of the exchange of the ratifications of this treaty; and those who shall remain in the said territories after the expiration of that year, without having declared their intention to retain the character of Mexicans, shall be considered to have elected to become citizens of the United States.

In the said territories, property of every kind, now belonging to Mexicans now established there, shall be inviolably respected. The present owners, the heirs of these, and all Mexicans who may hereafter acquire said property by contract, shall enjoy with respect to it guarantees equally ample as if the same belonged to citizens of the United States.

ARTICLE IX (original draft)

The Mexicans who, in the territories aforesaid, shall not preserve the character of citizens of the Mexican republic conformably with what is

* *Treaties and Other International Acts of the United States* . . . (Washington, D.C., Government Printing Office, 1937), Vol. V, pp. 217-218; 219; 241-43.

stipulated in the preceding article, shall be incorporated into the Union of the United States, and admitted as soon as possible, according to the principles of the federal constitution, to the enjoyment of all the rights of citizens of the United States. In the meantime they shall be maintained and protected in the enjoyment of their liberty their property, and the civil rights now vested in them according to the Mexican laws. With respect to political rights, their condition shall be on an equality with that of the inhabitants of the other territories of the United States and at least equally good as that of the inhabitants of Louisiana and the Floridas, when these provinces, by transfer from the French republic and the crown of Spain, became territories of the United States.

The same most ample guaranty shall be enjoyed by all ecclesiastics and religious corporations or communities, as well as in the discharge of the offices of their ministry, as in the enjoyment of their property of every kind, whether individual or corporate. This guaranty shall embrace all temples, houses, and edifices dedicated to the Roman Catholic worship; as well as all property destined to its support, or to that of schools, hospitals, and other foundations for charitable or beneficent purposes. No property of this nature shall be considered as having become the property of the American government, or as subject to be by it disposed of, or diverted to other uses.

Finally, the relations and communications between the Catholics living in the territories aforesaid, and their respective ecclesiastical authorities, shall be open, free, and exempt all hindrance whatever, even although such authorities should reside within the limits of the Mexican republic, as defined by this treaty; and this freedom shall be continued, so long as a new demarcation of ecclesiastical districts shall not have been made, conformably with the laws of the Roman Catholic church.

ARTICLE IX (Senate draft)

Mexicans who, in the territories aforesaid, shall not preserve the character of the Mexican republic, conformably with what is stipulated in the preceding article, shall be incorporated in the Union of the United States, and be admitted at the proper time (to be judged of by the Congress of the United States) to the enjoyment of all the rights of citizens of the United States, according to the principles of the Constitution; and in the meantime shall be maintained and protected in the free enjoyment of their liberty and property, and secured in the free exercise of their religion without restriction.

ARTICLE X (deleted by Senate)

All grants of land made by the Mexican government, or by the competent authorites, in territories previously appertaining to Mexico, and remaining for the future within the limits of the United States, shall be respected as valid to the same extent that the same grants would be valid if the said territories had remained within the limits of Mexico. But the grantees of the land in Texas, put in possession thereof, who, by reason of the circumstances of the country since the beginning of the troubles between Texas and the Mexican government, may have been prevented from fulfilling all the conditions of their grants, shall be under the obligation to fulfill the said conditions within the periods limited in the same respectively; such periods to be now counted from the date of the exchange of ratifications of this treaty; in default of which, the said grants shall not be obligatory upon the State of Texas, in virtue of the stipulations contained in this article.

The foregoing stipulation in regard to grantees of land in Texas is extended to all grantees of land in territories aforesaid, elsewhere than in Texas, put in possession under such grants; and, in default of the fulfillment of the conditions of any such grant within the new period which as is above stipulated begins with the day of the exchange of ratifications of this treaty, the same shall be null and void.

The Mexican government declares that no grant whatever of lands in Texas has been made since the second day of March, one thousand eight hundred and thirty-six; and that no grant whatever of lands in any of the territories aforesaid has been made since the thirteenth day of May, one thousand eight hundred and forty-six.

3. Civil Rights Amendments to the United States Constitution

ARTICLE XIII (declared ratified December 18, 1865)

Section 1. Neither slavery nor involuntary servitude, except as a punishment for crime whereof the party shall have been duly convicted, shall exist within the United States, or any place subject to their jurisdiction.

Section 2. Congress shall have power to enforce this article by appropriate legislation.

ARTICLE XIV (declared ratified July 28, 1868)

Section 1. All persons born or naturalized in the United States, and subject to the jurisdiction thereof, are citizens of the United States and of the State wherein they reside. No State shall make or enforce any law which shall abridge the privileges or immunities of citizens of the United States; nor shall any State deprive any person of life, liberty, or property, without due process of law; nor deny to any person within its jurisdiction the equal protection of the laws.

Section 2. Representatives shall be apportioned among the several States according to their respective numbers, counting the whole number of persons in each State, excluding Indians not taxed. But when the right to vote at any election for the choice of electors for President and Vice President of the United States, Representatives in Congress, the Executive and Judicial officers of a State, or the members of the Legislature thereof, is denied to any of the male inhabitants of such State, being twenty-one years of age, and citizens of the United States, or in any way abridged, except for participation in rebellion, or other crime, the basis of representation therein shall be reduced in the proportion which the number of such male citizens shall bear to the whole number of male citizens twenty-one years of age in such State. . . .

Section 5. The Congress shall have power to enforce, by appropriate legislation, the provisions of this article.

ARTICLE XV (declared ratified March 30, 1870)

Section 1. The right of citizens of the United States to vote shall not be denied or abridged by the United States or by any State on account of race, color, or previous condition of servitude.

Section 2. The Congress shall have power to enforce this article by appropriate legislation.

4. "An Act to Protect All Citizens in Their Civil and Legal Rights" (March 1, 1875)*

Whereas, it is essential to just government to recognize the equality of all

* *The Statutes at Large of the United States* . . . (Washington, D.C., Government Printing Office, 1875), Vol. XVIII, part 3, pp. 335-37.

men before the law, and hold that it is the duty of government in its dealings with the people to mete out equal and exact justice to all, of whatever nativity, race, color, or persuasion, religious or political; and it being the appropriate object of legislation to enact great fundamental principles into law: Therefore,

Be it enacted by the Senate and House of Representatives of the United States of America in Congress assembled, That all persons within the jurisdiction of the United States shall be entitled to the full and equal enjoyment of the accommodations, advantages, facilities, and privileges of inns, public conveyances on land or water, theaters, and other places of public amusement; subject only to the conditions and limitations established by law, and applicable alike to citizens of every race and color, regardless of any previous condition of servitude.

SEC. 2. That any person who shall violate the foregoing section by denying to any citizen, except for reasons by law applicable to citizens of every race and color, and regardless of any previous condition of servitude, the full enjoyment of any of the accommodations, advantages, facilities, or privileges in said section enumerated, or by aiding or inciting such denial, shall, for every such offense, forfeit and pay the sum of five hundred dollars to the person aggrieved thereby, to be recovered in an action of debt, with full costs; and shall also, for every such offense, be deemed guilty of a misdemeanor, and, upon conviction thereof, shall be fined not less than five hundred nor more than one thousand dollars, or shall be imprisoned not less than thirty days nor more than one year: *Provided,* That all persons may elect to sue for the penalty aforesaid or to proceed under their rights at common law and by State statutes; and having so elected to proceed in the one mode or the other, their right to proceed in the other jurisdiction shall be barred. But this proviso shall not apply to criminal proceedings, either under this act or the criminal law of any State: *And provided further,* That a judgment for the penalty in favor of the party aggrieved, or a judgment upon an indictment, shall be a bar to either prosecution respectively.

SEC. 3. That the district and circuit courts of the United States shall have, exclusively of the courts of the several States, cognizance of all crimes and offenses against, and violations of, the provisions of this act; and actions for the penalty given by the preceding section may be prosecuted in the territorial, district, or circuit courts of the United States wherever the defendant may be found, without regard to the other party; and the district attorneys, marshals, and deputy marshals of the United States, and commissioners appointed by the circuit and territorial courts of the United States, with powers of arresting and imprisoning or bailing offenders against the laws of the United States, are hereby specially authorized and required to institute proceedings against every person who shall violate the provisions of this act, and cause him to be arrested and imprisoned or bailed, as the case may be, for trial before such court of the United States, or territorial court, as by law has cognizance of the offense, except in respect of the right of action accruing to the person aggrieved; and such district attorneys shall cause such proceedings to be prosecuted to their termination as in other cases: *Provided,* That nothing contained in this section shall be construed to deny or defeat any right of civil action accruing to any person, whether by reason of this act or otherwise; and any district attorney who shall willfully fail to institute and prosecute the proceedings herein required, shall, for every such offense, forfeit and pay the sum of five hundred dollars to the person aggrieved thereby, to be recovered by an action of debt, with full costs, and shall, on conviction thereof, be deemed guilty of a misdemeanor, and be fined not less than one thousand nor more than five thousand dollars: *And provided further,* That a judgment for the penalty in favor of the party aggrieved against any such district attorney, or a judgment upon an indictment against any such district attorney, shall be a bar to either prosecution respectively.

SEC. 4. That no citizen possessing all other qualifications which are or may be prescribed by law shall be disqualified for service as grand or petit juror in any court of the United States, or of any State, on account of race, color, or previous condition of servitude; and any officer or other person charged with any duty in the selection or summoning of jurors who shall exclude or fail to summon any citizen for the cause aforesaid shall, on conviction thereof, be deemed guilty of a misdemeanor, and be fined not more than five thousand dollars.

SEC. 5. That all cases arising under the provisions of this act in the courts of the United States shall be reviewable by the Supreme Court of the United States, without regard to the sum in the controversy, under the same provisions and regulations as are now provided by law for the review of other causes in said court.

Approved, March 1, 1875.

B. THE REALITIES: DESTRUCTION OF ETHNIC POWER

Although it does some violence to their true complexity, it is possible to gain insight into Anglo relations with Indians, Blacks, and Mexican Americans in the context of two fundamental issues— land and race. Originally Indians possessed all of America, and from the beginning the motivating energy of Anglo relations with Native Americans was the desire for Indian land; the issue of cultural inferiority went arm-in-arm with that of enduring passion. The principal element contributing to Negro misfortune in America has been race. Afro-Americans have traditionally been considered a race apart, inferior to whites, and properly relegated to the bottom of society. The troubles of Mexican Americans derive from a combination of elements. Like the Indians they possessed vast areas of desirable land and, like both Indians and Blacks, they possessed cultural and racial "characteristics" that Anglos considered inferior. American treaties, laws, and promises meant little as long as ethnics were set off racially, as long as their cultures were demeaned by Anglos, as long as they controlled land Anglos wanted, and as long as they lacked the power to compel compliance with laws and guarantees.

This section illustrates the systematic destruction of ethnic power in nineteenth-century America, despite government promises to the contrary. One of the saddest chapters in the book of Indian sorrows was the eviction of the Cherokees, Creeks, Choctaws, Chickasaws, and Seminoles from their ancestral homes in the Southern states during the presidency of Andrew Jackson. Mary F. Young describes the process by which peaceful, "civilized" tribes were forced from their homelands by the naked greed of land-hungry whites. For decades American settlers had encircled and pushed across Indian lands in the South, and by the 1830s the pressures on Native Americans to relinquish their lands had become too great for most to resist. In the frauds, subterfuges, and blatant breaches of faith perpetuated on the Indians, land speculators received full support from the Jackson administration.

Using the concept of colonialism, sociologist Joan M. Moore examines the destruction of Mexican-American political power in New Mexico, Texas, and California. She observes different patterns of colonial exploitation—"classic," "conflict," and "economic"—but notes that in each case the result was the same. Through one form of conquest or another indigenous Spanish-speaking leadership groups were replaced by encroaching Anglos, and the structure of Mexican-American political life was totally disrupted. Today's Chicano movement, she says, is in part an attempt to restore lost political power and identity to the Mexican Americans.

In the third selection Vernon Lane Wharton describes the problems faced by Mississippi Blacks in the 1870s. The moral and political reforms of post-Civil War Reconstruction were rarely supported in Mississippi because of the refusal of whites to deal with Blacks as political or social equals. Without vigorous federal enforcement civil rights legislation was meaningless. By 1875, through intimidation, violence, and federal reluctance to act in support of the law, the rule of white supremacy was reestablished in Mississippi.

1. MARY E. YOUNG

Indian Removal and Land Allotment: The Civilized Tribes and Jacksonian Justice*

By the year 1830, the vanguard of the southern frontier had crossed the Mississippi and was pressing through Louisiana, Arkansas, and Missouri. But the line of settlement was by no means as solid as frontier lines were classically supposed to be. East of the Mississippi, white occupancy was limited by Indian tenure of northeastern Georgia, enclaves in western North Carolina and southern Tennessee, eastern Alabama, and the northern two thirds of Mississippi. In this twenty-five-million-acre domain lived nearly 60,000 Cherokees, Creeks, Choctaws, and Chickasaws.

The Jackson administration sought to correct this anomaly by removing the tribes beyond the reach of white settlements, west of the Mississippi. As the President demanded of Congress in December, 1830: "What good man would prefer a country covered with forests and ranged by a few thousand savages to our extensive Republic, studded with cities, towns, and prosperous farms, embellished with all the improvements which art can devise or industry execute, occupied by more than 12,000,000 happy people, and filled with all the blessings of liberty, civilization, and religion?"

The President's justification of Indian removal was the one usually applied to the displacement of the Indians by newer Americans—the superiority of a farming to a hunting culture, and of Anglo-American "liberty, civilization, and religion" to the strange and barbarous way of the red man. The superior capacity of the farmer to exploit the gifts of nature and of nature's God was one of the principal warranties of the triumph of westward-moving "civilization."

Such a rationalization had one serious weakness as an instrument of policy. The farmer's right of eminent domain over the lands of the savage could be asserted consistently only so long as the tribes involved were "savage." The southeastern tribes, however, were agriculturists as well as hunters. For two or three generations prior to 1830, farmers among them

*Mary E. Young, "Indian Removal and Land Allotment: The Civilized Tribes and Jacksonian Justice," *American Historical Review,* Vol. LXIV (1958), pp. 31-45. Reprinted by permission of Mary E. Young.

fenced their plantations and "mixed their labor with the soil," making it their private property according to accepted definitions of natural law. White traders who settled among the Indians in the mid-eighteenth century gave original impetus to this imitation of Anglo-American agricultural methods. Later, agents of the United States encouraged the traders and mechanics, their half-breed descendants, and their fullblood imitators who settled out from the tribal villages, fenced their farms, used the plow, and cultivated cotton and corn for the market. In the decade following the War of 1812, missionaries of various Protestant denominations worked among the Cherokees, Choctaws, and Chickasaws, training hundreds of Indian children in the agricultural, mechanical, and household arts and introducing both children and parents to the further blessings of literacy and Christianity.

The "civilization" of a portion of these tribes embarrassed United States policy in more ways than one. Long-term contact between the southeastern tribes and white traders, missionaries, and government officials created and trained numerous half-breeds. The half-breed men acted as intermediaries between the less sophisticated Indians and the white Americans. Acquiring direct or indirect control of tribal politics, they often determined the outcome of treaty negotiations. Since they proved to be skillful bargainers, it became common practice to win their assistance by thinly veiled bribery. The rise of the half-breeds to power, the rewards they received, and their efforts on behalf of tribal reform gave rise to bitter opposition. By the mid-1820's, this opposition made it dangerous for them to sell tribal lands. Furthermore, many of the new leaders had valuable plantations, mills, and trading establishments on these lands. Particularly among the Cherokees and Choctaws, they took pride in their achievements and those of their people in assimilating the trappings of civilization. As "founding Fathers," they prized the political and territorial integrity of the newly organized Indian "nations." These interests and convictions gave birth to a fixed determination, embodied in tribal laws and intertribal agreements, that no more cessions of land should be made. The tribes must be permitted to develop their new way of life in what was left of their ancient domain.

Today it is a commonplace of studies in culture contact that the assimilation of alien habits affects different individuals and social strata in different ways and that their levels of acculturation vary considerably. Among the American Indian tribes, it is most often the families with white or half-breed models who most readily adopt the Anglo-American way of life. It is not surprising that half-breeds and whites living among the Indians should use their position as go-betweens to improve their status and power among the natives. Their access to influence and their efforts toward reform combine with pressures from outside to disturb old life ways, old securities, and established prerogatives. Resistance to their leadership and to the cultural alternatives they espouse is a fertile source of intratribal factions.

To Jacksonian officials, however, the tactics of the half-breeds and the struggles among tribal factions seemed to reflect a diabolical plot. Treaty negotiators saw the poverty and "depravity" of the common Indian, who suffered from the scarcity of game, the missionary attacks on his accustomed habits and ceremonies, and the ravages of "demon rum" and who failed to find solace in the values of Christian and commercial civilization. Not unreasonably, they concluded that it was to the interest of the tribesman to remove west of the Mississippi. There, sheltered from the intruder and the whisky merchant, he could lose his savagery while improving his nobility. Since this seemed so obviously to the Indian's interest, the negotiators conveniently concluded that it was also his desire. What, then, deterred emigration? Only the rapacity of the half-breeds, who were unwilling to give up their extensive properties and their exalted position.

These observers recognized that the government's difficulties were in part of its own making. The United States had pursued an essentially contradictory policy toward the Indians, encouraging both segregation and assimilation. Since Jefferson's administration, the government had tried periodically to secure the emigration of the eastern tribes across the Mississippi. At the same time, it had paid agents and subsidized missionaries who encouraged the Indian to follow the white man's way. Thus it had helped create the class of tribesmen skilled in agriculture, pecuniary accumulation, and political leadership. Furthermore, by encouraging the southeastern Indians to become cultivators and Christians, the government had undermined its own moral claim to eminent domain over tribal lands. The people it now hoped to displace could by no stretch of dialectic be classed as mere wandering savages.

By the time Jackson became President, then, the situation of the United States vis-à-vis the southeastern tribes was superficially that of irresistible force and immovable object. But the President, together with such close advisers as Secretary of War John H. Eaton and General John Coffee, viewed the problem in a more encouraging perspective. They believed that the government faced not the intent of whole tribes to remain near the bones of their ancestors but the selfish determination of a few quasi Indian leaders to retain their riches and their ill-used power. Besides, the moral right of the civilized tribes to their lands was a claim not on their whole domain but rather on the part cultivated by individuals. Both the Indian's natural right to his land and his political capacity for keeping it were products of his imitation of white "civilization." Both might be eliminated by a rigorous application of the principle that to treat an Indian fairly was to treat him like a white man. Treaty negotiations by the tried methods of purchase and selective bribery had failed. The use of naked force without the form of voluntary agreement was forbidden by custom, by conscience, and by fear that the administration's opponents would exploit religious sentiment which cherished the rights of the red man. But within the confines of legality and the formulas of voluntarism it was still possible to acquire the lands of the civilized tribes.

The technique used to effect this object was simple: the entire population of the tribes was forced to deal with white men on terms familiar only to the most acculturated portion of them. If the Indian is civilized, he can behave like a white man. Then let him take for his own as much land as he can cultivate, become a citizen of the state where he lives, and accept the burdens which citizenship entails. If he is not capable of living like this, he should be liberated from the tyranny of his chiefs and allowed to follow his own best interest by emigrating beyond the farthest frontiers of white settlement. By the restriction of the civilized to the lands they cultivate and by the emigration of the savages millions of acres will be opened to white settlement.

The first step dictated by this line of reasoning was the extension of state laws over the Indian tribes. Beginning soon after Jackson's election, Georgia, Alabama, Mississippi, and Tennessee gradually brought the Indians inside their borders under their jurisdiction. Thus an Indian could be sued for trespass or debt, though only in Mississippi and Tennessee was his testimony invariably acceptable in a court of law. In Mississippi, the tribesmen were further harassed by subjection—or the threat of subjection—to such duties as mustering with the militia, working on roads, and paying taxes. State laws establishing county governments within the tribal domains and, in some cases, giving legal protection to purchasers of Indian improvements encouraged the intrusion of white settlers on Indian lands. The laws nullified the legal force of Indian customs, except those relating to marriage. They provided heavy penalties for anyone who might enact or enforce tribal law. Finally, they threatened punishment to any person who might attempt to deter another from signing a removal treaty or enrolling for emigration. The object of these laws was to destroy the tribal governments and to thrust upon individual Indians the uncongenial alternative of adjusting to the burdens of citizenship or removing beyond state jurisdiction.

The alternative was not offered on the unenlightened supposition that the Indians generally were capable of managing their affairs unaided in a white man's world. Governor Gayle of Alabama, addressing the "former chiefs and headmen of the Creek Indians" in June of 1834 urged them to remove from the state on the grounds that

> you speak a different language from ours. You do not understand our laws and from your habits, cannot be brought to understand them. You are ignorant of the arts of civilized life. You have not like your white neighbors been raised in habits of industry and economy, the only means by which anyone can live, in settled countries, in even tolerable comfort. You know nothing of the skill of the white man in trading and making bargains, and cannot be guarded against the artful contrivances which dishonest men will resort to, to obtain your property under forms of contracts. In all these respects you are unequal to the white men, and if your people remain where they are, you will soon behold them in a miserable, degraded, and destitute condition.

The intentions of federal officials who favored the extension of state laws are revealed in a letter written to Jackson by General Coffee. Referring to the Cherokees, Coffee remarked:

> Deprive the chiefs of the power they now possess, take from them their own code of laws, and reduce them to plain citizenship . . . and they will soon determine to move, and then there will be no difficulty in getting the poor Indians to give their consent. All this will be done by the State of Georgia if the U. States do not interfere with her law— . . . This will of course silence those in our country who constantly seek for causes to complain—It may indeed turn them loose upon Georgia, but that matters not, it is Georgia who clamors for the Indian lands, and she alone is entitled to the blame if any there be.

Even before the laws were extended, the threat of state jurisdiction was used in confidential "talks" to the chiefs. After the states had acted, the secretary of war instructed each Indian agent to explain to his charges the meaning of state jurisdiction and to inform them that the President could not protect them against the enforcement of the laws. Although the Supreme Court, in *Worcester* vs. *Georgia*, decided that the state had no right to extend its laws over the Cherokee nation, the Indian tribes being "domestic dependent nations" with limits defined by treaty, the President refused to enforce this decision. There was only one means by which the government might have made "John Marshall's decision" effective—directing federal troops to exclude state officials and other intruders from the Indian domain. In January, 1832, the President informed an Alabama congressman that the

United States government no longer assumed the right to remove citizens of Alabama from the Indian country. By this time, the soldiers who had protected the territory of the southeastern tribes against intruders had been withdrawn. In their unwearying efforts to pressure the Indians into ceding their lands, federal negotiators emphasized the terrors of state jurisdiction.

Congress in May, 1830, complemented the efforts of the states by appropriating $500,000 and authorizing the President to negotiate removal treaties with all the tribes east of the Mississippi. The vote on this bill was close in both houses. By skillful use of pamphlets, petitions, and lobbyists, missionary organizations had enlisted leading congressmen in their campaign against the administration's attempt to force the tribes to emigrate. In the congressional debates, opponents of the bill agreed that savage tribes were duty-bound to relinquish their hunting grounds to the agriculturist, but they argued that the southeastern tribes were no longer savage. In any case, such relinquishment must be made in a freely contracted treaty. The extension of state laws over the Indian country was coercion; this made the negotiation of a free contract impossible. Both supporters and opponents of the bill agreed on one cardinal point—the Indian's moral right to keep his land depended on his actual cultivation of it.

A logical corollary of vesting rights in land in proportion to cultivation was the reservation to individuals of as much land as they had improved at the time a treaty was signed. In 1816, Secretary of War William H. Crawford had proposed such reservations, or allotments, as a means of accommodating the removal policy to the program of assimilation. According to Crawford's plan, individual Indians who had demonstrated their capacity for civilization by establishing farms and who were willing to become citizens should be given the option of keeping their cultivated lands, by fee simple title, rather than emigrating. This offer was expected to reconcile the property-loving half-breeds to the policy of emigration. It also recognized their superior claim, as cultivators, on the regard and generosity of the government. The proposal was based on the assumption that few of the Indians were sufficiently civilized to want to become full-time farmers or state citizens. . . .

The Choctaws were the first to cede their eastern lands. The treaty of Dancing Rabbit Creek, signed in September, 1830, provided for several types of allotment. Special reservations were given to the chiefs and their numerous family connections; a possible 1,600 allotments of 80 to 480 acres, in proportion to the size of the beneficiary's farm, were offered others who intended to emigrate. These were intended for sale to private persons or to the government, so that the Indian might get the maximum price for his improvements. The fourteenth article of the treaty offered any head of an Indian family who did not plan to emigrate the right to take up a quantity of land proportional to the number of his dependents. At the end of five years' residence those who received these allotments were to have fee simple title to their lands and become citizens. It was expected that approximately two hundred persons would take land under this article.

The Creeks refused to sign any agreements promising to emigrate, but their chiefs were persuaded that the only way to put an end to intrusions on their lands was to sign an allotment treaty. In March, 1832, a Creek delegation in Washington signed a treaty calling for the allotment of 320 acres to each head of a family, the granting of certain supplementary lands to the chiefs and to orphans, and the cession of the remaining territory to the United States. If the Indian owners remained on their allotments for five years, they were to receive fee simple titles and become citizens. Returning to Alabama, the chiefs informed their people that they had not actually sold the tribal lands but "had only made each individual their own guardian, that they might take care of their own possessions, and act as agents for themselves."

Unlike the Creeks, the Chickasaws were willing to admit the inevitability of removal. But they needed land east of the Mississippi on which they might live until they acquired a home in the west. The Chickasaw treaty of May, 1832, therefore, provided generous allotments for heads of families, ranging from 640 to 3,200 acres, depending on the size of the family and the number of its slaves. These allotments were to be auctioned publicly when the tribe emigrated and the owners compensated for their improvements out of the proceeds. Although the fullblood Chickasaws apparently approved of the plan for a collective sale of the allotments, the half-breeds, abetted by white traders and planters, persuaded the government to allow those who held allotments to sell them individually. An amended treaty of 1834 complied with the half-breeds' proposals. It further stipulated that leading half-breeds and the old chiefs of the tribe comprise a committee to determine the competence of individual Chickasaws to manage their property. Since the committee itself disposed of the lands of the "incompetents," this gave both protection to the unsophisticated and additional advantage to the half-breeds.

Widespread intrusion on Indian lands began with the extension of state laws over the tribal domains. In the treaties of cession, the government promised to remove intruders, but its policy in this respect was vacillating and ineffective. Indians whose allotments covered valuable plantations proved anxious to promote the sale of their property by allowing buyers to enter the ceded territory as soon as possible. Once this group of whites was admitted, it became difficult to discriminate against others. Thus a large number of intruders settled among the Indians with the passive connivance of the War Department and the tribal leaders. The task of removing them was so formidable that after making a few gestures the government generally evaded its obligation. The misery of the common Indians, surrounded by intruders and confused by the disruption of tribal authority, was so acute that any method for securing their removal seemed worth trying. Furthermore, their emigration would serve the interest of white settlers, land speculators, and their representatives in Washington. The government therefore chose to facilitate the sale of allotments even before the Indians received fee simple title to them.

The right to sell his allotment was useful to the sophisticated tribesman with a large plantation. Such men were accustomed to selling their crops and hiring labor. Through their experience in treaty negotiations, they had learned to bargain over the price of lands. Many of them received handsome payment for their allotments. Some kept part of their holdings and remained in Alabama and Mississippi as planters—like other planters, practicing as land speculators on the side. Nearly all the Indians had some experience in trade, but to most of them the conception of land as a salable commodity was foreign. They had little notion of the exact meaning of an "acre" or the probable value of their allotments. The government confused them still further by parceling out the lands according to Anglo-American, rather than aboriginal notions of family structure and land ownership. Officials insisted, for example, that the "father" rather than the "mother" must be defined as head of the family and righteously refused to take cognizance of the fact that many of the "fathers" had "a plurality of wives."

Under these conditions, it is not surprising that the common Indian's legal freedom of contract in selling his allotment did not necessarily lead him to make the best bargain possible in terms of his pecuniary interests. Nor did the proceeds of the sales transform each seller into an emigrant of large independent means. A right of property and freedom to contract for its sale did not automatically invest the Indian owner with the habits, values, and skills of a sober land speculator. His acquisition of property and freedom actually increased his dependence on those who traditionally mediated for him in contractual relations with white Americans.

Prominent among these mediators were white men with Indian wives who made their living as planters and traders in the Indian nations, men from nearby settlements who traded with the leading Indians or performed legal services for them, and interpreters. In the past, such individuals had been appropriately compensated for using their influence in favor of land cessions. It is likely that their speculative foresight was in part responsible for the allotment features in the treaties of the 1830's. When the process of alloting lands to individuals began, these speculative gentlemen made loans of whisky, muslin, horses, slaves, and other useful commodities to the new property-owner. They received in return the Indian's written promise to sell his allotment to them as soon as its boundaries were defined. Generally they were on hand to help him locate it on "desirable" lands. They, in turn, sold their "interest" in the lands to men of capital. Government agents encouraged the enterprising investor, since it was in the Indian's interest and the government's policy that the lands be sold and the tribes emigrate. Unfortunately, the community of interest among the government, the speculator, and the Indian proved largely fictitious. The speculator's interest in Indian lands led to frauds which impoverished the Indians, soiled the reputation of the government, and retarded the emigration of the tribes.

An important factor in this series of complications was the government's fallacious assumption that most of the "real Indians" were anxious to emigrate. Under the Choctaw treaty, for example, registration for fee simple allotments was optional, the government expecting no more than two hundred registrants. When several hundred full-bloods applied for lands, the Choctaw agent assumed that they were being led astray by "designing men" and told them they must emigrate. Attorneys took up the Choctaw claims, located thousands of allotments in hopes that Congress would confirm them, and supported their clients in Mississippi for twelve to fifteen years while the government debated and acted on the validity of the claims. There was good reason for this delay. Settlers and rival speculators, opposing confirmation of the claims, advanced numerous depositions asserting that the attorneys, in their enterprising search for clients, had materially increased the number of claimants. Among the Creeks, the Upper Towns, traditionally the conservative faction of the tribe, refused to sell their allotments. Since the Lower Towns proved more compliant, speculators hired willing Indians from the Lower Towns to impersonate the unwilling owners. They then bought the land from the impersonators. The government judiciously conducted several investigations of these frauds, but in the end the speculators outmaneuvered the investigators. Meanwhile, the speculators kept the Indians from emigrating until their contracts were approved. Only the outbreak of fighting between starving Creeks and their settler neighbors enabled the government, under pretext of a pacification, to remove the tribe.

Besides embarrassing the government, the speculators contributed to the demoralization of the Indians. Universal complaint held that after paying the tribesman for his land they often borrowed back the money without serious intent of repaying it, or recovered it in return for overpriced goods, of which a popular article was whisky. Apprised of this situation, Secretary of War Lewis Cass replied that once the Indian had been paid for his land, the War Department had no authority to circumscribe his freedom to do what he wished with the proceeds.

Nevertheless, within their conception of the proper role of government, officials who dealt with the tribes tried to be helpful. Although the Indian must be left free to contract for the sale of his lands, the United States sent agents to determine the validity of the contracts. These agents sometimes refused to approve a contract that did not specify a fair price for the land in question. They also refused official sanction when it could not be shown that the Indian owner had at some time been in possession of the sum stipulated. This protective action on the part of the government, together with its several investigations into frauds in the sale of Indian lands, apparently did secure the payment of more money than the tribesmen might otherwise have had. But the effort was seriously hampered by the near impossibility of obtaining disinterested testimony.

In dealing with the Chickasaws, the government managed to avoid most of the vexing problems which had arisen in executing the allotment program among their southeastern neighbors. This was due in part to the improvement of administrative procedures, in part to the methods adopted by speculators in Chickasaw allotments, and probably most of all to the inflated value of cotton lands during the period in which the Chickasaw territory was sold. Both the government and the Chickasaws recognized that the lands granted individuals under the treaty were generally to be sold, not settled. They therefore concentrated on provisions for supervising sales and safeguarding the proceeds. Speculators in Chickasaw lands, having abundant resources, paid an average price of $1.70 per acre. The Chickasaws thereby received a better return than the government did at its own auctions. The buyers' generosity may be attributed to their belief that the Chickasaw lands represented the last first-rate cotton country within what were then the boundaries of the public domain. In their pursuit of a secure title, untainted by fraud, the capitalists operating in the Chickasaw cession established a speculators' claim association which settled disputes among rival purchasers. Thus they avoided the plots, counterplots, and mutual recriminations which had hampered both speculators and government in their dealings with the Creeks and Choctaws.

A superficially ironic consequence of the allotment policy as a method of acquiring land for white settlers was the fact that it facilitated the engrossment of land by speculators. With their superior command of capital and the influence it would buy, speculators acquired 80 to 90 per cent of the lands allotted to the southeastern tribesmen.

For most of the Indian beneficiaries of the policy, its most important consequence was to leave them landless. After selling their allotment, or a claim to it, they might take to the swamp, live for a while on the bounty of a still hopeful speculator, or scavenge on their settler neighbors. But ultimately most of them faced the alternative of emigration or destitution, and chose to emigrate. The machinations of the speculators and the hopes they nurtured that the Indians might somehow be able to keep a part of their allotted lands made the timing of removals less predictable than it might otherwise have been. This unpredictability compounded the evils inherent in a mass migration managed by a government committed to economy and unversed in the arts of economic planning. The result was the "Trail of Tears."

The spectacular frauds committed among the Choctaws and Creeks, the administrative complications they created and the impression they gave that certain self-styled champions of the people were consorting with the avaricious speculator gave the allotment policy a bad reputation. The administration rejected it in dealing with the Cherokees, and the policy was not revived on any considerable scale until 1854, when it was applied, with similar consequences, to the Indians of Kansas. In the 1880's, when allotment in severalty became a basic feature of American Indian policy, the "civilized tribes," then in Oklahoma, strenuously resisted its application to them. They cited their memories of the 1830's as an important reason for their intransigence.

2. JOAN W. MOORE

Colonialism: The Case of the Mexican Americans*

American social scientists should have realized long ago that American minorities are far from being passive objects of study. They are, on the contrary, quite capable of defining themselves. A clear demonstration of this rather embarrassing lag in conceptualization is the current reassessment of

*Joan W. Moore, "Colonialism: The Case of the Mexican Americans," *Social Problems*, Vol. XVII (1970), pp. 463-71. Reprinted by permission of Joan W. Moore and The Society for the Study of Social Problems.

sociological thought. It is now plain that the concepts of "acculturation," of "assimilation," and similar paradigms are inappropriate for groups who entered American society not as volunteer immigrants but through some form of involuntary relationship.

The change in thinking has not come because of changes within sociology itself. Quite the contrary. It has come because the minorities have begun to reject certain academic concepts. The new conceptual structure is not given by any academic establishment but comes within a conceptual structure derived from the situation of the African countries. In the colonial situation, rather than either the conquest or the slave situation, the new generation of black intellectuals is finding parallels to their own reactions to American society.

This exploration of colonialism by minority intellectuals has met a varied reaction, to say the least, but there have been some interesting attempts to translate these new and socially meaningful categories into proper academic sociologese. Blauner's (1969) article . . . is one of the more ambitious attempts to relate the concept of "colonialism" as developed by Kenneth Clark, Stokely Carmichael and Eldridge Cleaver to sociological analysis. In the process, one kind of blurring is obvious even if not explicit: that is, that "colonialism" was far from uniform in the 19th Century, even in Africa. In addition, Blauner (1969) makes explicit the adaptations he feels are necessary before the concept of colonialism can be meaningfully applied to the American scene. Common to both American internal colonialism of the blacks and European imperial expansion, Blauner argues, were the involuntary nature of the relationship between the two groups, the transformation or destruction of indigenous values, and, finally, racism. But Blauner warns that the situations are really different: "the . . . culture . . . of the (American black) colonized . . . is less developed; it is also less autonomous. In addition, the colonized are a numerical minority, and furthermore, they are ghettoized more totally and are more dispersed than people under classic colonialism."

But such adaptations are not needed in order to apply the concept fruitfully to America's second largest minority—the Mexican Americans. Here the colonial concept need not be analogized and, in fact, it describes and categorizes so accurately that one suspects that earlier "discovery" by sociologists of the Mexican Americans, particularly in New Mexico, might have discouraged uncritical application of the classic paradigms to all minorities. The initial Mexican contact with American society came by conquest, not by choice. Mexican American culture *was* well developed; it *was* autonomous; the colonized *were* a numerical majority. Further, they were—and are—less ghettoized and more dispersed than the American blacks. In fact, their patterns of residence (especially those existing at the turn of the century) are exactly those of "classic colonialism." And they were indigenous to the region and not "imported."

In at least the one state of New Mexico, there was a situation of comparatively "pure" colonialism. Outside of New Mexico, the original conquest colonialism was overlaid, particularly in the 20th century, with a grossly manipulated voluntary immigration. But throughout the American Southwest where the approximately five million Mexican Americans are now concentrated, understanding the Mexican minority requires understanding both conquest colonialism and "voluntary" immigration. It also requires understanding the interaction between colonialism and voluntarism.

In this paper I shall discuss a "culture trait" that is attributed to Mexican Americans both by popular stereotype and by social scientists—that is, a comparatively low degree of formal voluntary organization and hence of organized participation in political life. This is the academic form of the popular question: "What's wrong with the Mexicans? Why can't they organize for political activity?" In fact, as commonly asked both by social scientist and popular stereotype, the question begs the question. There is a great deal of variation in three widely different culture areas in the Southwest. And these culture areas differ most importantly in the particular variety of colonialism to which they were subjected. In the "classically" colonial situation, New Mexico, there has been in fact a relatively high order of political participation, especially by comparison with Texas, which we shall term "conflict colonialism," and California, which we shall term "economic colonialism."

New Mexico.—An area that is now northern New Mexico and parts of southern Colorado was the most successful of the original Spanish colonies. At the beginning of the war between the United States and Mexico, there were more than 50,000 settlers, scattered in villages and cities with a strong upper class as well as a peasantry. There were frontier versions of Spanish colonial institutions that had been developing since 1600. The conquest of New Mexico by the United States was nearly bloodless and thus allowed, as a consequence, an extraordinary continuity between the Mexican period and the United States period. The area became a territory of the United States and statehood was granted in 1912.

Throughout these changes political participation can be followed among the elite and among the masses of people. It can be analyzed in both its traditional manifestations and in contemporary patterns. In all respects it differs greatly in both level and quality from political participation outside this area. The heritage of colonialism helps explain these differences.

On the elite level, Spanish or Mexican leadership remained largely intact through the conquest and was shared with Anglo leadership after the termination of military rule in 1851. The indigenous elite retained considerable strength both in the dominant Republican party and in the state legislature. They were strong enough to ensure a bilingual provision in the 1912 Constitution (the only provision in the region that guarantees Spanish speakers the right to vote and hold office). Sessions of the legislature were—by law—conducted in both languages. Again, this is an extraordinary feature in any part of the continental United States. Just as in many Asian nations controlled by the British in the 19th century, the elite suffered little—either economically or politically.

On the lower-class level, in the villages, there was comparatively little articulation of New Mexican villages with the developing urban centers. What there was, however, was usually channeled through a recognized local authority, a *patrón*. Like the class structure, the *patrón* and the network of relations that sustained him were a normal part of the established local social system and not an ad hoc or temporary recognition of an individual's power. Thus political participation on both the elite and the lower-class levels were outgrowths of the existing social system.

Political participation of the elite and the *patrón* system was clearly a colonial phenomenon. An intact society, rather than a structureless mass of individuals, was taken into a territory of the United States with almost no violence. This truly colonial situation involves a totally different process of relationship between subordinate and superordinate from either the voluntary or the forced immigration of the subordinate—that is, totally different from either the "typical" American immigrant on the eastern seaboard or the slave imported from Africa.

A final point remains to be made not about political participation but about proto-political organization in the past. The villages of New Mexico had strong internal organizations not only of the informal, kinship variety but of the formal variety. These were the *penitente* sects and also the cooperative associations, such as those controlling the use of water and the grazing of livestock. That such organizations were mobilized by New Mexican villagers is evidenced by the existence of terrorist groups operating against both Anglo and Spanish landowners. González (1967) mentions two: one functioning in the 1890's and one in the 1920's. Such groups could also act as local police forces.

Let us turn to the present. Political participation of the conventional variety is very high compared to that of Mexican Americans in other states of the Southwest. Presently there is a Spanish American in the United States Senate (Montoya, an "old" name), following the tradition of Dennis Chavez (another "old" name). The state legislature in 1967 was almost one-third Mexican American. (There were no Mexican American legislators in California and no more than six percent in the legislature of any other Southwest state.) This, of course, reflects the fact that it is only in very recent years that Mexican Americans have become a numerical minority in New Mexico, but it also reflects the fact that organized political participation has remained high.

Finally, New Mexico is the locus of the only mass movement among Mexican Americans—the *Alianza Federal de Mercedes,* headed by Reies Tijerina. In theme, the *Alianza,* which attracted tens of thousands of members, relates specifically to the colonial past, protesting the loss of land and its usurpation by Anglo interests (including, most insultingly, those of the United States Forest Service). It is this loss of land which has ultimately been responsible for the destruction of village (Spanish) culture and the large-scale migration to the cities. In the light of the importance of the traditional village as a base for political mobilization, it is not really surprising that the *Alianza* should have appeared where it did. In content the movement continues local terrorism (haystack-burning) but has now extended beyond the local protest as its members have moved to the cities. Rather than being directed against specific Anglo or Spanish landgrabbers, it has lately been challenging the legality of the Treaty of Guadalupe Hidalgo. The broadening of the *Alianza's* base beyond specific local areas probably required the pooled discontent of those immigrants from many villages, many original land grants. It is an ironic feature of the *Alianza* that the generalization of its objectives and of its appeal should be possible only long after most of the alleged land-grabbing had been accomplished.

Texas.—Mexican Americans in Texas had a sharply contrasting historical experience. The Mexican government in Texas was replaced by a revolution of the American settlers. Violence between Anglo-American settlers and Mexican residents continued in south Texas for generations after the annexation of Texas by the United States and the consequent full-scale war. Violence continued in organized fashion well into the 20th Century with armed clashes involving the northern Mexican *guerilleros* and the U.S. Army.

This violence meant a total destruction of Mexican elite political participation by conquest, while such forces as the Texas Rangers were used to suppress Mexican American participation on the lower status or village levels. The ecology of settlement in south Texas remains somewhat reminiscent of that in northern New Mexico: there are many areas that are predominantly Mexican, and even some towns that are still controlled by Mexicans. But there is far more complete Anglo economic and political dominance on the local level. Perhaps most important, Anglo-Americans outnumbered Mexicans by five to one even before the American conquest. By contrast, Mexicans in New Mexico remained the numerical majority for more than 100 years after conquest. . . .

California.—The California transition between Mexican and American settlement falls midway between the Texas pattern of violence and the relatively smooth change in New Mexico. In northern California the discovery of gold in 1849 almost immediately swamped a sparse Mexican population in a flood of Anglo-American settlers. Prior to this time an orderly transition was in progress. Thus the effect was very much that of violence in Texas: the indigenous Mexican elite was almost totally excluded from political participation. A generation later when the opening of the railroads repeated this demographic discontinuity in southern California the Mexicans suffered the same effect. They again were almost totally excluded from political participation. The New Mexico pattern of social organization on a village level had almost no counterpart in California. Here the Mexican settlements and the economy were built around very large land holdings rather than around villages. This meant, in essence, that even the settlements that survived the American takeover relatively intact tended to lack internal social organization. Villages (as in the Bandini rancho which became the modern city of Riverside) were more likely to be clusters of ranch employees than an independent, internally coherent community.

In more recent times the peculiar organization of California politics has tended to work against Mexican American participation from the middle and upper status levels. California was quick to adopt the ideas of "direct democracy" of the Progressive era. These tend somewhat to work against ethnic minorities. But this effect is accidental and can hardly be called "internal colonialism," coupled as it was with the anti-establishment ideals of the Progressive era. The concept of "colonialism," in fact, appears most useful with reference to the extreme manipulation of Mexican immigration in the 20th Century. Attracted to the United States by the hundreds of thousands in the 1920's, Mexicans and many of their U.S.-born children were deported ("repatriated") by welfare agencies during the Depression, most notably from California. (Texas had almost no welfare provisions; hence no repatriation.) The economic expansion in World War II required so much labor that Mexican immigration was supplemented by a contract labor arrangement. But, as in the Depression, "too many" were attracted and came to work in the United States without legal status. Again, in 1954, massive sweeps of deportations got rid of Mexicans by the hundreds of thousands in "Operation Wetback." New Mexico was largely spared both waves of deportation; Texas was involved primarily in Operation Wetback rather than in the welfare repatriations. California was deeply involved in both.

This economic manipulation of the nearly bottomless pool of Mexican labor has been quite conscious and enormously useful to the development of California extractive and agricultural enterprises. Only in recent years with increasing—and now overwhelming—proportions of native-born Mexican Americans in the population has the United States been "stuck" with the Mexicans. As one consequence, the naturalization rate of Mexican immigrants has been very low. After all, why relinquish even the partial protection of Mexican citizenship? Furthermore the treatment of Mexicans as economic commodities has greatly reduced both their motivation and their effectiveness as political participants. The motivations that sent Mexican Americans to the United States appear to have been similar to those that sent immigrants from Europe. But the conscious dehumanization of Mexicans in the service of the railroad and citrus industries in California and elsewhere meant an assymmetry in relationship between "host" and immigrant that is less apparent in the European patterns of immigration. Whatever resentment that might have found political voice in the past had no middle class organizational patterns. California was structurally unreceptive and attitudinally hostile. . . .

How useful, then, is the concept of colonialism when it is applied to these three culture areas? We argue here that both the nature and extent of political participation in the state of New Mexico can be understood with reference to the "classical" colonial past. We noted that a continuity of elite participation in New Mexico from the period of Mexican rule to the period of American rule paved the way for a high level of conventional political participation. The fact that village social structure remained largely intact is in some measure responsible for the appearance of the only mass movement of Mexicans in the Southwest today—the *Alianza*. But even this movement is an outcome of colonialism; the expropriation of the land by large-scale developers and by federal conservation interests led ultimately to the destruction of the village economic base—and to the movement of the dispossessed into the cities. Once living in the cities in a much closer environment than that of the scattered small villages, they could "get together'' and respond to the anti-colonialist protests of a charismatic leader.

Again following this idea, we might categorize the Texas experience as ''conflict colonialism.'' This would reflect the violent discontinuity between the Mexican and the American periods of elite participation and the current struggle for the legitimation of ethnic politics on all levels. In this latter aspect, the ''conflict colonialism'' of Texas is reminiscent of black politics in the Deep South, although it comes from different origins.

To apply the colonial concept to Mexicans in California, we might usefully use the idea of ''economic colonialism.'' The destruction of elite political strength by massive immigration and the comparative absence of local political organization meant a political vacuum for Mexican Americans. Extreme economic manipulation inhibited any attachment to the reality or the ideals of American society and indirectly allowed as much intimidation as was accomplished by the overt repression of such groups as the Texas Rangers.

To return to Blauner's use of the concept of ''internal colonialism'': in the case of the Mexicans in the United States, a major segment of this group who live in New Mexico require no significant conceptual adaptation of the classic analyses of European overseas colonialism. Less adaptation is required in fact than in applying the concepts to such countries as Kenya, Burma, Algeria, and Indonesia. Not only was the relationship between the Mexican and the Anglo-American ''involuntary,'' involving ''racism'' and the ''transformation . . . of indigenous values,'' but the culture of the Spanish American was well developed, autonomous, a majority numerically, and contained a full social system with an upper and middle as well as lower class. The comparatively non-violent conquest was really almost a postscript to nearly a decade of violence between the United States and Mexico which began in Texas.

The Texas pattern, although markedly different, can still be fitted under a colonialist rubric, with a continuous thread of violence, suppression, and adaptations to both in recent political affairs.

The Mexican experience in California is much more complicated. Mexicans lost nearly all trace of participation in California politics. Hence, there was no political tradition of any kind, even the purely negative experience in Texas. Then, too, the relationship between imported labor and employer was ''voluntary,'' at least on the immigrants' side. The relationships were much more assymmetrical than in the ''classic colonial'' case. . . .

3. VERNON LANE WHARTON

The "Revolution of 1875": The End of Black Reconstruction in Mississippi*

From the beginning of Reconstruction, there were in Mississippi a large number of white men who insisted upon the necessity of accepting the results of the war and of complying with the requirements of the national government. This group, made up largely of old Whigs, and generally men of property, desired above all else order, prosperity, and harmonious relations within the Union. Guaranteeing to the Negro those minimum rights set up in the amendments to the Constitution, they would seek to gain his confidence and his vote by convincing him that their leadership was for the best interests of both races. Such distinguished citizens as A. G. Brown, C. C. Shackleford, H. F. Simrall, Amos R. Johnston, J. A. P. Campbell, Joshua Morris, and J. L. Alcorn were by temperament members of this group, although some worked with the Democratic party and some with the Republican. The essence of their failure lay in the fact that almost none of them could bring himself to deal with a Negro, however able or honest that Negro might be, as a political or social equal. In later years, J. L. Alcorn often dcclared that he had never been a "negro Republican." Exactly the same was true of such Northern leaders as H. R. Pease, George C. McKee, and R. C. Powers. By 1874, men of this class had to recognize either their failure to make Democrats of the Negroes, or the repudiation of their leadership in the Republican party. Given the assurance that the national government would not intervene, most of these conservatives were then ready to join the mass of the white Democrats in any methods they might use to drive the Negroes from power.

The majority of the white citizens, brought up on the belief that the Negro was an inferior creature who must be kept in subjection, found themselves unable from the beginning to endorse the program of the Conservatives. In December, 1869, the editor of the Columbus *Index* made a bid for the leadership of this group with the declaration: "We have given the negro a fair trial. He has voted solidly against us, and we hoist, from this day, the white man's flag, and will never take it down so long as we have a voice in the government of the State." The year 1870 saw the organization of a

*From Vernon Lane Wharton, *The Negro in Mississippi, 1869-1890* (Chapel Hill, University of North Carolina Press, 1947), pp. 181-98. Reprinted by permission of University of North Carolina Press.

number of "White Men's Clubs" throughout the state. One at Bellefountaine, with 152 members, pledged its subscribers to a perpetual and uncompromising opposition to social and political equality of the white and black races, and to all measures tending thereto. Believing that Negro suffrage was "wrong in principle and disastrous in effect," they pledged themselves to labor unceasingly, from year to year, for the restoration of white supremacy in Mississippi and in the United States. A similar club at West Point agreed to follow a policy that would ignore the Negro as a voter and as an element in politics. The Columbus *Democrat,* advocating the union of these groups in a revitalized Democratic party, declared:

> . . . Its leading ideas are, that white men shall govern, that niggers are not rightly entitled to vote, and that when it gets into power, niggers will be placed upon the same footing with white minors who do not vote or hold office.
>
> There are professed Democrats who do not understand Democratic principles, that want the party mongrelized, thinking that the less difference between the two parties will give them a better chance for the spoils. They are willing for the niggers to vote, but not to hold office. . . . Nigger voting, holding office and sitting in the jury box, are all wrong, and against the sentiment of the country. There is nothing more certain to occur than that these outrages upon justice and good government will soon be removed, and the unprincipled men who are now their advocates will sink lower in the social scale than the niggers themselves.

Here was sheer racial antagonism. There was no consideration of the undesirability of the participation of ignorant and poverty-stricken masses in the government of the state; the line was drawn on the basis of race.

In the face of the decrepitude of the Democratic party, and of the certainty of Federal intervention in case of a state-wide movement based on violence, the program was held in check during 1871, 1872, and 1873. But with the rejection of Alcorn in the election of 1873, and the great increase in office holding by Negroes after that election, the movement gained new strength. Native and Northern whites whose leadership had been rejected by the Negroes now joined in the demand for white supremacy. The great financial depression of 1873 was reflected in the state by increased unpleasantness in political and social relations, and in the nation by a decline of interest in affairs of the South. Furthermore this financial collapse, along with the discovery of scandals in the Federal government, served greatly to weaken the power of the Republican party in the nation. There were predictions of a

Democratic president in 1876. When these predictions were strengthened by the great Democratic victories which gained control of the House of Representatives in 1874, conservative leaders in Mississippi at last agreed to abandon their caution. The word went out that the time for revolution was at hand, and the efforts of such men as A. G. Brown and L. Q. C. Lamar to halt the movement were of no avail.

Greater and greater numbers of white Republicans in Mississippi were now deserting the party and joining the opposing conventions. As Charles Nordhoff was told in the spring of 1875, the Democrats were making it "too damned hot for them to stay out." Economic pressure and threats of physical violence were used, but the most powerful force was that of social ostracism. Colonel James A. Lusk, a prominent native Republican, said to a Negro leader: "No white man can live in the South in the future and act with any other than the Democratic party unless he is willing and prepared to live a life of social isolation and remain in political oblivion." In consideration of the future happiness of his sons and daughters, he felt it necessary to announce his renunciation of all Republican connections. The Canton *Mail* published the names of those whites who must no longer be recognized on the streets, and whose attentions must be scorned by "every true woman."

At the same time that white Republicans were abandoning their party, more and more of the conservative Democratic leaders and newspapers were accepting the "white-line" program. The transition could be seen clearly in most cases. Editors who for several years had written of the Negroes in terms of sympathy, impatience, or friendly ridicule, and who had even praised them at times in an effort to gain their votes, came to speak of them during the summer of 1874 with open dislike, and finally with hatred. By May of 1875, such original color liners as the Vicksburg *Herald,* Columbus *Index,* Handsboro *Democrat,* Yazoo City *Banner,* Vicksburg *Monitor,* and Okolona *Southern States,* had been joined by the conservative Hinds County *Gazette,* Newton *Ledger,* Brandon *Republican,* Forest *Register,* and Jackson *Clarion,* and by the Republican Meridian *Gazette.*

The general charge made by papers and individuals in renouncing their former conservatism was that the color line had already been drawn by the Negro. As evidence, they offered the fact that almost none of the Negroes ever voted with the whites [Democrats], that in some of the counties the Negroes had taken most of the offices, that in the Republican convention of 1873 Negroes had absolutely demanded three of the seven state offices, and that, on such questions as the reduction of the tax for schools, Negroes in the legislature had voted almost as a unit against the whites. In making these charges, the Democrats ignored the fact that the Negroes had from the beginning welcomed the leadership of almost any white who would serve with them, that in so doing they had taken into their party from ten to twenty thousand white Mississippians and that they could not be expected to join in any numbers a party which had from the beginning opposed all of the rights upon which their hopes were built.

As time went on the attack became more and more bitter. The Forest *Register* carried at its masthead the slogan: "A white man in a white man's place. A black man in a black man's place. Each according to the 'eternal fitness of things.' " The Yazoo City *Banner* declared, *"Mississippi is a white man's country, and by the Eternal God we'll rule it."* The Handsboro *Democrat* called for *"A white man's Government, by white men, for the benefit of white men."* All of these papers justified their stand in editorials describing the depravity and innate bestiality of the Negro. These reached a climax in one published by the Forest *Register.*

> A negro preacher is an *error loci.* God Almighty, in farming out his privileges to mankind, drew a line as to qualifications.
> He never exacted from a nation or tribe an impossibility. . . . Does any sane man believe the negro capable of comprehending the ten commandments? The miraculous conception and the birth of our Savior? The high moral precepts taught from the temple on the mount?
> Every effort to inculcate these great truths but tends to bestialize his nature, and by obfuscating his little brain unfits him for the duties assigned him as a hewer of wood and drawer of water. The effort makes him a demon of wild fanatical destruction, and consigns him to the fatal shot of the white man.

Declarations by the rapidly dwindling group of conservative Democrats that the votes of the Negroes could be secured by treating them fairly and reasoning with them met the scorn of the white liners. The editor of the Newton *Democrat* declared that he would just as soon try to reason with a shoal of crocodiles or a drove of Kentucky mules. From Colonel McCardle of the Vicksburg *Herald* came the answer: "The way to treat Sambo is not to argue to him or to reason with him. If you do that, it puffs his vanity and it only makes him insolent. Say to him, 'Here, we are going to *carry* this election; you may vote as you like; but we *are* going to carry it. Then we are going to look after ourselves and our friends; you can look after yourself,' and he will vote with you." Furthermore, when Lamar succeeded in inserting in the Democrat-Conservative platform a vague statement recognizing "the civil and political equality of all men," and inviting the Negroes to vote with the party for good government, the white liners were quick to deny any allegiance. As a Democratic leader declared the following year, ". . . [The] only issue in the election was whether the whites or the blacks should predominate; there was no other politics that I could see in it. Men that had been republicans all their lives just laid aside republicanism and said that they had to go into the ranks then." In the words of J. S. McNeily, "It was a part of the creed of a desperate condition, one easily understood, that any white man, however odious, was preferable . . . to any negro however unobjectionable individually."

Once the general policy had been adopted that Negro and Republican control of the state government was to be broken at any cost, a number of methods were followed for its accomplishment. One of these involved the intimidation of those whites who still worked with the Republican party. There was a general understanding that in the case of the outbreak of a "race war," carpet-baggers would be the first to be killed. As early as December, 1874, the Hinds County *Gazette* declared that death should be meted out to those who continued their opposition. "All other means having been exhausted to abate the horrible condition of things, the thieves and robbers, and scoundrels, white and black, deserve death and ought to be killed. . . . The thieves and robbers kept in office by Governor Ames and his robber associates . . . ought to be compelled to leave the State, or abide the consequences." After the Clinton "riot," Colonel McCardle of the *Herald* urged that in future cases of violence white Republicans be killed and the deluded Negroes spared. . . .

Against the Negroes themselves one of the most powerful forces used was economic pressure. All over the state, Democratic clubs announced that no Negro who voted Republican could hope for any form of employment the following year. It was also urged that the boycott be extended to the wives of Negro Republicans. In some cases, doctors announced that they would no longer serve Negroes who did not vote the Democratic ticket. Lists of Negroes who were pledged for or against the party were prepared, and arrangements were made for checkers to be present at the polls. After the election, the names of Negroes marked for discharge were printed in the various papers, along with the names of those who deserved special consideration for having refrained from voting or for having worked with the Democrats.

At the same time, except in the counties where the Democrats had a safe majority, strenuous efforts were being made to get the Negroes into the various Democratic clubs. For those Negroes who would take this step, and participate in the processions and other functions of the clubs, there were pledges of protection and of continued employment. There were also abundant supplies of flags, transparencies, uniforms, and badges. The Democratic badge in Lafayette County not only protected the wearer from physical violence, but also allowed him to "boss" other Negroes. There were numerous barbecues and picnics at which Negro bands and glee clubs furnished entertainment, and at which Negroes either volunteered or were hired to speak. In some of the counties, no expense was spared. In Monroe, the candidates for the legislature gave $1,000.00 each, and subscriptions from private citizens ranged up to $500.00. In Panola, the Democratic committee supplied $5,000.00 in addition to subscriptions from individuals. According to one of the leaders in that county, "Our purpose was to overawe the negroes and exhibit to them the ocular proof of our power . . . by magnificent torchlight processions at night and in the day by special trains of cars . . . loaded down with white people with flags flying, drums beating, and bands playing, the trains being chartered and free for everybody. . . ."

Much more successful was the use of threats and actual violence. It is not to be imagined that this campaign of violence involved all who called themselves Democrats. Many members of the party undoubtedly opposed it, and many more probably considered it regrettable but necessary. It did involve directly thousands of young men and boys of all classes, a large part of the poor white element, and many local political leaders of some importance. Furthermore, it must be admitted that the Democratic leaders of the state, while they often denied the existence of violence, or tried to shift the blame for it to the Negroes, never actually repudiated its use, and in some cases encouraged it. In the meantime, the Democratic press adopted the slogan, "Carry the election peaceably if we can, forcibly if we must." Urged on by newspapers and political leaders, young men all over the state formed militia companies, and Democratic clubs provided themselves with the latest style of repeating rifles. By September, 1875, the Hinds County *Gazette* could announce, "The people of this State are now fully armed, equipped, and drilled. . . ."

With this powerful military force at its command, the white Democracy was ready for its campaign against a mass of Negroes who were timorous, unarmed, and largely unorganized. The program involved extensive processions and drills, and much firing of cannon, at least one of which was owned by every club of any importance. As the campaign of intimidation went on, Negro Republicans were ostentatiously enrolled in "dead books." Negro political leaders were warned that another speech would mean death. Republican political meetings were broken up by violent attacks, or prevented by armed force. Committees of "active young men" waited on Negroes who tried to prevent others of their race from deserting their party. Negroes were prevented from registering by sham battles and the firing of pistols at registration points, or by armed pickets who met them on the roads. Democrats adopted a policy of appearing in force at all Republican meetings, demanding the privilege of presenting Democratic speakers, and compelling Republican speakers to "tell the truth or quit the stand."

In the political, economic, and social subjugation of the freedmen, the most effective weapon ever developed was the "riot." Because this fact was discovered in the Meridian riot of 1871, that incident deserves some attention. In the spring of 1871, Meridian, a rapidly growing railroad town in the eastern part of the state, was under the control of white Republicans appointed to office by Governor Alcorn, and of Negro leaders including J. Aaron Moore, William Clopton, and Warren Tyler. The population of this new town could best be described as "tough," and relations between the races were bad. For the purpose of discussing the situation, the Negroes were brought together in a mass meeting early in March, and were addressed by the three Negro leaders and William Sturgis, the white Republican mayor. While the meeting was going on, a fire alarm was heard, and it was discovered that a store owned by Sturgis was on fire. In the resultant excitement, there was further unpleasantness between the whites and the blacks. On the following morning, white citizens persuaded a lawyer who had not been present at the Republican meeting to prepare an affidavlt to the effect that the speeches of Warren Tyler, Bill Dennis [Clopton], and Aaron Moore had been of an incendiary character. The trial of these men was held the following Sunday afternoon before Judge Bramlette, a native white Republican, in a crowded court room. According to the prosecutor, one of the Negroes, Warren Tyler, interrupted James Brantley, a white witness, to say, "I want three colored men summoned to impeach your testimony." Brantley then seized the city marshal's stick and started toward the Negro. Tyler, moving toward a side door, reached back as though to draw a pistol, and general firing immediately began in the rear of the court room. Although it seems that no one actually saw Tyler fire, and although Negroes stoutly denied that he did so, the available evidence indicates that he probably shot at the advancing Brantley and, missing him, killed Judge Bramlette. W. H. Hardy, a local Democratic leader, later wrote a description of the affair in which he attributed the shot that killed Bramlette to the Negro Bill Dennis. In this he was probably incorrect, but to the rest of his story there is general agreement.

> As quick as a flash the white men sitting in the rear drew their pistols and

> fired upon Dennis. [Tyler had run through the side door and leaped to the ground from a second-floor veranda.] By the time the smoke cleared away the court room had but few people left in it. Judge Bramlette was found dead and Bill Dennis mortally wounded. The riot [sic] was on and white men and negroes were seen running in every direction; the white men to get their arms and the negroes in mortal terror to seek a place of hiding. Every man that could do so got a gun or a pistol and went on the hunt for negroes. The two men left to guard the wounded Bill Dennis in the sheriff's office grew tired of their job and threw him from the balcony into the middle of the street, saying that their services were needed elsewhere, and they could not waste time guarding a wounded negro murderer. Warren Tyler was found concealed in a shack and shot to death. Aaron Moore had escaped from the courthouse in the confusion and lay out in the woods that night, and the next day made his way to Jackson. . . . It was not known how many negroes were killed by the enraged whites, but the number has been estimated at from twenty-five to thirty. . . .
>
> The mayor, Bill Sturgis, was thoroughly overcome with terror at the vengeance of the people and concealed himself in the garret of his boarding house. Being a member of the Odd Fellows' order he opened communication with a member of the lodge, and it resulted in a cartel by which Sturgis was to resign the office of mayor and was to leave the State in twenty-four hours. . . .

This affair marked the end of Republican control in the area surrounding Meridian. According to Dunbar Rowland, "The Meridian riot marks an epoch in the transition period of reconstruction, and was a forecast of the end of carpetbag rule in Mississippi. . . ." The lesson learned was that the Negroes, largely unarmed, economically dependent, and timid and unresourceful after generations of servitude, would offer no effective resistance to violence. Throughout the period, any unpleasant incident was likely to produce such a "riot." During the bad feeling of 1874 and 1875 there were a great number of unpleasant incidents, and after each resulting riot Negro resistance to white domination in the surrounding area completely collapsed.

With the development of the white-line program in the summer of 1874, the newspapers began to carry a constantly increasing number of stories about clashes between the races. Some of these were reports of real incidents growing out of increasing bitterness; others seem to have been the product of exaggerated rumors, or of an effort to arouse feeling against the Negroes. Soon blood began to flow. In Austin, Negroes raised violent objections to the release of a white man who, in shooting at a Negro man, had killed a Negro girl. In the quarrel which followed, six Negroes were killed; no whites were wounded. In Vicksburg, where the white militia had overthrown Republican control in the municipal election, a number of Negroes prepared to come into town in answer to a call from the Negro sheriff. After they had agreed to go back to their homes, firing started. About thirty-five Negroes were killed. Two whites met death, one possibly by accident. This was in December, 1874. Three months later, the Vicksburg *Monitor* announced, *"The same tactics that saved Vicksburg will surely save the State, and no other will."* In the same city, in the following July, the Republicans held a celebration of Independence Day. Trouble developed with white Democrats. Two Negroes were killed; no whites were wounded. Water Valley was disturbed by a rumor that Negroes were going to attack the town. An exploring party found a group of Negroes concealed under a cliff. An unknown number of Negroes were killed; no whites were wounded. In August, Negroes at a Republican meeting in Louisville "succeeded in raising a disturbance." "Result, two negroes wounded, no white men hurt. Will the negro never learn that he is always sure to be the sufferer in these riots?" Late in the same month, a group of whites near Macon, including more than a hundred horsemen from Alabama, were out looking for a Negro political meeting. After they had failed to find one, they were told by a runner that several hundred Negroes had gathered at a church, where they were preparing to carry aid to those of their race in Vicksburg, on the other side of the state. When the church was found, the Alabamians disobeyed the order of the deputy sheriff and fired into the crowd. Twelve or thirteen Negroes were killed; no white was hurt.

A few nights later, the Republicans endeavored to hold a meeting in Yazoo City. Their hall was invaded by a number of Democrats, led by their "rope-bearer," H. M. Dixon. In the confusion which followed, a native white Republican was killed, and several Negroes were wounded. The white sheriff escaped with his life by fleeing to Jackson. White militia then took charge of the county, and systematically lynched the Negro leaders in each supervisor's district. Three days later, Democrats obtained their customary division of time at a large Republican meeting and picnic at Clinton. Trouble developed between a Negro policeman and a young white who was drunk. In the shooting which followed, two young white Democrats and a white Republican were killed. The number of Negroes killed is unknown; estimates varied from ten to thirty. Two thousand Negroes in wild panic rushed to the woods or to Jackson. By nightfall, armed whites, including the Vicksburg "Modocs," had control of the entire area. During the next four days they scoured the surrounding country, killing Negro leaders. Estimates of the number killed varied between ten and fifty. On the day of the Clinton affair, white Democrats captured a Republican meeting at Utica and compelled a thousand Negroes to listen to Democratic speakers for several hours. There seems to have been no bloodshed. A few days later, there was a minor skirmish at Satartia in which one Negro was killed. Early in the following month, the Negro sheriff was run out of Coahoma County after an encounter in which five Negroes were killed and five wounded. One white was killed from ambush; another shot himself by accident. The final clash of the campaign came at Columbus, a large town with a heavy Negro majority, on the night before the election. A crowd of young whites rushed from a drug store to attack a Negro parade, cutting the heads out of the drums and scattering the marchers. About an hour later, two old sheds in the Negro section were found to be burning, and the rumor was spread that the blacks were trying to burn the town. The Columbus Riflemen and a large number of visiting Alabamians immediately took charge, and Negroes began to flee for safety. Those who refused to halt were fired upon; four men were killed, and several men and one woman were wounded. No whites were hurt.

Long before the day of the election, a Democratic victory was assured. In many of the counties, all efforts to hold Republican meetings were abandoned. In several of the black counties, the sheriffs had fled or were powerless. White military units held the towns, and pickets patrolled the roads. The Negroes, with many of their leaders either dead or in hiding, faced the proposition of voting with the Democrats or staying away from the polls.

Letters to Governor Ames revealed the panic of the Negroes. . . . From Warren County came a letter from 108 Negroes who could not and would not register and vote, "for we cannot hold a meeting of no description without being molested and broken up; and further our lives are not safe at nor in our cabins, and therefore we deem it unwise to make a target of our body to be shot down like dogs and have no protection. . . ." From Vicksburg came the plea, "The rebles turbulent; are aiming themselves here now to-day to go to Sartartia to murder more poor negroes. Gov., aint the no pertiction?"

There was not any protection. In January, the administration had endeavored to secure the passage of a bill to allow the governor to set up special police bodies in towns where they were needed. Passed in the house by a vote of forty to thirty-eight, it was killed on a color-line vote in the senate. In the desperate days of September, Governor Ames made the formal gesture of commanding the private military bands to disperse. From the *Clarion*, there came a scornful answer that was echoed all over the state:

" 'Now, therefore, I, A.A., do hereby command all persons belonging to such organizations to disband.' Ha! ha!! ha!!! 'Command.' 'Disband.' That's good."

The Governor then turned to the Federal government, although he knew his request would be unpopular, eve' in the North. To Attorney-General Edward Pierrepont, he wrote: "Let the odium, in all its magnitude descend on me. I cannot escape. I am conscious in the discharge of my duty toward a class of American citizens whose only offense consists in their color, and which I am powerless to protect." The plea was hopeless. Negro suffrage, or even Negro freedom, had never been really popular with the masses in the North. Negro suffrage had appeared to be necessary, and had been accepted as such. It had been inaugurated to save a party that a majority of the voters in a number of the Northern states now considered hardly worth saving. Its maintenance had proved to be a troublesome problem. Why should the Negro majority in Mississippi be constantly crying for help? The sending of Federal troops into a state simply to prevent white men from ruling Negroes was distasteful to the average Northern voter. In the final moment of his decision, Grant was visited by a delegation of politicians from Ohio, a pivotal state which was to have an election in October. Mississippi, these visitors declared, was already lost to the party; troops would arrive too late to save the state. Even worse, the order that sent troops to Mississippi would mean the loss of Ohio to the party. The Negroes must be sacrificed. Grant's answer to Ames was a statement that aid could not be sent until all local resources had been exhausted. In the midst of the negotiations, Pierrepont declared, "The whole public are tired of these annual autumnal outbreaks in the South." "This flippant utterance of Attorney-General Edward Pierrepont," wrote Adelbert Ames twenty years later, "was the way the executive branch of the National government announced that it had decided that the reconstruction acts of congress were a failure. . . ."

On the day of the election, a peculiar quiet prevailed in many of the counties. "It was a very quiet day in Jackson—fearfully quiet." According to a witness at Yazoo City, "Hardly anybody spoke aloud." In Columbus, where many of the Negroes were still in the swamps as a result of the riot on the preceding night, the Democratic mayor reported everything as "quiet as a funeral." Similar reports came from Bolton, Lake, and Boswell. At Holly Springs, about 250 Negroes voted with the Democrats, offering their open ballots as proof. At Meridian, the White League seized the polls, while the Negroes, "sullen and morose," gathered in a mass across the street. Any Negro who approached without a white Democrat at his side was immediately crowded away from the ballot box.

In other sections, the day was not so peaceful. In Scott County, Negroes who were carrying the Republican tickets for distribution at the polls were fired on "by accident" by Democratic squirrel hunters. They fled, abandoning both the tickets and their mules. At Forest, the county seat, it was arranged for boys with whips to rush suddenly into the crowd of Negroes. The voters, already frightened and nervous, feared that this was the beginning of an outbreak, and left in a panic. In Monroe County, on the day before the election, the Negro candidate for chancery clerk saved himself and several friends by a promise to leave the state and not to return. At Okolona, the Negroes, with women and children, gathered at a church in the edge of town, intending to go from there to the polls in groups. The Democratic army marched up and formed near the church. When guns went off by accident, the Negroes stampeded, paying no attention to Democratic invitations for them to come back and vote. At Aberdeen, in spite of the fact that the heavy Negro population in the eastern part of the county was cut off by an open bridge and pickets along the Tombigbee, a large number gathered at the polls early in the morning. E. O. Sykes, in charge of the Democratic war department, posted the cavalry he had imported from Alabama, surrounded the Negroes with infantry, loaded a cannon with chains and slugs, and then sent a strong-arm squad into the crowd to beat the Negroes over the head. They broke and ran, many of them swimming the river in search of safety. The Republican sheriff, an ex-Confederate, locked himself in his own jail. The Democrats then carried the box "very quietly," turning a Republican majority of 648 in 1871 into a Democratic majority of 1,175. . . .

The Democrats came very close to sweeping the state. In some places they used fraud, but this method was generally unnecessary. In Yazoo County, the center of an overwhelming Negro majority, Republican candidates received only seven votes. In Kemper they received four, and in Tishomingo twelve. They received two votes at Utica, in the black county of Hinds, and none at Auburn. Democrats carried the first, third, fourth, and fifth congressional districts. The second went to G. Wiley Wells, renegade Republican who was working with the Democrats. In the sixth, John R. Lynch, with much white support, held his majorities in the black counties of Adams, Jefferson, and Wilkinson to win by a slim margin over Roderick Seal. In the state senate, of which only half the members had been involved in the election, there were now twenty-six Democrats and ten Republicans. Only five, all of them hold-overs, were Negroes. In the new house of representatives there were twenty Republicans and ninety-five Democrats. Sixteen of the representatives were Negroes; of these, fifteen were Republicans and one was a Democrat. Sixty-two of the seventy-four counties elected Democrats as their local officials. In the only race for a state office, that for state treasurer, the Democrat, W. L. Hemingway, polled 96,596 votes to 66,155 for George M. Buchanan, a popular and widely known ex-Confederate who was his Republican opponent.

When the Democratic legislature met in the following January, it quickly completed the work by impeaching and removing the Lieutenant-Governor, and by securing the resignations of the Governor and the Superintendent of Education. Thus ended the successful revolution of 1875. In its preparation and execution, economic and political motives played a large part. Essentially, however, it was a racial struggle. . . .

C. MINORITY RESPONSES

As official guarantees collapsed before United States expansionism and racial attitudes, the hopes of ethnics diminished. Instead of enjoying the rights of full citizenship granted to them, Blacks were systematically discriminated against and exploited. As Anglos broke promise after promise, Native Americans and Mexican Americans became degraded aliens in their own lands. The problem was what to do about it. Answers ranged from patient, enduring trust in the promise of America to armed resistance and rebellion.

To Booker T. Washington—probably the best-known Black in America at the time of his Atlanta Exposition Address—the lesson of Reconstruction was clear. In America social legislation—"artificial forcing," as he put it—would not produce equality for Blacks. The only workable solution was for Blacks temporarily to accept their low status, be patient with white society, and rise through their own efforts. Eschewing social integration as a goal, Washington believed that with legal rights, hard work, and education Blacks would some day be able to earn equality by virtue of their material accomplishments.

In the next selection Nez Percé Chief Young Joseph describes with unsurpassable eloquence the history of white transgressions against his tribe. Believing in honesty and fair dealing, the Nez Percés expected the same in return; but time after time white men violated that trust. Left with the bitter alternatives of acquiescing to removal from tribal homelands or fighting to retain them, Joseph suffered a special agony—no matter what he did the Nez Percés would lose their country and traditional way of life.

The same was true for Mexican Americans. Some tried to adjust peacefully to the circumstances of Yanqui colonization in the southwest, but many reacted violently to the brutalities of Anglo occupation. Two notable examples of this resistance were the guerrilla movement of Juan N. Cortina and the clandestine revolutionary plan of San Diego, Texas. Cortina, born of a prominent Texas-Mexican family, rose up against Anglo policies and practices in Texas in 1859. As expressed in his Proclamation of 1859, he viewed Yanquis as "vampires" who fed on Mexican land and labor. Justice under Yanqui law did not exist for Mexican Americans, and the only realistic alternative left was to try to exterminate the "tyrants." Half a century later the same solution was attempted. Bitter over generations of abuse and excited by the reformist ideals emanating from revolutionary Mexico, a group of Chicanos in south Texas agreed to rise up against their Yanqui oppressors. Although the precise origins of the Plan of San Diego (1915) are unclear, the document reflects a well-developed third-world consciousness and reveals the depth of Chicano frustrations and hostility to Anglo America resulting from decades of discrimination and exploitation.

1. BOOKER T. WASHINGTON

The Atlanta Exposition Address, 1895*

MR. PRESIDENT AND GENTLEMEN OF THE BOARD OF DIRECTORS AND CITIZENS.

One-third of the population of the South is of the Negro race. No enterprise seeking the material, civil, or moral welfare of this section can disregard this element of our population and reach the highest success. I but convey to you, Mr. President and Directors, the sentiment of the masses of my race when I say that in no way have the value and manhood of the American Negro been more fittingly and generously recognized than by the managers of this magnificent Exposition at every stage of its progress. It is a recognition that will do more to cement the friendship of the two races than any occurrence since the dawn of our freedom.

Not only this, but the opportunity here afforded will awaken among us a new era of industrial progress. Ignorant and inexperienced, it is not strange that in the first years of our new life we began at the top instead of at the

*From Booker T. Washington, *Up From Slavery, an Autobiography* (New York, Doubleday, Page & Co., 1902), pp. 218-25.

bottom; that a seat in Congress or the state legislature was more sought than real estate or industrial skill; that the political convention or stump speaking had more attractions than starting a dairy farm or truck garden.

A ship lost at sea for many days suddenly sighted a friendly vessel. From the mast of the unfortunate vessel was seen a signal, "Water, water; we die of thirst!" The answer from the friendly vessel at once came back, "Cast down your bucket where you are." A second time the signal, "Water, water; send us water!" ran up from the distressed vessel, and was answered, "Cast down your bucket where you are." And a third and fourth signal for water was answered, "Cast down your bucket where you are." The captain of the distressed vessel, at last heeding the injunction, cast down his bucket, and it came up full of fresh, sparkling water from the mouth of the Amazon River. To those of my race who depend on bettering their condition in a foreign land or who underestimate the importance of cultivating friendly relations with the Southern white man, who is their next-door neighbour, I would say: "Cast down your bucket where you are"—cast it down in making friends in every manly way of the people of all races by whom we are surrounded.

Cast it down in agriculture, mechanics, in commerce, in domestic service, and in the professions. And in this connection it is well to bear in mind that whatever other sins the South may be called to bear, when it comes to business, pure and simple, it is in the South that the Negro is given a man's chance in the commercial world, and in nothing is this Exposition more eloquent than in emphasizing this chance. Our greatest danger is that in the great leap from slavery to freedom we may overlook the fact that the masses of us are to live by the productions of our hands, and fail to keep in mind that we shall prosper in proportion as we learn to dignify and glorify common labour and put brains and skill into the common occupations of life; shall prosper in proportion as we learn to draw the line between the superficial and the substantial, the ornamental gewgaws of life and the useful. No race can prosper till it learns that there is as much dignity in tilling a field as in writing a poem. It is at the bottom of life we must begin, and not at the top. Nor should we permit our grievances to overshadow our opportunities.

To those of the white race who look to the incoming of those of foreign birth and strange tongue and habits for the prosperity of the South, were I permitted I would repeat what I say to my own race, "Cast down your bucket where you are." Cast it down among the eight millions of Negroes whose habits you know, whose fidelity and love you have tested in days when to have proved treacherous meant the ruin of your firesides. Cast down your bucket among these people who have, without strikes and labour wars, tilled your fields, cleared your forests, builded your railroads and cities, and brought forth treasures from the bowels of the earth, and helped make possible this magnificent representation of the progress of the South. Casting down your bucket among my people, helping and encouraging them as you are doing on these grounds, and to education of head, hand, and heart, you will find that they will buy your surplus land, make blossom the waste places in your fields, and run your factories. While doing this, you can be sure in the future, as in the past, that you and your families will be surrounded by the most patient, faithful, law-abiding, and unresentful people that the world has seen. As we have proved our loyalty to you in the past, in nursing your children, watching by the sick-bed of your mothers and fathers, and often following them with tear-dimmed eyes to their graves, so in the future, in our humble way, we shall stand by you with a devotion that no foreigner can approach, ready to lay down our lives, if need be, in defence of yours, interlacing our industrial, commercial, civil, and religious life with yours in a way that shall make the interests of both races one. In all things that are purely social we can be as separate as the fingers, yet one as the hand in all things essential to mutual progress.

There is no defence or security for any of us except in the highest intelligence and development of all. If anywhere there are efforts tending to curtail the fullest growth of the Negro, let these efforts be turned into stimulating, encouraging, and making him the most useful and intelligent citizen. Effort or means so invested will pay a thousand per cent interest. These efforts will be twice blessed—"blessing him that gives and him that takes."

There is no escape through law of man or God from the inevitable:—

The laws of changeless justice bind
Oppressor with oppressed;
And close as sin and suffering joined
We march to fate abreast.

Nearly sixteen millions of hands will aid you in pulling the load upward, or they will pull against you the load downward. We shall constitute one-third and more of the ignorance and crime of the South, or one-third its intelligence and progress; we shall contribute one-third to the business and industrial prosperity of the South, or we shall prove a veritable body of death, stagnating, depressing, retarding every effort to advance the body politic.

Gentlemen of the Exposition, as we present to you our humble effort at an exhibition of our progress, you must not expect overmuch. Starting thirty years ago with ownership here and there in a few quilts and pumpkins and chickens (gathered from miscellaneous sources), remember the path that has led from these to the inventions and production of agricultural implements, buggies, steam-engines, newspapers, books, statuary, carving, paintings, the management of drug-stores and banks, has not been trodden without contact with thorns and thistles. While we take pride in what we exhibit as a result of our independent efforts, we do not for a moment forget that our part in this exhibition would fall far short of your expectations but for the constant help that has come to our educational life, not only from the Southern states, but especially from Northern philanthropists, who have made their gifts a constant stream of blessing and encouragement.

The wisest among my race understand that the agitation of questions of social equality is the extremest folly, and that progress in the enjoyment of all the privileges that will come to us must be the result of severe and constant struggle rather than of artificial forcing. No race that has anything to contribute to the markets of the world is long in any degree ostracized. It is important and right that all privileges of the law be ours, but it is vastly more important that we be prepared for the exercises of these privileges. The opportunity to earn a dollar in a factory just now is worth infinitely more than the opportunity to spend a dollar in an opera-house.

In conclusion, may I repeat that nothing in thirty years has given us more hope and encouragement, and drawn us so near to you of the white race, as this opportunity offered by the Exposition; and here bending, as it were, over the altar that represents the results of the struggles of your race and mine, both starting practically empty-handed three decades ago, I pledge that in your effort to work out the great and intricate problem which God has laid at the doors of the South, you shall have at all times the patient, sympathetic help of my race; only let this be constantly in mind, that, while from representations in these buildings of the product of field, of forest, of mine, of factory, letters, and art, much good will come, yet far above and beyond material benefits will be that higher good, that, let us pray God, will come, in a blotting out of sectional differences and racial animosities and suspicions, in a determination to administer absolute justice, in a willing obedience among all classes to the mandates of law. This, this, coupled with our material prosperity, will bring into our beloved South a new heaven and a new earth.

2. CHIEF YOUNG JOSEPH

An Indian's View of Indian Affairs*

My friends, I have been asked to show you my heart. I am glad to have a chance to do so. I want the white people to understand my people. Some of you think an Indian is like a wild animal. This is a great mistake. I will tell you all about our people, and then you can judge whether an Indian is a man or not. I believe much trouble and blood would be saved if we opened our hearts more. I will tell you in my way how the Indian sees things. The white man has more words to tell you how they look to him, but it does not require many words to speak the truth. What I have to say will come from my heart, and I will speak with a straight tongue. Ah-cum-kin-i-ma-me-hut (the Great Spirit) is looking at me, and will hear me.

My name is In-mut-too-yah-lat-lat (Thunder traveling over the Mountains). I am chief of the Wal-lam-wat-kin band of Chute-pa-lu, or Nez Percés (nose-pierced Indians). I was born in eastern Oregon, thirty-eight winters ago. My father was chief before me. When a young man, he was called Joseph by Mr. Spaulding, a missionary. He died a few years ago. There was no stain on his hands of the blood of a white man. He left a good name on the earth. He advised me well for my people.

Our fathers gave us many laws, which they had learned from their fathers. These laws were good. They told us to treat all men as they treated us; that we should never be the first to break a bargain; that it was a disgrace to tell a lie; that we should speak only the truth; that it was a shame for one man to take from another his wife, or his property without paying for it. We were taught to believe that the Great Spirit sees and hears everything, and that he never forgets; that hereafter he will give every man a spirit-home according to his deserts: if he has been a good man, he will have a good home; if he has been a bad man, he will have a bad home. This I believe, and all my people believe the same.

We did not know there were other people besides the Indian until about one hundred winters ago, when some men with white faces came to our country. They brought many things with them to trade for furs and skins. They brought tobacco, which was new to us. They brought guns with flint stones on them, which frightened our women and children. Our people could not talk with these white-faced men, but they used signs which all people

*Chief Young Joseph, "An Indian's View of Indian Affairs," *North American Review*, Vol. CXXVIII (1879), pp. 415-33; reprinted in New Series, 6 (Spring 1969), pp. 56-64. Reprinted with permission of *North American Review*.

understand. These men were Frenchmen, and they called our people "Nez Percés," because they wore rings in their noses for ornaments. Although very few of our people wear them now, we are still called by the same name. These French trappers said a great many things to our fathers, which have been planted in our hearts. Some were good for us, but some were bad. Our people were divided in opinion about these men. Some thought they taught more bad than good. An Indian respects a brave man, but he despises a coward. He loves a straight tongue, but he hates a forked tongue. The French trappers told us some truths and some lies.

The first white men of your people who came to our country were named Lewis and Clarke. They also brought many things that our people had never seen. They talked straight, and our people gave them a great feast, as a proof that their hearts were friendly. These men were very kind. They made presents to our chiefs and our people made presents to them. We had a great many horses, of which we gave them what they needed, and they gave us guns and tobacco in return. All the Nez Percés made friends with Lewis and Clarke, and agreed to let them pass through their country, and never to make war on white nen. This promise the Nez Percés have never broken. No white man can accuse them of bad faith, and speak with a straight tongue. It has always been the pride of the Nez Percés that they were the friends of the white men. When my father was a young man there came to our country a white man (Rev. Mr. Spaulding) who talked spirit law. He won the affections of our people because he spoke good things to them. At first he did not say anything about white men wanting to settle on our lands. Nothing was said about that until about twenty winters ago, when a number of white people came into our country and built houses and made farms. At first our people made no complaint. They thought there was room enough for all to live in peace, and they were learning many things from the white men that seemed to be good. But we soon found that the white men were growing rich very fast, and were greedy to possess everything the Indian had. My father was the first to see through the schemes of the white men, and he warned his tribe to be careful about trading with them. He had suspicion of men who seemed so anxious to make money. I was a boy then, but I remember well my father's caution. He had sharper eyes than the rest of our people.

Next there came a white officer (Governor Stevens), who invited the Nez Percés to a treaty council. After the council was opened he made known his heart. He said there were a great many white people in the country, and many more would come; that he wanted the land marked out so that the Indians and white men could be separated. If they were to live in peace it was necessary, he said, that the Indians should have a country set apart for them, and in that country they must stay. My father, who represented his band, refused to have anything to do with the council, because he wished to be a free man. He claimed that no man owned any part of the earth, and a man could not sell what he did not own.

Mr. Spaulding took hold of my father's arm and said, "Come and sign the treaty." My father pushed him away, and said: "Why do you ask me to sign away my country? It is your business to talk to us about spirit matters, and not to talk to us about parting with our land." Governor Stevens urged my father to sign his treaty, but he refused. "I will not sign your paper," he said; "you go where you please, so do I; you are not a child, I am no child; I can think for myself. No man can think for me. I have no other home than this. I will not give it up to any man. My people would have no home. Take away your paper. I will not touch it with my hand."

My father left the council. Some of the chiefs of the other bands of the Nez Percés signed the treaty, and then Governor Stevens gave them presents of blankets. My father cautioned his people to take no presents, for "after a while," he said, "they will claim that you have accepted pay for your country." Since that time four bands of the Nez Percés have received annuities from the United States. My father was invited to many councils, and they tried hard to make him sign the treaty, but he was firm as the rock, and would not sign away his home. His refusal caused a difference among the Nez Percés.

Eight years later (1863) was the next treaty council. A chief called Lawyer, because he was a great talker, took the lead in this council, and sold nearly all the Nez Percés country. My father was not there. He said to me: "When you go into council with the white man, always remember your country. Do not give it away. The white man will cheat you out of your home. I have taken no pay from the United States. I have never sold our land." In this treaty Lawyer acted without authority from our band. He had no right to sell the Wallowa (*winding water*) country. That had always belonged to my father's own people, and the other bands had never disputed our right to it. No other Indians ever claimed Wallowa.

In order to have all people understand how much we owned, my father planted poles around it and said:

"Inside is the home of my people—the white man may take the land outside. Inside this boundary all our people were born. It circles around the graves of our fathers, and we will never give up these graves to any man."

The United States claimed they had bought all the Nez Percés country outside of Lapwai Reservation, from Lawyer and other chiefs, but we continued to live on this land in peace until eight years ago, when white men began to come inside the bounds my father had set. We warned them against this great wrong, but they would not leave our land, and some bad blood was raised. The white men represented that we were going upon the war-path. They reported many things that were false.

The United States Government again asked for a treaty council. My father had become blind and feeble. He could no longer speak for his people. It was then that I took my father's place as chief. In this council I made my first speech to white men. I said to the agent who held the council:

"I did not want to come to this council, but I came hoping that we could save blood. The white man has no right to come here and take our country. We have never accepted any presents from the Government. Neither Lawyer nor any other chief had authority to sell this land. It has always belonged to my people. It came unclouded to them from our fathers, and we will defend this land as long as a drop of Indian blood warms the hearts of our men."

The agent said he had orders, from the Great White Chief at Washington, for us to go upon the Lapwai Reservation, and that if we obeyed he would help us in many ways. "You *must* move to the agency," he said. I answered him: "I will not. I do not need your help; we have plenty, and we are contented and happy if the white man will let us alone. The reservation is too small for so many people with all their stock. You can keep your presents; we can go to your towns and pay for all we need; we have plenty of horses and cattle to sell, and we won't have any help from you; we are free now; we can go where we please. Our fathers were born here. Here they lived, here they died, here are their graves. We will never leave them." The agent went away, and we had peace for a little while.

Soon after this my father sent for me. I saw he was dying. I took his hand in mine. He said: "My son, my body is returning to my mother earth, and my spirit is going very soon to see the Great Spirit Chief. When I am gone, think of your country. You are the chief of these people. They look to you to guide them. Always remember that your father never sold his country. You must stop your ears whenever you are asked to sign a treaty selling your home. A few years more, and white men will be all around you. They have their eyes on this land. My son, never forget my dying words. This country holds your father's body. Never sell the bones of your father and your mother." I pressed my father's hand and told him I would protect his grave with my life. My father smiled and passed away to the spirit-land.

I buried him in that beautiful valley of winding waters. I love that land more than all the rest of the world. A man who would not love his father's grave is worse than a wild animal.

For a short time we lived quietly. But this could not last. White men had found gold in the mountains around the land of winding water. They stole a great many horses from us, and we could not get them back because we were Indians. The white men told lies for each other. They drove off a great many of our cattle. Some white men branded our young cattle so they could claim them. We had no friend who would plead our cause before the law councils. It seemed to me that some of the white men in Wallowa were doing these things on purpose to get up a war. They knew that we were not strong enough to fight them. I labored hard to avoid trouble and bloodshed. We gave up some of our country to the white men, thinking that then we could have peace. We were mistaken. The white man would not let us alone. We could have avenged our wrongs many times, but we did not. Whenever the Government has asked us to help them against other Indians, we have never refused. When the white men were few and we were strong we could have killed them all off, but the Nez Percés wished to live at peace.

If we have not done so, we have not been to blame. I believe that the old treaty has never been correctly reported. If we ever owned the land we own it still, for we never sold it. In the treaty councils the commissioners have claimed that our country had been sold to the Government. Suppose a white man should come to me and say, "Joseph, I like your horses, and I want to buy them." I say to him, "No, my horses suit me, I will not sell them." Then he goes to my neighbor, and says to him: "Joseph has some good horses. I want to buy them, but he refuses to sell." My neighbor answers, "Pay me the money, and I will sell you Joseph's horses." The white man returns to me, and says, "Joseph, I have bought your horses, and you must let me have them." If we sold our lands to the Government, this is the way they were bought.

On account of the treaty made by the other bands of the Nez Percés, the white men claimed my lands. We were troubled greatly by white men crowding over the line. Some of these were good men, and we lived on peaceful terms with them, but they were not all good.

Nearly every year the agent came over from Lapwai and ordered us on to the reservation. We always replied that we were satisfied to live in Wallowa. We were careful to refuse the presents or annuities which he offered.

Through all the years since the white men came to Wallowa we have been threatened and taunted by them and the treaty Nez Percés. They have given us no rest. We have had a few good friends among white men, and they have always advised my people to bear these taunts without fighting. Our young men were quick-tempered, and I have had great trouble in keeping them from doing rash things. I have carried a heavy load on my back ever since I was a boy. I learned then that we were but few, while the white men were many, and that we could not hold our own with them. We were like deer. They were like grizzly bears. We had a small country. Their country was large. We were contented to let things remain as the Great Spirit Chief made them. They were not; and would change the rivers and mountains if they did not suit them.

Year after year we have been threatened, but no war was made upon my people until General Howard came to our country two years ago and told us that he was the white war-chief of all that country. He said: "I have a great many soldiers at my back. I am going to bring them up here, and then I will talk to you again. I will not let white men laugh at me the next time I come. The country belongs to the Government, and I intend to make you go upon the reservation."

I remonstrated with him against bringing more soldiers to the Nez Percés country. He had one house full of troops all the time at Fort Lapwai.

The next spring the agent at Umatilla agency sent an Indian runner to tell me to meet General Howard at Walla Walla. I could not go myself, but I sent my brother and five other head men to meet him, and they had a long talk.

General Howard said: "You have talked straight, and it is all right. You can stay in Wallowa." He insisted that my brother and his company should go with him to Fort Lapwai. When the party arrived there General Howard sent out runners and called all the Indians in to a grand council. I was in that council. I said to General Howard, "We are ready to listen." He answered that he would not talk then, but would hold a council next day, when he would talk plainly. I said to General Howard: "I am ready to talk to-day. I have been in a great many councils, but I am no wiser. We are all sprung from a woman, although we are unlike in many things. We can not be made over again. You are as you were made, and as you were made you can remain. We are just as we were made by the Great Spirit, and you can not change us; then why should children of one mother and one father quarrel—why should one try to cheat the other? I do not believe that the Great Spirit Chief gave one kind of men the right to tell another kind of men what they must do."

General Howard replied: "You deny my authority, do you? You want to dictate to me, do you?"

Then one of my chiefs—Too-hool-hool-suit—rose in the council and said to General Howard: "The Great Spirit Chief made the world as it is, and as he wanted it, and he made a part of it for us to live upon. I do not see where you get authority to say that we shall not live where he placed us."

General Howard lost his temper and said: "Shut up! I don't want to hear any more of such talk. The law says you shall go upon the reservation to live, and I want you to do so, but you persist in disobeying the law'' (meaning the treaty). ''If you do not move, I will take the matter into my own hand, and make you suffer for your disobedience.''

Too-hool-hool-suit answered: ''Who are you, that you ask us to talk, and then tell me I shan't talk? Are you the Great Spirit? Did you make the world? Did you make the sun? Did you make the rivers to run for us to drink? Did you make the grass to grow? Did you make all these things, that you talk to us as though we were boys? If you did, then you have the right to talk as you do.''

General Howard replied, ''You are an impudent fellow, and I will put you in the guard-house,'' and then ordered a soldier to arrest him.

Too-hool-hool-suit made no resistance. He asked General Howard: ''Is that your order? I don't care. I have expressed my heart to you. I have nothing to take back. I have spoken for my country. You can arrest me, but you can not change me or make me take back what I have said.''

The soldiers came forward and seized my friend and took him to the guard-house. My men whispered among themselves whether they should let this thing be done. I counseled them to submit. I knew if we resisted that all the white men present, including General Howard would be killed in a moment, and we would be blamed. If I had said nothing, General Howard would never have given another unjust order against my men. I saw the danger, and, while they dragged Too-hool-hool-suit to prison, I arose and said: ''*I am going to talk now.* I don't care whether you arrest me or not.'' I turned to my people and said: ''The arrest of Too-hool-hool-suit was wrong, but we will not resent the insult. We were invited to this council to express our hearts, and we have done so.'' Too-hool-hool-suit was prisoner for five days before he was released.

The council broke up for that day. On the next morning General Howard came to my lodge, and invited me to go with him and White-Bird and Looking-Glass, to look for land for my people. As we rode along we came to some good land that was already occupied by Indians and white people. General Howard, pointing to this land, said: ''If you will come on to the reservation, I will give you these lands and move these people off.''

I replied: ''No. It would be wrong to disturb these people. I have no right to take their homes. I have never taken what did not belong to me. I will not now.''

We rode all day upon the reservation, and found no good land unoccupied. I have been informed by men who do not lie that General Howard sent a letter that night, telling the soldiers at Walla Walla to go to Wallowa Valley, and drive us out upon our return home.

In the council, next day, General Howard informed me, in a haughty spirit, that he would give my people *thirty days* to go back home, collect all their stock, and move on to the reservation, saying, "If you are not here in that time, I shall consider that you want to fight, and will send my soldiers to drive you on."

I said: "War can be avoided, and it ought to be avoided. I want no war. My people have always been the friends of the white man. Why are you in such a hurry? I can not get ready to move in thirty days. Our stock is scattered, and Snake River is very high. Let us wait until fall, then the river will be low. We want time to hunt up our stock and gather supplies for winter."

General Howard replied, "If you let the time run over one day, the soldiers will be there to drive you on to the reservation, and all your cattle and horses outside of the reservation at that time will fall into the hands of the white men."

I knew I had never sold my country, and that I had no land in Lapwai; but I did not want bloodshed. I did not want my people killed. I did not want anybody killed. Some of my people had been murdered by white men, and the white murderers were never punished for it. I told General Howard about this, and again said I wanted no war. I wanted the people who lived upon the lands I was to occupy at Lapwai to have time to gather their harvest.

I said in my heart that, rather than have war, I would give up my country. I would give up my father's grave. I would give up everything rather than have the blood of white men upon the hands of my people.

General Howard refused to allow me more than thirty days to move my people and their stock. I am sure that he began to prepare for war at once. . . .

When I returned to Wallowa I found my people very much excited upon discovering that the soldiers were already in the Wallowa Valley. We held a council, and decided to move immediately, to avoid bloodshed.

Too-hool-hool-suit, who felt outraged by his imprisonment, talked for war, and made many of my young men willing to fight rather than be driven like dogs from the land where they were born. He declared that blood alone would wash out the disgrace General Howard had put upon him. It required a strong heart to stand up against such talk, but I urged my people to be quiet, and not to begin a war.

We gathered all the stock we could find, and made an attempt to move. We left many of our horses and cattle in Wallowa, and we lost several hundred in crossing the river. All of my people succeeded in getting across in safety. Many of the Nez Percés came together in Rocky Cañon to hold a grand council. I went with all my people. This council lasted ten days. There was a great deal of war-talk, and a great deal of excitement. There was one young brave present whose father had been killed by a white man five years before. This man's blood was bad against white men, and he left the council calling for revenge.

Again I counseled peace, and I thought the danger was past. We had not complied with General Howard's order because we could not, but we intended to do so as soon as possible. I was leaving the council to kill beef for my family, when news came that the young man whose father had been killed had gone out with several other hot-blooded young braves and killed four white men. He rode up to the council and shouted: "Why do you sit here like women? The war has begun already." I was deeply grieved. All the lodges were moved except my brother's and my own. I saw clearly that the war was upon us when I learned that my young men had been secretly buying ammunition. I heard then that Too-hool-hool-suit, who had been imprisoned by General Howard, had succeeded in organizing a war-party. I knew that their acts would involve all my people. I saw that the war could not then be prevented. The time had passed. I counseled peace from the beginning. I knew that we were too weak to fight the United States. We had many grievances, but I knew that war would bring more. We had good white friends, who advised us against taking the war-path. My friend and brother, Mr. Chapman, who has been with us since the surrender, told us just how the war would end. Mr. Chapman took sides against us, and helped General Howard. I do not blame him for doing so. He tried hard to prevent bloodshed. We hoped the white settlers would not join the soldiers. Before the war commenced we had discussed this matter all over, and many of my people were in favor of warning them that if they took no part against us they should not be molested in the event of war being begun by General Howard. This plan was voted down in the war-council.

There were bad men among my people who had quarreled with white men, and they talked of their wrongs until they roused all the bad hearts in the council. Still I could not believe that they would begin the war. I know that my young men did a great wrong, but I ask, Who was first to blame? They had been insulted a thousand times; their fathers and brothers had been killed; their mothers and wives had been disgraced; they had been driven to madness by whisky sold to them by white men; they had been told by General Howard that all their horses and cattle which they had been unable to drive out of Wallowa were to fall into the hands of white men; and, added to all this, they were homeless and desperate.

I would have given my own life if I could have undone the killing of white men by my people. I blame my young men and I blame the white men. I blame General Howard for not giving my people time to get their stock away from Wallowa. I do not acknowledge that he had the right to order me to leave Wallowa at any time. I deny that either my father or myself ever sold that land. It is still our land. It may never again be our home, but my father sleeps there, and I love it as I love my mother. I left there, hoping to avoid bloodshed.

If General Howard had given me plenty of time to gather up my stock, and treated Too-hool-hool-suit as a man should be treated, there *would have been no war.*

My friends among white men have blamed me for the war. I am not to blame. When my young men began the killing, my heart was hurt. Although I did not justify them, I remembered all the insults I had endured, and my blood was on fire. Still I would have taken my people to the buffalo country without fighting, if possible.

I could see no other way to avoid a war. We moved over to White Bird Creek, sixteen miles away, and there encamped, intending to collect our stock before leaving; but the soldiers attacked us, and the first battle was fought. We numbered in that battle sixty men, and soldiers a hundred. The fight lasted but a few minutes, when the soldiers retreated before us for twelve miles. They lost thirty-three killed, and had seven wounded. When an Indian fights, he only shoots to kill; but soldiers shoot at random. None of the soldiers were scalped. we do not believe in scalping, nor in killing wounded men. Soldiers do not kill many Indians unless they are wounded and left upon the battle-field. Then they kill Indians. . . .

We had no knowledge of General Miles's army until a short time before he made a charge upon us, cutting our camp in two, and capturing nearly all of our horses. About seventy men, myself among them, were cut off. My little daughter, twelve years of age, was with me. I gave her a rope, and told her to catch a horse and join the others who were cut off from the camp. I have not seen her since, but I have learned that she is alive and well.

I thought of my wife and children, who were now surrounded by soldiers, and I resolved to go to them or die. With a prayer in my mouth to the Great Spirit Chief who rules above, I dashed unarmed through the line of soldiers. It seemed to me that there were guns on every side, before and behind me. My clothes were cut to pieces and my horse was wounded, but I was not hurt. As I reached the door of my lodge, my wife handed me my rifle, saying: "Here's your gun. Fight!"

The soldiers kept up a continuous fire. Six of my men were killed in one spot near me. Ten or twelve soldiers charged into our camp and got possession of two lodges, killing three Nez Percés and losing three of their men, who fell inside our lines. I called my men to drive them back. We fought at close range, not more than twenty steps apart, and drove the soldiers back upon their main line, leaving their dead in our hands. We secured their arms and ammunition. We lost, the first day and night, eighteen men and three women. General Miles lost twenty-six killed and forty wounded. The following day General Miles sent a messenger into my camp under protection of a white flag. I sent my friend Yellow Bull to meet him.

Yellow Bull understood the messenger to say that General Miles wished me to consider the situation; that he did not want to kill my people unnecessarily. Yellow Bull understood this to be a demand for me to surrender and save blood. Upon reporting this message to me, Yellow Bull said he wondered whether General Miles was in earnest. I sent him back with my answer, that I had not made up my mind, but would think about it and send word soon. A little later he sent some Cheyenne scouts with another message. I went out to meet them. They said they believed that General Miles was sincere and really wanted peace. I walked on to General Miles's tent. He met me and we shook hands. He said, "Come, let us sit down by the fire and talk this matter over." I remained with him all night; next morning Yellow Bull came over to see if I was alive, and why I did not return.

General Miles would not let me leave the tent to see my friend alone.

Yellow Bull said to me: "They have got you in their power, and I am afraid they will never let you go again. I have an officer in our camp, and I will hold him until they let you go free."

I said: "I do not know what they mean to do with me, but if they kill me you must not kill the officer. It will do no good to avenge my death by killing him."

Yellow Bull returned to my camp. I did not make any agreement that day with General Miles. The battle was renewed while I was with him. I was very anxious about my people. I knew that we were near Sitting Bull's camp in King George's land, and I thought maybe the Nez Percés who had escaped would return with assistance. No great damage was done to either party during the night.

On the following morning I returned to my camp by agreement, meeting the officer who had been held a prisoner in my camp at the flag of truce. My people were divided about surrendering. We could have escaped from Bear Paw Mountain if we had left our wounded, old women, and children behind. We were unwilling to do this. We had never heard of a wounded Indian recovering while in the hands of white men.

On the evening of the fourth day General Howard came in with a small escort, together with my friend Chapman. We could now talk understandingly. General Miles said to me in plain words, "If you will come out and give up your arms, I will spare your lives and send you to your reservation." I do not know what passed between General Miles and General Howard.

I could not bear to see my wounded men and women suffer any longer; we had lost enough already. General Miles had promised that we might return to our own country with what stock we had left. I thought we could start again. I believed General Miles, or *I never would have surrendered.* I have heard that he has been censured for making the promise to return us to Lapwai. He could not have made any other terms with me at that time. I would have held him in check until my friends came to my assistance, and then neither of the generals nor their soldiers would have ever left Bear Paw Mountain alive.

On the fifth day I went to General Miles and gave up my gun, and said, "From where the sun now stands I will fight no more." My people needed rest—we wanted peace.

I was told we could go with General Miles to Tongue River and stay there until spring, when we would be sent back to our country. Finally it was decided that we were to be taken to Tongue River. We had nothing to say about it. After our arrival at Tongue River, General Miles received orders to take us to Bismarck. The reason given was, that subsistence would be cheaper there.

General Miles was opposed to this order. He said: "You must not blame me. I have endeavored to keep my word, but the chief who is over me has given the order, and I must obey it or resign. That would do you no good. Some other officer would carry out the order."

I believe General Miles would have kept his word if he could have done so. I do not blame him for what we have suffered since the surrender. I do not know who is to blame. We gave up all our horses—over eleven hundred—and all our saddles—over one hundred—and we have not heard from them since. Somebody has got our horses.

General Miles turned my people over to another soldier, and we were taken to Bismarck. Captain Johnson, who now had charge of us, received an order to take us to Fort Leavenworth. At Leavenworth we were placed on a low river bottom, with no water except river-water to drink and cook with. We had always lived in a healthy country, where the mountains were high and the water was cold and clear. Many of my people sickened and died, and we buried them in this strange land. I can not tell how much my heart suffered for my people while at Leavenworth. The Great Spirit Chief who rules above seemed to be looking some other way, and did not see what was being done to my people.

During the hot days (July, 1878) we received notice that we were to be moved farther away from our own country. We were not asked if we were willing to go. We were ordered to get into the railroad-cars. Three of my people died on the way to Baxter Springs. It was worse to die there than to die fighting in the mountains.

We were moved from Baxter Springs (Kansas) to the Indian Territory, and set down without our lodges. We had but little medicine, and we were nearly all sick. Seventy of my people have died since we moved there.

We have had a great many visitors who have talked many ways. Some of the chiefs (General Fish and Colonel Stickney) from Washington came to see us, and selected land for us to live upon. We have not moved to that land, for it is not a good place to live.

The Commissioner Chief (E.A. Hayt) came to see us. I told him, as I told every one, that I expected General Miles's word would be carried out. He said it "could not be done; that white men now lived in my country and all the land was taken up; that, if I returned to Wallowa, I could not live in peace; that law-papers were out against my young men who began the war, and that the Government could not protect my people." This talk fell like a heavy stone upon my heart. I saw that I could not gain anything by talking to him. Other law chiefs (Congressional Committee) came to see me and said they would help me to get a healthy country. I did not know who to believe. The white people have too many chiefs. They do not understand each other. They do not all talk alike.

The Commissioner Chief (Mr. Hayt) invited me to go with him and hunt for a better home than we have now. I like the land we found (west of the Osage reservation) better than any place I have seen in that country; but it is not a healthy land. There are no mountains and rivers. The water is warm. It is not a good country for stock. I do not believe my people can live there. I am afraid they will all die. The Indians who occupy that country are dying off. I promised Chief Hayt to go there, and do the best I could until the Government got ready to make good General Miles's word. I was not satisfied, but I could not help myself.

Then the Inspector Chief (General McNiel) came to my camp and we had a long talk. He said I ought to have a home in the mountain country north, and that he would write a letter to the Great Chief at Washington. Again the hope of seeing the mountains of Idaho and Oregon grew up in my heart.

At last I was granted permission to come to Washington and bring my friend Yellow Bull and our interpreter with me. I am glad we came. I have shaken hands with a great many friends, but there are some things I want to know which no one seems able to explain. I can not understand how the Government sends a man out to fight us, as it did General Miles, and then breaks his word. Such a Government has something wrong about it. I can not understand why so many chiefs are allowed to talk so many different ways, and promise so many different things. I have seen the Great Father Chief (the President), the next Great Chief (Secretary of the Interior), the Commissioner Chief (Hayt), the Law Chief (General Butler), and many other law chiefs (Congressmen), and they all say they are my friends, and that I shall have justice, but while their mouths all talk right I do not understand why nothing is done for my people. I have heard talk and talk, but nothing is done. Good words do not last long unless they amount to something. Words do not pay for my dead people. They do not pay for my country, now overrun by white men. They do not protect my father's grave. They do not pay for all my horses and cattle. Good words will not give me back my children. Good words will not make good the promise of your War Chief General Miles. Good words will not give my people good health and stop them from dying. Good words will not get my people a home where they can live in peace and take care of themselves. I am tired of talk that comes to nothing. It makes my heart sick when I remember all the good words and all the broken promises. There has been too much talking by men who had no right to talk. Too many misrepresentations have been made, too many misunderstandings have come up between the white men about the Indians. If the white man wants to live in peace with the Indian he can live in peace. There need be no trouble. Treat all men alike. Give them all the same law. Give them all an even chance to live and grow. All men were made by the same Great Spirit Chief. They are all brothers. The earth is the mother of all people, and all people should have equal rights upon it. You might as well expect the rivers to run backward as that any man who was born a free man should be contented when penned up and denied liberty to go where he pleases. If you tie a horse to a stake, do you expect he will grow fat? If you pen an Indian up on a small spot of earth, and compel him to stay there, he will not be contented, nor will he grow and prosper. I have asked some of the great white chiefs where they get their authority to say to the Indian that he shall stay in one place, while he sees white men going where they please. They can not tell me.

I only ask of the Government to be treated as all other men are treated. If I can not go to my own home, let me have a home in some country where my people will not die so fast. I would like to go to Bitter Root Valley. There my people would be healthy; where they are now they are dying. Three have died since I left my camp to come to Washington.

When I think of our condition my heart is heavy. I see men of my race treated as outlaws and driven from country to country, or shot down like animals.

I know that my race must change. We can not hold our own with the white men as we are. We only ask an even chance to live as other men live. We ask to be recognized as men. We ask that the same law shall work alike on all men. If the Indian breaks the law, punish him by the law. If the white man breaks the law, punish him also.

Let me be a free man—free to travel, free to stop, free to work, free to trade where I choose, free to choose my own teachers, free to follow the religion of my fathers, free to think and talk and act for myself—and I will obey every law, or submit to the penalty.

Whenever the white man treats the Indian as they treat each other, then we will have no more wars. We shall all be alike—brothers of one father and one mother, with one sky above us and one country around us, and one government for all. Then the Great Spirit Chief who rules above will smile upon this land, and send rain to wash out the bloody spots made by brothers' hands from the face of the earth. For this time the Indian race are waiting and praying. I hope that no more groans of wounded men and women will ever go to the ear of the Great Spirit Chief above, and that all people may be one people.

In-mut-too-yah-lat-lat has spoken for his people.

WASHINGTON CITY, D.C. YOUNG JOSEPH

3. JUAN N. CORTINA

Proclamation*

County of Cameron,

Camp in the Rancho del Carmen, November 23, 1859.

COMPATRIOTS: A sentiment of profound indignation, the love and esteem which I profess for you, the desire which you have for that tranquillity and

*U.S. House of Representatives, *Difficulties on the Southwestern Frontier,* Ex. Doc. No. 52, 36th Congress, 1st Session, pp. 79-82.

those guarantees which are denied you, thus violating the most sacred laws, is that which moves me to address you these words, hoping that they may prove some consolation in the midst of your adversity, which heretofore has borne the appearance of predestination.

The history of great human actions teaches us that in certain instances the principal motive which gives them impulse is the natural right to resist and conquer our enemies with a firm spirit and lively will; to persist in and to reach the consummation of this object, opening a path through the obstacles which step by step are encountered, however imposing or terrible they may be.

In the series of such actions, events present themselves which public opinion, influenced by popular sentiment, calls for deliberation upon their effects, to form an exact and just conception of the interests which they promote; and this same public opinion should be considered as the best judge, which, with coolness and impartiality, does not fail to recognize some principle as the cause for the existence of open force and immutable firmness, which impart the noble desire of coöperating with true philanthropy to remedy the state of despair of him who, in his turn, becomes the victim of ambition, satisfied at the cost of justice.

There are, doubtless, persons so overcome by strange prejudices, men without confidence or courage to face danger in an undertaking in sisterhood with the love of liberty, who, examining the merit of acts by a false light, and preferring that of the same opinion contrary to their own, prepare no other reward than that pronounced for the "bandit," for him who, with complete abnegation of self, dedicates himself to constant labor for the happiness of those who, suffering under the weight of misfortunes, eat their bread, mingled with tears, on the earth which they rated.

If, my dear compatriots, I am honored with that name, I am ready for the combat.

The Mexicans who inhabit this wide region, some because they were born therein, others because since the treaty Guadalupe Hidalgo, they have been attracted to its soil by the soft influence of wise laws and the advantages of a free government, paying little attention to the reasoning of politics, are honorably and exclusively dedicated to the exercise of industry, guided by that instinct which leads the good man to comprehend, as uncontradictory truth, that only in the reign of peace can he enjoy, without inquietude, the fruit of his labor. These, under an unjust imputation of selfishness and churlishness, which do not exist, are not devoid of those sincere and expressive evidences of such friendliness and tenderness as should gain for them that confidence with which they have inspired those who have met them in social intercourse. This genial affability seems as the foundation of that proverbial prudence which, as an oracle, is consulted in all their actions and undertakings. Their humility, simplicity, and docility, directed with dignity, it may be that with excess of goodness, can, if it be desired, lead them beyond the common class of men, but causes them to excel in an irresistible inclination towards ideas of equality, a proof of their simple manners, so well adapted to that which is styled the classic land of liberty. A man, a family, and a people, possessed of qualities so eminent, with their heart in their hand and purity on their lips, encounter every day renewed reasons to know that they are surrounded by malicious and crafty monsters, who rob them in the tranquil interior of home, or with open hatred and pursuit; it necessarily follows, however great may be their pain, if not abased by humiliation and ignominy, their groans suffocated and hushed by a pain which renders them insensible, they become resigned to suffering before an abyss of misfortunes.

Mexicans! When the State of Texas began to receive the new organization which its sovereignty required as an integrant part of the Union, flocks of vampires, in the guise of men, came and scattered themselves in the settlements, without any capital except the corrupt heart and the most perverse intentions. Some, brimful of laws, pledged to us their protection against the attacks of the rest; others assembled in shadowy councils, attempted and excited the robbery and burning of the houses of our relatives on the other side of the river Bravo; while others, to the abusing of our unlimited confidence, when we intrusted them with our titles, which secured the future of our families, refused to return them under false and frivolous pretexts; all, in short, with a smile on their faces, giving the lie to that which their black entrails were meditating. Many of you have been robbed of your property, incarcerated, chased, murdered, and hunted like wild beasts, because your labor was fruitful, and because your industry excited the vile avarice which led them. A voice infernal said, from the bottom of their soul, "kill them: the greater will be our gain!" Ah! this does not finish the sketch of your situation. It would appear that justice had fled from this world, leaving you to the caprice of your oppressors, who become each day more furious towards you; that, through witnesses and false charges, although the grounds may be insufficient, you may be interred in the penitentiaries, if you are not previously deprived of life by some keeper who covers himself from responsibility by the pretence of your flight. There are to be found criminals covered with frightful crimes, but they appear to have impunity until opportunity furnish them a victim; to these monsters indulgence is shown, because they are not of our race, which is unworthy, as they say, to belong to the human species. But this race, which the Anglo-American, so ostentatious of its own qualities, tried so much to blacken, depreciate, and load with insults, in a spirit of blindness, which goes to the full extent of such things so common on this frontier, does not fear, placed even in the midst of its very faults, those subtle inquisitions which are so frequently made as to its manners, habits, and sentiments; nor that its deeds should be put to the test of examination in the land of reason, of justice, and of honor. This race has never humbled itself before the conqueror, though the reverse has happened, and can be established; for he is not humbled who uses among his fellow-men those courtesies which humanity prescribes; charity being the root whence springs the rule of his actions. But this race, which you see filled with gentleness and inward sweetness, gives now the cry of alarm throughout the entire extent of the land which it occupies, against all the artifice interposed by those who have become chargeable with their division and discord. This race, adorned with the most lovely disposition towards all that is good and useful in the line of progress, omits no act of diligence which might correct its many imperfections, and lift its grand edifice among the ruins of the past, respecting the ancient traditions and the maxims bequeathed by their ancestors, without being dazzled by brilliant and false appearances, nor crawling to that exaggeration of institution which, like a sublime statue, is offered for their worship and adoration.

Mexicans! Is there no remedy for you? Inviolable laws, yet useless, serve, it is true, certain judges and hypocritical authorities, cemented in evil and injustice, to do whatever suits them, and to satisfy their vile avarice at the cost of your patience and suffering; rising in their frenzy, even to the taking of life, through the treacherous hands of their bailiffs. The wicked way in which many of you have been oftentimes involved in persecution, accompanied by circumstances making it the more bitter, is now well known; these crimes being hid from society under the shadow of a horrid night, those implacable people, with the haughty spirit which suggests impunity for a life of criminality, have pronounced, doubt ye not, your sentence, which is, with accustomed insensibility, as you have seen, on the point of execution.

Mexicans! My part is taken, the voice of revelation whispers to me that to me is entrusted the work of breaking the chains of your slavery, and that the Lord will enable me, with powerful arm, to fight against our enemies, in compliance with the requirements of that Sovereign Majesty, who, from this day forward, will hold us under His protection. On my part, I am ready to offer myself as a sacrifice for your happiness; and counting upon the means necessary for the discharge of my ministry, you may count upon my cooperation, should no cowardly attempt put an end to my days. This undertaking will be sustained on the following bases:

First. A society is organized in the State of Texas, which devotes itself sleeplessly until the work is crowned with success, to the improvement of the unhappy condition of those Mexicans resident therein; exterminating their tyrants, to which end those which compose it are ready to shed their blood and suffer the death of martyrs.

Second. As this society contains within itself the elements necessary to accomplish the great end of its labors, the veil of impenetrable secrecy covers "The Great Book" in which the articles of its constitution are written; while so delicate are the difficulties which must be overcome that no honorable man can have cause for alarm, if imperious exigencies require them to act without reserve.

Third. The Mexicans of Texas repose their lot under the good sentiments of the governor elect of the State, General Houston, and trust that upon his elevation to power he will begin with care to give us legal protection within the limits of his powers.

Mexicans! Peace be with you! Good inhabitants of the State of Texas, look on them as brothers, and keep in mind that which the Holy Spirit saith: "Thou shalt not be the friend of the passionate man; nor join thyself to the madman, lest thou learn his mode of work and scandalize thy soul."

JUAN N. CORTINA

4. The Plan of San Diego, Texas (1915)*

We, who in turn sign our names, assembled in the revolutionary plot of San Diego, Tex., solemnly promise each other, on our word of honor, that we will fulfill, and cause to be fulfilled and compiled with, all the clauses and provisions stipulated in this document, and execute the orders and the wishes emanating from the provisional directorate of this movement and recognize as military chief of the same Mr. Agustin S. Garza, guaranteeing with our lives the fruitful accomplishment of what is here agreed upon.

*U.S. Senate, Committee on Foreign Relations, Preliminary Reports and Hearings, *Investigation of Mexican Affairs*, Senate Doc. 285, 66th Congress, 2nd Session, I, pp. 1205-7.

1. On the 20th day of February, 1915, at 2 o'clock in the morning, we will rise in arms against the Government and the country of the United States of North America, one as all and all as one, proclaiming the liberty of the individuals of the black race and its independence of Yankee tyranny which has held us in iniquituous slavery since the remote times; and at the same time and in the same manner we will proclaim the independence and segregation of the States bordering on the Mexican Nation, which are: Texas, New Mexico, Arizona, Colorado, and Upper California, of which States the Republic of Mexico was robbed in a most perfidious manner by North American imperialism.

2. In order to render the foregoing clause effective, the necessary army corps will be formed under the immediate command of military leaders named by the Supreme Revolutionary Congress of San Diego, Tex., which shall have full power to designate a supreme chief, who shall be at the head of said army. The banner which shall guide us in this enterprise shall be red, with a white diagonal fringe, and bearing the following inscription: "Equality and independence," and none of the subordinate leaders or subalterns shall use any other flag (except only the white flag for signals). The aforesaid army shall be known by the name of "liberating army for races and peoples."

3. Each one of the chiefs will do his utmost, by whatever means possible, to get possession of the arms and funds of the cities which he has beforehand been designated to capture, in order that our cause may be provided with resources to continue the fight with better success, the said leaders each being required to render an account of everything to his superiors, in order that the latter may dispose of it in the proper manner.

4. The leader who may take a city must immediately name and appoint municipal authorities, in order that they may preserve order and assist in every way possible the revolutionary movement. In case the capital of any State we are endeavoring to liberate be captured, there will be named in the same manner superior municipal authorities for the same purpose.

5. It is strictly forbidden to hold prisoners, either special prisoners (civilians) or soldiers; and the only time that should be spent in dealing with them is that which is absolutely necessary to demand funds (loans) of them; and whether these demands are successful or not, they shall be shot immediately without any pretext.

6. Every stranger who shall be found armed and who can not prove his right to carry arms shall be summarily executed, regardless of his race or nationality.

7. Every North American over 16 years of age shall be put to death, and

only the aged men, the women, and children shall be respected; and on no account shall the traitors to our race be spared or respected.

8. The Apaches of Arizona, as well as the Indians (redskins) of the Territory shall be given every guaranty; and their lands which have been taken from them shall be returned to them, to the end that they may assist us in the cause which we defend.

9. All appointments and grades in our army which are exercised by subordinate officers (subalterns) shall be examined (recognized) by the superior officers. There shall likewise be recognized the grades of leaders of other complots which may be connected with this, and who may wish to cooperate with us; also those who may affiliate with us later.

10. The movement having gathered force, and once having possessed ourselves of the States above alluded to, we shall proclaim them an independent republic, later requesting (if it be thought expedient) annexation to Mexico, without concerning ourselves at the time about the form of government which may control the destinies of the common mother country.

11. When we shall have obtained independence for the Negroes, we shall grant them a banner, which they themselves shall be permitted to select, and we shall aid them in obtaining six States of the American Union, which States border upon those already mentioned, and they may form from these six States a republic, and they may therefore be independent.

12. None of the leaders shall have power to make terms with the enemy, without first communicating with the superior officers of the army, bearing in mind that this is a war without quarter; nor shall any leader enroll in his ranks any stranger, unless said stranger belong to the Latin, the Negro, or the Japanese race.

13. It is understood that none of the members of this complot (or any one who may come in later) shall, upon the definite triumph of the cause which we defend, fail to recognize their superiors, nor shall they aid others who, with bastard designs, may endeavor to destroy what has been accomplished by such great work.

14. As soon as possible each local society (junta) shall nominate delegates who shall meet at a time and place beforehand designated, for the purpose of nominating a permanent directorate of the revolutionary movement. At this meeting shall be determined and worked out in detail the power and duties of the permanent directorate and this revolutionary plan may be revised or amended.

15. It is understood among those who may follow this movement that we shall carry in a singing voice the independence of the negroes, placing obligations upon both races and that on no account will we accept aid, either

moral or pecuniary, from the Government of Mexico; and it need not consider itself under any obligation in this, our movement.

Equality and independence.

SAN DIEGO, TEX., *January 6, 1919.*

(Signed)

L. PERRIGO, *President.*
A. GONZALES, *Secretary.*
A. A. SAENZ,
E. CISNEROS.
PORFIRIO SANTOS
A. S. GARZA.
MANUEL FLORES.
B. RAMOS, JR.
A. G. ALMARAZ.

III. Migration and the Effects of Urbanization

This chapter examines the question of ethnic displacement from the land, patterns of migration to the city, effects of urbanization on minorities, and ethnic reactions to life in the city.

The experience of Blacks, Chicanos, and Native Americans in the United States has been closely linked to the process of urbanization. Like all Americans, members of these minority groups have steadily become urbanized, although with variations in causes, phases, and impact. This process has been particularly disruptive for minorities because of their special connection with the land.

Long before the arrival of Europeans in North America, for example, Indian life and culture had developed deep, powerful roots in the soil. In a similar manner Mexicans regarded the land as a basic ingredient in their lives. In the Southern United States, Blacks were forced into an involuntary relationship with the land; enslaved in Africa and brought to the Western Hemisphere to work the soil for others, they became strongly linked with the land.

The nineteenth century disrupted these landed relationships. The westward movement of American pioneers resulted in the displacement of Indians from their homelands. The Mexican-American War (1846-48), in which the United States took one-third of Mexico's territory, led eventually to the collapse of Mexican landholding patterns in the conquered lands. The American Civil War (1861-65) ended legalized slavery and inaugurated the Black search for a new, freedman's relationship to the land. The development of mining, railroads, and agriculture in the American Southwest drew thousands of immigrants from Mexico to provide human energy in the building of a new economy.

The attempt to maintain their land-based existence became more difficult and unrewarding for ethnic minorities in the twentieth century. Reservation life for Indians grew steadily more impoverished. Black farmers found it increasingly difficult to survive in the face of mounting socioeconomic pressures. In the Southwest, Mexican Americans struggled to slow the loss of land, while Mexican immigrants, mostly from farms or small towns, left behind political and economic disruptions as they crossed the border in search of new opportunities, often entering the agricultural migrant-labor stream. With urban industry clamoring for labor and with a growing need for urban support services, minorities saw the city as a possible road to escape from their difficulties. Reservation Indians, Black farmers, and Mexican Americans thus turned from the land and entered the city full of hope.

For some ethnics city life was not an entirely new experience. Blacks, either as slaves of urban masters or as freedmen, had lived in cities long before the Civil War. Mexicans had built cities throughout their northern provinces long before the coming of the Anglo, and as nineteenth-century Mexican immigrants generally labored for agricultural, mining, and railroad enterprises, many formed and settled in urban barrios.

But it was not until the twentieth century that minority groups became urbanized in massive numbers, and there was little in the urban experience of the relatively few to prepare the majority of migrants for modern American city life. For some the move to the city did bring upward economic and social mobility; for most, however, it brought bewilderment, disorientation, and psychological shock. Not only did they lose their cultural moorings, but urban ethnic minorities suffered chronic unemployment, poor housing, segregation in ghettos or barrios, and the debilitating effects of racism. For most the city brought not fulfillment but unhappiness and frustration.

A. THE LAND: THE ETHNIC STRUGGLE FOR EXISTENCE

Over the years and by one means or another Anglo-Americans have continuously pressured ethnic groups from their lands. This section examines that process as it affected Californio ranchers in the 1850s, one group of California Indians in the 1860s, and contemporary Southern Black sharecroppers. It also describes a variety of ethnic responses to these challenges. Some, for example, refused to leave their lands and fought Anglo incursions in the courts or by arms. Others accepted the inevitable, gave in, and did what they could to salvage their land-based existence on reservations or in rural enclaves. Still others attempted to adjust to dispossession by establishing entirely new relationships with the land or by seeking a new life in the city.

Leonard Pitt portrays the destruction of the Mexican-American rancho system in northern California during the 1850s. Faced with Anglo land hunger and hostility, the Californio ranchers tried in a variety of ways to preserve their property and way of life. But the force they struggled against was too powerful. Massive migration following the United States acquisition of California in 1848 and the discovery of gold the same year spelled the end of the great Mexican land grants in northern California.

Indians suffered a similar fate. Although details may vary from group to group, the story of Indian displacement is one of bitter repetition. As whites moved onto their ancestral lands, Indians were either killed, driven off, or led away to distant reservations. Through Chief José Pacheco, we learn the experience of the Kern River Indians of California. Some resisted white land grabs and scattered to fight the encroachers. Others left the land and put themselves at the mercy of Indian agents and the military. And some, like Pacheco himself, tried to adopt the white man's ways. But as his letter makes clear, Pacheco's success was not significantly greater than that of the others.

The last selection describes the question of ethnic land-alienation in its contemporary American setting. Gene Roberts deals with the problems of post-World War II Southern Black sharecroppers who have lost their small farms not to scheming whites but to mechanized agriculture. These "off-farm" migrants have inevitably drifted to the city, where, disoriented and untrained, they must compete in the urban job market.

1. LEONARD PITT

THE DECIMATION OF THE NORTHERN CALIFORNIA RANCHOS*

A puzzle greeted the sojourner near San Leandro in the summer of 1853: Why should a fence patrol the desolate stretch of coastal road? Fences normally signal agricultural enterprise, yet this one surrounded no homes, no crops, no cattle—only a limitless expanse of ripe brown forage grass rolling inland toward a distant mountain range. Close inspection of the wooden barrier as it turned a corner and marched away from the highway, heading for the mountains, revealed that its purpose was negative—to prevent, rather than encourage, the use of the land. On the unenclosed property grazed a herd of gaunt-looking longhorns, sniffing hungrily at the unattainable feed and biting at soil as bare of grass as the dirt road itself.

Inquiry at nearby Union City or San Leandro clarified the mystery. The residents confirmed the suspicion that the fence was the work of settlers

*Leonard Pitt, *The Decline of the Californios* (Berkeley, University of California Press, 1966), pp. 83-103. Originally published by the University of California Press; reprinted by permission of the regents of the University of California.

(more bluntly known as squatters), and that the cattle belonged to Californios. The land was claimed by the Peraltas and the Estudillos, who had occupied it since 1830, and by about 1,500 Americans who had hammered their stakes into it after 1851. The property had been in limbo since the beginnings of the Land Law of 1851. While the Californios pleaded their case before the Land Commission, the Americans watched and waited. Lawyers had meantime picked a flaw in an original claimant's will by means of which some settlers hoped to gain possession. Besides, the Americans knew that the legislature had recently granted settlers entry rights to land which "to the best of one's knowledge" was unused. The settlers thus put the law to the test and spoke candidly of seeing the Peraltas "in hell" before removing their fences.

Here and everywhere near San Francisco Bay lives had been lost, property seized, and cattle killed, while the land itself lay idle. A leading gubernatorial candidate complimented the San Leandro settlers and urged them to stay put until the Land Commission awarded a favorable decision. An aspiring local assembly candidate, who laughingly boasted of once shooting a "Spanish cow" for "trespassing," promised, if elected, to introduce for the settlers' relief a "fence act," an act preventing cattle from drinking at certain streams, and still another act compelling the old claimants—"semi-barbarians," he called them—to pay immediately for settlers' improvements. If they refused to pay, his law would eject them when their titles were confirmed and permit settlers to take possession.

Nobody in California five years earlier seems to have anticipated this sort of social, political, and legal conflict. The Treaty of Guadalupe Hidalgo of 1848 had optimistically promised that the Californians would be "admitted . . . to the enjoyment of all the rights of the United States according to the principles of the Constitution; and . . . shall be maintained and protected in the free enjoyment of their liberty and property." An early draft of the treaty had spelled out the provision on the California land titles, but for extraneous reasons the provision was later dropped. Yet both signatories implied that the deletion in no way compromised the Californians' rights. Secretary of State James Buchanan generously amplified this point, asserting that "if no stipulation whatever were contained in the Treaty to secure to the Mexican inhabitants and all others protection in the free enjoyment of their liberty, property and . . . religion . . . these would be amply guaranteed by the Constitution and laws of the United States. These invaluable blessings, under our form of government, do not result from Treaty stipulations, but from the very nature and character of our institutions." The spirit, if not the letter, of the document promised full protection; its main fault thus was vagueness rather than prejudice against the Californians.

But, if the Treaty of Guadalupe Hidalgo itself did not create the land-tenure trouble of 1853, the Land Law of 1851 was more culpable. Of course, the originator of that act, Senator William Gwin, renounced all intention of harming the "happy and contented race" of Californians who faced a "prosperous and glorious" future; his bill would not cause them to feel "either distressed, oppressed or frightened." Yet in it he proposed a fine-toothed combing of all the titles without exception, for he believed them to be largely inchoate and fraudulent—or so he said. The other California senator, John C. Frémont, believed that the defeat of Gwin's bill was of "vital importance to the security of our property"—that is, of the property of the landed class—for he owned 44,000-acre gold-rich Rancho Mariposa. He discreetly kept his seat as an interested party, however, and let his father-in-law, Senator Thomas Hart Benton, take up the cudgels in behalf of the grantees.

Benton thundered that Gwin's bill was "the most abominable attempt at legislation that has ever appeared in a civilized nation"; it would force the Californians into costly litigation and compel them to divide, sell, or simply give away parcels to pay their lawyers. They would arise in bloody insurrection and possibly assassinate Gwin himself. The Missouri senator presented an alternative bill, based on the premise that the present grants were generally sound. Let the law substantiate all the claims in one grand sweep, he proposed, and afterward let the challengers file suits in local courts to question the soundness of each individual holding. Gwin ignored Benton's first charge and said of the second that if any Californian killed him, Benton would have to bear the blame for having voiced such incendiary thoughts on the Senate floor.

Gwin's bill passed handily. As Senator Henry Clay declared in its behalf, while Californians deserved some consideration in the matter of land, the new "enterprising [Yankee] citizens" of the West deserved more. As Gwin later admitted, what he had really sought in 1851 was an act to encourage his fellow Yankees to "homestead" directly on the land of the old claimants and thereby force the latter to pack up and relocate on public land. Had his modest proposal been enacted into law, the acres beyond the fence at San Leandro would have been occupied instead of withdrawn from entry—by Yankees. Yet the present act was a good start in the direction he eventually hoped to go.

In brief, the Land Law of 1851 established a three-man commission, the

Board of Land Commissioners, to sit in San Francisco for two years (a period later extended) and weigh the proofs of all the titleholders who chose to come before it. Should the claimants or the government dispute the board's rulings, they could appeal to the district court and all the way to the United States Supreme Court. Both rejected and unclaimed land would revert to the public domain and could be seized by settlers. The board's function was to weed out the valid titles as defined by Spanish and Mexican law, the provisions of the Treaty of Guadalupe Hidalgo, the principles of equity, and the precedents of the United States Supreme Court.

The resulting disturbances differed in kind and order of magnitude from those Benton had predicted. He had not envisioned the squatterism, the waste of land, or the bodily attack on the Californians. Moreover, their expected uprising simply did not materialize. The real aggressors were not Benton, Gwin, or the Californians, but the Yankee Argonauts bursting with explosive energies. Tired of grubbing for gold, desiring to possess more nourishing soil, and feeling the weight of history on their side, they tried to adjust the land question swiftly and drastically. In fact, the Yankees' land hunger far outran the bounds of the Land Law.

Preliminary reports in 1849 showed great inequities in the land-tenure system. An estimated two hundred California families owned 14 million acres in parcels of from 1 to 11 leagues (nearly 4,500 acres to the league). This, cried the Yankee, was simply unfair. Many of the titles reportedly overlapped, or melted together in bewildering confusion; some had dubious legality. Governor Pico, it was rumored, had dreamed up some eighty new grants *after* the American occupation and had doled them out to his "worthless cronies"; certainly, all such grants must be retracted at once. The newly arrived Yankee argued that real estate in California, a province wrung from the enemy by blood, was formerly cheap; that "we [Americans] have actually made the land of its present value." If rancheros deserved recompense for their acreage—and that was doubtful—then let them get only the prices current before July, 1846.

According to the traditions of humid-area agriculture in Anglo-America, ranchers—by comparison with farmers—generally stood accused of using land uneconomically. California provided an object lesson of this sort. While "idly living on a revenue" the rancheros were wasting "rich pasture land for unchecked herds." This situation could be remedied only by yeomen. Thus, with unfailing regularity, public spokesmen began intoning praises to the "hearty and industrious" farmers; the "hardy immigrants . . . the industrious settlers"; "the hardy and industrious settlers"; "the hardy and industrious hand which . . . turns the rich sod with the ploughshare";

"the sturdy New Englander, who with his family leaves the home of his childhood and goes into the wild woods of the far west or on to her unbroken prairies and builds himself up a new home among the haunts of the deer and the buffalo."

However inappropriate for arid California, this poetic imagery served the purpose of evoking tradition, especially the freeholder tradition. It also advanced the Jacksonian idea that a few men of "immoderate wealth" and "special privilege" must not interfere with the equality of opportunity. In all fairness to the more well-intentioned squatters, it must be said that they probably did not mean to turn the Californians out into the cold. They proposed to let the rancheros keep as much land as an ordinary farmer—a quarter section—but to take away the "excess." While relinquishing their luxuries, the rancheros could learn to share the "modest but respectable comforts" of the farmer; let them "look for their future advancement through the enterprise of their American fellow-citizen," one newspaper advised. Perhaps they could join agricultural societies and learn to "ply the sledge" themselves.

To supplement the Land Law, which was only a beginning, the settlers wanted specific agrarian reforms; above all, they wanted protection for newcomers who hewed out farms on apparently unused private ranchos. To this end the settlers sought enactment of two laws: First, a law guaranteeing the right of occupancy, that is, permission to enter upon and improve "vacant" land with the guarantee of recovering the value of improvements from the titleholder should the court rule for the latter; second, a law of preemption, that is, a guarantee of the option to buy the land they had improved, should the courts reject the original claim, and to buy it at a minimum price (say, $1.25 an acre) before it went up for public auction. "Rights that had been . . . generally recognized elsewhere would," the American immigrants felt, "surely be granted in California by state and federal legislation."

As it happened, Congress and the state legislature failed to satisfy the squatters; even the Land Law seemed inadequate. For a time the squatters actually demanded abolition of the Land Commission for its "dilatory behavior." Neither Gwin in Congress, John Bigler in the state house, nor the hosts of sympathetic local officials seemed to accomplish quite enough for them. A state preemption law did pass the legislature in April, 1852, permitting a settler to make $200 worth of improvements and then absent himself for a while without losing his presumed rights. (This explains the ghostly aspect of the landscape near San Leandro in the fall of 1853.) Gwin, moreover, in March, 1853, secured two encouraging congressional measures giving preemption to settlers on unsurveyed land and on land whose titles the United States Supreme Court might invalidate later. Yet, despite these improvements, the absence of more immediate and more generous laws distressed the squatters and provoked excessive litigation and direct action, including violence. . . .

The ranchero never understood, much less accepted, the gringo's concept of land tenure. The Land Law, preemption and occupancy rights, and the "jungle-thickets" of land litigation made him not only violently angry but also mystified him. Even if he did comprehend the basic logic of owning land for speculative purposes or for family farming, the seeming heartlessness of the speculators and yeomen repelled him. Indeed, the more sanguine Californians had hoped to rent or to sell some land, raise cattle and crops on the remainder, and live according to custom—in a symbiotic relationship with the settlers. The relative peace and prosperity on the ranchos from 1848 to 1851 had reinforced such hopes; even the most pessimistic and farseeing Californians had not anticipated the wholesale land trouble after 1851.

The Californians felt sure they could prove their equity if given half a chance. Even when they realized that the Yankee demanded solid, "gold-plated" documentary proof of ownership, which they had either never possessed or had misplaced or lost, the Californios nevertheless still banked on "common knowledge." Had not most of them earned their property through hard labor as soldiers and colonists? Salvador Vallejo, for one, dared any Yankees to say that he had not won his property fairly; and he proudly noted that none of them did. Were not herds and homes sound enough proofs of tenure? Was it justice that a man lose his patrimony because he lacked some papers?

As for the accusation that their land was vaguely defined, they agreed. Undeniably, most ranchos overlapped or were bounded by lines ambling indefinitely from perhaps a bullock's skull to a fork in a cow path, then to a brush hut and on to a sycamore, to end at a hatchet-blazed stump. But then, in the early days no other boundaries had been necessary, and with a little patience most vagaries could be adjusted. What the Yankee had to understand was that California had been a wilderness, and that when colonists open a wilderness, judicial niceties hardly matter. What did matter was that men raise cattle and serve their king, God, and country, and this the Californios felt they had done.

As to the charge of fraud, the Californios avoided coming down to cases but retorted that, since land originally had been plentiful and easy to come by, no man had needed to forge papers or to lie to get his title, and few men had done so; the rancheros had executed all legal steps in "simplicity and good faith.'' Although few Californios held a brief for Pio Pico, they refused flatly to agree that his eleventh-hour grants were illegal, since he had still been the rightful governor of California when he drew them up. But even if the Pico grants were questionable, how could the Yankees begin to doubt the legitimacy of solid old grants, such as that of the Peraltas, which went back twenty or more years and which any fool could plainly see were sound? Insofar as they admitted to swearing falsely in court, the Californios claimed that they used this Yankee trick only to defend otherwise legitimate claims, and only in desperation. If the ''squatter courts'' would accept none but the ironclad titles, what else could Californios do but ''doctor'' the record a little?

The Californians generally took an equally dim view of the personnel and the procedures of the land courts. The judges, the juries, and the ''forensic judicature'' of the courts were bad enough. Even worse, though, were the lawyers, who customarily picked at trivia, intimidated witnesses, flattered the jury, and even harangued the audience with patriotic speeches when they ran out of legitimate arguments. Land-law attorneys, in particular, seemed to give the lie to the professed beauties of Yankee justice.

Nevertheless, since most Californians scarcely understood English, much less the technical language of the courts, they had to depend greatly on their attorneys, whom they usually paid in land itself, and only rarely in cash. Sad to say, of the fifty or so attorneys who specialized in claim law in the 1850's, most were shysters who lacked not only honesty but also knowledge and experience. The names of William Carey Jones, Elisha Oscar Crosby, Henry W. Halleck, Henry Hittell, and Joseph Lancaster Brent nearly exhaust the list of worthy counsels. These few men pleaded for moderation. They wanted a legal compromise between the rights of the grantees and those of the settlers, not so much as spokesmen for an oppressed ethnic minority but as defenders of a Whiggish social philosophy. Since most of these honest lawyers owned land themselves, they crusaded with conviction for the defense of established property rights against upstart adventurers and scheming politicians. Their briefs, pamphlets, and articles articulated the only public defense the ruling class ever obtained in its time. . . .

The total wealth devoured by lawyers and swept away by the raps of the gavel in judicial chambers is hard to judge. Benton's estimate of one-third of the rancheros' land runs too high; Professor Gates's figure of 5 or 10 percent seems too low; Theodore Hittell's projection of two-fifths to one-fourth probably comes closer to the truth.

The Board of Land Commissioners itself generally was fair, but its entire operation, from January, 1852, until March, 1856, took far too long and produced eccentric decisions. Owing to its members' lack of fluency in Spanish, incompetency in Mexican law, and vulnerability to lawyers who dealt in technicalities alone, the board never discovered an equitable rule of thumb for measuring usufructuary interest.

The very act under which the board operated prevented an equitable outcome. The Land Law rested on a legal fiction, according to which the California titles were assumed to be so utterly confusing that only judges deliberating in Olympian detachment could distinguish valid from false claims. Actually, at a week's notice, dozens of trustworthy men of all nationalities—Thomas Larkin, Abel Stearns, William E. Hartnell, Pablo de la Guerra—could have drawn up lists and produced sketches of the best-known ranchos in their communities and told which were sound and which were not. Such pragmatic information, based on the "honesty and efficiency of average business clerks," would have produced results quicker and no less sound than those of the Land Commission.

The Land Law prolonged an agony when speed was of the essence. As time dragged on, the gentry sustained outside the chamber of the Land Commission losses that were much more damaging than anything that went on inside. Ultimately, the Land Law did not cripple them half as much as the adventurism that accompanied the legal proceedings.

The Californians had to engage in relentless backyard guerrilla warfare with settlers bent on outright confiscation. At first the settlers would encroach only on the outskirts of an estate, often taking up uninhabited land in good faith and paying rent for it, even though they refused to buy it. The first waves of settlers were quite tractable, but with each passing week in 1852 the number of settlers increased, and their field of battle grew wider and their mood more grim. Prospective farmers first headed for the green and fertile ranchos such as San Antonio, Napa, and Petaluma. Entrepreneurs could easily calculate from boats plying San Francisco Bay which points of land, inlets, and river outlets on these properties might make the best trading ports; they staked out their claims accordingly. The Peralta's Rancho San Antonio had the special advantage of fertile and naturally irrigated soil, thick stands of timber, and a strategic location directly east of San Francisco. Vallejo's Petaluma, besides its orchardlike appearance and proximity to the port city, was a proposed site of the state capital.

Bay-region settlers quit paying rent as soon as the Land Law took effect, on grounds that nobody owned the land. Initially, if a ranchero claimed 12 square leagues, they left him a sanctuary of 4 leagues and nibbled at the remaining 8, each squatter staking out 160 acres. In addition, they appropriated the rancheros' goods and crops for their own use or sold them in

San Francisco. The Peralta squatters cut and milled orchard trees and took cattle to slaughter pens in an altogether businesslike fashion. Later they invaded the last 4 leagues, designated 160-acre parcels to the owner and his sons, and thus made yeomen out of ranchers. As though to emphasize their muscular reforms, they burned the Californians' crops, shot stray cattle, chased off vaqueros, tore down or occupied outlying buildings, blocked off gates, and fenced in access routes. Now and again, to show their "magnanimity," squatters leased range space to the claimants. But some rancheros could not fetch drinking water and firewood or hold a rodeo without a fight. Several Californios, like Señor Peña's son who went out to seed his father's field, and the thirty-year-old José Suñol, were killed. One sheriff died attempting to restore order.

Meanwhile, mushrooming settlers' leagues institutionalized the breakup of the ranchos. The leagues sometimes hired professional squatters who used strong-arm methods on legitimate settlers as well as on claimants. After the Californios had fled in fear, land jobbers bought up and consolidated squatter claims. Intimidation often included third-party suits—suits supplementary to those submitted by claimants against the government. League attorneys produced numerous writs, injunctions, and counterclaims in the lower courts, sometimes valid but more often "smelling rankly of injustice and determined robbery." In this way adventurers hoped to win a legal draw by some technicality, even if the courts confirmed the original titles.

When the squatters on Rancho San Antonio finally blocked off the very doorways to the Peralta homes, the old clan had to move from land it had occupied since the Spanish days. Salvador Vallejo also fled into exile, although he managed to salvage some cash. By selling some of his cattle, he paid his lawyers $80,000 to defend Napa. Although they secured him a favorable verdict before the Land Commission, the government's appeal to the district court gave the settlers courage to move into the remaining 4 leagues of the ranch. But, when they kept burning his crops, Salvador reached the limit of his patience: he sold his last 4 leagues and his home for a "paltry" $160,000 and moved to San Francisco. His brother Mariano, although similarly besieged, stood fast pending court action.

By 1853, every rancho within a day's march of San Francisco Bay had its contingent of uninhibited nonpaying guests, and within the next three years ranchos in all seven northern counties—Sonoma, Napa, Solano, Contra Costa, Santa Clara, Santa Cruz, and Monterey—were to experience at least some of the typical settlers' agitation. For all the hullabaloo about "hearty settlers," however, yeomen did precious little farming in northern California in the early 1850's. Even the more honest settlers were unwilling to risk putting in fences, crops, and homes only to be ejected on short notice, or to be ordered to pay some as yet unstipulated price for land.

Probably even more pernicious than the squatters were the lawyers and adventurers who outsmarted the Californians while posing as their benefactors. Unlike the "Hallecks" of their days, they used any legal dodge to avail themselves of land and welcomed the Land Law as a smoke screen. Through friendly conversation and paperwork with the rancheros they sometimes accomplished more than a legion of armed squatters sniping from behind trees.

For all his suspicion of gringos, the typical Californian was intrigued by their worldly airs and freely opened his door to them. This naïveté took its toll, however. Swindlers hired on as secretaries, managers, or lawyers and ensnared the rancheros in "sure-fire" business deals. One smooth-talking lawyer, Horace Carpentier, and two of his associates, Edson Adams and James Moon, ingeniously divested the Peralta family of its 19,000-acre Rancho San Antonio, with an estimated worth of $3 million. Not content to stake out quarter sections, slaughter cattle, fell orchard trees, and otherwise harass the titleholder, Carpentier aimed for bigger stakes: control over the entire waterfront and the community it served. He craftily gained control over the settlers' league while at the same time acting as the Peraltas' "benefactor." He appeared in the family casts with a cross dangling from his neck, talked of religion, and unrolled legal papers that would "make the family rich." Happily for him, Vicente Peralta was going mad, but he was still rational enough to think he needed a manager for the purpose of leasing, selling, codeveloping, and defending the title in the courts. At one point Carpentier drew up for Peralta's signature a "lease" that later turned out to be a mortgage *against* the signer. When the don refused to pay, Carpentier bought the property he wanted at a sheriff's sale.

Carpentier's shrewd personal accession of some of the most valuable real estate on the eastern shore irked many members of the settlers' league. Nonetheless, he platted on Rancho San Antonio the town of Oakland, of which he became the first mayor, incidentally promising his constituents to stamp out bear-baiting and bullfighting which "belong to a people and a generation that are past." With his associates installed as aldermen, he made the town his private bailiwick. The Peraltas, meanwhile, started legal action to recover their land and were still doing so as late as 1910. From Oakland's founding fathers they got little more than a street named after them.

Beside legal and financial counsel, a benefactor could play other roles—even that of husband: he need only seek out an estate held by a widow. More than likely the *señora* was entangled in a web of tax liens, litigation, debts, and ranching problems which threatened to destroy her home—a prospect that made her vulnerable. As a result, distaff property that remained intact after a few years of the Yankee régime was a rarity. . . .

The activity of Henry Miller, California's greatest land and cattle baron, illustrates yet a third method of gobbling up rancho land. The German-born butcher made his start by buying San Joaquin Valley cattle and bringing them to San Francisco. He soon branched out into the land business, however, in the hope of securing good sites for resting, watering, and fattening his herds along a trail that stretched from Santa Rita through Pacheco Pass and Gilroy all the way to San Francisco. Sometimes he rented grazing land; more often he used the technique of buying into a rancho that had several owners, retaining joint possession for a time, and then gradually easing out the co-owners or demanding a partition. The trick was to pay his associates no profits from the cattle trade and yet use all their land. Eventually, Miller and a partner of his named Charles Lux acquired all or substantial parts of fifteen northern Spanish-Mexican ranchos. These holdings constituted the core of the Miller and Lux empire, which eventually stretched it mosaic fashion from the Oregon to the Mexican border.

A fourth and altogether painless method of acquiring rancho land in California was through moneylending. The rancheros wanted nothing more desperately than cash to enable them to pay their legal fees and taxes and still live grandly, and they would almost certainly forfeit land rather than pay their debts. By foreclosing a mortgage, a moneylender might accomplish his end more painlessly than hosts of squatters and lawyers.

The export of gold from California, and certain other economic factors as yet badly understood, made cash scarce and capital dear. While titles lay in the "purgatory" of the Land Law, they had little worth as collateral and were good only for short-term, high-interest loans, with rates compounded monthly or even weekly. One claimant who needed cash for taxes and lawyers' fees was so hemmed in by squatters in 1853 that he could no longer raise and sell cattle and had to take a $10,000 mortgage payable at 10 percent monthly; *weekly* interest of 12 percent on loans and of 3 percent on mortgages was common in the 1850's. Furthermore, any ranchero planning to borrow money normally had his compadres underwrite his note. When the note went unpaid, cosigners whose own finances were relatively sound were sucked into the vortex of debt. In Los Angeles county, Andrés and Pio Pico had involved so many of their friends that, when they themselves defaulted, they caused the severance of thousands of acres of rancho land. . . .

Throughout northern California, scores of estates changed hands in the modes just described. The most tragic struggle for land, however, the one that distorted all the usual tendencies until it assumed the dimensions of a Spanish tragedy, involved the Berreyesa family. The scene of the battle was Rancho Milpitas, a green sward near San Jose where the bay divides the land. Yankee squatters began coming there in numbers in 1852. Like Vicente Peralta, Nicolás Berreyesa was going mad; the wartime deaths of his nephews and brother had undermined his stability. Now, as Horace Carpentier had done to Peralta, a cunning character named James Jakes took advantage of Nicolás Berreyesa's weakness. Jakes convinced the don and his three sons to respond to the Land Law by emulating the settlers and squatting on their own land. He even obligingly hired a surveyor to officially mark off one plot for each Berreyesa family. This accomplished, Jakes promptly claimed the vacated property, including Don Nicolás adobe. Berreyesa sued to get it back but lost his case and had to pay $500 court costs. The pathetically deranged man thereupon sent protest letters to Governor Alvarado, believing that the governor still had some power in these matters.

The neighboring rancho belonging to the Alviso family also was at the mercy of a gringo "benefactor." This man, a butcher by trade, was engaged in pleading the title to the Alviso property before the Land Commission. He not only succeeded in confirming that title, but his measurements conveniently swallowed up a valuable piece of Berreyesa land, including buildings and crops. Don Nicolás filed a third-party suit but lost it. In this way, the butcher-lawyer systematically created a private fortune and was elected to the legislature.

This by no means ended the troubles of the Berreyesa family. Nemasio Berreyesa was having equal difficulty substantiating a title to the New Almadén quicksilver mine. One night masked raiders seized him, purportedly on a charge of murder, and hanged him from an oak near San Jose. Nemasio had not been the murdering kind, and the Berreyesas maintained that rival claimants hanged him simply to remove him from the scene. Two other Berreyesas were lynched, one in 1854 and the other in 1857. Furthermore, lawyers representing Don Nicolás before the United States Supreme Court disappeared in Washington along with irreplaceable documents, whereupon the don himself burned other papers in an insane rage. A year later, rival claimants ordered the family evicted from Milpitas. Two of Don Nicolás' sons who barricaded themselves against the town marshal were bodily ejected. They rented a home from the widow Alviso, but when she remarried, her Sonoran husband ejected the brothers.

That was not all, however. Three other Berreyesa brothers were bedridden with measles when a squatter deliberately grazed his cattle on their newly seeded fields, thus driving the men from their sickbeds to save their crops. The family's congenital weakness now caught up with them: all three became insane. One of them ran into the hills and nearly died of exposure, and another succumbed shortly thereafter in an asylum. In lucid moments the old man, brooding over the incredible tragedies that had befallen his kin since the Bear Flag Rebellion, begged the remainder of his dear ones to flee to Mexico while time permitted. They refused, however, in faint hope of a favorable decision in district court. In 1869, District Judge Ogden Hoffman ruled against them, although partly on the grounds that Nicolás had squatted on his own property. In 1873 the don died.

Three years later, the United States Supreme Court upheld Judge Hoffman's decision, and the seventy members of the once-powerful Berreyesa family, now completely landless and virtually penniless, threw themselves at the mercy of the San Jose town government and begged some small plot as a homesite. Concluding the saddest saga of all, Antonio Berreyesa estimated that of all the old families, his was the "one which most justly complained of the bad faith of the adventurers and squatters and of the treachery of American lawyers."

In the north of California, then, the basis of landownership had changed drastically by 1856. Through armed struggle, legislation, litigation, financial manipulation, outright purchase, and innumerable other tactics, Yankees had obtained a good deal of interest in the land. The transfer of property destroyed the irenic vision provided by the Treaty of Guadalupe Hidalgo, which guaranteed the Californios the "free enjoyment of their liberty and property"—an obligation that did not worry many Yankees.

In the eyes of the Californios, on the other hand, the results of the land transfers amounted to something akin to social revolution. Whom did they blame? Doubtless each victim had his own answer, but it is noteworthy that many of them spoke of the land settlement as a massive betrayal. They charged the Mexican government with having sold them in 1848 as a "shepherd turns over his flock to a purchaser," and the gringo buyer with having led them to slaughter. Bitterly they alluded to the biblical tale of Joseph and his brothers; among Mexicans they were "Our Brothers Who Were Sold."

2. CHIEF JOSÉ PACHECO

Letter to General George Wright*

Fort Trion, April 16, 1864

To his Excellency General Wright—My Dear General:

I am an Indian, and Chief of the Kern river Indians; my father was a great Chief, and owned all the land on Kern river from the Lakes to the tops of the big mountains, until the white man came to dig for gold. The miners laid waste our lands and destroyed our means of living. My people did not know how to work, and some of my best warriors became discontented and went over the mountains and joined the Owens river Indians to fight the white man. I am a friend to the whites—I think their ways are the best; but I could not make my people think so. I made me a little farm on the south branch of the Kern river, above Keysville, where I lived very happy with my wife and children. I planted potatoes, corn, wheat, squashes, enough for myself and some to sell to the miners. I also had two horses and four cows. Last Summer, when I had got my farm planted and watered, Colonel Evans and Captain McLaughlin came to my house and told me that I must go with them to Owens river to act as guide and interpreter. I did not wish to go on this expedition. I was much better contented to remain on my farm with my family. They told me that I should have fifty dollars per month as long as I would stay with them, and I concluded to go. I was once before all over that country with Captain Davidson of the 1st Dragoons, and was promptly paid for my services in cash. I left my farm without any one to take care of it, and getting a little money from the officers to leave with my children, I went with them to Owens river, and after a hard Summer's work, building a fort and fighting the Indians there, they were induced to give themselves up as prisoners, with the promise that they should be provided with food and clothing and protected from any further violence. They were no sooner in the power of the soldiers, however, than I was required to point out the Kern river Indians who had been engaged in the war, and they were all (thirty-four in number) immediately taken outside the camp and shot and sabered by the soldiers. The Owens river Indians, numbering about 900, were carried to Fort Tejon, where a small portion of them still remain. While in charge of the soldiers they were well fed, but since they have been turned over to the

*Chief José Pacheco to General George Wright, San Francisco *Evening Bulletin,* April 27, 1864.

agents here they have had very little to eat except acorns and such roots and game as they could procure themselves. Some of the children used to come about the fort and get what the soldiers had left when they were done eating, but now there is an order against it, and a sentry posted to keep them away; and what is still worse, the acorns are all gone, and the game is very scarce and hard to be got, and there is little else to eat than tule roots and a little clover, which you must know is very poor living. They have had no clothing except about 100 very poor blankets and a little calico, which was distributed soon after they were brought to the fort. They are nearly naked and have had hard work to keep warm this cold Winter. I have tried hard to keep the Indians here, and told them that they would be shot if they ran away, but they are discontented, and nearly every day some of them leave without my knowing it, and if they are not better cared for I think they will all be gone in less than two months. We are willing to work if we had anything to do, and need not be an expense to the Government. We do not want to go to war, because we know that you have more warriors than we have, and could easily beat us and drive us from our country, even if we were united, which we are not.

I should not have troubled you with this letter dear General, did I not think that the agents here had wronged us. You and our Great Father at Washington do not know how bad we fare, or you would give us food or let us go back to our own lands where we can get plenty of fish and game. I do not think we get the provisions and clothing intended for us by our Great Father; the agents keep it from us, and sell it to make themselves rich, while we and our children are very poor, and hungry and naked.

I will now tell you more about myself. When Colonel Evans, Major O'Neal and Captain McLaughlin was here, they all told me that I should be paid for my services, and they also permitted me to draw provisions for myself and family, and Captain McLaughlin paid me $185 in cash; but since he left I have received no food or money from the officers here (it being about three months), and my money is all gone. I had a talk with Major Sprague, but he said he could not pay me now, and Captain Smith said he would write to you about it. But I do not know whether he did or did not write, as I have not heard anything more about it. I have now been with the soldiers a little more than thirteen months, and the officers agreed to pay me $50 per month; and besides this I sustained damages on my farm by leaving when I did, in the loss of crops of wheat, corn, potatoes, etc., amounting to $220—as everything was destroyed, no one being left to take care of them.

All I have told you is the truth and I hope you will see about it.

Wentworth was here last week but I could not get a chance to talk with him. He did not call at my house and he was gone before I knew he was going. I do not think he will do anything for the Indians here. He is too proud and likes to make money and don't care anything about us. I have had to borrow a little money from the soldiers to buy bread, but my children often have nothing to eat and I do not know what I shall do unless I am paid. I expect very little from the Agents, and will soon have to go and take care of myself. The Indians will all soon scatter off. I cannot persuade them to stay here much longer. There are only two hundred and fifty seven here now, nearly all squaws and little children.

I have no more to say, but am, very respectfully yours, etc.

JOSÉ PACHECO

3. GENE ROBERTS

Sharecropping Doomed*

ATLANTA, July 15—Keever Suit pulled a pencil stub from the bib of his overalls, totaled the money he had earned as a day laborer during the last week and said it came to "just under $16."

"Where I ought to be is back in the country," said the 44-year-old former sharecropper who has moved to Durham, N.C. from a tobacco farm, "but I can't find me enough crop to tend."

Mr. Suit's employment dilemma has been faced by many of the three million persons who have left Southern farms since 1840. Hundreds of thousands of others will face it within the next decade.

Some farm population experts are now predicting that "virtually all" of the 1.5 million Negroes now in Southern and Border state farms will have to look elsewhere for employment within the next 10 to 25 years.

The prospect of increased migration to cities and towns in both the South and the North is alarming civil rights leaders, who already consider the lack of jobs the chief civil rights problem.

Selz B. Mayo, chairman of the department of rural sociology at North Carolina State College—the University of North Carolina at Raleigh—offers them little encouragement. He expects a major wave of off-farm

*Gene Roberts, "Sharecropping Doomed," New York *Times*, July 19, 1965.

migration within the next five years and predicts that "within 10 years there will not be any Negroes left on Southern farms."

Calvin Beale, head of a farm population analysis section of the Department of Agriculture in Washington, agrees that the Negro farmer will "virtually disappear," but says the process will take 20 to 25 years.

The beginning of the end for the Negro, they both agree, will come with the development of a mechanical tobacco harvester.

Will Slash Man-Hours

This will cut the man-hours involved in tobacco farming by more than half, they say, and will speed the departure of the Negro from the bright-leaf tobacco belt, the last stronghold of the Southern sharecropper.

The belt begins in Virginia and stretches through the Carolinas into Georgia and Florida.

Dr. Francis J. Hassler, head of the department of agricultural engineering at North Carolina State, predicts that the mechanical harvester will be available commercially within the next five years—a semi-mechanical one is already on the market—and will come into widespread use soon after in the bright-leaf belt.

A bulk curing process developed by Dr. Hassler is already coming into use and is cutting about 125 man-hours off the 400 normally required to grow and harvest an acre of tobacco. The mechanical harvester would cut the total man-hours required to "little more than 100," Dr. Hassler says.

Deep South Picture

Mechanical cotton pickers and grain harvesters have "all but erased" the sharecropper in the Deep South, Mr. Beale reports, leaving only about 500,000 Negroes on farms there as day laborers. Most of the million other Negroes on Southern and Border state farms are tobacco sharecroppers and their families.

Sharecropping, which has been widespread in the South since the end of the Civil War, is being replaced by a new system that sociologists are calling owner-renter.

Junius Evans of Freemont, N. C. near the heart of the bright-leaf belt, is typical of the new breed of farmer (almost all of them white because of the capital involved) who own tractors, other mechanized equipment and a small farm and rent additional land to take maximum advantage of the equipment.

A Reasonable Living

Mr. Evans owns a farm with 50 cultivated acres and a Government tobacco allotment of 4.7 acres. He rents enough additional acreage to raise his total commercial crop to 15.7 acres of tobacco, 70 acres of corn and 10 acres of soybeans.

With an average production of 2200 pounds of tobacco an acre and at an average price of 40 cents a pound, Mr. Evans can expect to gross $20,000 from tobacco alone.

"Expenses are heavy," Mr. Evans says, "but you can make a reasonable living."

Before the tractor began coming into wide use 25 years ago, at least three farm families, possibly four, would have worked full time to cultivate the Evans acreage. Now Mr. Evans does it himself with tractors, mechanical grain harvesters and occasional day labor from two families who live on his farm rent free.

Even the day laborers may go when the mechanical tobacco harvester is developed.

Public Works Urged

The Rev. Dr. Martin Luther King Jr., head of the Southern Christian Leadership Conference, sees little hope of stemming the off-farm migration. He believes instead that public works and "other imaginative, job-producing programs are necessary" to aid those leaving the farms.

Another civil rights leader, Bayard Rustin of New York, also sees public works as an answer. "The machine," he says, "has become as great an enemy of the Negro people as segregation and discrimination ever were."

James Farmer, the national director of the Congress of Racial Equality also favors public works but says his organization is studying "the type of collective farm in use in Israel" as one possible way of keeping some of the Negroes on the farm.

Mr. Beale of the Department of Agriculture expects many Negroes, perhaps one family in three, to remain on the farm and commute to jobs in the city.

He says such a trend is already pronounced among whites. Although Southern white farmers and their families have declined from about eight million in 1840 to slightly more than two million, they are continuing to live in rural areas in large numbers.

B. MIGRATION AND DISLOCATION: PHYSICAL AND PSYCHOLOGICAL

Migration has been a central element of American minority life since the late nineteenth century. For Mexicans moving to the United States and for native Americans and Southern Blacks forsaking rural for urban life, the process has involved not only physical disorientation, but also the psychic impact of conflicting life-styles. The enduring problems—especially acute for those migrants who do not speak English—have been how to sustain themselves in a hostile society and at the same time accommodate their traditional mores with those of urban America.

In the first selection Manuel Gamio gives us firsthand accounts of two Mexican immigrants to the United States in the 1920s. Their search for decent jobs and lives was one of unending frustration. Confronted on all sides by prejudice and exploitation, Elías Garza and Nivardo del Río illustrate what life was like for most Mexicans seeking a better life to the north.

Similar hardships faced Southern Blacks who migrated North around the turn of the century. A generation removed from slavery, feeling no strong attachment to the soil, and seeing that the farm had produced few rewards for their parents, many Blacks forsook rural life and traveled northward in search of opportunity. The results of the change were mixed. Though their problems were great and the city was harsh, life in the North, according to Gilbert Osofsky, was still better than what many had left behind.

1. MANUEL GAMIO

The Mexican Immigrant: His Life Story*

ELIA GARZA

Elias Garza is a native of Cuernavaca, Morelos, white.

"My life is a real story, especially here in the United States where they drive one crazy from working so much. They squeeze one here until one is left useless, and then one has to go back to Mexico to be a burden to one's countrymen. But the trouble is that is true not only here but over there also. It

*Manuel Gamio, *The Mexican Immigrant: His Life Story* (Chicago, University of Chicago Press, 1931), pp. 149-59. Reprinted by permission of The University of Chicago Press.

is a favor that we owe Don Porfirio [President Porfirio Díaz] that we were left so ignorant and so slow minded that we have only been fit for rough work. I began to work when I was twelve years old. My mother was a servant and I worked in one of those old mills which ground sugar cane. I took charge of driving the oxen. They called me the driver. This was on the estate of La Piedad, Michoacán. I think that they paid me $0.25 a day and I had to go round and round the mill from the time the sun rose until it set. My mother, as well as I, had to work, because my father died when I was very small. I went on in that way until when I was fifteen or sixteen I planted corn on my own account on shares. The owners gave us the seed, the animals and the land, but it turned out that when the crop was harvested there wasn't anything left for us even if we had worked very hard. That was terrible. Those land-owners were robbers. At that time I heard that there were some good jobs here in the United States and that good money could be made. Some other friends accompanied me and we went first to Mexico City and from there we came to Ciudad Juárez. We then went to El Paso and there we took a *renganche* for Kansas. We worked on the tracks, taking up and laying down the rails, removing the old ties and putting in new, and doing all kinds of hard work. They only paid us $1.50 and exploited us without mercy in the Commissary camp, for they sold us everything very high. Nevertheless as at that time things generally were cheap I managed to make a little money with which I went back to La Piedad to see my mother. She died a little later and this left me very sad. I decided to come back to the United States, and I came to Los Angeles, California. Here I married a Mexican young lady. I went to work in a stone quarry. I placed the dynamite and did other work which took some care. They paid me $1.95 a day but I worked 10 hours. Later I worked at a railroad station. I worked as a riveter, working a pressure gun for riveting. At that work I earned $1.50 a day for nine hours, but it was very hard. My wife died at that time. I then got work in a packing plant. I began by earning $1.25 a day there for nine hours of work and I got to earn $4.00 a day for eight hours work. I learned to skin hogs there and slaughter them also. The work was very hard. Later I was married to a woman from San Antonio, Texas. She was young, beautiful, white, and she had two little children who became my step-children. We went to Mexico together. We boarded ship at San Pedro and from there went to Mazatlán until we got to Michoacán. We saw that things were bad there, for that was in 1912, and the disorders of the revolution had already started; so we came back to the United States by way of Laredo, Texas. In San Antonio we were under contract to go and pick cotton in a camp in the Valley of the Rio Grande. A group of countrymen and my wife and I went to pick. When we arrived at the camp the planter gave us an old hovel which had been used as a chicken house before, to live in, out in the open. I didn't want to live there and told him that if he didn't give us a little house which was a little better we would go. He told us to go, and my wife and I and my children were leaving when the sheriff fell upon us. He took me to the jail and there the planter told them that I wanted to leave without paying him for my passage. He charged me twice the cost of the transportation, and though I tried first not to pay him, and then to pay him what it cost, I couldn't do anything. The authorities would only pay attention to him, and as they were in league with him they told me that if I didn't pay they would take my wife and my little children to work. Then I paid them. From there we went to Dallas, Texas, from where we worked on the tracks as far as El Paso. I kept on at the same work towards Tucson, Arizona, until I got to Los Angeles. I have worked in the packing plants here since then, in cement and other jobs, even as a farm laborer. In spite of it all I have managed to save some money with which I have bought this automobile and some clothes. I have now decided to work in the colony in Mexico and not come back to this country where I have left the best of my youth. I learned a little English here from hearing it so much. I can read and write it, but I don't even like to deal with those *bolillos* for the truth is that they don't like the Mexicans. Even the *pochos* don't like us. I have scarcely been able to stand up for my rights with the little English that I have learned, but I would like to know a lot of English so as to tell them what they are and in order to defend my poor countrymen.

"I am going to tell you what happened to me one day. Coming out of a packing plant in Alhambra where I worked, a Mexican policeman and an American stopped me, saying that I had escaped from I don't know where. I told them that no, that I was coming out from my work. Then the *pocho* policeman gave me a push, and put me in the machine which he had and there began to insult me in English and told me that if I didn't shut up he was going to break my snout. They took me in the police-station and there made me fill my hand and thumbs with ink and put them down on a white paper. After they had examined that they let me go free without doing anything else. Once a poor Mexican bought a bottle of whisky to take to his house to drink it. He had put it in the back pocket of his trousers. That was at night and he was going home. He stopped in front of a work-shop to see some goods when he noticed that a policeman was drawing near. Then he slyly put his hand to his back pocket in order to take the little bottle out and perhaps throw it away when the policeman, without more ado, fired a shot at him and killed him. They didn't do anything to that policeman; he is going about free. And there have been an infinite number of cases like that. I know of others who at work in the factories have lost an arm or a leg, and they haven't been given a thing. What they do is to take away their jobs. That is why we don't like these people.

"I almost am, and almost am not, a Catholic. I remember that when I was very little, over there in Cuernavaca, my mother took me to some exercises of Holy Week and that the priest told all those who were in the Church that they should cry for their sins before Christ there in the temple and they all began to weep and to cry out all that they had done, even my own mother. But I couldn't weep nor did I want to cry out my sins. Since that time I have almost not gone back to the church nor do I pray at home.

"I read few newspapers for they almost don't say anything but lies and one comes out from work so tired that one doesn't even want to read papers of any kind. I have almost never read books; once in a long time I do read books of stories of Mexicans.

"I have always tried to be close to my countrymen and defend them, but there are some who are neither united nor do they want to defend themselves; that is why the Americans look down on us as they do."

NIVARDO DEL RÍO

This man is a *mestizo*, a miner, a native of Chihuahua.

"As my parents were very poor I had no schooling, no education. I got only as far as the third grade, and that was only because we lived in the capital of the state, for in the time of Don Porfirio [Díaz], there were almost no schools and those who lived in the villages and in the rural districts didn't even have that chance. I was only a kid when I had to begin to work. I served first in various homes doing house work. When I had grown some and could say that I was a young man, I went to work in the mines, in the house of an American family. My work wasn't very hard, for although sometimes I worked in the mine I spent most of the time running errands for the lady of the house and doing house work. This family was very good to me and they had me there because they wanted to learn Spanish and in return they taught me English. The lady especially took pains to teach me the names of things in English. She even taught me the alphabet and I could almost read in English. I worked a good many years at the mine until at last I got tired, and as I always had been ambitious and wanted to work for myself, I managed to set up a little store in Chihuahua. There I managed to make a little money and was getting along well when the revolution came. Then business began to go to pieces and one began to lose money rather than to make it. I had to join the revolution with Villa because they took me almost by main force, but by good luck I was put in the supply camp so that I hardly ever had to fight. Of course I went around armed with a pistol so that I would be respected. All that I had to do was to see that the supplies were properly distributed. So I went around with the forces of Villa from place to place, and it was at that time that the opportunity offered itself to go to the United States. Ever since then I haven't liked the system of things in this country. I came with a colonel; we went to Chicago, to New York, Minneapolis, St. Louis and other places buying trucks, munitions and equipment for Villa's army. As the colonel didn't know more than just a few words of English, I practically served him as an interpreter, for I remembered what the American family had taught me at the mine. I did have a good time when traveling through the country and spending quite a little money. But as I have always been observant, I kept observing how they worked and how they lived here, and it all disgusted me. The truth is that we hate these people and they hate us and that is why we are different. We have different languages, don't understand each other and shan't, no matter how much we may wish to. It doesn't matter how much good will there is, for at bottom we hate each other. At least I feel dislike towards everything that is American and know that they, although they may not say so, also dislike us. That about the governments, that they are friends, that they are sister nations and the rest, is nothing but lies. But it is well that way, because in that way they have peace and get along as nations. But they know well enough that they dislike each other. The Americans want to take everything that we have and we won't let them. Therefore the governments say that they treat everything diplomatically and in that they are wise. As I am a man of some ambitions I have worked very hard, but either hard luck or my lack of brains has carried me to nothing but failure. I have made a fortune three times and three times have I lost it, so that it seems that I shall never be independent. I shall always have to be working for others and that is what I most hate, having to be a slave. I sacrifice more now that I am married and have two adopted children. They are nephews of my wife and I have to work for their schooling so that they can go to school. They have progressed a great deal according to what we have been told by the "Palmore" school of El Paso—which is where they are. My wife is from Chihuahua. We were married there some years ago but we haven't had a single child. We have extra obligations with these adopted children, because if they don't have anyone to help them now when they grow up they could say that they hadn't learned anything because they had had no father and I don't want them to say that about me. They are sons of a colonel who died in the revolution. This colonel was married to the sister of my wife; that is how they are her nephews. The mother also died, and they were left to us, so that we are forced to bring them up, and that is why we are here. Before coming here and a little before we were married and when I failed for the third time, I had a saloon. At first there was a lot of business but then the business began to fail; so that I decided that it was better to come to the United States. This was during the crisis of 1921 and 1922. By 1923 when the situation had become unbearable I told my wife that we should come to Los Angeles or any other place in the United States in order to look for work at anything and thus earn our livelihood. Coming in search for work, I expected to go to Los Angeles, California, for I had been told that there was work there. I also had many friends there and I expected that they would help me in case of need. But in Torreón I met a friend who was the agent who sold me the beer for the saloon and he asked me where I was going. When I had told him, he said that instead of going to Los Angeles I should go to Miami for he lived there, and he would help me to get work in the mines. As I was looking for work and for security, I came to Miami with my wife and left the children in the school. I only brought one little fellow who has since died. Well, we arrived, and I found my friend who got work for me in the 'Miami' mine. Since then I have been here. The work here is very hard and the most that they pay even to one like me who knows how to work the drills, is $5.00. In order to make a few cents extra I have to kill myself working. And I really mean kill myself. That is why all the *paisanos* get sick with consumption and other diseases even when they don't have an accident, for some break a foot, or a hand or are even killed. Here the work is very different from what it is in Mexico. There the man who is able to get a contract can make as much as $20.00 a day if he is skilled and wants to, but here they have one's capacity so measured that even if one gets a contract one can earn only a few cents more than the usual wages. It is a shame that in Mexico the mines are closed and so much disorder exists. If it wasn't for that I would go back at once and could work with better success. I have thought at times of starting a little store here but it wouldn't work for there wouldn't be any profits. All the miners buy in the company stores and I know by experience that in the grocery business there are no profits except for those who have money enough to buy on a large scale. Those certainly make money. Here in front of my house there lives a man who has a little grocery store. He has supported himself for three years but he only gets by and isn't able to get ahead. That is why I haven't been able to do anything. It is not because I haven't thought about it. On the other hand the way one lives here it might be said that one lives from hand to mouth. These people have one tied down so that it seems as though they did it with the idea of fixing it up so that one can't go. In the house, rent, food, and other little expenses use up everything, so that one can't save even if one wants to. In my case the wages are hardly enough to save a few pennies and pay for the education of the children and at that I kill myself in order to earn something extra. If I confined myself to the small regular wages I might not even have enough to eat because I am always making payments on this thing and that. Around here one doesn't have any security, the police do whatever they want, they beat up everybody. This is what happened to me the other day. I was at my work, being on the shift from seven in the morning to three in the afternoon, and my wife had gone to El Paso to see the boys at the school, and the police came to see us. When I came back from my work the neighbors told me about it and I went to see the police and talked with the sergeant. I asked him at once why they had gone to my house to look for me, and he said that he had been told that there had been a commotion there at one o'clock in the morning. I then told him that if he had been notified of that at that hour he should have gone then and not at one o'clock in the afternoon the next day. Then he told me to shut up. I answered that he had no business going to my house without an order from the proper authorities and that I wouldn't shut up because I had a right to stand up for my rights. He then said that the police didn't lie. I then asked if he could know better than I who lived in my house and I made him see that he should be more careful about the homes of honest working people and should pay more attention to what was going on in the gambling halls of the mining camp. In that way I showed that I knew how to stand up for my rights. I told him that if I had violated any law it was then well that they go to look for me at my house but not when I was at my work. A few days later it so happened that the consul came to my house with a lawyer. They left their automobile there and after a while a police came hollering. The lawyer then came out and told the policeman to be quiet for he had no right to shout that way, for he was going to take his automobile away right away, but that he was going to go to the police headquarters to complain to the sergeant and he was going to tell him about the treatment which the police give the Mexicans, so that it seems as if they were dealing with thieves rather than working people. We went to headquarters, and there the lawyer and the consul told them that the police were many times to blame for having Mexicans kill them because they were the first in offending by their way of treating them so roughly. The major begged the Consul to excuse him and made himself very humble in praising them.

"As to the matter of religion, I have studied practically all of them and I haven't found a one which would convince me. No one has seen God, although I believe in Him, but not in religions. I believe that one should do harm to no one and that is everything. I see that the priests and the Protestants say one thing and another but no one tells the truth for no one is absolutely sure. So that I for that reason say that I don't have any religion. I have read many works of Victor Hugo and of Vargas Vila and of others of which I don't remember the titles, and not even the names of the authors. I do know that Victor Hugo told Vargas Vila that his works would never become classic, as is quite true, for the works of Victor Hugo are read everywhere while those of Vargas Vila are not. I like Victor Hugo the best. Vargas Vila has some things which I like and others which I don't. I believe that in this work one gets stupider and stupider, for the truth is I am even losing my memory. I almost always read *La Prensa* of San Antonio, *El Heraldo de México* of Los Angeles and other papers from Mexico, when I have time, but there are months at a time that I go without reading a thing, for I come from my work very tired and all that I wish is to rest. I haven't changed from what I was in Mexico. I eat according to Mexican style, for my wife makes my food. I only buy my lunch in the restaurants. In everything I am like the Mexicans, that is to say, like they live over there. I don't like anything about this country and I am only waiting until the boys are educated or till things get better to go from this country. The climate here is rather good, for in Chihuahua it gets much colder than it does here. The heat is the most bothersome, especially in those little wooden houses in which both the heat and the cold enter."

2. GILBERT OSOFSKY

"Come Out from Among Them": Negro Migration and Settlement, 1890-1914

The most important factor underlying the establishment of Harlem as a Negro community was the substantial increase of Negro population in New York City in the years 1890-1914. That Harlem became the specific center of Negro settlement was the result of circumstance; that *some* section of the city was destined to become a Negro ghetto was the inevitable consequence of the Negro's migration from the South. This pre-World War I population movement, the advance guard of the Great Migration (as the movement of Negroes during the First World War is generally called), laid the foundations for present-day Negro communities in Chicago and Philadelphia as well.

*Gilbert Osofsky, " 'Come Out from Among Them': Negro Migration and Settlement, 1890-1914," in *Harlem: The Making of a Ghetto*. Copyright © 1966 by Gilbert Osofsky. Reprinted by permission of Harper & Row, Publishers, Inc.

These were the formative years for the development of Negro communities throughout the North.

In spite of the high Negro death rate, the colored population increased by "leaps and bounds" in New York City in the early twentieth century. By 1910 there were 91,709 Negroes in the metropolis, the majority southern-born: "A Census of the Negroes in any city of the North," said a speaker at the first organizational meeting of the NAACP in 1909, "would show that the majority of . . . them . . . were more or less recent arrivals from the South." Mary White Ovington, in her excellent study *Half A Man: The Status of the Negro in New York,* found that most of the Negro neighborhoods were populated by southerners. Only 14,309 of the 60,534 Negroes in Manhattan in 1910 were born in New York State. The majority of the others (61 per cent) came from other states, practically all in the South. Virginia, North Carolina, South Carolina, Georgia and Florida, in perfect geographical order, were the major southern sources of New York's migrant population.

Contemporaries in both the North and South, Negro and white, were aware of this movement. Unable to foresee that the First World War would bring even larger numbers of Negroes northward, they were staggered by the myriad problems this migration created for them: "There are more Southern Negroes in the North and West than original Northern ones, and they are coming all . . . the time," wrote a Negro journalist in 1913. "What to do with the needy and those who fall by the wayside is becoming a problem of the greatest magnitude. . . ." Historians, impressed by the enormity of changes that occurred at the time of the "Great War," have tended to overlook or underestimate the significance of the pre-World War I migration of Negroes to northern cities. . . .

There were as many individual and varied reasons for migration as there were people who moved. The less respectable as well as the educated came north. Negroes themselves characterized some as a "hoodlum element," "rovers," "wanderers," "vagrants," "criminals in search of a sporting life." "Many of the worthless people of the race are making their way northward," said *The New York Age* in an editorial. Some wayward husbands—the "travelin' men" of Negro folk songs—abandoned their families and responsibilities and sought the anonymity of a city: "I was raised in the country, I been there all my life/ Lord I had to run off and leave my children and my wife."

Others came north on excursion trains to get a look at the big city and never returned. One man "heard so much of this town," he said, "that he decided to look it over.'' Another stated that he ''didn't want to remain in one little place all my days. I wanted to get out and see something of the world.'' Migratory laborers found work on New Jersey, Pennsylvania and New York farms every spring and summer. Some traveled back and forth each year; others simply went to the nearest city when winter came. ''Tired of the South,'' ''Wanted to make a change,'' ''Ran away from home,'' were some of the reasons advanced by Negroes for coming north. All received nominally higher wages in the North, and this was certainly a great attraction. One woman who came to New York City from Virginia, for example, said she was ''willing to live anywhere, if the wages were good.''

There were also those who fled social proscription and violence in the South. C. Vann Woodward has described the ''Capitulation to Racism'' that characterized the southern attitude toward the Negro from the late 1880's through the early twentieth century. Vast numbers of Jim Crow laws were passed in these years as the forces which held virulent southern racism in check suddenly crumbled. The conservative, *noblesse oblige* attitude of former Whig leaders (''it is a mark of breeding to treat Negroes with courtesy'') was replaced by a violently racist white supremacy movement; the paternalism of a Wade Hampton was followed by the viciousness of a Ben Tillman (whose racist tirades even embarrassed his southern colleagues). Free rein was given to mass aggressions as all forces joined together in an active program of ''keeping the Negro down.'' The great heresy that proclaimed the Negro capable of attaining equality with the white had to be rooted out at all costs, it was argued. There were more Negroes lynched, burned, tortured and disfranchised in the late eighties, nineties and first decade of the twentieth century than at any other time in our history. The militant Negro Ida B. Wells graphically and sadly described this *Red Record* in 1895. It was not surprising to find that the American Colonization Society, organized in 1817, experienced a long-hoped-for revival in the 1890's, and various other plans to colonize Negroes in Africa were rekindled in these years. ''I used to love what I thought was the grand old flag, and sing with ecstasy about the stars and stripes,'' wrote Negro Bishop Henry McNeal Turner of Georgia, ''but to the Negro in this country today the American flag is a dirty contemptible rag. . . . Hell is an improvement upon the United States when the Negro is involved.'' ''No man hates this Nation more than I do,'' Turner said on another occasion. He looked longingly to Africa as the only possible place of Negro freedom.

Negro leaders and the Negro press continually stressed their belief that migration was primarily a movement away from racism: ''The large cities of the North and West have had a marvelous increase of Afro-American population in the last ten years, and the increase is growing . . . because of the conditions in the Southern States which make for unrest''; ''the terrors of mob wrath.'' When T. Thomas Fortune, William Lewis Bulkley, and North Carolina educator and politician Edward A. Johnson came north, each emphasized he could no longer live under Jim Crow and racial violence. George Henry White said he left North Carolina because he ''couldn't live there and be a man and be treated like a man.'' He believed that thousands of others would follow him. Booker T. Washington told the Board of Trustees of Tuskegee, in 1903, that ''for every lynching that takes place . . . a score of colored people leave . . . for the city.''

In general, however, the migration could best be considered not so much a flight from racial violence, as it was a desire for expanded opportunity. This is best summarized in a phrase commonly used by the migrants themselves—the attempt ''to better my condition.'' People moved away from the South in search of a better and more fulfilling life. A Negro shoemaker came north, for example, because he felt ''choked'' by the ''narrow and petty life'' he was forced to lead in a small Virginia town. To him, the great attraction of New York City was the ''wider scope allowed the Negro.'' One woman who ''never could work . . . in a menial way'' was proud that she could earn a living as an independent seamstress in New York. Moving north, wrote DuBois in 1907, offered ''the possibility of escaping caste at least in its most aggravating personal features. . . . A certain sort of soul, a certain kind of spirit, finds the narrow repression and provincialism of the South simply unbearable.''

> Where I come from
> folks work hard
> all their lives
> until they die
> and never own no part
> of earth nor sky.

The *possibilities* for such movement resulted from two basic changes in American life. One was the overwhelming industrial expansion of the late nineteenth century. The Industrial Revolution created economic opportunities for rural people, Negro and white, and both migrated to industrial and urban centers in the North. For the Negro, hedged about by union restrictions and racial antagonism, employment was usually found in the fringe jobs that an industrial and commercial society creates—as janitors, elevator operators, general laborers of all kinds, longshoremen, servants.

Negro women almost always worked as domestics. During periods of labor disputes, Negroes were commonly found among the strikebreakers.

There was, however, an added factor that influenced Negro migration and distinguished it from the general rural migration to cities. Why, it might be asked, had Negroes not moved in similar numbers in response to industrialization in the 1870's—the period of great social upheaval and dislocation that followed the destruction of slavery? The answer undoubtedly lies in an understanding of the differences between the slave and post-slave generations. The Negroes who came north now were the first descendants of former slaves. They had listened to tales of slavery, gentle and harsh, but had not experienced and lived its blight—the denial of full manhood. To them, "*War, Hell, and Slavery were but childhood tales. . . .*" Their parents and grandparents, psychologically and economically unprepared to enter what contemporaries called the "competition for life," tended to remain as tenants, sharecroppers or laborers on their former plantations or on places similar to them. They continued in freedom to live the only life they had knowledge of. "There were great upheavals in political and labor conditions at the time of emancipation, but there was little shifting in the populations. For the most part, the freedmen stayed on in the states and counties where they had formerly existed as slaves," writes one historian of Negro life. In 1900, practically all southern Negroes continued to work on the land and some 75 per cent remained sharecroppers, tenants and laborers. On one Georgia plantation in 1901, as on others, lived many Negroes who had been slaves there: "I have men," the white owner testified, "who were slaves on the place. . . . They have always lived there and will probably die there, right on the plantation where they were born." "It was predicted [during the Civil War] that the Negroes would leave the . . . fields and fill the towns in case of emancipation," said a southern planter at the turn of the century. "That prediction has not been realized suddenly as we anticipated it would be, but it seems to be approaching."

Those who migrated to the North in the 1890's were a new generation. Many Negroes no longer felt any strong attachment to the soil. They could at least *conceive* of life in a new and different way. For some, the discontented and restless, there was now both the ability and willingness to move. They left a South in which their futures were sealed: "There is absolutely nothing before them on the farm. . . . Working year in and year out with . . . no prospect . . . but to continue until they die." In many rural communities of the South, it was reported in 1907, a "number of youths have expressed their conviction that since their fathers and mothers have accumulated nothing after years on the land, they did not intend to stay on the plantation to repeat the process.'' A leading Republican politician and defender of Negro civil rights, James S. Clarkson, took a trip to the South in the 1890's and ''saw many a grey head . . . talking to the young people . . . encouraging the young people to become content,'' he wrote a Negro confidant. The migrants who came north were aptly described by George Edmund Haynes as ''groping seekers for something better. . . .'' To southerners this seemed to be a different and puzzling kind of Negro—not a people especially educated or skilled, but a group willing to make some change in the traditional patterns of its life. To the stereotype of the docile, irresponsible, immoral, dishonest Negro was now added a new ''racial'' characteristic—''a migratory disposition.'' Philip A. Bruce, Virginia historian, called the ''new generations'' worthless. They ''rarely remain long enough under the supervision of any planter to allow him sufficient time to teach them,'' he wrote. ''Habits of diligence, order, faithfulness''—all the qualities of a good slave—were absent in the ''new generation,'' said another. There exists ''a certain unrest and discontent,'' a white planter commented. ''Under its influence the boys and girls are beginning to drift to the cities.'' To contrast the supposedly ''faithful old darkies'' with ''the new generation, which has become restless, dissatisfied, and worthless'' (and ''migrated from the plantations to the cities'') was a standard and hackneyed statement found throughout the racial literature of the time. . . .

Most southern farmers who testified before the United States Industrial Commission in 1899-1901 expressed similar opinions. They spoke of the differences in attitudes between the freed slave and his children. The ''good old negroes, as we call them . . . negroes about grown before the war,'' ''old-time negroes'' (''before-the-war negroes,'' they were sometimes called), were touted as the best farm workers and tenants. ''The younger ones'' are ''discontented and want to be roaming.'' ''The older class of colored labor,'' repeated a West Virginia farmer, ''men that are pretty well up in years—are a first rate class of labor. The younger class . . . are . . . very trifling. . . .'' The Negro ''is not as steady as he was,'' thought another. ''The South laments to-day the slow, steady disappearance of a certain type of Negro—the faithful, courteous slave of other days, with his dignified . . . humility,'' W. E. B. DuBois commented at the turn of the century. ''He is passing away just as surely as the old type of Southern gentleman is passing. . . .''

Related to the belief of the emergence of a new and different Negro generation was the revival of scientific attempts to prove the Negro a degraded being. During this same period Darwinism invaded the South (as well as the North) to revive the debate over the place of the Negro in the human community. Arguments strikingly similar to the old proslavery diatribes of natural Negro inferiority were dressed up in the new scientific garb and presented to the public by "objective social scientists" who claimed to be uninfluenced by "preconceived ideas." The improvident, dishonest, immoral, lazy, lascivious Negro was shown to be incapable of education: "he is a fungus growth that the white man will totally destroy. . . . The only race that has never made any progress in any respect," more similar in mind to the chimpanzee than to man. The greatest menace and curse to our Anglo-Saxon civilization, some thought, was its pollution with the blood of the "depraved Ethiopian." Aryan supremacy could only be achieved, it was argued, after total separation, by colonization or extermination, of the entire Negro race.

This ideology combined with the reality of Negro migration and encouraged southerners to attempt to replace Negro laborers with European immigrants. The substitution of immigrants for Negroes was an integral part of the philosophy that preached southern progress through industrialization—the New South. It was in these very years that the South attempted to rejuvenate its efforts, first begun in Reconstruction, to attract European immigrants. State immigration bureaus were created and offices established in the principal port cities to direct the newest arrivals to southern farms. Southern emigration agents were even sent abroad. There was more myth than reality in the conception of a New South—a South where factories were to spring up "like stars after twilight." The movement to encourage settlement of immigrants to replace Negro labor was an almost total failure.

This reality presented southerners with a major paradox. The new generation of Negroes seemed unreliable (even inhuman) and yet, at the same time, it was also clearly recognized that the southern economy was largely dependent upon them: "I think the Negro is a necessity in the South as a farm laborer," stated a South Carolinian. "*We have no other. . . .*" "I do not know how the South could live without negro labor," a Georgia plantation owner said. "It is the life of the South; it is the foundation of its prosperity. . . . God pity the day when the negro leaves the South. . . ." "Think twice, before committing the State to a policy which may strip the land of its best . . . laborers," editorialized a North Carolina newspaper opposed to European immigration. In the minds of most southerners, Negroes seemed racially adapted to agricultural life, permanently tied to the soil. To forsake farm life would necessarily lead to their degradation. This was their only "proper calling," their "proper place."

Negro farmers in the South cultivated twice as much acreage as did all the farmers in New England combined. Nearly one-half of all farms under fifty acres in the South Atlantic states and one-fourth of all those between fifty and one hundred were operated by Negroes. Negroes were also the most important farm laborers throughout the South.

If Negroes began leaving the South in great numbers, Senator George F. Hoar of Massachusetts predicted, "there would be a general alarm on the part of the men who now depend on their labor, and they would find themselves pretty earnestly solicited to change their minds." It was the reality of this practical dependence on Negro farm labor that produced a series of laws limiting the free movement of Negro workers and tenants and heavily taxing all labor agents sent south to "entice" them away. From the late 1880's through the first decade of the twentieth century such legislation was passed in Alabama, Arkansas, Florida, Georgia, Kentucky, Mississippi, North Carolina, South Carolina, Louisiana, Tennessee and Virginia. Southern courts generally interpreted these laws for the benefit of the white farm owner, forcing Negro workers to remain on the land. The Department of Justice in 1907, for example, received eighty-three complaints from Negroes protesting what they considered to be their practical peonage. Although the Supreme Court outlawed peonage in 1911, the practice continued through subterfuge for decades. (As late as 1947 the President's Committee on Civil Rights documented a case of forced labor.)

Exaggerated accounts of the destitute conditions of migrants were commonly published in the press and every hint of failure was described as destitution. The high Negro mortality rate in northern cities was presented as absolute proof that the Negro could not live in cold climates: "They will take colds and develop pneumonia and consumption . . . and will die there." The Southern Negro Anti-Exodus Association was founded in Virginia in 1905 to "preach the gospel of contentment to the colored people South of Mason and Dixon's line. . . ." When a labor agent was arrested in Georgia, an editorial in the *Age* said: "If there is one thing the Southern man preaches all the time it is that the young Negro is worthless and is not to be mentioned in the same breath with the older. . . . The young Negro is pictured as worthless and a general nuisance that has been tolerated too long. . . . But as yet no one can be found to deny the cold fact that this agent was arrested to put a stop to the exodus. . . . In spite of all this talk, there is a desire to keep the Negro help in the South."

These reactions were a reflection of a basic dichotomy in southern thought. On the one hand, it was believed that the Negro was worthless, inefficient, untrustworthy, less faithful than the slave. The failure to use improved agricultural machinery and in industrialization in general was often blamed on his ignorance. On the other hand, the Negro was encouraged to remain in the South (and sometimes forced to do so) as the only source of labor available—"the backbone of the South when it comes to labor"; the best labor we could have in the South." With the failure of attempts to attract European immigrants the reliance of the South on Negro farmers and laborers became even more evident. In reality, Southern society fundamentally distrusted the very people it seemed most hopelessly dependent upon. It was caught in a vise of restricting the migration of Negroes who, at the same time, were looked upon with the utmost disdain, even denied fully human qualities. This paradox in southern thought provided a seedbed for bitter racial antagonism. It added an emotionalism to the racial hatreds of these years that make them stand out, above all others, as a period of great violence.

Most of the Negro migrants who came to New York City prior to the 1930's settled in Manhattan. The Negro population of that borough increased by 24,288 between 1900 and 1910, whereas that of Brooklyn expanded by 4,341. Seventy-eight per cent of the city's industry was located in Manhattan in the early twentieth century and the migrants filled many of the unskilled jobs that these factories created.

The typical Negro migrant to the metropolis originally came from some rural area in the South. Most grew up on farms or in small southern towns. In 1913 a study was made of thirty-five Negroes in Harlem. Thirty-four came from the rural South, and only one grew up in a town whose population exceeded 10,000. Of the twenty-one born on farms, only three were children of parents who owned their land outright. The others were sons and daughters of sharecroppers and farm laborers. The majority of Negroes in this group were indirect migrants—they had lived in some large town or city for a time before coming to New York. All but four were presently employed as domestics, servants or laborers. Similar findings were made in other surveys of northern cities.

Among the immigrants who settled in New York City were young women who came north on what were sometimes called "Justice's Tickets." These were tickets supplied to them by employment and labor agents. In exchange for transportation and the guarantee of a job on arrival, the women signed contracts to work where the agent placed them and swore to pay a fee usually equal to one or two months' wages. These employment agents thus collected money from both employers and workers. . . .

Social service organizations founded to assist Negroes in the city were vitally interested in protecting these girls from "the agents with oily tongues [who] come about and offer flattering inducements. . . ." "Many of them,'' concluded one report, ''are brought from the South, consigned like merchandise to Northern agents.'' Trunks, ''slender satchels,'' clothing, trinkets—personal possessions of all kinds—were often kept as security until fees were paid. Migrants commonly complained of extortionate charges and generally shoddy treatment.

These women who worked as domestics and most of the Negroes who came to the city prior to World War I made the trip on boats that ran along the Atlantic Coast. ''Negroes,'' observed one man in 1898, ''are coming on every boat from southern waters.'' ''Nobody knows how it happened,'' an old resident of the Tenderloin recalled, ''but [on] every old Dominion Steamship that docked there [were] from two to three hundred negroes landed in New York.'' This was the cheapest means of transportation from the South, and New York's migrant population was, and would continue to be, primarily composed of Virginians or people from states bordering the Atlantic. Steerage fare, with meals, from Norfolk or Richmond cost $5.50 or $6.00—the approximate equivalent of a week's wages in New York City. Cabin fares were $9.00. The Old Dominion Steamship Company (migrants called it the ''O.D. Line'') had a bi-weekly service between Virginia and New York. The Baltimore, Chesapeake and Atlantic Railway ran steamers from Washington and Baltimore, and others went as far south as Florida. Many of the waiters and seamen on these ships were Negroes, some of whom lived in New York City. Negroes were generally berthed in separate quarters, ate at separate tables, and were served food inferior to that given white passengers. Some migrants complained that, besides these indignities, the Negro sections of the boats were also reserved for the dogs and pets of other travelers.

It was common practice for migrants, who lived within a day's journey of their former homes, to shuttle back and forth for regular visits. If European immigrants found the Atlantic no great barrier to such journeys (as evidenced by what contemporaries called the ''birds of passage''), the Negro migrant was even less restricted by distance and cost. Practically every issue of *The New York Age* carried some report of such movement: ''R. C. Turner the barber, is back in the city after two months' vacation to his old home, Hillsboro, North Carolina''; ''Mrs. Mary E. Swan . . . has gone to Virginia to bury her niece. . . . She will soon return.'' Many migrants wrote home of their supposedly glowing successes in the North. Some returned to their birthplaces dressed in the latest fashion, pockets full of cash, to tell the rural folk of their exploits. George Edmund Haynes described ''the exaggerated stories of prosperity which relatives and friends in these cities write to friends at home and the prosperity shown by those returning home in their display of clothes and cash.'' Negro students and teachers from the South regularly came to study in New York City during their summer vacations. Some attended the summer session at Columbia University and lived in segregated quarters in Hartley Hall. Others came in search of summer jobs, lived at the Negro YMCA and YWCA, saved their money and returned south when school began: ''New York is . . . crowded with a host of young men and women students from . . . southern schools . . . These young [people] come North every season and work. . . .''

For those who remained permanently, the city was a strange and often hostile place—it was so noisy and unfriendly, so cold, so full of ''temptations and moral perils,'' a ''pernicious influence,'' a ''fast and wicked place.'' ''Many of those who have come North complain of cold and chills from the like of which they had not previously suffered,'' wrote one scholar. The oft-told tale of the sale of the Brooklyn Bridge to the rural hayseed had a basis in fact. One naive migrant wanted to know how it was done: ''I heard about 'selling the Brooklyn Bridge,' '' he said, ''and I wondered how it was sold, and asked questions about it.'' In 1902 Paul Laurence Dunbar published a novel, *The Sport of the Gods,* which described the dissolution and eventual destruction of a southern Negro family in the ''fast life'' of the ''great alleys of New York.'' Southern Negroes were commonly subject to intraracial as well as interracial prejudice.

Confronted with this estrangement and antagonism many migrants banded together to try to retain as much contact with the patterns of their former lives as possible:

> I'm a poor boy and I'm a stranger blowed in your town,
> Yes I am,
> I'm a poor boy and I'm a stranger blowed in your town,
> I'm a poor boy and I'm a stranger blowed in your town,
> I'm goin' where a friend can be found.

Negroes, foreign-born and native, established benevolent, fraternal and protective societies to keep up old friendships and provide insurance for themselves and families in sickness and death. The vast majority of New York's Negro population belonged to insurance and fraternal societies. The largest Negro insurance company of Virginia, the True Reformers, had a branch office in the city. Prior to World War I, New York City had its Sons and Daughters of South Carolina, Sons of North Carolina, Sons of Virginia, Sons of the South, Southern Beneficial League. When one North Carolinian was appointed Assistant District Attorney of New York County a celebration was given for him "in the fullness of the North Carolinian pride." Storefront churches revived the spirit of southern preaching. These and other churches held special services and celebrations in honor of communicants from individual southern states. There were regular South Carolina days, Virginia days, and so on. When the World War drew migrants in greater numbers from the Deep South and the West Indies, new societies were founded by Floridians, Georgians and the varieties of West Indians.

The entire Negro community of New York City took on a southern flavor. Businesses expanded to service the wants of a growing population: "The great influx of Afro-Americans into New York City within recent years from all parts of the South has made . . . possible a great number and variety of business enterprises," editorialized *The New York Age* in 1907. Negro restaurants, undertaking establishments, saloons, barbershops—the plethora of small businesses necessary to satisfy a community's needs—catered to the newcomers. Restaurants advertised special "southern-style" breakfasts and dinners. Negro grocers specialized in Virginia fruits, vegetables and chickens. Migrants asked friends to send them special southern delicacies. . . .

Migration to the city created possibilities for economic mobility that were largely absent from southern life. Many of the businesses which provided services for Negroes were owned by migrants themselves. Some recent arrivals began as small entrepreneurs but made modest fortunes in a relatively short time.

Perhaps the most interesting and among the most successful was Lillian Harris, born in a shanty on the Mississippi Delta in 1870. She came north as a teenager and, in 1901, after having knocked around many northern cities for a decade, hitched her way from Boston to New York City on hay, milk and vegetable wagons. Miss Harris had $5.00, and with this capital went into business. She spent $3.00 for an old baby carriage and boiler and $2.00 for pigs' feet. This was the beginning of her career as New York's most widely known Negro peddler. Her converted buggy became a "traveling restaurant."

Hawking her wares in Negro sections, specializing in southern cooking (hog-maws, chitterlings), Lillian Harris was popularly called "Pig Foot Mary." She lived in a tiny room and scrimped and saved for years: "Saving for a respectable old age," she always said. When Negroes began moving to Harlem this astute street-corner saleswoman grasped at opportunity and invested her savings in Harlem property. By the First World War "Pig Foot Mary" (now Mrs. Lillian H. Dean) was a wealthy landlord—"one of the wealthiest women in Harlem;" "one of the most successful colored business women in New York." "Send it and send it damn quick," she wrote tenants who fell behind in their rent. "Pig Foot Mary" spent her "respectable old age" in retirement in California, where she died in 1929.

William Mack Felton was another southern Negro who made good in New York. He arrived in the city in 1898 with a dollar tucked away in his shoe: "Heeding the call to the Big City," he said. Felton grew up on a small farm in Georgia with little opportunity for formal education. He was naturally bright, however, and gifted with mechanical ability. When he came to New York he worked as a longshoreman long enough to save some money to open a repair shop. The first big job that came his way called for the repair of dozens of clocks left in a Manhattan pawnshop. Most of them had simply stopped running because they had picked up dust and dirt lying around the shelves. Felton realized this, bought a large washtub, filled it with gallons of kerosene and oil and cleaned all the stripped-down clocks in one day. He used this same ingenuity to fix watches, pistols bicycles—anything that needed repairing. In 1901, when wealthy New Yorkers began to buy the new automobile, Felton opened an auto school and garage. He later invented a device that washed cars automatically. By 1913 his Auto Transportation and Sales Company employed fifteen people and was housed in a seven-story building which he owned. Felton rode back to Georgia in his new car to visit his family and old friends and tell them of life in the "Big City."

Success came to other southern migrants who arrived in New York City in these years. Madame C.J. Walker, born in Louisiana in 1867, was a laundress before she discovered a hair-straightening process (the "Walker System") which brought her great fortune, In 1913 she built a mansion for herself on West One Hundred and Thirty-sixth Street and four years later built a manificent country estate, Villa Lewaro, in exclusive Irvington-on-the-Hudson. H.C. Haynes, formerly a southern barber, founded a company which manufactured razor strops; Edward E. Lee, a Virginian, was Negro Democratic leader of New York County for fifteen years; J. Franklin Smallwood became chief collector of the State Bank of New York; J.S. Montague ran a mortgage and loan company on Wall Street; Ferdinand Q. Morton, of Macon, Mississippi, was prominent in Democratic politics and ruled "Black Tammany" from the First World War through the Great Depression.

Practically all of these migrants were born in the direst southern poverty and achieved their postions, as the Reverend Dr. Adam Clayton Powell, Sr., later wrote, "Against the Tide." Very few southern Negroes had such fortune, however. The majority of those who came to New York City ended in the ranks of the poor and swelled the slum populations of the Tenderloin, San Juan Hill or Harlem. To many nothern Negroes, who had never known or had since forgotton the restrictive conditions in the South, the life of the typical migrant seemed no great improvement on his former conditions.

The average Negro migrant to New York City obviously found life harsh and difficult. For those who came, however, conditions in the North did offer a measure of self-respect and the possibility for future advancement that was generally denied the Negro in the South. "To many of them oppressed within the limitations set up by the south," wrote Ray Stannard Baker, "it is indeed the promised land."

C. THE CITY: EXPLOSION OF A DREAM

For most ethnic minorities the city provided neither escape nor fulfillment. Rather, it became a nightmare of unemployment, inadequate housing, and racism and meant a continuous struggle for cultural survival. Over the years these problems have fed on themselves, producing frustrations and feelings of helplessness and anger among urban minorities. Occasionally violence has occurred as Anglos have attempted to keep minorities "in their place" and as ethnic underclasses have struggled to find decent, more meaningful lives in urban ghettos.

In the first selection Stan Steiner discusses the problem of Indians in adapting to the urban environment. Driven to the city by the poverty of their reservations and encouraged to move by the Bureau of Indian Affairs relocation program, Native Americans arrive without money, training, or knowledge of the ways of city life. Moreover, as a people whose lives and culture are rooted in the land, Native Americans have had an especially hard time adjusting to urban America.

The last two selections examine the potential of urban racism for spawning violence by focusing on two historic episodes of race rioting in American cities. Horace R. Cayton and St. Clair Drake show that post-World War I Southern Black migrants to Chicago experienced extreme hostility from whites and were none too warmly welcomed by Black "Old Settlers." From the spark of a summer beach incident, racial antagonisms exploded in a six-day black-white conflagration that caused hundreds of casualties, destroyed hundreds of thousands of dollars in property, but left the root causes of the violence unaltered.

Chicanos in Los Angeles have felt hostility of the same order. Carey

McWilliams describes the Los Angeles "Zoot Suit Riots" of 1943 in which Anglo-American servicemen, encouraged by an anti-Mexican police department and Anglo public opinion, established a reign of terror over Chicano youths in the West Coast metropolis.

1. STAN STEINER

Cement Prairies*

> In Billings, Montana, there is a hill. In Sioux it is called Place of Many Sorrows. There a child dies every week. A wife dies too young. A man he is old and sad at 30, and the sick are too many. The dead songs are singed there till a tall man runs from his shack, from all his family, and he drinks not to hear. Now he sits, drunk so much he cannot talk, and too sad to not sing the same hard songs. He cannot go away. There is no place to go. These men, these people, are Indians who have sold their land.

The unlettered Indian had written his anguish on the back of an unused government form. He had not signed his name. He had mailed his outcry to the Denver *Post*, which sent a reporter, Robert W. Fenwick, to find the Dantesque inferno—the Place of Many Sorrows. Fenwick found not one but several.

One of these, known as "Hill 57," in Great Falls, Montana, was typical of the rest:

"It's an Indian village of shocking filth, poverty and degradation. Its outstanding features are the frail huts, the battered hulks of automobiles, the ever-present outhouses, a hand-pump which is the sole water supply for the entire community, and an almost unbelievable sea of junk resembling a city rubbish disposal," Fenwick wrote.

"Now, the Indian sits on the White Man neck," the nameless Indian had written, "and the White Man is saddened because of this. We are both sad because only grief has come to both of us because of sale [of Indian land]. Soon, if this goes on, all Indians must come to town.

"What town want one more Place of Many Sorrows? Who will fight this thing? What man is so brave? Now something must be done. Who will do it?"

One young Sioux in San Francisco, who was shown a copy of the pathetic

*From Stan Steiner, *The New Indians*, abridgment of "Cement Prairies."

letter, scoffed at it. "Man, I think that letter is a put-on," he said. "For one thing that's not how a Sioux thinks. There's no Sioux I know of who would say, 'He cannot go away. There is no place to go.' He can go home to his reservation any time. If he can crawl, they'll take him home. For another thing living in towns, lousy as it may be, doesn't scare us into writing gibberish. Man, we been doing the towns ever since Sitting Bull laid down the tools of his trade on the Little Big Horn and joined the touring Wild West Show of Buffalo Bill.

"Every town has a hellhole like that. Every town in the West has its 'native quarter.' " the San Francisco Sioux said. "That's not the problem. You see, living in the city is your problem, really. We just come visiting to make a little money. Our problem is making it."

Interestingly enough, when the Denver *Post* reporter searched Billings, Montana, asked everywhere, he could not find the Place of Many Sorrows.

Are the city Indians invisible?

The tribal Indians are unquestionably coming to town. Half of the Indians in the country may be city Indians, Vine Deloria, Jr., has estimated. There are a quarter of a million living in the metropolitan areas alone, thought Mel Thom. And the San Francisco Indian Center publication *The American Indian*, has reported that the Indian adults living "off-reservation"—estimated at 198,000— outnumbered those "on-reservation"; for many job-seeking parents left their children at home with grandparents.

One decade ago, The *Harvard Law Review* estimated that "about 100,000 Indians [reside] in American cities and towns" ("American Indians: People Without a Future," by Ralph Nader, May 10, 1956). Even if the statistic was a reasonably inaccurate guess, the urban population of tribesmen has doubled within ten years.

But the city Indians have always been invisible statistics. The U.S. Census Bureau counts Indians only when they so identify themselves, or are identifiable. And the city Indians often "pass" as whites, when it is economically necessary, or socially desirable. Those who don't "pass" have been usually counted as "nonwhite"—a nearly invisible shade, it seems, when they happen to be Indians.

The statistics of the Bureau of Indian Affairs have been as equalitarianly invisible, for the Bureau's concern has traditionally been the reservation Indian, and the cajoling of him to leave the reservation. Once he goes, however, the Bureau no longer counts him.

So the city Indian has been an invisible man. He has not even become a statistic.

"Chicago does not realize they have a 'reservation of Indians' right in their own backyard,'' commented an official of the American Indian Center on the near North Side. ''There are better than ten thousand Indians representing seventy tribes in Chicago.'' Half of these are wedged into a few-block area between the Puerto Rican ghetto and the luxury apartment houses on the Lake Shore Drive.

''We don't riot,'' said Nathan Bird, one of the Chicago Indian leaders, ''so no one knows we're here.''

Brooklyn, New York, Cleveland, Detroit, St. Louis, Minneapolis, Omaha, Denver, Phoenix, Los Angeles, San Francisco, and Seattle all have their own ''native quarters'' of Indians. Many of these have more than ten thousand tribal residents. And in the smaller cities of the Rocky Mountains, the Plains, and the Southwest, there are repetitious ''Hill 57's.'' ''The Cement Prairies'' was what some of the city Indians nicknamed these homeless homes away from home. . . .

In the eyes of an Indian what does the city look like? He has seen villages and he has seen towns. Nowhere has he seen one million people, five million, living in houses like great tombstones, row upon row, and running about like little mechanical ants, to and fro, on streets full of cars like plagues of grasshoppers. He has lived most of his life without a sidewalk, without a subway, without a superhighway, and often without a supermarket.

He has lived beside the still waters.

Living in the city is then not something he can adjust to with a street map, an orientation course, and a job. It is beyond his imagination, beyond his emotions.

Within a few miles of the metropolitan areas of Los Angeles and New York City more human beings live than in the more than one million square miles of all the states of the Western mountains and plains and deserts, where most of the tribal Indians come from.

So the tribesmen come into the metropolis with its glass and steel office buildings, where the twentieth century is on perpetual display like a living museum piece.

How exotic are the artifacts of the urban civilization! Its rituals of folk-rock chants, commercial ceremonials, and automobile worship were fascinating. The tribal Indians come with the curiosity of tourists. It is like visiting a circus in a foreign country.

Richard McKenzie, a young Sioux who lived in San Francisco for several years—successfully—and was a leader of the Indian Center in that city, cast a dubious eye on this citifying of the tribesmen. ''The reservation Indian has not been prepared to make his way in the city of 1860's—much less the demanding fast-paced and cold-blooded city of 1960's,'' he said.

Life in the city whetted the Indian's curiosity, McKenzie said, but he faced a ''hopeless situation.'' Most of the Indians he met were lost. ''The simplest facts of life in the city were new to them: gearing your entire day by a clock, when to go to work, when to eat lunch. They don't even understand where you board a bus, how to pay, and how to open and close the doors.

''Because they have been sent from the reservation with the lack of training, information, and money,'' he said, they would be victims of ''the hardships and loneliness of the disillusioned Indian in the city.''

Why then, if the city Indian faces a ''hopeless situation,'' do more and more rural Indians come to the cities?

''Lots of the younger kids want to leave the reservation and get a job,'' said Mary Lou Payne, a Cherokee girl who made the journey to the city herself. ''It's not that they really want to get away from the reservation, but that they want to have an income. Everyone is *encouraged* to go away. To leave. To become a working American. To join the 'rat race,' really. What they call the 'mainstream.' ''

The exodus has been not wholly voluntary. ''It reflects a policy the Bureau of Indian Affairs has had and still has: to get the Indians off the reservation,'' Mary Lou Payne said.

''Relocation'' is the term given to this trek. It was instituted by Commissioner of Indian Affairs Dillon Myer, who, as has been noted, was director of the Relocation Centers where Japanese-Americans were imprisoned during World War II. Thus, the term had a disquieting connotation to young Indians, many of whom had fought in that war. Nonetheless, tens of thousands of tribal Indians have been ''relocated'' since the early 1950's.

Vice President Hubert Humphrey has written optimistically about the ''Relocation'' Program: It is aimed at ''encouraging Indians to move off the less promising reservations and into industrial centers where work opportunities are more plentiful. . . . A package program—vocational training and job placement, with all expenses paid for trainee and family—has lured 50,000 Indians into successful urban living.''

The former Commissioner of Indian Affairs, Philleo Nash, who guided the program during the administration of the late President John F. Kennedy, was more cautious and less optimistic: ''Relocation by itself solves nothing,'' Nash said. ''. . . As long as relocation was merely a program to transport people from one pocket of poverty to another, little was accomplished. Not everyone likes city living—not everyone is suited to it. To combat poverty successfully will require programs that relate people to jobs wherever they choose to live."

Some of the relocated Indians were even more skeptical. The Sioux Richard McKenzie said that when a reservation Indian arrived in San Francisco he was referred by the Relocation Office to "the few boarding houses available to Indians under the Bureau pogram [that were] usually ill-run, often short on food, and in bad districts—especially for girls."

The jobs that the Bureau found for "the usually unskilled Indians" were often with "fly-by-night outfits who enjoy getting as much labor as possible from their workers, while paying them as little as possible," McKenzie said. Since the Indians did not know union rules, many were working up to twelve hours a day without overtime pay. When "the pitifully small cash given him to make the trip" ran out, the relocated Indian was often penniless and lost.

His own family, McKenzie said, had housed and fed "many Indians who were in dire need, but somehow did not qualify for aid from any [welfare] agency."

"Mr. Indian," said the irate Sioux, "your 'Green Pastures' in the city will be even worse than what you have now at home. Sending Indians [to the city] on a sink or swim basis is the way to guarantee most will sink."

"It was shameful," Mary Lou Payne said, "to force rural Indians into urban ghettos. It's no answer to poverty to dump these people into the cities. They are so unprepared for city life, paying bills every month, going to work every day, that they filter out to the very bottom of society.

"This shipping out of unprepared people is just shameful. It doesn't work out. They just go back to what they did before. Which is picking up odd jobs. But doing it in the cities."

Vice President Hubert Humphrey sounded an official note of concern: "Most of them [those Indians who go on their own] have never held jobs of any duration and are almost totally unequipped for industrial work. They seek to escape from poverty on the reservation without realizing that they may be making another and worse trap for themselves. Unless we take measures to help this group, we will find new ghettos being established in our cities and towns, new slum children growing up, a new breed of unemployed unemployables, taxing our welfare services." . . .

Relocation had become a fancy word for "dumping the rural poor into the ghettos," said Mel Thom. The idea of urbanizing and integrating the tribal Indian was forgotten, momentarily, and practical reality was recognized by changing the name of the Bureau of Indian Affairs, Branch of Relocation, to Branch of Employment Assistance.

The Vocational Education Act for Indians was intensified when Congress increased the appropriation from $12 to $15 million. Under this act, originally part of the Relocation Program, tribal Indians were job-trained and paid to leave their reservations. Yet, in the first ten years of its operation, but thirteen thousand of the tens of thousands of Indians who went to the cities benefited from its largess. "Usually Indians must leave the reservation to take advantage of it," *Eyapaha,* the Rosebud Sioux newspaper, complained.

Mary Lou Payne was less polite: "I have gripes about the on-the-job training programs. On the Cherokee Reservation back home we have two factories. One of them is a stitching plant, they make bed clothing; and the other is a bobby pin factory. They run the Indian kids through the training courses, the government picks up part of their salary while they're training, and then when they're through training, the company employs them for a month, or two months, and drops them, and hires another crew for training.

"How many jobs are there on the Cherokee Reservation where they can go and make stitched bed clothing? It's so impractical. They should be trained to become plumbers, carpenters, electricians, television repairmen."

Joe Maday, a young Chippewa boy on the Bad River Reservation in Wisconsin, had just come home from an on-the-job-training project, two thousand miles from his home.

He sat in his father's gas station, on a muddy river flat, near the wild-rice fields of his tribe on Lake Superior. He reminisced and he cursed the government for sending him to Seattle.

"Couldn't they send me to Milwaukee?" the boy said. He had gone wide-eyed and eager to see the country, on a $130-a-month government allowance, paying $90 a month for boarding-house rent. "Who could live on what was left? That rent for a dormitory-type room," he said. But it was exciting, anyway, being with Indians from a dozen tribes he had never heard of. "It was like a big powwow all the time. It didn't ever stop."

What did he learn? "Nothing!" he shrugged. "They wanted to teach me mechanics. But I didn't want to work as a mechanic way out there. So far away from home. And mechanics are a dime a dozen around here. So I come back. I'm going to learn electronics this time. If there's a job around here, I rather stay. But maybe I will go away. There's no work here. No one stays.". . .

"That lonesome path that leads to Nowhere is taking me away from this lonesome place" was the lament of the Plains Indian boy Calvin O'John, who had come to a very different city, in a very different era. He too had felt the cold hand of the "lonely people." So did his fellow student at the Santa

Fe Institute of American Indian Arts, Donna Whitewing, who thought of the city as a "blank cold wall":

> *Against a blank cold wall*
> *room enough for many flowers*
> *to grow and bloom.*
> *Feel the heart hesitate*
> *as flowers and buds*
> *wilt and die with pain.*

Where was the warmth and love of the kinship family? In the impersonal and cold efficiency of the city there is no such human touch. The "lonely people" do not touch one another.

Donna Whitewing wrote:

> *The essence of death*
> *is the untouched sense*
> *of being felt.*

Loyal Shegonee, another of the young city Indians, poignantly cried out: "Where are my friends? What is there to do? Would someone, anyone, please come and talk to me?" He heard, the young man said, "the deafening tick-tick of the clock." He felt "the dark room crowding its silence upon me."

"Oh God," he cried out. "Someone, please come and talk to me!"

Who in the city talks to strangers? The "lonely people" prefer to talk to their machinery; for didn't they say "the medium is the message"? Kathryn Polacca, a Navajo teacher who has been to many cities, said: "Your people have so many ways of communication: IBM machines, telephones, newspapers, telegraphs, radios, and television. In the Navajo ways the most important communication is still person to person. This is the way we solve many of our problems. This is the way we enjoy life." The Indian way of talking and living, she said, was based on human values, not on mechanical or monetary values.

Unlike so many newcomers to the cities the tribal Indians "are not with it," Mel Thom said. "He doesn't think of making money. He just wants to make a living and live." That is why, though there are an estimated twenty thousand Indians in the environs of San Francisco, and perhaps thirty thousand in Los Angeles, Thom said he knew of only two or three Indian-owned establishments in either city. One was a bar.

"Money! Money! Money! That is all the white man thinks of when it comes to the Indian," said a Pomo Indian of California. "The only thing they see is money. For me a heartbeat is enough.". . .

Those Indians who chose to stay in the "cold-blooded city" had to protect themselves—politically, economically, and culturally. They were often abandoned by the federal bureaus, with little knowledge of the city agencies, left on their own, uncomfortable with urban life, separated from their tribes, and something had to be done for them, by themselves. The invisible city Indian had to become visible.

Where Indians have come, they have built Indian centers. The men and women from tribes throughout the country, with different cultures and different languages, would get together and establish a meeting place where they could meet relatives and tribesmen, reminisce about life back at home, discuss the frustrations of city life, and help and protect themselves. The Indian center might be a tiny, dreary storefront, or an elaborate and well-equipped community hall. But, whatever it looked like, it was run by and financed by tribal Indians, for tribal Indians.

Powwows in the city? A nostalgic attempt to transplant tribal life to the cement prairie? These Indian centers are not governmental or social-work-sponsored, not tribal nor intertribal. In coming to these community halls the Indians come as Indians, not representing their tribes. The city Indians have created something new and independent and yet Indian. They speak of the "Indian language"—"Let's talk Indian," they say; though there is, of course, no such language—and seek to preserve their "Indian traditions," and they dance in powwows, doing "Indian dances," and they fight for their "Indian rights."

In doing these things they are not only building an Indian urban community, but are building an Indian consciousness that is no longer tribal, but is extratribal. It too is an embryo of Indian nationalism.

Chicago's Indian Center, one of the oldest and largest of these urban, extratribal groups, is typical in its goals of most. Its aim is to help tribesmen in becoming "a functioning part of the social fabric of the city," while "sustaining cultural values perhaps uniquely their own."

The Indians of Chicago are seeking, in other words, to become urban citizens outwardly, but to remain Indians inwardly. And these Indians wish to do this not by urbanizing the tribal life, nor by tribalizing the urban life, but by combining both. Fascinating are the combinations. Rock 'n' roll and tribal dances. Potlatch dinners and auto-mechanic classes. . . .

The invisibility of the city Indian belongs to the past. He is becoming visible. He may have been lost in the city; but the longer he has stayed the more he has begun to feel it is the city that is lost—not he. When the city Indian began to build urban tribal communities he discovered the Indian way of life filled the lonely void of "the cement prairies." And he began to wonder if "the lonely crowd" might learn neighborliness from him.

"The very values the Indian represents may contribute to the improvement of our frantic cities," said Richard McKenzie. He thought the values of tribal humanism might "make the cities more human." And one young Pueblo Indian in the Chicago Indian Center said: "Instead of giving Indians these urban-orientation courses, maybe they ought to give Chicagoans human-orientation courses."

Has the "alienation" of the city Indian been too convenient and self-comforting a concept? It has been used by non-Indians to define the feelings of the Indian, but it has described the effect and not the cause. It has placed the onus on the Indian for his failure to conform to urban life and for his return home to the reservation. But, at a time when the disappearance of communities and the demise of neighborhoods are troubling city planners, the communal feeling of the city Indian has something to be said for it.

If the "alienation" of urban life becomes too overwhelming, the city Indian returns to his tribal community, and home to the reservation many had gone.

"The return to the reservations," former Commissioner of Indian Affairs Philleo Nash, estimated, "was about as frequent as the permanent relocation." Mary Lou Payne thought it even greater: "On this relocation the return home is fantastic. I bet it is 60 percent and up who return to the reservations." Richard McKenzie said it was his experience that 90 percent returned home as soon as there were jobs on the reservations.

A young girl of the Laguna Pueblo, Pat Pacheco, who returned to her pueblo from college, where she had studied psychology, said: "It's almost impossible to adjust to the outside world, and many of our people are coming back from Cleveland, Chicago, and Los Angeles, because they can work here now."

Not only are the relocated Indians beginning to go home, the *Wall Street Journal* observed, but "there's evidence Indians aren't moving off reservations as readily as a short while ago."

Into the Indian Center of San Francisco, up the shabby stairs, one day walked an unknown tribesman. He was welcomed, as every Indian was, a tall man, with a tight face and puzzled eyes. The man was a newcomer;

perhaps he had just arrived from the reservation, and was ill at ease.

The stranger was something more, however. He was a relocation officer of the government who had been sent from the reservation to see how the tribal Indians were being urbanized.

"He was told we took a rather dim view of the program," a San Francisco Indian recalled. "I pinned him down about the lack of adequate orientation on the reservation. And he said they did indeed tell people about buses, housing, and so forth. I told him that John Glenn could tell me in six orientation lessons how to fly a space ship and I wouldn't know a thing about it if I got in one."

That broke up the official meeting. "Last three hours of our visit were spent talking about hunting, fishing, and wide-open spaces on the reservation. The cheaper cost of living and better life in general back home," the relocated Indian said. "Naturally, many of the things the relocation officer said, and many of the things he saw, will never be included in his written report to D.C., or for that matter in his verbal report to his superintendent on the reservation.

"One wonders, after seeing relocation at the other end, if he will not be more reluctant about sending Indian people out. Will the relocation officer relocate himself?" The city Indian laughed.

The most unusual tale of relocation-in-reverse, however, occurred in Los Angeles. In that multiplicity of the Angels lived a group of Cherokees. Some of the families were well established and some were well to do. They were all Los Angeles boosters; for they had done well enough and lived quite happily.

Yet the hills of eastern Oklahoma of the Cherokee Nation haunted them. "Twelve years ago a group of Indians, many of us children, or grandchildren, of Oklahomans, decided to 'put down a fire' in California," said Dr. John Harris Jeffries, a lawyer and chiropractic doctor who was a leader of these Los Angeles Cherokees. He explained that to "put down a fire," in the Cherokee tradition, meant just that. A ceremonial ground was prepared and a fireplace dug in the earth. There the fire was lighted for religious rituals. There a stomping ground for religious dances was established around the fire.

In the city of Los Angeles, the Western Keetoowah Society was founded. The Keetoowah Society is the nativist religious group of the Cherokees. Its traditional worship, with masks and robes and rites, was not only sacred, but in the urban frenzy was an island of the Indian spirit. Though the city Cherokees were separated by miles of freeways, they held regular religious ceremonies and prayers. In the kinship families they kept their matriarchal clans intact. The old customs of the tribe were practiced, and the children given Cherokee names in the traditional way.

One of the Western Keetoowah Society of Los Angeles members was a lawyer. One was an insurance salesman. One was the owner of an electrical firm. One was a professional golfer. One was a professional artist. One was a surveyor. One was a doctor. One was a computer analyst. And yet—business suits off, ties loosened, brief cases left in the foyers of the suburban houses—they were traditionalist Indians.

"Suddenly we began to think about coming home," Dr. Jeffries said. "I don't know with whom the idea originated. We knew we wanted to get out of the rat race in Los Angeles. There just wasn't any discussion about where we should go. It was Tahlequah."

And so to Tahlequah, Oklahoma, the old capital of the Cherokee Nation, the families began to come. In the beginning just seven families moved. Then four more came. Soon forty of the Cherokees had come. Dr. Jeffries expected that in all one hundred and fifty would come home.

"It was home instantly," he said. "No one has mentioned moving back." Somehow it was as though they had never left.

The coals of the sacred fires that they had "put down" in Los Angeles were unearthed. In their cars the coals were carefully carried halfway across the continent, once more to be buried, but this time in the earth of their Cherokee homeland. Once more, the fires would flame.

2. ST. CLAIR DRAKE AND HORACE R. CAYTON

Race Riot and Aftermath*

RIOT (1919)

Here and there throughout America, the tensions of postwar readjustment flared into open violence. On the labor front and along the color-line, deep-laid frustrations, uneasy fears, and latent suspicions bobbed to the surface. Group antagonisms suppressed and sublimated by the war effort now returned with doubled fury. For labor, there were the "Palmer raids"; for the Negro, lynchings and riots. The South, particularly, was nervous.

*From St. Clair Drake and Horace R. Cayton, *Black Metropolis,* copyright © 1945 by St. Clair Drake and Horace R. Cayton. Reprinted by permission of Harcourt Brace Jovanovich, Inc.

Returning Negro soldiers, their horizons widened through travel, constituted a threat to the caste system. They must be kept in their place. A wave of interracial conflicts swept the country involving communities in the North as well as in the South.

Chicago was not spared its measure of violence. The sporadic bombing of Negro homes in 1918 was but the prelude to a five-day riot in 1919 which took at least thirty-eight lives, resulted in over five hundred injuries, destroyed $250,000 worth of property, and left over a thousand persons homeless. For the first time since 1861 the Negro was the center of a bloody drama. Then he was the hero; now he was the villain.

The generally disturbed background out of which the Chicago riot exploded is revealed in a news item in the Chicago *Tribune* for July 4, 1917, reporting a protest meeting against a bloody riot which had occurred in East St. Louis, Illinois. The article, headlined, "LAWYER WARNS NEGROES HERE TO ARM SELVES" quoted one of Chicago's most respected and conservative Negro leaders as saying, "Arm yourselves now with guns and pistols." Another equally prominent leader was quoted as declaring that he "hoped God would demand 100,000 white lives in the War for each Negro slaughtered in East St. Louis."

The Chicago riot began on a hot July day in 1919 as the result of an altercation at a bathing beach. A colored boy swam across the imaginary line which was supposed to separate Negroes from whites at the Twenty-ninth Street beach. He was stoned by a group of white boys. During the ensuing argument between groups of Negro and white bathers, the boy was drowned. Colored bathers were enraged. Rumor swept the beach, "White people have killed a Negro." The resulting fight, which involved the beach police and the white and colored crowd, set off six days of rioting.

Pitched battles were fought in the Black Belt streets. Negroes were snatched from streetcars and beaten; gangs of hoodlums roamed the Negro neighborhood, shooting at random. Instead of the occasional bombings of two years before, this was a pogrom. But the Negroes fought back.

Attacks and reprisals were particularly bitter up and down the western and southern boundary between the Irish neighborhoods and the Black Belt. Here youthful white gangs—the so-called athletic clubs—functioning with the tacit approval of the ward politicians who sponsored them, raided the Negro community, attacking the people whom for years they had derided as "jigs," "shines," "dinges," "smokes," and "niggers," and who were now fair game. The rising smoke from burning homes in the white neighborhoods around the stockyards and the railroad tracks, during the next two days, was silent evidence of the embittered Negroes' reprisals.

The reaction of most colored civic leaders was ambivalent. Publicly they were constrained to be conciliatory and to curb the masses who did the actual fighting. Privately, despite a recognition of the horrors of the riot, like Negroes of all classes they justified the fighting as self-defense and as proof that Negroes would not supinely suffer mistreatment. They did not view a riot as unmitigated evil if it focused attention upon injustices. To them it held the same paradoxical elements of good emerging from evil that Wilson saw in the First World War or Lenin in the Russian Revolution.

There were some, however, particularly among Old Settlers [blacks who settled in Chicago before World War I—ED.] who viewed the riot as the tragic end of a golden age of race relations. They were very bitter against the southern Negroes, who, they felt, had brought this catastrophe upon them. A group of representative business and professional men met to devise means for ending the disorder. Among the speakers was a lawyer who had come to Chicago from Georgia by way of Canada in 1893, studied law, and amassed some wealth. He insisted that "a lot of the trouble is due to Negroes from the South" and called upon "some representative Negroes from the same part of the country [to] do what they can to help quiet things down."

Many Negroes expressed their resentment against one Old Settler who began his address by placing the blame for the riot on the colored population, stating that "One of the chief causes of the trouble is that the colored men have been taught they must act on the policy of an eye for an eye and a tooth for a tooth."

["Uncle Tom," the hero of Harriet Beecher Stowe's famous novel of the abolitionist era, has become for colored people a symbol of the subservient Negro. The term thus serves as a satirical condemnation of any Negro who is thought to be currying favor with white people.—ED.]

They condemned him as an "Uncle Tom" when he continued:

"This starts a series of reprisals that is likely to go on until the white man will get mad, and if he does we know what will happen to the man of color. Some of us forget that the white man has given us freedom, the right to vote, to live on terms of equality with him, to be paid well for our work, and to receive many other benefits."

They ridiculed him as a "white man's nigger" for his warning:

"If the white man, should decide that the black man has proved he is not fit to have the right to vote, that right may be taken away. We might also find it difficult to receive other favors to which we have been accustomed, and then what would happen to us? We must remember that this is a white man's country. Without his help we can do nothing. When we fight the white man we fight ourselves. We can start a riot but it takes the white man to stop it. We are not interested now in what started the riot, but how to stop it. The Germans thought these same people were so easy-going that they wouldn't fight, and they kept stirring things up until the Americans got mad. That ought to be warning enough! If this thing goes on for three days more there will be no jobs for our men to go back to."

They agreed, however, with his solution, provided it were impartially applied: "If the city cannot restore order then let us with the aid of the militia, have martial law, and take the arms away from the hoodlums."

The bitterness felt by even the more conservative Negro leaders is plainly revealed in the tone of the annual report of Providence Hospital for 1919. Proud of the efficiency with which it handled riot casualties, the hospital board detailed its activities as follows:

> . . . A crowd of young white toughs from in and near Wentworth Avenue, mainly mere boys, began raids into the colored district, destroying, wounding and killing as they went. On one of these trips the raiders shot into the hospital. That evening fifteen victims were treated at the hospital, one white, the rest colored . . . the majority stabbed or clubbed, and a few shot.
>
> As early as three o'clock in the afternoon on Monday, a mob gathered about the hospital. Feeling was running high. Many of the nurses, worn and tired by long hours of excitement and hard work, found human nature too weak to stand the hideous sights and bloodshed and begged to be taken away . . . but except for short spells of hysteria they were at their posts every minute of the time without sleep and without proper nourishment, for it was difficult from the start to get food into the hospital.
>
> During the twenty-four hours from midnight Sunday to midnight Monday, seventy-five victims were taken care of. A number were taken by friends after having received treatment and a number died. Of these patients nine were white. Cots were placed in the wards and in the emergency room until every available space was occupied; then the victims had to lie upon the floor.
>
> The demand on the hospital surgical supplies and food supplies was heavy; furnishings and equipment suffered; surgical instruments were lost and broken; mattresses were ruined, and furniture was wrecked.

The references to the treatment of white patients were a deliberate build-up for two devastating paragraphs:

> It should be borne in mind that the conditions in the colored district were

> exactly reversed in certain white localities where any offending colored person who appeared was ruthlessly slaughtered, whether man, woman, or baby. From these localities came the raiding parties that caused substantially all the trouble.
>
> The white doctors, of course, were not in attendance during this time and many of the colored staff doctors and the three colored house interns workgd day and night; sometimes six operations were in progress at one time.

The daily newspapers headlined the Riot as big news, at the same time editorializing against it. The *New Majority*, organ of the Chicago Federation of Labor, prominently displayed an article, "FOR WHITE UNION MEN TO READ," reminding the workers of their "hatred of violence on the picket line" and insisting that a heavy responsibility rested on them "not because they had anything to do with starting the present trouble, but because of their advantageous position to help end it." The general public watched and read, but did not participate. Probably its sympathies were divided and its loyalties coofused.

The Riot was ended on its sixth day by the state militia, belatedly called after the police had shown their inability, and in some instances their unwillingness, to curb attacks on Negroes.

RECONCILIATION (1920-1922)

One result of the Riot was an increased tendency on the part of white Chicagoans to view Negroes as a "problem." The rapid influx from the South had stimulated awareness of their presence. The elections of 1915 and 1917 had indicated their growing political power in the Republican machine—a circumstance viewed with apprehension by both the Democratic politicians and the "good government" forces. Now the Riot, the screaming headlines in the papers, the militia patrolling the streets with fixed bayonets, and the accompanying hysteria embedded the "Negro problem" deeply in the city's consciousness.

Civic leaders, particularly, were concerned. They decided that the disaster demanded study, so Governor Lowden appointed the nonpartisan, interracial Chicago Commission on Race Relations to investigate the causes of the Riot and to make recommendations. For the next twenty years its suggestions set the pattern of activity for such civic groups as the Urban League, the YMCA, and various public agencies. The Commission's report was the first formal codification of Negro-white relations in Chicago since the days of the Black Code.

After a year of study the Commission reported that it could suggest no "ready remedy," no "quick means of assuring harmony between the races," but it did offer certain suggestions in the hope that "mutual understanding and sympathy between the races will be followed by harmony and co-operation." It based its faith on "the civic conscience of the community" and opined that "progress should begin in a direction steadily away from the disgrace of 1919."

Immediately after the Riot there had been some sentiment favoring a segregation ordinance. The alderman of one white ward introduced a resolution in the City Council asking for an interracial commission to investigate the causes of the Riot and "to equitably fix a zone or zones . . . for the purpose of limiting within its borders the residence of only colored or white persons." Alderman Louis B. Anderson, Mayor Thompson's colored floor leader, "spoke with acerbity and resentment" against the resolution, and it was referred to the judiciary committee and subsequently dropped. The Governor's Commission, too, was emphatic in its repudiation of such a solution, declaring that:

"We are convinced by our inquiry . . . that measures involving or approaching deportation or segregation are illegal, impracticable and would not solve, but would accentuate, the race problem and postpone its just and orderly solution by the process of adjustment."

The Negro had come to Chicago to stay!

The Commission was very specific in its charges and did not hesitate to allocate responsibility for the conditions which produced the Riot. Even governmental agencies were asked to assume their share of the blame. To the police, militia, state's attorney, and courts, the Commission recommended the correction of "gross inequalities of protection" at beaches and playgrounds and during riots; rebuked the courts for facetiousness in dealing with Negro cases, and the police for unfair discrimination in arrests. It suggested the closing of the white adolescent "athletic clubs." It asked the authorities to "promptly rid the Negro residence areas of vice resorts, whose present exceptional prevalence in such areas is due to official laxity." The City Council and administrative boards were asked to be more vigilant in the condemnation and razing of "all houses unfit for human habitation, many of which the Commission has found to exist in the Negro residence areas." In such matters as rubbish and garbage disposal, as well as street repair, Negro communities were said to be shamefully neglected. Suggestions were made that more adequate recreational facilities be extended to Negro neighborhoods, but also that Negroes should be protected in their right to use public facilities anywhere in the city.

The Board of Education was asked to exercise special care in selecting principals and teachers in Negro communities; to alleviate overcrowding and double-shift schools; to enforce more carefully the regulations regarding truancy and work-permits for minors, and to establish adequate night schools. Restaurants, theaters, stores, and other places of public accommodation were informed that "Negroes are entitled by law to the same treatment as other persons" and were urged to govern their policies and actions accordingly.

Employers and labor organizations were admonished in some detail against the use of Negroes as strike-breakers and against excluding them from unions and industries. "Deal with Negroes as workmen on the same plane as white workers," was the suggestion. Negroes were urged to join labor unions. "Self-seeking agitators, Negro or white, who use race sentiment to establish separate unions in trades where existing unions admit Negroes to equal membership" were roundly condemned.

As to the struggle for living space a section of the report directed toward the white members of the public reiterated the statement that Negroes were entitled to live anywhere in the city. It pointed out several neighborhoods where they had lived harmoniously with white neighbors for years, insisted that property depreciation in Negro areas was often due to factors other than Negro occupancy, condemned arbitrary advance of rents, and designated the amount and quality of housing as "an all-important factor in Chicago's race problem." The final verdict was that "this situation will be made worse by methods tending toward forcible segregation or exclusion of Negroes."

3. CAREY MCWILLIAMS

Blood on the Pavements: The Los Angeles "Zoot Suit" Riots of 1943*

On Thursday evening, June 3, 1943, the Alpine Club—made up of youngsters of Mexican descent—held a meeting in a police substation in Los Angeles. Usually these meetings were held in a nearby public school but, since the school was closed, the boys had accepted the invitation of a police

*Carey McWilliams, *North From Mexico, the Spanish-Speaking People of the United States* (Philadelphia, J.B. Lippincott Co., 1949), pp. 244-53. Reprinted by permission of Carey McWilliams.

captain to meet in the substation. The principal business of the meeting, conducted in the presence of the police captain, consisted in a discussion of how gang-strife could best be avoided in the neighborhood. After the meeting had adjourned, the boys were taken in squad cars to the street corner nearest the neighborhood in which most of them lived. The squad cars were scarcely out of sight, when the boys were assaulted, not by a rival "gang" or "club," but by hoodlum elements in the neighborhood. Of one thing the boys were sure: their assailants were not of Mexican descent.

Earlier the same evening a group of eleven sailors, on leave from their station in Los Angeles, were walking along the 1700 block on North Main Street in the center of one of the city's worst slum areas. The surrounding neighborhood is predominantly Mexican. On one side of the street the dirty brick front of a large brewery hides from view a collection of ramshackle Mexican homes. The other side of the street consists of a series of small bars, boarded-up store fronts, and small shops. The area is well off the beaten paths and few servicemen found their way this far north on Main Street. As they were walking along the street, so they later stated, the sailors were set upon by a gang of Mexican boys. One of the sailors was badly hurt; the others suffered minor cuts and bruises. According to their story, the sailors were outnumbered about three to one.

When the attack was reported to the nearest substation, the police adopted a curious attitude. Instead of attempting to find and arrest the assailants, fourteen policemen remained at the station after their regular duty was over for the night. Then, under the command of a detective lieutenant, the "Vengeance Squad," as they called themselves, set out "to clean up" the gang that had attacked the sailors. But—miracle of miracles!—when they arrived at the scene of the attack they could find no one to arrest—not a single Mexican—on their favorite charge of "suspicion of assault." In itself this curious inability to find anyone to arrest—so strikingly at variance with what usually happened on raids of this sort—raises an inference that a larger strategy was involved. For the raid accomplished nothing except to get the names of the raiding officers in the newspapers and to whip up the anger of the community against the Mexican population, which may, perhaps, have been the reason for the raid. . . .

Thus began the so-called "Zoot-Suit Race Riots" which were to last, in one form or another, for a week in Los Angeles.

I. THE TAXICAB BRIGADE

Taking the police raid as an official cue,—a signal for action,—about two hundred sailors decided to take the law into their own hands on the following night. Coming down into the center of Los Angeles from the Naval Armory in Chavez Ravine (near the "Chinatown" area), they hired a fleet of twenty taxicabs. Once assembled, the "task force" proceeded to cruise straight through the center of town en route to the east side of Los Angeles where the bulk of the Mexicans reside. Soon the sailors in the lead-car sighted a Mexican boy in a zoot-suit walking along the street. The "task force" immediately stopped and, in a few moments, the boy was lying on the pavement, badly beaten and bleeding. The sailors then piled back into the cabs and the caravan resumed its way until the next zoot-suiter was sighted, whereupon the same procedure was repeated. In these attacks, of course, the odds were pretty uneven: two hundred sailors to one Mexican boy. Four times this same treatment was meted out and four "gangsters,"—two seventeen-year-old youngsters, one nineteen, and one twenty-three,—were left lying on the pavements for the ambulances to pick up.

It is indeed curious that in a city like Los Angeles, which boasts that it has more police cars equipped with two-way radio than any other city in the world (Los Angeles *Times,* September 2, 1947), the police were apparently unable to intercept a caravan of twenty taxicabs, loaded with two hundred uniformed, yelling, bawdy sailors, as it cruised through the downtown and east-side sections of the city. At one point the police did happen to cross the trail of the caravan and the officers were apparently somewhat embarrassed over the meeting. For only nine of the sailors were taken into custody and the rest were permitted to continue on their merry way. No charges, however, were ever preferred against the nine.

Their evening's entertainment over, the sailors returned to the foot of Chavez Ravine. There they were met by the police and the Shore Patrol. The Shore Patrol took seventeen of the sailors into custody and sent the rest up to the ravine to the Naval Armory. The petty officer who had led the expedition, and who was not among those arrested, gave the police a frank statement of things to come. "We're out to do what the police have failed to do," he said; "we're going to clean up this situation. . . . Tonight [by then it was the morning of June fifth] the sailors may have the marines along."

The next day the Los Angeles press pushed the war news from the front page as it proceeded to play up the pavement war in Los Angeles in screaming headlines. "Wild Night in L.A.—Sailor Zooter Clash" was the headline in the *Daily News.* "Sailor Task Force Hits L.A. Zooters" bellowed the *Herald-Express.* A suburban newspaper gleefully reported that "zoot-suited roughnecks fled to cover before a task force of twenty taxicabs." None of these stories, however, reported the slightest resistance, up to this point, on the part of the Mexicans.

True to their promise, the sailors were joined that night, June fifth, by scores of soldiers and marines. Squads of servicemen, arms linked, paraded through downtown Los Angeles four abreast, stopping anyone wearing zoot-suits and ordering these individuals to put away their "drapes" by the following night or suffer the consequences. Aside from a few half-hearted admonitions, the police made no effort whatever to interfere with these heralds of disorder. However, twenty-seven Mexican boys, gathered on a street corner, were arrested and jailed that evening. While these boys were being booked "on suspicion" of various offenses, a mob of several hundred servicemen roamed the downtown section of a great city threatening members of the Mexican minority without hindrance or interference from the police, the Shore Patrol, or the Military Police.

On this same evening, a squad of sailors invaded a bar on the east side and carefully examined the clothes of the patrons. Two zoot-suit customers, drinking beer at a table, were peremptorily ordered to remove their clothes. One of them was beaten and his clothes were torn from his back when he refused to comply with the order. The other—they were both Mexicans—doffed his "drapes" which were promptly ripped to shreds. Similar occurrences in several parts of the city that evening were sufficiently alarming to have warranted some precautionary measures or to have justified an "out-of-bounds" order. All that the police officials did, however, was to call up some additional reserves and announce that any Mexicans involved in the rioting would be promptly arrested. That there had been no counterattacks by the Mexicans up to this point apparently did not enter into the police officers' appraisal of the situation. One thing must be said for the Los Angeles police: it is above all consistent. When it is wrong, it is consistently wrong; when it makes a mistake, it will be repeated.

By the night of June sixth the police had worked out a simple formula for action. Knowing that wherever the sailors went there would be trouble, the police simply followed the sailors at a conveniently spaced interval. Six carloads of sailors cruised down Brooklyn Avenue that evening. At Ramona Boulevard, they stopped and beat up eight teenage Mexicans. Failing to find any Mexican zoot-suiters in a bar on Indiana Street, they were so annoyed that they proceeded to wreck the establishment. In due course, the police made a leisurely appearance at the scene of the wreckage but could find no one to arrest. Carefully following the sailors, the police arrested eleven boys who had been beaten up on Carmelita Street; six more victims were arrested a few blocks further on, seven at Ford Boulevard, six at Gifford Street—and so on straight through the Mexican east-side settlements. Behind them came the police, stopping at the same street corners "to mop up" by arresting the injured victims of the mob. By morning, some forty-four Mexican boys, all severely beaten, were under arrest.

2. Operation "Dixie"

The stage was now set for the really serious rioting of June seventh and eighth. Having featured the preliminary rioting as an offensive launched by sailors, soldiers, and marines, the press now whipped public opinion into a frenzy by dire warnings that Mexican zoot-suiters planned mass retaliations. To insure a riot, the precise street corners were named at which retaliatory action was expected and the time of the anticipated action was carefully specified. In effect these stories announced a riot and invited public participation. "Zooters Planning to Attack More Servicemen," headlined the *Daily News*; "Would jab broken bottlenecks in the faces of their victims. . . . Beating sailors' brains out with hammers also on the program." Concerned for the safety of the Army, the Navy, and the Marine Corps, the *Herald-Express* warned that "Zooters . . . would mass 500 strong."

By way of explaining the action of the police throughout the subsequent rioting, it should be pointed out that, in June, 1943, the police were on a bad spot. A man by the name of Beebe, arrested on a drunk charge, had been kicked to death in the Central Jail by police officers. Through the excellent work of an alert police commissioner, the case had finally been broken and, at the time of the riots, a police officer by the name of Compton Dixon was on trial in the courts. While charges of police brutality had been bandied about for years, this was the first time that a seemingly airtight case had been prepared. Shortly after the riots, a Hollywood police captain told a motion picture director that the police had touched off the riots "in order to give Dixie (Dixon) a break." By staging a fake demonstration of the alleged necessity for harsh police methods, it was hoped that the jury would acquit Dixon. As a matter of fact, the jury did disagree and on July 2, 1943, the charges against Dixon were dismissed.

On Monday evening, June seventh, thousands of *Angelenos,* in response to twelve hours' advance notice in the press, turned out for a mass lynching. Marching through the streets of downtown Los Angeles, a mob of several thousand soldiers, sailors, and civilians, proceeded to beat up every zoot-suiter they could find. Pushing its way into the important motion picture theaters, the mob ordered the management to turn on the house lights and then ranged up and down the aisles dragging Mexicans out of their seats. Street cars were halted while Mexicans, and some Filipinos and Negroes, were jerked out of their seats, pushed into the streets, and beaten with sadistic frenzy. If the victims wore zoot-suits, they were stripped of their clothing and left naked or half-naked on the streets, bleeding and bruised. Proceeding down Main Street from First to Twelfth, the mob stopped on the edge of the Negro district. Learning that the Negroes planned a warm reception for them, the mobsters turned back and marched through the Mexican east side spreading panic and terror.

Here is one of numerous eye-witness accounts written by Al Waxman, editor of *The Eastside Journal:*

> At Twelfth and Central I came upon a scene that will long live in my memory. Police were swinging clubs and servicemen were fighting with civilians. Wholesale arrests were being made by the officers.
>
> Four boys came out of a pool hall. They were wearing the zoot-suits that have become the symbol of a fighting flag. Police ordered them into arrest cars. One refused. He asked: "Why am I being arrested?" The police officer answered with three swift blows of the night-stick across the boy's head and he went down. As he sprawled, he was kicked in the face. Police had difficulty loading his body into the vehicle because he was one-legged and wore a wooden limb. Maybe the officer didn't know he was attacking a cripple.
>
> At the next corner a Mexican mother cried out, "Don't take my boy, he did nothing. He's only fifteen years old. Don't take him." She was struck across the jaw with a night-stick and almost dropped the two and a half year old baby that was clinging in her arms. . . .
>
> Rushing back to the east side to make sure that things were quiet here, I came upon a band of servicemen making a systematic tour of East First Street. They had just come out of a cocktail bar where four men were nursing bruises. Three autos loaded with Los Angeles policemen were on the scene but the soldiers were not molested. Farther down the street the men stopped a streetcar, forcing the motorman to open the door and proceeded to inspect the clothing of the male passengers. "We're looking for zoot-suits to burn," they shouted. Again the police did not interfere. . . .Half a block away . . . I pleaded with the men of the local police substation to put a stop to these activities. "It is a matter for the military police," they said.

Throughout the night the Mexican communities were in the wildest possible turmoil. Scores of Mexican mothers were trying to locate their youngsters and several hundred Mexicans milled around each of the police substations and the Central Jail trying to get word of missing members of their families. Boys came into the police stations saying: "Charge me with vagrancy or anything, but don't send me out there!" pointing to the streets where other boys, as young as twelve and thirteen years of age, were being beaten and stripped of their clothes. From affidavits which I helped prepare at the time, I should say that not more than half of the victims were actually wearing zoot-suits. A Negro defense worker, wearing a defense-plant identification badge on his workclothes, was taken from a street car and one of his eyes was gouged out with a knife. Huge half-page photographs, showing Mexican boys stripped of their clothes, cowering on the pavements, often bleeding profusely, surrounded by jeering mobs of men and women, appeared in all the Los Angeles newspapers. Al Waxman more truthfully reported, blood had been "spilled on the streets of the city."

At midnight on June seventh, the military authorities decided that the local police were completely unable or unwilling to handle the situation, despite the fact that a thousand reserve officers had been called up. The entire downtown area of Los Angeles was then declared "out of bounds" for military personnel. This order immediately slowed down the pace of the rioting. The moment the Military Police and Shore Patrol went into action, the rioting quieted down. On June eighth the city officials brought their heads up out of the sand, took a look around, and began issuing statements. The district attorney, Fred N. Howser, announced that the "situation is getting entirely out of hand," while Mayor Fletcher Bowron thought that "sooner or later it will blow over." The chief of police, taking a count of the Mexicans in jail, cheerfully proclaimed that "the situation has now cleared up." All agreed, however, that it was quite "a situation."

Unfortunately "the situation" had not cleared up; nor did it blow over. It began to spread to the suburbs where the rioting continued for two more days. When it finally stopped, the Eagle Rock *Advertiser* mournfully editorialized: "It is too bad the servicemen were called off before they were able to complete the job. . . . Most of the citizens of the city have been delighted with what has been going on." County Supervisor Roger Jessup told the newmen: "All that is needed to end lawlessness is more of the same action as is being exercised by the servicemen!" While the district attorney of Ventura, an outlying county, jumped on the bandwagon with a statement to the effect that "zoot suits are an open indication of subversive character." This was also the opinion of the Los Angeles City Council which adopted a resolution making the wearing of zoot-suits a misdemeanor! On June eleventh, hundreds of handbills were distributed to students and posted on bulletin boards in a high school attended by many Negroes and Mexicans which read: "Big Sale. Second-Hand Zoot Suits, Slightly Damaged. Apply at Nearest U.S. Naval Station. While they last we have your Size."

3. WHEN THE DEVIL IS SICK . . .

Egging on the mob to attack Mexicans in the most indiscriminate manner, the press developed a fine technique in reporting the riots. "44 Zooters Jailed in Attacks on Sailors" was the chief headline in the *Daily News* of June seventh; "Zoot Suit Chiefs Girding for War on Navy" was the headline in the same paper on the following day. The moralistic tone of this reporting is illustrated by a smug headline in the Los Angeles *Times* of June seventh: "Zoot Suiters Learn Lesson in Fight with Servicemen." The riots, according to the same paper, were having "a cleansing effect." An editorial in the *Herald-Express* said that the riots "promise to rid the community of . . . those zoot-suited miscreants." While Mr. Manchester Boddy, in a signed editorial in the *Daily News* of June ninth excitedly announced that "the time for temporizing is past. . . . The time has come to serve notice that the City of Los Angeles will no longer be terrorized by a relatively small handful of morons parading as zoot suit hoodlums. To delay action *now* means to court disaster later on." As though there had been any "temporizing," in this sense, for the prior two years!

But once the Navy had declared the downtown section of Los Angeles "out of bounds," once the Mexican ambassador in Washington had addressed a formal inquiry to Secretary of State Hull, and once official Washington began to advise the local minions of the press of the utterly disastrous international effects of the riots, in short when the local press realized the consequences of its own lawless action, a great thunderous cry for "unity," and "peace," and "order" went forth. One after the other, the editors began to disclaim all responsibility for the riots which, two days before, had been hailed for their "salutary" and "cleansing" effect.

Thus on June eleventh the Los Angeles *Times,* in a pious mood, wrote that,

> at the outset, zoot-suiters were limited to no specific race; they were Anglo-Saxon, Latin and Negro. The fact that later on their numbers seemed to be predominantly Latin was in itself no indictment of that race at all. No responsible person at any time condemned Latin-Americans as such.

Feeling a twinge of conscience, Mr. Boddy wrote that "only a ridiculously small percentage of the local Mexican population is involved in the so-called gang demonstrations. Every true Californian has an affection for his fellow citizens of Mexican ancestry that is as deep rooted as the Mexican culture that influences our way of living, our architecture, our music, our language, and even our food." This belated discovery of the Spanish-Mexican cultural heritage of California was, needless to say, rather ironic in view of the fact that the ink was not yet dry on Mr. Boddy's earlier editorial in which he had castigated the Mexican minority as "morons." To appreciate the ironic aspects of "the situation," the same newspapers that had been baiting Mexicans for nearly two years now began to extol them.

As might have been expected, this post-mortem mood of penitence and contrition survived just long enough for some of the international repercussions of the riots to quiet down. Within a year, the press and the police were back in the same old groove. On July 16, 1944, the Los Angeles *Times* gave front-page prominence to a curious story under the heading: "Youthful Gang Secrets Exposed." Indicating no source, identifying no spokesman, the story went on to say that "authorities of the Superior Court" had unearthed a dreadful "situation" among juvenile delinquents. Juveniles were using narcotics, marihuana, and smoking "reefers." Compelled to accept drug addiction, "unwilling neophytes" were dragooned into committing robberies and other crimes. Young girls were tatooed with various "secret cabalistic symbols" of gang membership. The high pompadours affected by the *cholitas,* it was said, were used to conceal knives and other "weapons." Two theories were advanced in the story by way of "explaining" the existence of these dangerous gangs: first, that "subversive groups" in Los Angeles had organized them; and second, that "the gangs are the result of mollycoddling of racial groups." In view of the record, one is moved to inquire, what mollycoddling? by the police? by the juvenile authorities? by the courts? Backing up the news story, an editorial appeared in the *Times* on July eighteenth entitled: "It's Not a Nice Job But It Has To Be Done." Lashing out at "any maudlin and misguided sympathy for the 'poor juveniles,' " the editorial went on to say that "stern punishment is what is needed; stern and sure punishment. The police and the Sheriff's men *should be given every encouragement* to go after these young gangsters" (emphasis mine).

Coincident with the appearance of the foregoing news story and editorial, the Juvenile Court of Los Angeles entered a most remarkable order in its minutes on July 31, 1944. The order outlined a plan by which Mexican wards of the Juvenile Court, over sixteen years of age, might be turned over to the Atchison, Topeka, and Santa Fe Railroad for a type of contract-employment. A form of contract, between the parents of the youngsters and the railroad, was attached to the order. The contract provided that the ward was to work "as a track laborer" at 58-1/2¢ per hour; that $1.03 per day was to be deducted for board, $2.50 per month for dues in a hospital association, and 10¢ a day for laundry. It was also provided that one-half of the pay was to be turned over to the probation officers to be held in trust for the ward. That this order was specifically aimed at *Mexican* juveniles is clearly shown by the circumstance that the court, prior to approving the arrangement, had first secured its approval by a committee of "representative" leaders of the Mexican-American community.

IV. Twentieth Century: Impact of United States Institutions

The ethnic experience in America cannot be fully understood without an analysis of minorities' relations with the major institutions of American life. Because of space limitations we focus in this chapter on four critical institutions: government and the law, the military, education, and labor.

These institutions have had both positive and negative effects on minorities, for they have served as agencies of both progress and exploitation. Government has the power and the bureaucratic means either to improve the conditions of life or to impede change; our system of law can be applied equally and fairly to all citizens or be used discriminatorily; the military can provide economic security and improved social status or it can be a source of humiliation, segregation, and bitterness; our educational system has the potential for producing trained, perceptive, sensitive, socially conscious, and self-confident citizens or it can belittle minorities and suppress their aspirations; and organized labor can be an agency of material self-improvement for ethnic underclasses or, when twisted to serve the selfish interests of labor bosses or to maintain racial barriers, it can become an engine of extortion and degradation. The regrettable fact that emerges from the selections in this chapter is that on balance Blacks, Mexican Americans, and Native Americans, have been more often abused than helped by these institutions.

Minority groups have not been mere passive victims of institutional neglect and maltreatment. Over the years they have struggled for change in America's institutions, often through various forms of protest and resistance. However, as we have seen in earlier chapters, for years these attempts produced relatively few long-lasting results. Entrenched hostility to minority liberation and progress was too strong to overcome, and minorities rarely succeeded in securing significant positive change.

The picture has been altered somewhat in the decades since World War II. At the same time that America's governmental, military, industrial, labor, and educational systems have grown enormously, ethnics have become more aware of institutional structures, the realities of institutional power, and the institutional potential for good as well as harm. Ethnic minorities have also become more aware of their own potential power and have sought to mobilize it in the struggle for institutional change—demanding equitable treatment from the government and the courts, calling on churches to be more active in the quest for social justice, organizing themselves to get equal status in the armed forces, demanding better education for their children, and becoming vocal elements in the labor movement.

As a result of these pressures America's institutions have begun to react positively, and in recent years public relations campaigns, magazine advertisements, and articles in trade journals have called attention to the progress made by major institutions in the private and public sectors in employing and assisting minorities to achieve their full rights. But as the readings in this chapter show, the response has too often been more rhetorical than material.

A. GOVERNMENT AND THE LAW

No institution has had a greater impact on ethnic minorities than the various levels and branches of American government. At times government has succeeded in initiating changes beneficial to minority groups. But it has also been a force of repression and discrimination, particularly the police agencies that enforce the law and the courts that interpret and apply it.

At the federal level hope and progress have come through such massive programs as the New Deal of the 1930s and the War on Poverty of the 1960s. But substantial long-lasting changes have been few. Congressional ambivalence toward ethnic minorities, shifts in public awareness and concern for minority rights and aspirations, and changes in national policy from administration to administration have created an ongoing crisis of confidence among minorities in their quest for progress through governmental institutions.

Government's potential for good with respect to minorities is examined in the first selection, in which John Collier, Commissioner of Indian Affairs under Franklin Delano Roosevelt, describes the New Deal approach to problems faced by Native Americans. As Commissioner, Collier dealt with these problems in the manner of an enlightened social engineer. He advocated careful and comprehensive social planning, but recognized the limits of governmental intervention. Realizing that Indians knew what was best for themselves he pressed for the restoration of tribal lands, therein enabling native Americans to control their own affairs more effectively. It should be pointed out, however, that the Indian Act of 1934 replaced tribal leadership with a "democratic tribal council" form of reservation government that was foreign to the very way of life Collier's Indian reconstruction program was supposed to reinstate. By imposing the white man's ideas of self-government on the tribes, the New Deal provided a means by which the younger "progressive" Indians, out of touch with ancient tribal ways, could wrest control from the tribal elders and place their reservations on a progressive-pragmatic-democratic footing. This produced dislocations in tribal unity and control that today are still critical issues on numerous reservations.

The potential of the federal government for conscious harm is discussed in the next selection—Dorothy Bohn's examination of the Eisenhower administration's attempt to reverse New Deal Indian reforms. Special interest groups, anxious to get their hands on valuable timber lands, lobbied in Congress for an end to the reservation system. The "termination policy" ultimately accepted by the Eisenhower administration was nothing but an updated version of the land-grab technique employed against the Cherokees in the 1830s—the destruction of reservations by distributing tribal land among individual Indians from whom whites could more easily obtain it and the transfer of control of Indian affairs from the federal to state and local government.*

The next group of selections illustrates the realities of minorities' relations with America's judicial system. Sometimes, as Dorothy Bohn illustrated, the problem is that the laws themselves are bad. Often, however, the problem is with their application. Here, the prejudices of those entrusted with safeguarding the laws, from policemen to judges, become crucial. Américo Paredes, in his discussion of the Texas Rangers, describes how "law enforcers" victimized rather than protected Mexican Americans in the Lone Star State.

Anti-minority attitudes in the law enforcement system may also be discovered in courtrooms across the nation. Fred P. Graham's article, " 'Jim Crow Justice' on Trial in the South," describes how Blacks have been systematically excluded from Southern juries by hostile white communities.

1. JOHN COLLIER

The Indian New Deal**

In March, 1933, Franklin D. Roosevelt entered into office as President of

*See Mary E. Young, "Indian Removal and Land Allotment: The Civilized Tribes and Jacksonian Justice," Chapter II, section B above.

**From John Collier, *Indians of the Americas*, Copyright © 1947 John Collier. Reprinted by arrangement with the New American Library, New York, N.Y.

the United States. Harold L. Ickes became the new Secretary of the Interior. I was appointed the new Indian Commissioner.

I had been learning a great deal about the American Indian himself, and about other men and women who knew the Indian, for over twelve years; and my staff and I, always with the firm support of Harold L. Ickes and the active and personal interest of tht President, formulated a set of principles that have remained dominant. They may be summarized this way:

First, Indian societies must and can be discovered in their continuing existence, or regenerated, or set into being *de novo* and made use of. This procedure serves equally the purposes of those who believe the ancient Indian ways to be best and those who believe in rapid acculturation to the higher rather than the lower levels of white life.

Second, the Indian societies, whether ancient, regenerated or created anew, must be given status, responsibility and power.

Third, the land, held, used and cherished in the way the particular Indian group desires, is fundamental to any lifesaving program.

Fourth, each and all of the freedoms should be extended to Indians, and in the most convincing and dramatic manner possible. In practice this included repeal of sundry espionage statutes, guarantee of the right to organize, and proclamation and enforcement of cultural liberty, religious liberty, and unimpeded relationships of the generations.

Fifth, the grant of freedom must be more, however, than a remission of enslavements. Free for what? Organization is necessary to freedom: help toward organizing must be extended by the government. Credit is necessary to freedom; co-operatively managed credit must be supplied. Knowledge is necessary to freedom: education in terms of live local issues and problems must be supplied through activity programs in the schools; technological and business and civic education must be supplied to adults; professional and collegiate training must be opened to the post-adolescent group. Responsibility is necessary to freedom: one responsibility is perpetuation of the natural resources, and conservation must be made mandatory on the tribes, by statute. Capital goods are necessary to freedom, and responsibility must be applied to capital goods: a tribe that handles its revolving credit fund irresponsibly must know that shrunken credit will be its lot tomorrow.

And now, the sixth principle: The experience of responsible democracy, is, of all experiences, the most therapeutic, the most disciplinary, the most dynamogenic and the most productive of efficiency. In this one affirmation we, the workers who knew so well the diversity of the Indian situation and its incalcitrancy toward monistic programs, were prepared to be unreserved, absolute, even at the risk of blunders and of turmoil. We tried to extend to the tribes a self-governing self-determination without any limit beyond the need to advance by stages to the goal. Congress let us go only part way, but the part way, when administrative will was undeviating, proved to be enough. Often the administrative will was not undeviating, often the administrative resourcefulness was not enough, often the Gulliver's threads of the land allotment system and of civil service and the appropriation systems kept the administrator imprisoned. The establishment of living democracy, profound democracy, is a high art; it is the ultimate challenge to the administrator. The Indian Service since 1933 has practiced the art, has met the challenge, in ways varied enough and amid situations diversified enough to enable one to give a verdict which seems genuinely momentous: the democratic way has been proved to be enormously the efficient way, the genius-releasing and the nutritive and life-impelling way, and *the way of order.*

The seventh principle I would call the first and the last: That research and then more research is essential to the program, that in the ethnic field research can be made a tool of action essential to all the other tools, indeed, that it ought to be the master tool. But we had in mind a particular kind of research impelled from central areas of needed action. Since action is by nature not only specialized but also integrative of specialties, and nearly always integrative of more than the specialties, our needed research must be of the integrative sort. Again, since the findings of the research must be carried into effect by the administrator and the layman, and must be criticized by them through their experience, the administrator and the layman must themselves participate creatively in the research, impelled as it is from their own area of need. Through such integrative research, in 1933, the Soil Conservation Service directly originated in the ecological and economic problems of the Navajo Indian tribe. In current years integrative research (the administrator and layman always participating) has pushed far back our horizons of knowledge and understanding of a whole series of the tribes, and has searched our policies, administration, personnel and operating methods to their foundations. . . .

In 1934 the Indian Reorganization bill was laid before Congress, where the hearings on it lasted several months. Some people ridiculed this bill because it contained 52 printed pages. They forgot that it was offered as a successor to the greater part of several thousand pages of Indian law. Until 1934, Indian tribes rarely had been consulted on the legislation introduced for their supposed benefit. In preparing this bill, however, the Indian office first sent to all the tribes questions concerning the Indian problems deemed to be central. Then the bill was furnished them all. Finally, congresses of

Indians were held in all the regions, gatherings in which practically every tribe in the United States was represented.

As originally introduced in Congress the bill had six main parts.

1. The Indian societies were to be recognized, and be empowered and helped to undertake political, administrative and economic self-government.

2. Provision was made for an Indian civil service and for the training of Indians in administration, the professions and other vocations.

3. Land allotment was to be stopped, and the revestment of Indians with land was provided for.

4. A system of agricultural and industrial credit was to be established, and the needed funds authorized.

5. Civil and criminal law enforcement, below the level reached by federal court jurisdiction, was to be set up under a system of courts operating with simplified procedures and ultimately responsible to the tribes.

6. The consolidation of fractionalized allotted lands, and the delivery of allotments back into the tribal estate, was provided for under conditions which safeguarded all individual property rights and freedoms.

The first four parts of the Reorganization bill, as listed, became law. The fifth and sixth parts were lost. The fifth part may have been fortunately lost, because the tribes, under the enacted parts of the bill and under court decisions defining the unextinguished, inherent powers of Indian tribes, are coping with law and order more effectively with each passing year. But the loss of the sixth part was a major disaster to the Indians, the Indian service and the program. Congress has not yet righted that blunder of 1934. The fractionalizing of allotted Indian lands rushes on; the real estate operation of leasing these atomized parcels and collecting and accounting for and paying out the hundreds of thousands of vanishing incomes becomes increasingly costly, and increasingly a barrier against productive work or thinking in the allotted jurisdictions; millions of their best acres remain unusable to the Indians.

In the meantime, however, the Indian Service and the tribes are struggling to reverse the flood that is eating away the Indians' land-base. This is being done through voluntary exchanges and relinquishments, which require contact with each of the all but innumerable heirs—fifty heirship equities may vest in one Indian, and one allotment may have hundreds of scattered heirs. Despite the difficulties, the wasting flood has been checked and reversed in a few jurisdictions. It is only where this occurs that there can be a beginning of the positive program of using Indian lands through Indian effort. The situation was fully recognized in the report of the House Sub-committee on Indian Investigation, issued in December, 1944. In passing so lightly over this very important subject I wish only to add that in this matter, too, the Indians are wrestling with a problem widely encountered in other lands. One of the heavy drags on the agricultural economy of Asiatic India, for example, is the ever-increasing fractionalization of farm holdings. The formulae that are being successfully used here in the United States (but far too gradually, in the absence of the Congressional authority sought but not obtained) have application in Europe and in Asia.

The Reorganization bill, as finally enacted, contained a requirement that every tribe should accept or reject it in a referendum held by secret ballot. Those who accepted the act could organize under it for local self-government. Through a subsequent referendum they could organize themselves as federal corporations chartered for economic enterprise. Ultimately, about three-fourths of the Indians of the United States and Alaska came within the act. A related enactment, the Johnson-O'Malley Act, also passed in 1934, provided for the devolution of federal power to states and other political subdivisions, and for the enlistment of private agencies in the Indian task, through a flexible system of contracts and of grants-in-aid.

The Indian Service, on the basis of this legislation and impelled by the principles enumerated above, has striven to the end that every one of the particular programs—conservation, the cattle program, community organization, schools, the credit program, health, the Indian branch of the Civilian Conservation Corps and the other depression-years programs, the arts and crafts work—that every particular program should serve the primary aims of freeing or regenerating the Indian societies, and infusing them with the spirit of democracy, implementing them with democratic tools, and concentrating their attention upon their basic practical exigencies. Year after year, and cumulatively with the years, we who were doing the work observed sadly our partial failures, here and there our complete failures. Yet we also witnessed a development that has far outweighed the deficiences.

We have seen the Indian prove himself to be the best credit risk in the United States: of more than $10,300,000 loaned across ten years, only $69,000 is today delinquent. We have seen the Indian beef-cattle holdings (nearly always they are managed co-operatively) increase 105 per cent in number of animals and 2,300 per cent in yield of animal products; and we have seen this increase take place on ranges that in varying measures were gutted by erosion caused by overgrazing twelve years ago, and now, in general, are overgrazed and gutted no more. We have watched scores of ancient tribal systems reorient themselves toward modern tasks, while more than a hundred tribal democracies have been newly born and have lived and marched out into life; these democracies are political, industrial and social. We have witnessed the Indian peoples giving themselves with ardor and discipline to the war; 25,000 of their young people have served in the armed forces, with the highest volunteering record, we believe, of any population in the country. Finally, we have seen the Indian death rate more than cut in half, and for this achievement the expanded and improved clinical services supply only a partial explanation: the changed anticipation, from death to life, the world winds that blow at last within what were the reservation compounds, the happiness and excitement of democratic striving and clashing and living—this is the significant explanation of a 55 per cent decrease in the death rate in less than ten years. . . .

This task of the guardian government, to make free the peoples who are its dependencies, demands not only sincerity of disinterested purpose but also deep knowledge of what those peoples are, and of the material environment within which they have their being. In particular (and this is true of all human life) what they are must be known in relation to what they must conquer. Here we verge upon social planning, which is just now beginning, and upon administration as art and science, which is also just beginning. In dealing with pre-industrial and pre-literate peoples, with colonies and dependencies, it has been the rule to rush in where angels would tread very cautiously. I mean, customary for dominant and guardian governments and religious and social missionaries and investment bankers thus to rush. Acoma and the Navajos, both, out of somewhat opposite records, raise their voices for knowledge and more knowledge, wisdom and more wisdom, and all possible freedom from the panic of haste, in the dealings which are upon us—the inescapable dealings—with the ethnic groups of Oceania and Asia, the Caribbean and Africa and our Western Hemisphere countries. Hundreds of millions of people raise or will raise the same voice that Acoma and the Navajos raise now.

It is no contradiction that even blunderingly making dependent peoples free to grapple with real emergencies is hygienic, life-releasing and life-saving. The apparent contradiction is canceled out with time, if the administrator is faithful to the spirit of science, to the spirit of that knowledge which he has not yet mastered. It is from the needs of action that knowledge is dynamically empowered. Imperfect action is better for men and societies than perfection in waiting, for the errors wrought by action are cured by new action. When the people acted upon are themselves made true partners in the actions, and co-discoverers of the corrections of error, then through and through, and in spite of blunders or even by virtue of them, the vital energies are increased, confidence increases, power increases, experience builds toward wisdom, and the most potent of all principles and ideals, deep democracy, slowly wins the field. This presupposition of the Indian administration since 1933 has been borne out by all of the experience.

Another conclusion that holds significance for dependencies everywhere pertains to the technical instrument, the Indian Reorganization Act itself. Over Indian matters, as over offshore dependencies, Congress still holds plenary power. But in the Indian Reorganization Act, and in some other related Indian statutes, Congress through general legislation has adopted self-restraining ordinances. The Reorganization Act furnishes a flexible system for the devolution of authority from the government, including Congress, to the tribes. The Johnson-O'Malley Act furnishes the machinery for devolution from the federal institution to local subdivisions of government. The Pueblo Lands Act places the Pueblo tribal corporations in control of the communal monies. It is true that all three of these acts explicitly or by implication affirm that federal responsibility shall continue, no matter how far the devolution shall go. They contemplate that a single, integrated agency of administration shall continue to exist, charged with the effectuation and defense of the Congressional policies. At the same time, however, this power of defense includes defense against Congressional attack on the policies; and, in addition, the acts contemplate that the single, integrated agency shall procure the needed services rather than itself supplying them. The Reorganization Act offends many prejudices and blocks the ambitions of many and powerful groups, and therefore it has been under attack within Congress every year since it was enacted. Yet it has not been repealed or weakened in any item. The act which freed the Indians and moved the administration toward diversity of program and method has proved to be also a conserving and stabilizing measure.

The policies established by legislation in 1934 have withstood every attack, except the attack through appropriations. Increasingly in recent years the appropriations acts of Congress have been made vehicles of covert legislation. The appropriations sub-committees, especially in the House of Representatives, are all but autonomous; the House gives only a fiction of deliberative consideration to the annual supply bills. In numberless cases Congress has concluded after careful deliberation that such and such policies shall be law, and has then proceeded to rubber-stamp appropriation bills which nullify and reverse the policies.

Specifically, in the Indian field, land acquisition for Indians, authorized by Congress, is blocked through the appropriation bills; the situation is similar with respect to the expansion of the Indian co-operative credit system. Congress legislated that Indian tribes and corporations should be given technical advice and assistance in their operations, and then the appropriation act nullified the legislation. The United States entered into treaty with thirteen other Western Hemisphere countries, and by the treaty pledged herself to maintain a National Indian Institute; the House subcommittee on Interior Department appropriations has flaunted the treaty commitment. In general, the appropriation acts have handicapped the Indian Service and the Indians in the realization of every democratic, libertarian policy that Congress has established as the law of the land.

This anomaly of our Congressional system has effects, of course, far beyond Indians and dependencies and ethnic problems. Precisely because it is an evil of so universal a reach, we may expect it to be corrected in times ahead. While it lasts, it hangs like a gloomy shadow over the Indians and over territories and dependencies such as Alaska, the Virgin Islands and Puerto Rico.

From the Indian record we can draw these conclusions:

First, biological racehood, whether it exists or not, is without practical importance. There accumulate within and around races that are biologically distinguishable, and within and around races that are not biologically distinguishable, those in-group and out-group factors whose aggregate is called "racial." The factors are socially caused and socially transmitted.

Second, in ethnic matters, as in other vital matters, governmental intervention can be baneful or benign. In any field of human relations, when government tries to do the whole job, authoritatively and monopolistically, the result is baneful. The earlier Indian record is replete with evidence of this. But when government makes research an inseparable part of its ethnic operations, eschews monopoly, acts as a catalytic and co-ordinating agent, offers its service through grants-in-aid to local subdivisions, then government can be decisively benign, as the recent Indian record demonstrates. It is of national importance, and necessary to the good role of our Occidental governments in the world, that ethnic groups shall have equality of opportunity, shall be enabled to contribute their ideals and genius to the common task, shall not suffer discriminations, shall be free to breathe deeply the breath of public life. The Bill of Rights and the Constitution within the United States, the Charter of United Nations in the world, must be made good. It follows that governments and the federation of governments should and must concern themselves with ethnic matters, and that the methods should be right and not wrong.

Third, the individual fares best when he is a member of a group faring best. All human beings, in young childhood at least, are members of groups. The group is the tree and they are the fruit it bears. At least up to a certain age-level, the individual reft from his group is hurt or destroyed. The ruin inflicted on Red Indians through the white man's denial of their grouphood, and his leading them to deny their own grouphood, is only a special case of something that is universal. It may be that contemporary white life is being injured nearly as much by the submergence of its primary social groupings as the denial of Indian grouphood injured Indian life. If the primary social group in white life were regenerated for full functioning, through resourceful and sustained social effort, and were dynamically connected once more with the great society, the hygienic and creative results might be no less startling than those observed in the comeback of Indian societies.

Fourth, in ethnic groups of low prestige the apparent inferiority (acquired or innate) may mask an actual superiority. In most Indian groups the academic lag of children is pronounced, but if these children were given non-language tests that have been standardized on whites, they excel, even to a sensational extent. Their elder brothers excel when they are thrown into critical action, as they have been in the recent world war. In rhythm, so little regarded in our white society, the Indians excel. In public spirit they excel, and in joy of life, and in intensity realized within quietude. They excel in art propensities, and in truthfulness. These superiorities will be masked by an apparent inferiority until their group as a group moves into status and power. Then the mask will fall away. The application of this fact to underprivileged ethnic groups in general is readily apparent.

And last, the Indians and their societies disclose that social heritage is far more perduring than is commonly believed. On how small a life-base, on a diminished and starved life-base for how many generations, the motivations and expectations of a society, and its world-view and value system and loyalties, can keep themselves alive; how these social possessions, which are of the soul, can endure, like the roots and seeds on the Mojave desert, through long ages, without one social rain; and how they rush, like these roots and seeds, into surprising and wonderful blossom when the social rain does come at last. Perhaps no other ethnic groups have revealed this old, all-important truth so convincingly as the Indians have done. Indeed, this capacity for perdurance is one of the truths on which the hope of our world rests—our world grown so pallid in the last century, and now so deathly pallid, through the totalitarian horror. The sunken stream can flow again, the ravaged desert can bloom, the great past is not killed. The Indian experience tells us this.

2. DOROTHY BOHN

"Liberating" the Indian: Euphemism for a Land Grab*

On July 27, 1953, Congress, under pressure from the Department of the Interior, announced a change of policy toward the American Indian that appears, to Indians, as a sweeping betrayal of trust. Joint Resolution 108 declared that the long-existing relationship between the federal government and the Indians was to be terminated, regardless of Indian desires. In August, President Eisenhower signed Public Law 280, enacted in pursuance of this policy, though he termed it an "un-Christian" approach. The new law permits any state government to substitute itself for the federal government in civil and criminal matters involving Indians—which means, in effect, that the states will be able to pulverize tribal cultures.

Public Law 280 was only a beginning. The Interior Department has now sent to Congress separate bills that together affect 70,000 Indians, and more are to come. Each bill purports to deal on a local basis with a named group of Indians. The effect of all will be to abolish federal trusteeship, dissolve the tribal constitutions and charters through which Indians are entitled to defend their property, end all federal Indian services, and nullify, without Indian consent, the contractual commitments of the federal government toward the tribes. These commitments are formulated in numerous treaties, agreements, and statutes, and in the charters and constitutions worked out through the Indian Reorganization Act.

In 1922-23, when Albert B. Fall was Secretary of the Interior, a similar attack on Indian rights was launched through the medium of the Indian omnibus bill. Because this was an omnibus bill, the Indians and their friends could mobilize to defeat it, and they did. A hundred separate bills, each local in application, each ostensibly based on a special need, are far more difficult to defeat.

What is the purpose of these bills? Are they another "land grab" in the guise of "emancipation"? John Collier, former Commissioner of Indian Affairs, believes that private interests are behind them and that the American Indian is threatened with destructions. "As soon as the federal trust is dissolved," he said in a recent speech before the American Anthropological Association, "the land would be broken into individual ownership. In no time the white man would move in and take over this land that's worth so

*Dorothy Bohn, "'Liberating' the Indian: Euphemism for a Land Grab," *Nation,* 178 (February 20, 1954), pp. 150-51. Reprinted by permission of *Nation.*

many billions of dollars . . . I am not aware of any state pressures wanting to take over the Indians. It would bring nothing but misery for the states and the Indians.''

Montana, with 4 per cent of its population living on seven Indian reservations, is deeply concerned over the proposed laws. The first Montana reservation marked for liquidation is the Flathead, which includes some of America's finest timber lands, water resources, and dam sites. Other Montana reservations are rich in oil and mineral resources—prime targets for special interests. The issue was recently discussed in Great Falls at an open forum sponsored by the Cascade County Community Council before a packed gallery. Representatives of the government and of the Inter-Tribal Policy Board, which speaks for the eight Montana tribes, presented arguments pro and con. The apprehension of the Indians over their abandonment by the federal government and the impact of the change on state welfare and other agencies were the main points stressed by the opposition.

Walter McDonald, chairman of the Flathead Tribal Council, attacked the measure as sponsored by persons who cared only for money. He reported that a Congressional committee told the Flatheads that each member of the tribe was worth $17,000 and the tribe as a whole more than $77,000,000. McDonald asserted that the Congressmen attempted to use these statistics to get members to sign a petition favoring the plan. ''We have a sacred right to be on our reservation,'' he said. ''I can't see why Congress is so interested in our reservation.''

Steve DeMers of the Inter-Tribal Policy Board objected to the haste of the withdrawal as planned by the government. ''Liquidation could not be accomplished in two years,'' he said, ''the period allowed under the proposed bill.'' K. W. Bergen, state Coordinator of Indian Affairs, said it was not fair for the federal government to throw on to the states or county the problems that its new reservation system had created. The most dramatic note of the evening, which brought applause from the predominantly Indian audience, was sounded by Dave Higgins, chairman of the Inter-Tribal Policy Board, who had been allotted ten minutes of discussion time. ''Ten minutes,'' he said, ''is a short time to cover 175 years of wrongdoing.''

All over America people are waking up to this threat to our Indian citizens. National organizations like the Association on American Indian Affairs and the Indian Rights Association are leading protest movements. The three hundred delegates to the tenth annual convention of the National Congress of American Indians, held at Phoenix, Arizona, on December 7-9, adopted resolutions opposing any measures to end federal service to Indians.

Similar action has been taken by the Montana Conference of Social Welfare, the Montana Inter-Tribal Policy Board, and various civic and church groups. The Daughters of the American Revolution, at its sixty-second Continental Congress last April, passed a resolution asking that no federal services be withdrawn without the full consent of each tribe concerned.

At the Conference of Indian Rights and Resources held under the sponsorship of the University of Minnesota on November 9 and 10, the issues were clearly stated by D'Arcy McNickle, nationally known author and director of the American Indian Development Foundation. Mr. McNickle believed that the present situation in Congress had arisen because members were impatient with the slowness with which the Bureau of Indian Affairs and the Indians themselves were moving toward integration. But he pointed out that Congress itself and the administrative agency charged with responsibility for Indian affairs had failed to provide adequate health care, education, or aid in the development and proper use of Indian resources. As a result the Indian people were unprepared for full participation in our competitive society.

At the same conference Dr. Richard Schifter, a Washington, D.C., attorney who is general counsel of the Association on American Indian Affairs, stated that "in many respects this is a movement to liberate the Indian from his land." He affirmed that the Indian's right to his land was "a basic, natural right," first proclaimed by papal authority and subsequently upheld by Supreme Court decisions. "If we agree that we are here dealing with a moral rather than a legal principle," he continued, "we must recognize that Congress can neither repeal nor amend it. It is there for us to obey it or to violate it."

The white man's attitude toward the Indian has been inconsistent and vacillating. Though treaties have been made and laws have been passed to protect the Indian's sovereign right to the land, he has been inexorably pushed back until only a few scattered reservations remain to him.

Throughout the history of the United States conscience and Manifest Destiny have been at odds, but in the past two decades conscience appears to have had the upper hand. In 1934 Congress passed the Indian Reorganization Act, which halted the movement away from the land and encouraged development of Indian resources. In 1946 it set up the Indian Claims Commission to adjudicate claims against the federal government. Now the pendulum appears to be swinging the other way. When the Indian's culture and folkways have passed from the American scene, Congress can build monuments to his memory and eulogize him as a part of our "glorious past."

3. AMÉRICO PAREDES

The Texas Rangers*

The group of men who were most responsible for putting the Texan's pseudo folklore into deeds were the Texas Rangers. They were part of the legend themselves, its apotheosis as it were. If all the books written about the Rangers were put one on top of the other, the resulting pile would be almost as tall as some of the tales that they contain. The Rangers have been pictured as a fearless, almost superhuman breed of men, capable of incredible feats. It may take a company of militia to quell a riot, but one Ranger was said to be enough for one mob. Evildoers, especially Mexican ones, were said to quail at the mere mention of the name. To the Ranger is given the credit for ending lawlessness and disorder along the Rio Grande.

The Ranger did make a name for himself along the Border. The word *rinche,* from "ranger," is an important one in Border folklore. It has been extended to cover not only the Rangers but any other Americans armed and mounted and looking for Mexicans to kill. Possemen and border patrolmen are also *rinches,* and even Pershing's cavalry is so called in Lower Border variants of ballads about the pursuit of Villa. The official Texas Rangers are known as the *rinches de la Kineña* or Rangers of King Ranch, in accordance with the Borderer's belief that the Rangers were the personal strong-arm men of Richard King and the other "cattle barons."

What the Border Mexican thought about the Ranger is best illustrated by means of sayings and anecdotes. Here are a few that are typical.

1. The Texas Ranger always carries a rusty old gun in his saddlebags. This is for use when he kills an unarmed Mexican. He drops the gun beside the body and then claims he killed the Mexican in self-defense and after a furious battle.

2. When he has to kill an armed Mexican, the Ranger tries to catch him asleep, or he shoots the Mexican in the back.

3. If it weren't for the American soldiers, the Rangers wouldn't dare come to the Border. The Ranger always runs and hides behind the soldiers when real trouble starts.

4. Once an army detachment was chasing a raider, and they were led by a couple of Rangers. The Mexican went into the brush. The Rangers galloped

*From Américo Paredes, *With a Pistol in His Hand: A Border Ballad and Its Hero* (Austin, University of Texas Press, 1958), pp. 23-32. Reprinted by permission of the University of Texas Press.

up to the place, pointed it out, and then stepped back to let the soldiers go in first.

5. Two Rangers are out looking for a Mexican horse thief. They strike his trail, follow it for a while, and then turn at right angles and ride until they meet a half-dozen Mexican laborers walking home from the fields. These they shoot with their deadly Colts. Then they go to the nearest town and send back a report to Austin: "In pursuit of horse thieves we encountered a band of Mexicans, and though outnumbered we succeeded in killing a dozen of them after a hard fight, without loss to ourselves. It is believed that others of the band escaped and are making for the Rio Grande." And as one can see, except for a few omissions and some slight exaggeration, the report is true in its basic details. Austin is satisfied that all is well on the Border. The Rangers add to their reputation as a fearless, hard-fighting breed of men, and the real horse thief stays out of the surrounding territory for some time, for fear he may meet up with the Rangers suddenly on some lonely road one day, and they may mistake him for a laborer.

I do not claim for these little tidbits the documented authenticity that Ranger historians claim for their stories. What we have here is frankly partisan and exaggerated without a doubt, but it does throw some light on Mexican attitudes toward the Ranger which many Texans may scarcely suspect. And it may be that these attitudes are not without some basis in fact.

The Rangers have been known to exaggerate not only the numbers of Mexicans they engaged but those they actually killed and whose bodies could be produced, presumably. In 1859 Cortina was defeated by a combined force of American soldiers and Texas Rangers. Army Major Heintzelman placed Cortina's losses at sixty; Ranger Captain Ford estimated them at two hundred. In 1875 Ranger Captain McNelly climaxed his Red Raid on the Rio Grande by wiping out a band of alleged cattle rustlers at Palo Alto. McNelly reported fifteen dead; eight bodies were brought into Brownsville. One more instance should suffice. In 1915 a band of about forty *sediciosos* (seditionists) under Aniceto Pizaña raided Norias in King Ranch. Three days later they were said to have been surrounded a mile from the Rio Grande and wiped out to the last man by a force of Rangers and deputies. About ten years later, just when accounts of this Ranger exploit were getting into print, I remember seeing Aniceto Pizaña at a wedding on the south bank of the Rio Grande. He looked very much alive, and in 1954 I was told he was still living. Living too in the little towns on the south bank are a number of the Norias raiders.

It also seems a well-established fact that the Rangers often killed Mexicans who had nothing to do with the criminals they were after. Some actually were shot by mistake, according to the Ranger method of shooting first and asking questions afterwards. But perhaps the majority of the innocent Mexicans who died at Ranger hands were killed much more deliberately than that. A wholesale butchery of "accomplices" was effected twice during Border history by the Rangers, after the Cortina uprising in 1859 and during the Pizaña uprising of 1915. Professor Webb calls the retaliatory killings of 1915 an "orgy of bloodshed [in which] the Texas Rangers played a prominent part." He sets the number of Mexicans killed between 500 and 5,000. This was merely an intensification of an established practice which was carried on during less troubled years on a smaller scale.

Several motives must have been involved in the Ranger practice of killing innocent Mexicans as accomplices of the wrongdoers they could not catch. The most obvious one was "revenge by proxy," as Professor Webb calls it, a precedent set by Bigfoot Wallace, who as a member of Hays's Rangers in the Mexican War killed as many inoffensive Mexicans as he could to avenge his imprisonment after the Mier expedition. A more practical motive was the fact that terror makes an occupied country submissive, something the Germans knew when they executed hostages in the occupied countries of Europe during World War II. A third motive may have been the Ranger weakness for sending impressive reports to Austin about their activities on the Border. The killing of innocent persons attracted unfavorable official notice only when it was extremely overdone.

In 1954 Mrs. Josefina Flores de Garza of Brownsville gave me some idea how it felt to be on the receiving end of the Ranger "orgy of bloodshed" of 1915. At that time Mrs. Garza was a girl of eighteen, the eldest of a family that included two younger boy in theirlteens and several small children. The family lived on a ranch near Harlingen, north of Brownsville. When the Ranger "executions" began, other Mexican ranchers sought refuge in town. The elder Flores refused to abandon his ranch, telling his children, "El que nada debe nada teme." (He who is guilty of nothing fears nothing.)

The Rangers arrived one day, surrounded the place and searched the outbuildings. The family waited in the house. Then the Rangers called the elder Flores out. He stepped to the door, and they shot him down. His two boys ran to him when he fell, and they were shot as they bent over their father. Then the Rangers came into the house and looked around. One of them saw a new pair of chaps, liked them, and took them with him. They left immediately afterwards.

From other sources I learned that the shock drove Josefina Flores temporarily insane. For two days her mother lived in the house with a brood of terrified youngsters, her deranged eldest daughter, and the corpses of her husband and her sons. Then a detachment of United States soldiers passed through, looking for raiders. They buried the bodies and got the family into town.

The daughter recovered her sanity after some time, but it still upsets her a great deal to talk about the killings. And, though forty years have passed, she still seems to be afraid that if she says something critical about the Rangers they will come and do her harm. Apparently Ranger terror did its work well, on the peaceful and the inoffensive.

Except in the movies, ruthlessness and a penchant for stretching the truth do not in themselves imply a lack of courage. The Borderer's belief that all Rangers are shooters-in-the-back is of the same stuff as the Texan belief that all Mexicans are back-stabbers. There is evidence, however, that not all Rangers lived up to their reputation as a fearless breed of men. Their basic techniques of ambush, surprise, and shooting first—with the resultant "mistake" killings of innocent bystanders—made them operate at times in ways that the average city policeman would be ashamed to imitate. The "shoot first and ask questions later" method of the Rangers has been romanticized into something dashing and daring, in technicolor, on a wide screen, and with Gary Cooper in the title role. Pierce's *Brief History* gives us an example of the way the method worked in actuality.

> On May 17, 1885, Sgt. B. D. Lindsay and six men from Company D frontier battalion of rangers, while scouting near the Rio Grande for escaped Mexican convicts, saw two Mexicans riding along. . . . As the horses suited the description of those alleged to be in possession of the convicts, and under the impression that these two were the men he was after, Lindsay called to them to halt, and at once opened fire on them. The elder Mexican fell to the ground with his horse, but the younger, firing from behind the dead animal, shot Private Sicker through the heart, killing him instantly. B. C. Reilly was shot through both thighs and badly wounded. The Mexicans stood their ground until the arrival of men from the ranch of a deputy-sheriff named Prudencio Herrera, who . . . insisted that the two Mexicans were well known and highly respected citizens and refused to turn them over to the rangers. . . . The citizens of Laredo . . . were indignant over the act of the rangers in shooting on Gonzalez, claiming that he was a well-known citizen of good repute, and alleging that the rangers would have killed them at the outset but for the fact that they defended themselves. The rangers, on the other hand, claimed that unless they would have proceeded as they did, should the Mexicans have been the criminals they were really after they, the rangers, would have been fired on first.

There is unanswerable logic in the Ranger sergeant's argument, if one concedes him his basic premise: that a Mexican's life is of little value anyway. But this picture of seven Texas Rangers, feeling so defenseless in the face of two Mexicans that they must fire at them on sight, because the Mexicans might be mean and shoot at them first, is somewhat disillusioning to those of us who have grown up with the tradition of the lone Ranger getting off the train and telling the station hangers-on, "Of course they sent one Ranger. There's just one riot, isn't there?" Almost every week one reads of ordinary city policemen who capture desperate criminals—sometimes singlehandedly—without having to shoot first.

Sometimes the "shoot first" method led to even more serious consequences, and many a would-be Mexican-killer got his head blown off by a comrade who was eager to get in the first shot and mistook his own men for Mexicans while they all waited in ambush. Perhaps "shoot first and ask questions afterwards" is not the right name for this custom. "Shoot first and then see what you're shooting at" may be a better name. As such it has not been limited to the Texas Rangers. All over the United States during the deer season, Sunday hunters go out and shoot first.

Then there is the story about Alfredo Cerda, killed on Brownsville's main street in 1902. The Cerdas were prosperous ranchers near Brownsville, but it was their misfortune to live next to one of the "cattle barons" who was not through expanding yet. One day three Texas Rangers came down from Austin and "executed" the elder Cerda and one of his sons as cattle rustlers. The youngest son fled across the river, and thus the Cerda ranch was vacated. Five months later the remaining son, Alfredo Cerda, crossed over to Brownsville. He died the same day, shot down by a Ranger's gun.

Marcelo Garza, Sr., of Brownsville is no teller of folktales. He is a respected businessman, one of Brownsville's most highly regarded citizens of Mexican descent. Mr. Garza claims to have been an eyewitness to the shooting of the youngest Cerda. In 1902, Mr. Garza says, he was a clerk at the Tomás Fernández store on Elizabeth Street. A Ranger whom Mr. Garza identifies as "Bekar" shot Alfredo, Mr. Garza relates, as Cerda sat in the doorway of the Fernández store talking to Don Tomás, the owner. The Ranger used a rifle to kill Cerda, who was unarmed, "stalking him like a wild animal." After the shooting the Ranger ran into a nearby saloon, where other Rangers awaited him, and the group went out the back way and sought refuge with the federal troops in Fort Brown, to escape a mob of indignant citizens. The same story had been told to me long before by my father, now deceased. He was not a witness to the shooting but claimed to have seen the chasing of the Rangers into Fort Brown.

Professor Webb mentions the shooting in 1902 of an Alfredo Cerda in Brownsville by Ranger A. Y. Baker. He gives no details. Mr. Dobie also mentions an A. Y. Baker, "a famous ranger and sheriff of the border country," as the man responsible for the "extermination" of the unexterminated raiders of Norias.

The methods of the Rangers are often justified as means to an end, the stamping out of lawlessness on the Border. This coin too has another face. Many Borderers will argue that the army and local law enforcement agencies were the ones that pacified the Border, that far from pacifying the area Ranger activities stirred it up, that instead of eliminating lawlessness along the Rio Grande the Rangers were for many years a primary cause of it. It is pointed out that it was the army that defeated the major border raiders and the local authorities that took care of thieves and smugglers. . . .

That the Rangers stirred up more trouble than they put down is an opinion that has been expressed by less partisan sources. Goldfinch quotes a Captain Ricketts of the United States Army, who was sent by the War Department to investigate Cortina's revolt, as saying that "conditions that brought federal troops to Brownsville had been nourished but not improved by demonstrations on the part of some Rangers and citizens." In 1913 State Representative Cox of Ellis attempted to eliminate the Ranger force by striking out their appropriation from the budget. Cox declared "that there is more danger from the Rangers than from the men they are supposed to hunt down; that there is no authority of law for the Ranger force; that they are the most irresponsible officers in the State." John Garner, future Vice-President of the United States, was among those who early in the twentieth century advocated abolishing the Ranger force.

In *The Texas Rangers* Professor Webb notes that on the Border after 1848 the Mexican was "victimized by the law," that "the old landholding families found their titles in jeopardy and if they did not lose in the courts they lost to their American lawyers," and again that "the Mexicans suffered not only in their persons but in their property." What he fails to note is that this lawless law was enforced principally by the Texas Rangers. It was the Rangers who could and did furnish the fortune-making adventurer with services not rendered by the United States Army or local sheriffs. And that is why from the point of view of the makers of fortunes, the Rangers were so important to the "pacification" of the Border.

The Rangers and those who imitated their methods undoubtedly exacerbated the cultural conflict on the Border rather than allayed it. The assimilation of the north-bank Border people into the American commonwealth was necessary to any effective pacification of the Border. Ranger operations did much to impede that end. They created in the Border Mexican a deep and understandable hostility for American authority; they drew Border communities even closer together than they had been, though at that time they were beginning to disintegrate under the impact of new conditions.

Terror cowed the more inoffensive Mexican, but it also added to the roll of bandits and raiders many high-spirited individuals who would have otherwise remained peaceful and useful citizens. These were the heroes of the Border folk. People sang *corridos* about these men who, in the language of the ballads, "each with his pistol defended his right."

4. FRED P. GRAHAM

"Jim Crow Justice" on Trial in South*

In three hours and five minutes, two all-white juries in Hayneville, Ala., have given the civil rights movement a prime target for next year—"Jim Crow justice."

It took one jury an hour and thirty-five minutes to acquit volunteer deputy sheriff Thomas L. Coleman of the shotgun killing of young Jonathan Daniels. Last week another jury beat that record by five minutes—it acquitted Collie Leroy Wilkins of murder charges in the slaying of Mrs. Viola Gregg Liuzzo in an hour and a half. Both victims were white civil rights workers.

Dr. Martin Luther King rushed home from Europe to organize protests, and Negro leader James Farmer called for a new Federal law "to prevent the Southern jury system from continuing to deprive Negroes and whites of justice."

The Justice Department jumped Monday into a private suit against exclusion of Negroes from the Hayneville jury rolls, and it became quickly clear that a key goal of the civil rights movement during the next session of Congress will be legislation to get more Negroes on Southern juries.

No Prosecution

But how? The one existing U.S. law against jury discrimination is so puny that the Justice Department has yet to prosecute any official under it in

*Fred P. Graham, " 'Jim Crow Justice' on Trial in South," New York *Times,* October 31, 1965.

this century. Attorney General Nicholas deB. Katzenbach threatened last week to invoke the 1875 criminal law, but privately Justice Department officials said it could serve only as a prod to local officials.

Since the law punishes only past offenses, and allows only fines and not jail penalties, and since the official himself would get a trial by a Southern jury, the criminal statute is considered almost worthless.

The Federal courts have held for years (and the Mississippi Supreme Court agreed last week) that Negroes' convictions cannot stand if members of their race have been systematically excluded from the grand and petit jury rolls. This doesn't require that Negroes actually serve on the jury, and one Federal court has struck down a Negro's conviction because a Negro was deliberately put on the jury.

That these case-by-case appeals of convictions have little effect is shown by Carroll County, Miss., where Negroes comprise more than half the population. In 1959 the murder conviction of a Negro was reversed because of jury discrimination. Yet the Civil Rights Commission heard testimony last spring that Negroes still don't serve on juries there.

But civil rights advocates have been embarrassed to learn that, even when Southern officials stop excluding Negroes from jury lists and attempt to seek them out, few Negroes actually serve on juries.

When the American Civil Liberties Union sued to remedy the dearth of Negroes on Birmingham juries, its own brief confessed that jury officials had sought Negro jurors by mail and by knocking on Negroes' doors.

Few Negroes answered the letters, the brief said, and many were afraid to answer the door.

The common practice of picking jurors at random from telephone books, voter registration lists, club and church membership lists, automobile owners and real property taxpayers' lists results in the exclusion of poor persons.

The A.C.L.U. has asked the Court of Appeals for the Fifth Circuit to outlaw all lists and to require that prospective jurors be picked as the Gallup Poll is conducted—by scientific surveys that seek out an accurate cross section of the community.

Aside from the trouble and cost of this proposal, it raises an important policy question—should jury panels represent a cross section of the community (including, presumably, illiterates)? Or should it be enough that no groups are deliberately excluded?

Some civil rights advocates are pressing for the "cross section" theory because in communities such as Hayneville it would amount to a quota system on Negroes. Seven Negroes were on the jury panel in the Liuzzo murder trial last week—yet none of them made it through the selection process to serve on the jury. Since the Hayneville community is 60 per cent Negro, a quota system would have placed so many Negroes on the panel that some of them would necessarily have gone on the jury.

Whether this could have resulted in a conviction, or even prevented the acquittal, is a moot question. But indications this week were that the Justice Department would not consider a quota system.

Sources within the department confirmed that an anti-jury discrimination law will probably be submitted to Congress with other civil rights proposals next year. It will probably give the department the power to bring suit to bar local officials from excluding prospective jurors because of their race. It might also lay down some guidelines for use in selecting prospective jurors (now many officials just pick the friends of employees in the court house). It could prohibit discrimination in hiring court personnel.

In the meantime, the Justice Department was expected to spotlight the problem soon by indicating a few of the most discriminatory Southern jury officials, and by joining in other private suits by Negroes complaining about jury exclusions.

B. The Military

Minorities serving in the United States armed forces over the years have faced problems similar to those encountered in civilian life: segregation, discrimination, and the lack of equal opportunities. In recent decades the picture has changed somewhat. As the proportional number of ethnic minorities entering the armed services has grown, as civil rights groups have pressured for reforms, and as the nation has become more responsive to the issue of minority rights, the military has reacted positively. However, even though the armed forces can claim with some accuracy to be "equal opportunity employers," the military experience of minorities is still marked by tensions and frustrations not shared by their white comrades-in-arms.

The first selection, "Secret Information Concerning Black American Troops," describes the discrimination faced by Blacks in the United States Army during the First World War. This document demonstrates not only that Americans propagated the doctrine of Negro inferiority, but that they consciously sought to discourage Black aspirations for equality in American society. Recognizing this, and acting for the sake of good relations with the United States Army, the French command ordered French military personnel and civilians to treat Black soldiers just as Americans treated them.

Native Americans, too, have felt the pain of military discrimination. In addition they have had to endure serious cultural dislocations as a result of their military service. In the second selection Stan Steiner describes the hardships of Indian soldiers during World War II, the threat to tribal life posed by the war, and the difficult postwar adjustments Indian veterans were forced to make. Most Indians went willingly to fight and performed bravely in the white man's war. When the fighting ended they expected to return to good jobs and new opportunities provided by a grateful society. Instead, they found themselves ignored and unemployed. The tragic fate of Pima war hero Ira Hayes stands as a symbol of their betrayal.

The problems of minority servicemen in adjusting to civilian life is examined next within the context of the Vietnamese War. "The Great Society—in Uniform" describes the progress toward equality for Black servicemen since World War II. But if Blacks are generally pleased with the opportunities now available to them in the military, they are angered over the lack of opportunities for them once they are out of uniform. Having served their country as first-class soldiers, they resent being second-class citizens when they return home. This bitter reality caused many Black veterans of our most recent war to become militant in their demands for a better life in America.

The reason why military life has attracted so many ethnic minorities in recent years is examined in the last selection. According to Ralph Guzmán's "Mexican American Casualties in Vietnam," Chicano youths in the 1960s entered the service for reasons largely related to their socioeconomic backgrounds. They could not avoid service by qualifying for educational deferments as many Anglo youths could; the military offered economic benefits and social status they could not find at home; and it was important for them to prove their loyalty to America and dispel the lingering suspicion that they were a "foreign minority." It was for this last reason that so many Chicanos chose high-risk duty and why they suffered so many casualties in Vietnam.

1. French Military Mission Stationed with the American Army, August 7, 1918: Secret Information Concerning Black American Troops*

1. It is important for French officers who have been called upon to

*"French Military Mission Stationed with the American Army, August 7, 1918: Secret Information Concerning Black American Troops," *The Crisis,* 18 (May, 1919), pp. 16-18.

exercise command over black American troops, or to live in close contact with them, to have an exact idea of the position occupied by Negroes in the United States. The information set forth in the following communication ought to be given to these officers and it is to their interest to have these matters known and widely disseminated. It will devolve likewise on the French Military Authorities, through the medium of the Civil Authorities, to give information on this subject to the French population residing in the cantonments occupied by American colored troops.

2. The American attitude upon the Negro question may seem a matter for discussion to many French minds. But we French are not in our province if we undertake to discuss what some call "prejudice." American opinion is unanimous on the "color question" and does not admit of any discussion.

The increasing numbers of Negroes in the United States (about 15,000,000) would create for the white race in the Republic a menace of degeneracy were it not that an impassable gulf has been made between them.

As this danger does not exist for the French race, the French public has become accustomed to treating the Negro with familiarity and indulgence.

This indulgence and this familiarity are matters of grievous concern to the Americans. They consider them an affront to their national policy. They are afraid that contact with the French will inspire in black Americans aspirations which to them [the whites] appear intolerable. It is of the utmost importance that every effort be made to avoid profoundly estranging American opinion.

Although a citizen of the United States, the black man is regarded by the white Americans as an inferior being with whom relations of business or service only are possible. The black is constantly being censured for his want of intelligence and discretion, his lack of civic and professional conscience and for his tendency toward undue familiarity.

The vices of the Negro are a constant menace to the American who has to repress them sternly. For instance, the black American troops in France have, by themselves, given rise to as many complaints for attempted rape as all the rest of the army. And yet the [black American] soldiers sent us have been the choicest with respect to physique and morals, for the number disqualified at the time of mobilization was enormous.

CONCLUSION

1. We must prevent the rise of any pronounced degree of intimacy between French officers and black officers. We may be courteous and amiable with these last, but we cannot deal with them on the same plane as

with the white American officers without deeply wounding the latter. We must not eat with them, must not shake hands or seek to talk or meet with them outside of the requirements of military service.

2. We must not commend too highly the black American troops, particularly in the presence of [white] Americans. It is all right to recognize their good qualities and their services, but only in moderate terms, strictly in keeping with the truth.

3. Make a point of keeping the native cantonment population from "spoiling" the Negroes. [White] Americans become greatly incensed at any public expression of intimacy between white women with black men. They have recently uttered violent protests against a picture in the "Vie Parisienne" entitled "The Child of the Desert" which shows a [white] woman in a "cabinet particulier" with a Negro. Familiarity on the part of white women with black men is furthermore a source of profound regret to our experienced colonials who see in it an over-weening menace to the prestige of the white race.

Military authority cannot intervene directly in this question, but it can through the civil authorities exercise some influence on the population.

(Signed) LINARD.

2. STAN STEINER

The Warriors Return*

The youth, in his Eisenhower jacket, bowed his head.

In solemn arcs of the old man's hand the sacred cedar bark was waved back and forth above the boy's crew cut. The priest of the Newekwe, the Clown Society, purified the Zuñi GI. Until this rite of purification—the Hanasema Isu Waha—was performed the pueblo would not welcome home the warrior. High on the mountain plateau of New Mexico, on the rutted banks of the Zuñi River, where the rite was traditionally held, the family of the youth nodded in approval. He was no longer a soldier in the white man's army. He was a Zuñi.

It was the spring of 1946. The rite of Hanasema Isu Waha was performed repeatedly that year. Literally it meant "Bad luck, get rid of it."

Two hundred young men of the Zuñi pueblo had come home from the

*From Stan Steiner, "The Warriors Return," *The New Indians*. Copyright © 1968 by Stan Steiner. Reprinted by permission of Harper & Row, Publishers, Inc.

battlefields of World War II. Religious belief of the elders prescribed that these young soldiers, who had been contaminated by contact with "The War of the Whites" and by the world beyond, be cleansed at once. One Pueblo mother refused to touch her homecoming son, it was said, until he had undergone the rite of purification; for without the Hanasema Isu Waha the returning warriors could not dance again in the Kiva, nor know the peace of being Zuñi.

The Zuñis have a war prayer:

May your way be fulfilled.
May you be blessed with life.
Where the life-giving way
Of your Sun Father shines
May your way be reached.

Not a very warlike prayer, it was a prayer for the peaceful return of the warrior, for the peace that restores the warrior to his people, to his community.

In the farm village of the Rama Navajos, down the road, the returning warriors were similarly purified. These Navajo GI's were psychologically cleansed of their battle traumas and their urban traumas by the ceremonials known as the Blessing Way and the Enemy Way: the traditional rituals of welcome and blessing for returning soldiers. Life in the Navajo way had to be restored to those who had come near to alien death. One of the Navajo war veterans of Rama recalled: "The ceremony was arranged by my grandfather. He said we needed it because we had seen lots of dead Germans. Not only seen them, but stepped on them, and smelled some dead German bodies. He was afraid that later we might go loco if we don't have this ceremony."

The grandfathers said, "Let The War of the Whites be now forgotten. Let the white way of life, and death, be now cast out of you."

The grandfathers said, "Let The War of the Whites be now exorcised." In saying this it was not merely the enemy dead that the priests of the Navajo religion thought of as a threat, but everything that was foreign to Navajo ways. "This exposure to alien ghosts involved not only the Germans and Japanese, but also contact with white Americans," said the anthropologists John Adair and Evon Vogt in their study of the war veterans of Rama and Zuñi.

Rites of purification were widespread. Everywhere among the tribes the rituals were different. But everywhere the aim was the same: to purify the warriors of The War of the Whites and to celebrate their return to the Indian way of tribal life.

Homecoming Teton Sioux veterans of World War II journeyed to the Wind River Reservation of the Arapahos of Wyoming, late in the summer of 1946, to partake in the sacrificial sun dance. Later, when the once torturous ritual of rejuvenation was revived on the Sioux reservations of the Dakotas, in the 1950's a young man of the Northern Cheyenne of Montana offered himself in symbolic sacrifice for the return of the warriors of his tribe, who had fought in the Korean War.

Yet the rites of purification were inadequate. The young warrior who fought in World War II, or the Korean War, may or may not have brought home with him the ghosts of the alien dead that his elders feared. But he did bring home living ghosts. The war veteran—there were nearly 25,000 Indians who served in the armed forces—was a veteran of life, as well as of death, in the world beyond his reservation.

He was a "culture bearer" of the nomad caravans of the old hunters—the Marco Polos of the Indians—who brought home enticing tales of the modern world's curious beliefs and strange customs. When the warrior of World War II talked of the battles he had fought he talked not only of those fought on foreign battlefields but of those fought in the barracks of his own army, and on the streets of American cities.

A young Navajo remembered those years. He had been in the Marine Corps, and he had come home to edit his tribal paper. One day, sitting in his modernistic office, years after the war, Marshall Tome began to reminisce; but his war story, like that of so many Indians, was not about his heroism in battle. It was about his being an Indian in a white man's army. He said:

"When I went into the service I was told: 'Remember, you represent us, you represent the Dinés, you represent the Navajo, you represent the Indian. Not the rest of the country. Not the white man.' I remembered that. When I went overseas, to Asia, some of the fellows would be rough, you know, with the girls. And they would hit an old man with their rifle butts. But I would never do that.

"If a boy fell off a bike, I would pick him up. If an old man was hit with a rifle butt, I would pick him up. And people would say, 'He is different from the others. He has a brown skin.'

"And I would say, 'That's not why.'

"And people would say, 'Why are you different then?'

"And I would say, 'Because I am Indian.'

"I lived by that. I believed in that. The Indian, you see, looked at being in the services a little differently."

The Navajo artist Beatien Yazz—Little No Shirt—told his war story with more imagery. But it was the same story. He too had been in the Marine Corps during World War II. He had tasted the water of the far ocean, had tasted it with curiosity, and had found it "tasted salty." He had "to spit out the Pacific Ocean," Yazz said.

Yazz told of the initiation rites of the Marine Corps with similar disenchantment: "They say, 'How old are you?' I say, 'Old enough.' They say, 'Why do you want to be a Marine?' I say, 'I want to see the world.' So I pass my physical, then start taking fingerprint. Oh, my finger was thin, the man say. 'Papoose, go back to your ma.' . . . Two other men talk together about me. One say, 'You think he's tough enough to kill a Jap?' The other say, 'I think he kill several Japs. He's an Indian.' They just laugh at me. So they say, 'Okay, Chief.' "

"Chief"—the word was an endearment to the ears of the Indian equal to "kike" or "nigger." Yet this was the GI dogtag that invariably was hung about the neck of the Indian GI. In the barracks humor the Indian became the butt, or the teller, of wild jokes. He was portrayed with satiric accuracy as Chief White Halfoat in Joseph Heller's *Catch-22.* But, at the same time, on the battlefield he became known as a good man to stay near to. He was cool in combat, the legend said. He was a good soldier.

The "Noble Red Man" lived on; but the two roles he played, as clown and hero, were both white images of the Indian. He was neither.

Eyapaha, the tribal paper of the Upper Brûlé Sioux of the Rosebud Reservation of South Dakota, editorialized on how these attitudes he met in military life affected the Indian soldier: "Ask any Sioux serviceman serving his country in outposts or military bases or on ships or in planes what it feels like to live in a world surrounded by people of other races. He still feels like an Indian, and *he is the envy of all others who want to, but cannot be, Indian.*" [Emphasis added.]

The Indian soldier had not imitated the white soldier, said the Sioux editor. He had become stronger, not weaker, in his Indian self-esteem because of the insults; what were the insults but a hostile expression of envy?

For all that, he was lonely. The Sioux editor wrote: ". . . the Sioux serviceman stands and feels alone until he returns to his own people."

Coming home from the war, the young warrior brought little with him in his hands. A silken pillow bought in Tokyo, decorated with an embroidered wigwam, and inscribed: GOD BLISS YOU HAPPY HOME. The souvenir of the Statue of Liberty, in a feathered headdress, whose stomach opened to reveal a pencil sharpener.

He came home also with memories and ghosts. It was these ghosts that the elders feared. It was not that they thought the young men of the tribe had become white. "In four hundred years of fighting, no Indian has turned white," Peter La Farge was to sing. But they feared that, hidden in the warriors' souls, out of sight, was the embodiment of the white world, lurking there like a ghost that had to be exorcised. The young warriors had fought in two wars at once. One was military; one was cultural. Both left their wounds.

For the first time since the military defeat of their forefathers, the young warriors had left the reservations by the tens of thousands. Would they return to the ways of their forefathers? Would they return at all? Would they see themselves against the backdrop of the white world, as in a shadow play a puppet is defined against the white screen, and be able to redefine their unique Indianness? Would they become a shadow of themselves? Would they be more clearly visible as Indians? Would they disappear in illusion?

The elders were fearful.

Who knew what thoughts were in these young men? It was not easy for them to talk of these things. Many of them hardly knew the words for their thoughts; for there had been cases of boys on reservations who enlisted, or were drafted, though they could not read or write English. Life in the white world had overwhelmed them with experiences for which there were no words in their own languages. So the warriors were silent.

The upheaval in the life of the Indian was not, however, wholly due to the returning warriors. On the reservations too World War II had brought the white world home—to the doorstep.

In those years there were forty to fifty thousand Indians hired by the war factories. During the wartime labor shortage jobs were offered reservation Indians by industries that had not before, and have not since, needed to hire them. These too were war veterans, in their way, who came home with experiences, and the memories of incomes, that stirred the dust on the somnolent reservations. Jobs in town meant living in town. And radios. And cars. "The war years," chronicled the *Navajo Yearbook,* "opened up new sources of livelihood to the Navajos in the form of wage work on the railroads and in industry, and during that period the social and economic structure of Navajo society underwent important changes. The reservation agricultural base ceased to figure as the principal source of livelihood for a majority of the population, becoming instead a source of supplementary income."

The *Yearbook* noted: To a people to whom cash income was peripheral even soldiers' dependency payments "given to families of Navajos who joined [the armed forces] were a factor in this regard. . . ."

Hunting and herding and farming were still the sources of tribal prestige, but no longer were the sole source of tribal well-being. "We now have a wage economy," Maurice McCabe, the Navajo tribal manager, was able to say within a few years. And the scattering of industries that came to the reservations during the war and postwar years reflected, and intensified, this trend.

One old longhair, on the tribal council of the Navajos, was perhaps a bit premature, but he spoke of the new fear. "Soon we will not be Navajo any more."

It was the first time in history that so many—almost 100,000—Indians had participated in the world of the conquerors. The wars that had been fought for this continent, that had ended less than one hundred years ago, had been fought as against enemy nations. Since their military defeat they had been quite literally imprisoned, under guard, on the reservations. One of the Apaches who fought with Geronimo had called the tribes "prisoners of war." In many way they had been prisoners-of-war generations after the wars had ended.

War, this time to save the civilization of the conquerors, was ironically what had unlocked the reservation doors. The years of social imprisonment were ending. Peace brought new hope that the Indian would walk out of his isolation, into the triumphant society. He would be free "to be white." He would join the twentieth century. He would be beguiled by its wealth and progress. The vanishing Indian would vanish, as a tribal Indian, and become a sunburned suburbanite.

"We were looked down upon as a backward people, and the assumption was made that we must be like white men to find peace of mind," said the Paiute youth Mel Thom: "No one ever asked us what we wanted. There was always someone to put words in our mouths."

Historian William Hagan, in his *American Indians,* wrote hopefully: "The returned veterans did their part to hasten the end of the old way of life. Wartime incomes and experiences accelerated the detribalization process." The old ways were doomed.

The cultural conquest of the recalcitrant red man, by cajoling and by assimilation, was at hand. He was measured for the melting pot. It was with this hope in mind that the Hoover Commission on postwar governmental reorganization, which had been appointed by President Truman, recommended "complete integration." The Indian had, after all, proven himself, in war factory and on the battlefield, to be the equal of the white citizenry. "Complete integration" was to be his reward.

In its Task Force Report of 1947 the Hoover Commission proposed "a policy of rapid integration into American life" [*sic*]. Further, the commissioners urged the terminating of federal social services to the tribes and the transfer of these treaty obligations to the states. These thoughts were a muted echo of the Senate Indian Affairs Committee report of 1943, which had called for the liquidation of the Bureau of Indian Affairs and the termination of its services. Commissioner of Indian Affairs Zimmerman, in the Truman Administration, had similarly told a Senate hearing in 1947 that he believed the time had come to terminate federal services to the more "advanced" tribes. Evidently it was thought that if the Indian could fight and work like everyone else then he must be like everyone else.

However, it was not until the appointment of Dillon Myer, the former head of the Japanese-American Relocation Center camps during the war—a latter-day "prisoner of war" expert—as Indian Commissioner, in 1950, that these recommendations became policy. Myer was their loudest spokesman. It was under his aegis that the plans to terminate federal services and to relocate the reservation Indians were drawn up. That is, get them off their lands and into the cities.

Later, during the Eisenhower years, when the attempt was abortively made to put these policies into effect, they provoked an anguished outcry from the Indians, especially from the returned war veterans.

In the years after the war the economy of the country boomed, but not for the Indian. He was to rediscover that the Indian was not merely the last hired—he was not hired at all. The war heroes and the war jobs were too soon forgotten. If the young warrior had a brief dream of a new life, it quickly became a nostalgic reminiscence, to be bitterly swallowed in the bars of the reservation towns.

The *Navajo Yearbook* observed the desolation of the dream:

> With the close of hostilities and the sudden change to a peacetime economy, these sources of [wartime] livelihood disappeared. And the erstwhile wage earners, finding themselves without employment, were forced back to the Reservation, where there were no resources available to them beyond such meager aid as kinsmen might provide. As a result their plight became critical to the degree that it drew national attention.

Hunger, stark and unbelievable hunger, befell many of the tribes. The Hopis and the Navajos were particularly hard hit; for during the winter blizzards of 1947, at the very time that the Hoover Commission was recommending their "complete integration," these destitute Indians were suffering a famine. Food had to be airlifted to the starving Indians, much as it was airlifted to Berlin, that bitter winter.

On the reservations life was mired in hunger. Again. But the war veterans were no longer willing to endure stagnation as a way of life. Nor were they stoic in their misery, in fear of the dominant society, as their forefathers had been.

These Indian youths took to the roads, butrtherewas nowhere for them to go, and nothing for them to do. On the reservations, the interest in cars was a symbol of their unrest. In those postwar years, the use of cars eclipsed that of the horse and wagon; and this expressed the need to "get somewhere," to "get going," to escape the dtspair. Still, these restless youths hardly carried their discontent outside their reservations, into the outside world. The youths' angers rarely left home.

The hero of the U.S. Marine Corps, Ira Hayes, who had raised the flag at Iwo Jima, became the symbol of the defeat of the Indian war veterans. Hayes had been feasted and feted and bemedaled. Then he was forgotten. When he wandered home to the Pima Reservation, in the bleak and stark deserts of Arizona, he was destitute—without work, without hope.

Just a Pima Indian—
No water, no crops, no chance.

Hayes had been an exemplary soldier. It was not merely his courage, which had been honored and decorated, that indicated the kind of young man he was, but his behavior. He had been "a good boy"; he had been "a good Indian"; he had been "a good Christian."

The young Pima had abandoned his Indianness for the values and promises of the white society. It was this that rendered him defenseless and unprepared for the betrayal of his beliefs. He had nothing to sustain him in defeat. So he became "the drunken Ira Hayes," the "whiskey-drinking Indian." He drowned in a drainage ditch, in two inches of water, in that waterless desert wasteland in which he sought refuge. To the young warriors who returned from the glory of World War II, the fate of Ira Hayes was the final betrayal.

The betrayal and bitterness that the warriors felt was voiced by another Marine Corps veteran of Iwo Jima. Dennie Hosteen, a Navajo who fought in the Korean War as well, wrote some years later: "Today as I sit at home without a job I think of those Innocents in the Vietnam War that will be returning home soon, saying: What's our benefit? to their Fathers, Mothers, husbands, wives, children, friends. For us poor Indians there are none on our reservations lands and within our reservations.''

''For the Deads,'' Hosteen wrote of his comrades, ''surely there are none!''

Liquored dreams, the solace of the inertia and nothingness of jobless and hopeless days, became an obsessive disease of these defeated warriors.

The Paiute youth Mel Thom, who was to become a leader of the new Indians, remembered similar days of bitterness after the Korean War: ''For a long time we were just angry. So angry that we would get drunk for five days at a time, you know. What else could we do?''

Into the restless group of new Indians came several thousand new recruits. The Korean War veterans deepened and accelerated these upheavals in tribal life. Even less than the warriors of World War II were they willing to play the stoic, long-suffering Indian. It was a new era.

''Ten years ago you could have tromped on the Indians and they would have said, 'Okay, kick me again. I'm just an Indian,' '' said the young Sioux Vine Deloria, Jr. But those days of acquiescence were gone, he thought.

Deloria, Jr., was of the new generation. He was as well the director of the National Congress of American Indians, the United Nations of more than one hundred tribes, the most influential of all tribal federations: he spoke not merely for the young, but for tribes that represented four hundred thousand Indians. He was the Rousseau of the new Indians. He talked of a turning point in tribal history.

''Listen,'' Deloria, Jr., said, ''since World War II the Indian people, everywhere, have gotten out of the era where they were taught a set of [non-Indian] 'truths.'

''Now they are thinking for themselves, and they are going to decide, 'What do *I* choose? My Indianness and Indian culture? Or this myth that the rest of the country lives by?' ''

Said the Paiute Mel Thom: ''Awareness of our situation had brought out anger. With anger and concern 'hope' was born. We were aware [that] if we did not take action, in our time, future generations of Indians would be denied the right to share our own heritage. This was a direct threat to us, and we knew it. It was a matter of how to set up action to fight this threat and how we [would] rally our Indian forces together.''

There was ''a new Indian'' war, Thom said. It fittingly had begun with the return of the warriors from ''The War of the Whites.'' It was these warriors, disguised by their khaki fatigues, who had gone back to the villages of their forefathers from the alien and urban battlefields. It was these warriors who represented the traditional greatness of the Indians.

Warriors were of the tribal past. If the heritage of the tribal way of life was to be fought for, who better to do so than modern warriors?

3. The Great Society—in Uniform*

"You might say I'm military all the way," Air Force Capt. Randolph Sturrup, a 27-year-old Negro, said briskly as he fitted a white technical sergeant with a set of false teeth in his dentist's office at Ellington Air Force Base near Houston. "I hope to make it for 30 years. It's a chance to improve yourself professionally . . ." A world away from Captain Sturrup's air-conditioned clinic, First Sgt. Ollie Henderson Sr. shrugged out of his flak jacket after returning from a combat patrol in a steamy jungle near the headquarters of the Army's First Division at Di An, South Vietnam. Henderson, a gentle, 40-year-old father of four, has fought in three wars during his 22 years in the Army. If he survives Vietnam, he'll stay in for eight years more. "It's a place where a guy feels he's wanted," Sergeant Henderson said softly. Off the coast of Vietnam, Lt. (j.g.) Harold Robert Wise Jr. was stopped short when a NEWSWEEK reporter asked about racial discrimination in the Navy. "I never thought about it . . . until you came aboard," he said. "I'm just one of the guys, out here."

HAVEN: Captain Sturrup went to Fisk, Howard and Columbia universities. Lieutenant Wise is a 1964 graduate of West Chester State College in Pennsylvania (with a distinctly unmilitary degree in music education). Henderson's formal education stopped at 16 when he left the hardscrabble coal fields of Perry County, Kentucky. But like thousands of other Negroes of differing dreams and attainments, they have found a haven of regimented democracy in the U.S. armed forces, where the color of a man's uniform counts more than the color of his skin. "In the service," summed up Staff Sgt. Seman Jenkins, a thirteen-year Air Force veteran now stationed at Ellington AFB, "I have felt more a real part of the Great Society. I have been recognized as a man in every sense of the word."

That recognition is now eighteen years old. Master Sgt. Ralph Tann, 43, a recruiting supervisor at the Boston Army base, remembers the "old" army, which he left in disgust in 1946 (only to be recalled during the Korean War).

*"The Great Society—in Uniform," *Newsweek* (August 22, 1966).

"Negro units were getting the worst quarters and the worst equipment and were considered a necessary evil by most commanders," he recalls. "They weren't permitted to fight; they were thrown into service and supply units." But, with the sweep of a pen, President Truman desegregated the armed forces on July 26, 1948. And while the Negro in service must still contend with an occasional bigot as a commander—and suffer most of the humiliations of a Negro civilian once he leaves the base—his life in uniform is immeasurably better.

"In the Navy," declares Chief Petty Officer Joseph Jones, who supervises a crew of 50 Negro and white enlisted men at Da Nang, "promotion is as fair as it is possible to make it. You have to take written exams for promotion, and they're graded by machines that can't be programed to know your color." And indistinct as the on-base color line may be in the States, it is almost totally obscured by the smoke of battle in Vietnam. Pfc. Claude Weaver Jr., 22, an assistant squad leader in the First Cavalry Division, summed up his view of battlefield brotherhood: "You get shot at, you get hit equally out here . . . and everybody knows it."

Off the battlefield there is a sort of separation of the races—in Saigon where the Negroes tend to seek out their own bars, or in rest areas where whites and blacks often congregate in separate groups. But this is personal choice rather than imposed segregation. As one Negro GI chuckles: "We sometimes segregate ourselves from those white guys. We don't like their hillbilly music."

DISPROPORTION: Negroes—who constitute 11 per cent of the nation's population—currently make up 9.5 per cent of the armed forces. But last year Negroes accounted for a disproportionate 13.4 per cent of the draftees inducted. And the disproportion is even more evident in Vietnam. The last Defense Department study available shows that at the end of 1965, 12.5 per cent of all U.S. servicemen in Vietnam—and 14.6 per cent of the battle dead—were Negroes.

In the NEWSWEEK poll, civilian Negroes agree by a margin of 47 to 26 per cent that a young Negro stands a better chance in a military uniform than in civilian clothes. "In the armed forces, they really look at your ability," says Mary Oakley of Springfield, Mass. "In civilian life, it's your skin."

Yet a sizable number of Negroes have doubts about the fairness of the draft, or even whether Negroes should be fighting in Vietnam at all. Among rank-and-file Negroes in the NEWSWEEK survey, 25 per cent think the draft is unfair to their race, and this feeling rises to a hefty 58 per cent among Negroes in the NEWSWEEK leadership sample. For example, Jackie Robinson protests: "They're drafting people that have a lack of opportunity."

Similarly, 35 per cent of the rank-and-file Negroes and 22 per cent of the leadership group agree that the Negro should be against the war in Vietnam because he has less freedom to fight for. "What are we fighting for? I don't know," snaps a San Francisco housewife. "Communists? We should be fighting the white folks in Mississippi." Another 44 per cent object that the war in Vietnam means less money for poverty and civil-rights programs at home.

'WE LOVE HER': Perhaps because of their disaffection, 29 per cent of the Negroes (compared with 12 per cent for the nation as a whole) would like to see the U.S. withdraw from Vietnam. But 54 per cent approve of the way President Johnson is handling the war and—while less hawkish than American whites—Negroes proudly feel by 3 to 2 that their men make better combat soldiers than whites. And if the U.S. should become involved in another world war, there is no question about Negro loyalty. Fully 87 per cent (compared with 81 per cent in 1963) say their country is worth fighting for. "America is the Negro's country too," says a college graduate from Cartersville, Ga. "She's not perfect . . . but we love her."

What does the Negro serviceman think? Probably his patriotic fever chart would run a few points higher than the civilian's 87 per cent. To get a firmer fix on his feelings about more specific questions—the draft, the war and civil rights—NEWSWEEK reporters talked to dozens of servicemen in Vietnam and at Stateside points in Massachusetts, Alabama, Texas and California.

'ALL AMERICANS': Surprisingly, there seems to be little resentment of the draft. "A higher proportion of Negroes to whites is drafted because of a lower educational level," says Sam Steele, a 26-year-old Conroe, Texas, native who just finished a two-year hitch as an Army medic. And at Fort Ord, Calif., First Lt. Donald L. Holmes, 30, an Army career man, said the draft is not only fair—but might do some of the complainers some good in the long run. "If a young man is in college, and his grades are at a certain level, he should be allowed to finish his education," Holmes says. "A lot of these guys who just hang around poolrooms and street corners might get something out of the Army, anyway. Most of them wouldn't take an education if you offered it to them."

Assignment to Vietnam is hardly coveted by any GI—Negro or white. But most of the Negroes see nothing sinister in the fact that, proportionately, they are carrying a heavier share of the American load—and consequently suffering a larger share of the casualties. "Somebody's got to be here," shrugs Aircraft Maintenance Helper Second Class Walter Foster, on the carrier Intrepid. "We're all Americans." Other military sources point out that bonus pay (such as the $55 a month extra paid paratroopers) attracts poorer Negroes to volunteer; and these outfits are most often in the thick of the Vietnam fighting. From Saigon, NEWSWEEK's John Berthelsen adds another point: "Negroes tend to volunteer for tough duty in disproportionate numbers, as if they feel the need to prove their valor to themselves and to their race."

As to the war itself, most of the Negro soldiers, sailors and marines want to fight through to victory. But they don't feel—as do many Negro civilians —that America's shortcomings on civil rights should affect its role in Vietnam. "I've got a lot of friends who have been wounded and killed over here for America," says the Army's Sgt. Joseph Conner in Saigon. "The main thing is to do our job and get out of this damned country. Civil rights can wait, as far as soldiers are concerned." Added Navy Chief Joe Jones: "Most fighting men don't want to be here—not just Negroes. The only way you can look at it is that it is my country I am fighting for . . . whether you are black or white." Whatever his motive, the Negro's fighting quality has won a tribute from Gen. William C. Westmoreland, the U.S. commander in Vietnam. "One of the great stories to come out of this war," he has said, "is the magnificent job being done by the Negro soldier."

DON'T ROCK THE BOAT: As men trained to fight, most Negro servicemen sound surprisingly nonviolent when it comes to the civil-rights struggle at home. The Rev. Martin Luther King is universally admired as the leader with the right technique; black power and black nationalism are just as universally scorned. "My people have been told all their lives they are inferior," says Chief Petty Officer Jones. "Now to have someone tell them they are superior is a little silly. I don't think the movement [black power] will get far; most Negroes I know don't like it." Navy man Foster sums up even more succinctly: "Black power is a bunch of nuts."

Part of the Negro serviceman's seeming malaise on civil rights at home stems from the fact that he's out of touch. And for some who have found a home in the service, there is a certain don't-rock-the-boat attitude. "During the Emmett Till case," recalls Sgt. Maj. Garland Alston, 39, a Negro career man at Fort Ord, "I went around to all the day rooms and collected copies of a magazine that had a big story on the lynching. It was a good balanced story, but it might have stimulated some racial conflicts. That's something you can't afford to have in a military establishment."

STATUS: For all of them—career man and draftee—military service will end some day, and the Negro protectively colored in Army khaki, Marine green and Air Force or Navy blue will be just another black civilian face. Some, such as Lieutenant Holmes, have suffered through this humiliating shift in status once before. He enlisted in 1958 after two years of college, and in 1961 was discharged and started looking for a job. "I'd call for an appointment about a job I knew was open, and when I'd get there they'd say, 'I'm sorry, sir, this job is no longer open. But we have something in the janitorial field.' At 25, I saw no reason why I should accept a job as a garbage man." Holmes re-enlisted. Re-enlistment, in fact, has been the obvious answer for many Negroes; in 1965 the re-enlistment rate for whites was 17.1 per cent, for Negroes 45.7 per cent.

But one thing is clear: those Negroes who do leave the service—and especially those who have fought in Vietnam—are not going to be satisfied with second-class citizenship when they get home. "I feel right now I've qualified myself for anything anybody else has," says Sergeant Henderson, yearning to be home. "I've exposed myself to the same dangers." Navy Chief Jones, sweltering in Da Nang's 110-degree heat, declares: "I don't think I'm going to have as much patience as I had before when I go home. Why should I? There are some things due me and I want them." And M/Sgt. Frederick Robinson, resting at a Special Forces camp in the Mekong River Delta, puts it bluntly: "When I get back, I am as good as any son of a bitch in the States."

4. RALPH GUZMÁN

Mexican American Casualties in Vietnam*

Mexican American military personnel have a higher death rate in Vietnam than all other servicemen. Analysis of casualty reports for two periods of time: one between January, 1961 and February, 1967 and the other between December, 1967 and March, 1969, reveals that a disproportionate number of young men with distinctive Spanish names do not return from the Southeast Asia theatre of war. Investigation also reveals that a substantial number of them are involved in high-risk branches of the service such as the U.S. Marine Corps.

In the southwest, where the majority of the people of Mexican-American descent reside, Spanish named casualties remain consistently high in both periods. During the first period (January, 1961 to February, 1967) casualties with home addresses in the states of Arizona, California, Colorado, New Mexico, and Texas, totalled 1,631 deaths from all causes. Of these, 19.4

*Ralph Guzmán, "Mexican American Casualties in Vietnam," Research Report, University of California, 1970.

percent had distinctive Spanish names (see Table 1). In the second period (December, 1967 to March, 1969) there were 6,385 deaths. Casualties with distinctive Spanish names represented 19.0 percent of the total.

Casualty figures for each period are high when compared with the total Spanish surnamed population living in the southwestern United States. According to the 1960 report of the U.S. Bureau of the Census 11.8 percent of the total southwestern population had distinctive Spanish surnames and were, therefore, presumably Mexican American. The figures remain high when the comparison is based only on males of military age, meaning individuals between age 17 and 36 years. Mexican Americans are estimated to represent 13.8 percent of this age group.

While these figures are estimates, they are sufficient to indicate orders of magnitude. If one were to project birthrate, immigration, natural death and other factors, the statistical relationship would not be substantially different. It is probable that Spanish-surnamed individuals would be slightly more numerous. It is significant that the percentages of Spanish-named casualties for each period remains nearly constant at 19.0 percent.

War deaths by branch of service indicate that a great number of Mexican Americans choose high-risk duty. For example, during the first period, 23.3 percent of all southwest Marine Corps casualties had distinctive Spanish surnames. The Army also supplies an important number of ground troops; 19.4 percent of the casualties reported between January, 1961 and February, 1967, had Spanish surnames and were presumably of Mexican parentage. In the later period, between December, 1967 and March, 1969, Spanish surnames represented 17.5 percent of all southwest Army casualties.

When these figures are analyzed by state, California shows both the greatest number of total deaths from all causes and the greatest number of Mexican-American casualties. During the first period 821 servicemen from California were killed. Of these, 15.0 percent had Spanish surnames, which is well above the 10.0 percent estimate of Spanish surnames in the total population of the state. During the second period 3,543 servicemen from California were reported as casualties in Vietnam, 14.8 percent had Spanish surnames. The State of Texas ranks second in total deaths and in Mexican-American casualties. During the first period 554 Texans died in the war. Of these, 22.4 percent were presumably Mexican American. In the more recent period, between December, 1967 and March, 1969, there were 1,921 deaths with home addresses in Texas. Casualties from Texas with Spanish surnames represented 25.2 percent of the total. In both California and Texas, Mexican-American deaths are consistently high and disproportionate to the size of this minority group.

An adequate interpretation of the data is impossible without more information from official sources. For example, there is a gap between February, 1967 and December, 1967. Data were not available when this report was written. In a different sense, Spanish-surnamed servicemen may be over-represented in the Vietnam reports because they are over-represented among those who are drafted for military service and those who volunteer.

Historically, Mexican Americans have been a suspect, "foreign," minority. Like the Japanese Americans during World War II they have been under great pressure to prove loyalty to the United States. However, there are other reasons why Mexican Americans join the military. One is the desire for social status that military life offers. Another is economic. Many Mexican-Americans help their families with service allotments. Mexican-American organizations proclaim the sizeable military contributions of the Mexican-American soldier as proof of loyalty. They point to impressive records of heroism in time of war.

Only a relatively small number of Mexican Americans have avoided obligatory military service by attending college. Student deferments for residents of our southwestern *barrios* are scarce. The reason, of course, is the under-representation of Mexican Americans in institutions of higher learning. In 1968 the Department of Health, Education and Welfare investigated university and college compliance with the Civil Rights. HEW officials reported that in the University of California system only 1.57 percent of the total student enrollment was Mexican American. The HEW also reported that the California State College system's total student enrollment was 2.28 percent Mexican American.

Other factors motivate Mexican Americans to join the Armed Forces. Some may be rooted in the inherited culture of these people while others may be imbedded in poverty and social disillusion. Whatever the real explanation, we do know that Mexican Americans are over-represented in the death reports from Vietnam and under-represented in the classrooms of our institutions of higher learning.

TABLE 1

VIETNAM CASUALTIES FROM ALL CAUSES IN THE FIVE SOUTHWESTERN STATES BY BRANCH OF SERVICE BETWEEN
January 1962 and February 1967

	All Causes			Combat			Non-Combat		
	Total	Sp. Surname		Total	Sp. Surname		Total	Sp. Surname	
		No.	%		No.	%		No.	%
Total	1,631	316	19.4	1,335	274	20.5	296	42	14.2
Army	927	180	19.4	765	155	20.3	162	25	15.4
Air Force	88	8	9.1	55	5	9.1	33	3	9.1
Marine Corps	520	121	23.3	459	109	23.7	61	12	19.7
Navy	96	7	7.3	56	5	8.9	40	2	5.0

Source of this table: *List of Casualties Incurred by U.S. Military Personnel in Connection with the Conflict in Vietnam by Home State of Record*, Directorate for Statistical Services, Office Assistant Secretary of Defense (Comptroller), 20 April 1967. Figures for this table and for Table 2 differentiate between combat and non-combat deaths subsequent data derived from the *Congressional Record* do not permit this distinction.

TABLE 2

VIETNAM CASUALTIES FROM ALL CAUSES IN EACH OF THE FIVE SOUTHWESTERN STATES BETWEEN
January 1961 and February 1967

	All Causes			Combat			Non-Combat		
	Total	Sp. Surname		Total	Sp. Surname		Total	Sp. Surname	
		No.	%		No.	%		No.	%
Arizona									
Total	83	14	16.9	68	11	16.2	15	3	20.0
Army	50	8	16.0	41	7	17.1	9	1	11.1
Air Force	4	0	0.0	4	0	0.0	0	0	0.0
Marine Corps	26	5	19.2	22	4	18.2	4	1	25.0
Navy	3	1	33.3	1	0	0.0	2	1	50.0

An Annotated Bibliography of Chic

California									
Total	821	123	15.0	685	108	15.8	136	15	11.0
Army	454	75	16.5	383	65	17.0	71	10	14.1
Air Force	39	2	5.1	29	2	6.9	10	0	0.0
Marine Corps	270	45	16.7	235	40	17.0	35	5	14.3
Navy	58	1	1.7	38	1	2.6	20*	0	0.0
Colorado									
Total	108	26	24.1	85	22	25.9	23	4	17.4
Army	55	16	29.1	45	15	33.3	10	1	10.0
Air Force	6	1	16.7	2	0	0.0	4	1	25.0
Marine Corps	37	9	24.2	33	7	21.2	4	2	50.0
Navy	10	0	0.0	5	0	0.0	5	0	0.0
New Mexico									
Total	65	29	44.6	54	25	46.3	11	4	36.4
Army	35	12	34.3	28	10	35.7	7	2	28.6
Air Force	2	1	50.0	1	0	0.0	1	1	100.0
Marine Corps	25	13	52.0	23	13	56.5	2	0	0.0
Navy	3	3	100.0	2	2	100.0	1	1	100.0
Texas									
Total	554	124	22.4	443	108	24.4	111	16	14.4
Army	333	69	22.7	268	58	21.6	65	11	16.9
Air Force	37	4	10.8	19	3	15.8	18	1	5.6
Marine Corps	162	49	30.2	146	45	30.8	16	4	25.0
Navy	22	2	63.6	10	2	20.0	12*	0	0.0

*Includes 1 member of the Coast Guard

TABLE 3
VIETNAM CASUALTIES FROM ALL CAUSES IN THE FIVE SOUTHWESTERN STATES BY BRANCH OF SERVICE BETWEEN
December 1967 and March 1969

Branch of Service	Total Number of Casualties	Distinctive Spanish-Surnamed Casualties
Army	4056	753

Air Force	116	9
Marine Corps	1977	465
Navy	236	25
TOTAL	6385	1252

SSN % of Total	Non-Spanish-Surnamed Casualties	Non-SSN % of Total	Percent Totals
17.5	3303	82.5	100.0
7.8	107	92.2	100.0
23.5	1512	76.5	100.0
10.6	211	89.4	100.0
19.0	5133	81.0	100.0

SOURCE: *Congressional Record,* vol. 115, No. 51 (March 25, 1969), pp. H2048-H2169
Congressional Record, vol. 115, No. 57 (April 3, 1969), pp. H2509-H2526
Congressional Record, vol. 115, No. 122 (July 22, 1969), pp. H6173-H6186

TABLE 4
VIETNAM CASUALTIES FROM ALL CAUSES IN EACH OF THE FIVE SOUTHWESTERN STATES BETWEEN December 1967 and March 1969

State	Total Number of Casualties	Distinctive Spanish-Surnamed Casualties	SSN % of Total
Arizona	354	86	24.3
California	3543	525	14.8

Colorado	336	66	19.1
New Mexico	231	91	39.4
Texas	1921	484	25.2
TOTAL	6385	1252	19.6

Non-Spanish Surnamed Casualties	Non-SSN % of Total	Percent Totals
268	75.7	100.0
3018	85.2	100.0
270	80.9	100.0
140	60.6	100.0
1437	74.8	100.0
5133	80.4	100.0

SOURCE: *Congressional Record,* vol. 115, No. 51 (March 25, 1969), pp. H2048-H2169
Congressional Record, vol. 115, No. 57 (April 3, 1969), pp. H2509-H2526
Congressional Record, vol. 115, No. 122 (July 22, 1969), pp. H6173-H6186

C. Education

A longstanding goal of American education has been a system of schooling that helps fulfill the potential of all the nation's young people by developing their skills and preparing them for productive, satisfying lives. To this end billions have been spent and dynamic innovations employed. Yet in all too many instances America's educational institutions have failed their white youth, while in the overwhelming majority of cases they have failed their minority youth. This section examines the problems American minority groups have faced in seeking equal opportunities to learn and to reach their full potential as individuals and citizens.

In "Education in the Grapes of Wrath," Dennis Mangers describes the hostility to adequate Chicano education of a San Joaquin Valley school district in California, dominated by Anglo agribusinessmen. Lest education help children of farm laborers discover new vistas which might lead them from the fields or make them unwilling to work for low wages, these Anglo growers were committed to a backward, often brutal, "educational" system.

The difficulties of Indian children are well illustrated in P. Boyd Mather's "Tama Indians Fight for Their Own School." Required to attend a white public school in Tama, Iowa, after the forced closure of their own primary school in 1968, Mesquakie Indian children suffered the built-in discriminations of an alien educational system as well as hostility from their white classmates. What their parents wanted was the restoration of the old school, where their children could study reading, writing, and arithmetic in a nonhostile atmosphere and learn Mesquakie culture, language, and religion. To reach their full human potential, the children needed Indian, not white, education.

The term "relevant education" is the subject of the concluding selection, Charles V. Hamilton's "Now That You've Got Your Administration Building Back, What Do You Do Next?" Hamilton argues that Black youths want not merely an understanding of Black history and culture, but education that will provide skills and knowledge directly applicable to community problems. He outlines how this goal is possible and suggests the steps needed to achieve relevance in the education of Blacks.

1. DENNIS H. MANGERS

Education in the Grapes of Wrath*

It was one of those incredibly beautiful spring days that help the inhabitants of California's San Joaquin Valley forget the hard winter that had just passed

*Dennis H. Mangers, "Education in the Grapes of Wrath," *The National Elementary School Principal,* Vol. L (November, 1970), pp. 34-40. Copyright © 1970, National Association of Elementary School Principals. All Rights Reserved. Reprinted by permission of the National Association of Elementary School Principals.

and the almost intolerable summer that is soon to come. The endless rows of lush grapes lining Highway 99 precipitated a wave of nostalgia, as I recalled similar treks along this road as a child visiting grandparents in the northeastern part of the Valley.

This time I was on my way north through the Valley as an adult, heading for my first assignment as an elementary school principal. The four men and one woman who made up the governing board of the tiny Earlimart School District had selected me just a few weeks before to be the first principal of their one and only elementary school.

The school district saw its beginning around 1885 when the Dalton boys were holding up trains at the local station and had grown from just a handful of pupils until now when it boasts an elementary school of nearly 1,000 youngsters and a junior high school of 500.

The junior high school had had its own principal for many years but because the district offices were on the elementary school site and because money had always been tight, the superintendent doubled as elementary principal.

Now at last, with the infusion of some federal funds, the board determined to heed the plea of the superintendent for a new principal and, after screening a number of applicants, selected me. Just 28 years old with four years of teaching experience in Long Beach, California, and a brand new master's degree from the University of Southern California, I was on my way to what people in the city referred to as the "boonies" or boon docks, faced with a job many older colleagues labeled hopeless at best.

The first few weeks I stayed in a small motel while my wife attempted to sell our home in the city and while I sought housing somewhere in my school's attendance area. Each day in the late afternoon and evening I drove for miles on end searching out every nook and cranny of this central section of the Valley from which busloads of children were sent to my school every morning.

Returning to my motel room late each night, I lay stunned by what I'd seen. Hidden behind the lush growth along Highway 99 was a culture of poverty, degradation, and misery that awakened in me a profound social conscience that I had never really acknowledged before.

Just a few miles from the school could be found the $50,000 to $80,000 homes of the wealthy and powerful growers juxtaposed with the wretched little shacks of the laborers who worked, in many cases, from before sunup to sundown in the nearby fields. Soon I was to learn that there were even harder and more insidious realities with which I would have to deal than just the deplorable living conditions of the majority of my youngsters.

Speaking of majorities, the ethnic makeup of the school revealed that nearly 70 percent of our students were Mexican Americans; 10 percent, black; 5 percent, Filipino; approximately 12 percent, low socio-economic Anglo Americans; and around 3 percent, highly privileged boys and girls from grower families. Yet as I surveyed the political structure of the school district and community, it became abundantly clear that the power rested firmly in the hands of the grower class, power that I saw abused in ways that would offend anyone who ascribes to the principles of justice and equality.

I determined, in spite of countless daily examples of man's inhumanity to man, to become the change agent that would wrest this anachronistic school out of its antiquated and blatantly discriminatory educational program and expose it to the light of new research and practice. This, of course, was a big order for anyone, anywhere, but in Earlimart the struggle seemed titanic.

Time after time I went to the board to present a new program only to find them approving the project reluctantly in order to get their hands on federal monies, but all the while expressing an unbelievable hostility toward the Mexican American, who they assumed would be the major beneficiary of the proposal. Why this hatred, this fear of the Mexican American? I could not fathom the depth of suspicion on the part of each grower as I outlined proposals for "English as a Second Language" clinics and badly needed preschool experience.

After many tension-filled board meetings, the reasons for their stubborn reluctance to do anything constructive on behalf of the Mexican American became quite clear. It could be summed up very simply in a name—Cesar Chavez.

Cesar Chavez lives in a tiny frame house on Kensington Street in nearby Delano, where he directs the efforts of the United Farm Workers Organizing Committee. As a result, his very name is anathema to the growers. Despite the fact that the House Committee on Un-American Activities has repeatedly cleared Chavez of any trace of subversion, the growers insist that this mild-mannered Mexican American migrant laborer is indeed a Communist agent dedicated to the demise of the grower class.

Knowing little of the strike or boycott when I arrived in Earlimart, I took no side in this classic labor dispute. Later, in retrospect, and after considerable study of the issues involved, I resolved never to eat non-union grapes until the growers agreed to recognize the laborers' right to organize on their own behalf, which they only recently have.

One night the chairman of the school board decided to enunciate as candidly as possible his views with regard to this "Mexican problem" so that once and for all this "city boy" would understand the board's feelings.

He said, "Look, you've got to understand that we've built this Valley to what it is and we've gotten to where we are because there's always been cheap labor around. When you come in talking about raising the educational vista of the Mexican American and helping him to aspire beyond the fields, and curing the dropout problem, you're talking about jeopardizing our economic survival. What do you expect, that we'll just lie down and let you reformers come in here and wreck everything for us?"

If that one revealing comment had not been enough to make me fearful for the educational future of our beautiful students, many of the events that were to follow did the job once and for all.

It naturally became my duty to evaluate and inservice the 30 members of the certified staff. To appreciate this task in Earlimart, you have to understand the recruitment and selection procedures employed.

The dozens of tiny school districts that dot the Valley have some of the lowest salary schedules in the state. With the climate notoriously poor most of the year, with virtually no social or cultural opportunities available, and with no major four-year institution nearby in which to pursue graduate work, the Valley holds little allure for the bright young men and women graduating from our best teacher training institutions. The school districts in middle- and upper-class suburban areas around the major cities snap up the most promising candidates through student teacher programs, expensive recruitment drives, and, in many cases, just because of their desirable locations. State and federal fund allocations are simply not sufficient for remote rural districts like Earlimart to offer high enough salaries to compensate for what prospective teachers think of as disadvantages.

Faced with a turnover of anywhere from 50 to 80 percent and with September drawing nearer each day, Earlimart and its many counterparts often find themselves with as many as 15 or more positions still unfilled. At this time, a curious phenomenon takes place. Letters start dribbling in, a few at a time, in response to queries sent around the country months ago. Women and a few men of all ages and backgrounds start drifting by the school. Many have families in cars and their belongings in trailers behind. These are the people who have failed, for a variety of reasons, to get jobs elsewhere. Many have been fired from job after job; some are terribly overweight or have other physical defects; some come from tiny little communities very much like Earlimart only in geographical locations around the country where prejudice and blatant discrimination are a way of life. A few have the half-hearted favorable evaluations one of our administrative colleagues has given when trying to pawn off an undesirable but tenured teacher on someone else. Finally, in desperation, the superintendent begins to cull through this group of equally desperate applicants and chooses as best he can.

I interviewed many of these applicants my first summer in Earlimart. Many were lovely and sincere Filipino girls with impressive degrees and credentials from colleges and universities in the Philippines that are as yet unaccredited by the United States. Some of these girls had waited for years to come to this country and dreamed of walking right into the "highly paid" American teaching profession, only to find on arrival that most of their college units were unacceptable here and that several years of work in American institutions still lay before them. All had, of course, turned to other sources of employment in the interim, and few were very happy individuals. Most serious of all was that of the four Filipinos whom the superintendent ended up hiring that summer spoke English so poorly that there was little hope of their ever providing a suitable language model for their young Mexican American charges or the black youngsters who have a patois of their own that is often completely unintelligible to anyone but themselves. Some of the Anglo applicants were quick to assure me that they were expert in handling these "problem-type kids" from minority ethnic groups and would guarantee "good classroom control."

When the superintendent felt he had chosen the best of the bunch, he set about the agonizing process of getting them signed up with the county office. I couldn't understand how he would ever bring this off, for some of our applicants simply did not qualify for even the lowest credential and one, in fact, had just a few units above a junior college education, with not one teaching methodology course to her credit. I was soon to find that there are vagaries in the law and exceptions to policy that are commonly made to allow for the desperate plight of rural school districts that have such difficulty in recruiting qualified personnel.

In this way, the classrooms are finally "staffed," and preschool orientation workshops for both the new and returning teachers are planned.

The returning teachers presented, in many cases, more problems than some of the new ones. One dear lady of 73 years was, in many ways, a wonder with children. When faced with physical education periods or yard duty during the winter months, however, she fell very ill and was invariably absent for long periods of time. Others of this hardy group of Earlimart veterans were wives of growers and local merchants who demonstrated practically no understanding of, or sensitivity to, the Mexican American child. Many of this group had gained tenure only because of the infrequent classroom observations that result from not having a full-time building principal.

A few classroom visitations during the summer school session confirmed my suspicion that every discredited teaching technique ever known was prevalent in Earlimart. Truly brutal and indiscriminate corporal punishment was accepted practice. One teacher was a particularly evangelical-style preacher whose tiny congregation could not support hem, so during the week he taught in Earlimart. It was his practice to beat "transgressors" with a paddle, be they girl or boy, for the slightest infraction of what amounted to an impossibly rigid standard of behavior. It was common for children to receive one swat for each spelling word or math problem missed. I often found him sitting at his desk, Bible in hand, preparing a Sunday sermon or eulogy for a funeral, while his children sat quietly copying pages from encyclopedias they could not read. He constantly sought to be released early from his "teaching" responsibilities or faculty meetings so he could minister to one of his flock or officiate at a funeral.

I found most of the teachers sitting behind massive desks reading from teachers manuals and rarely if ever moving from that position all day. One particularly overweight teacher complained that if she got up out of her seat to help students, her legs ached terribly that night, so invariably she had a long line of youngsters waiting at her desk to consult with her on problems.

True, there is a handful of teachers in Earlimart who care and who have a desire to help, but even these realize how few skills they have to meet the needs of Mexican American children who year after year fall farther and farther behind.

Early in the year, I administered the "Minnesota Teacher Attitude Inventory" which erased any lingering doubts I may have had about the child-centeredness of this staff. The scores defied imagination. It was obvious that no efforts to inservice these teachers could truly be effective until they became sensitive to Mexican American children—sensitive to their needs, their background, their heritage.

With the aid of a federal grant, we were able to bring in from La Jolla, California, the brilliant young Mexican American educator, Dr. Uvaldo Palomares, and his associates to conduct a week-long series of sessions with teachers and members of the community. Dr. Palomares is himself the son of migrant farm workers. While in the third grade, he was labeled mentally retarded because of language difficulties and placed in special classes. He has subsequently earned his doctorate from the University of Southern California and is known internationally for his contributions to the Mexican American.

Dr. Palomares, his wife, and their associates, Dr. Besell and Dr. Carnivali, divided our staff into small groups and took them off into separate rooms. In the days that followed, I saw our teachers relating to one another for the first time. They were sharing their anxieties and secret fears with one another and feeling good about it. Mrs. Palomares brought in a group of our own little children and formed them into a "magic circle." The way they responded to her patient and loving techniques seemed magic indeed, and the demonstration was not wasted on even the least sensitive among us.

But, alas, the grower contingent known as the school board soon labeled Palomares and friends "imported troublemakers," and with that influence pervading every aspect of the school's life, most of the teachers retreated five steps back for every one they had gained.

My morale would have to withstand many such reversals in the months ahead, but one thing I shall never forget is the terrible spectre of hunger that hangs over the children of Earlimart and other communities in a valley that is one of this country's biggest producers of food.

The law required that the school district provide Class A lunches for children whose parents had no work and could not afford to pay. I soon noticed that very few youngsters ever received the benefit of a free lunch due to some rather elaborate criteria that successfully precluded most of them from qualifying. It seemed very strange to me that so many of our children announced daily that they were going home for lunch and then would reappear on the playground just five minutes later. In investigating further, I found that a great number of the children simply could not stand the embarrassment of being made to go through the lunch line when they had no money and could not qualify for a free lunch. Their ploy, then, was to say they were going home for lunch even though they knew very well there was no food at home and they would be back on the grounds in minutes, hungrier than ever.

Among those who did manage to eat in the cafeteria, I noticed many children having difficulty eating some of the food prepared by the exclusively Anglo staff of cooks. In questioning the children and many of their parents, I found that for years they had been asking if rice and beans could be substituted for mashed potatoes occasionally. When we called in a state consultant, she told us that since rice and beans were surplus commodities and available in huge quantities, there should be no problem. Furthermore, she provided our cooks with many Mexican-style recipes that were simple and economical.

The school board, however, soon got wind of the consultant's suggestions through a disgruntled cook, and in a meeting of unparalleled vitriol, one member lost his temper and said, "If these damn Mexican kids are too good for American food, then ship the little bastards back to Tiajuana [*sic*]."

The inevitable finally occurred. The school board had subverted the intent of the laws so openly that the state was obliged to cut the district off the surplus commodity program. When notified of the state's decision, the board was elated. Now they didn't even have to pretend to give free lunches. Since no big money was involved, just surplus rice and beans for hungry children, they callously let the program collapse.

Because the growers on the board accept huge subsidies from the government for letting land lie idle, it is impossible to comprehend how they can resent hungry Mexican American children getting a small subsidy for food unless you understand their ultimate aim: to preserve an abundance of cheap labor.

When proposing new programs to the board, I prepared meticulously but always found the reaction the same. After many a stormy board meeting, we discovered that proposed changes had been approved only because of the board's desire to get their hands on large amounts of federal money. Their hope was, of course, that later they could quietly divert the funds into the "regular district program" and cut their own tax rate.

Because of these funds, we were able to start a preschool for three- and four-year-olds, and move from two three-hour kindergarten sessions to four all-day sessions. A talented young Mexican American teacher was brought from New Mexico to open "English as a Second Language" classes. We began having Spanish lessons for a small group of teachers and met three mornings a week before school.

The PTA meetings, always poorly attended and totally dominated by the growers' wives, actually saw an increase in attendance from the Mexican American community for a short time as word was passed that the new principal was involving their children more than ever before. As no Spanish translation of the program was ever allowed, however, interest soon waned again.

The one change most vitally needed, but unfortunately the most sacrosanct of all the sacred cows, had to do with the reading program.

A reading levels program had been devised nearly ten years before when the number of Mexican American enrollments began to rise. Through a levels testing program, children were placed in classes homogeneously on the basis of scores. The result, of course, was that the growers' children were segregated into top "enrichment" groups while non-English-speaking Mexican children were lumped into "remedial" groups with other children of low IQ as measured by standardized tests. The levels system was inviolate; I couldn't crack it. The teachers who were considered the "best" of the returning crop were always assigned to the top groups as reward for signing on for another year. The lowest groups went to those least equipped to help them.

By going to county meetings and Phi Delta Kappa gatherings, I learned that other districts in the Valley less dominated by the growers were doing some very innovative things to alleviate the misery of the Mexican American and his black counterpart. But there was still Earlimart and many other school districts like it where these innovations cannot take place, and I, as an educator and an American, found the problem intolerable.

Sixteen months of batting my head against the proverbial stone wall convinced me that my effectiveness on behalf of the boys and girls in Earlimart was crippled beyond repair. The board felt I had chosen a side in "the war," and it was obviously the wrong side as far as they were concerned. My assessment of the scene was simple but painful. Hopeless. Reluctantly, I activated my placement file and was invited for an interview by the Fountain Valley School District.

One Monday morning shortly thereafter, word reached me that Fountain Valley wanted me to take an assignment as principal of an excitingly innovative new school for the coming year. The board in Earlimart seethed in quiet fury as my resignation was read. Their boat had been rocked. For whatever small changes I had been able to bring about, these board members wanted me punished and this new job opportunity seemed in every way a reward instead.

Soon the letters, vindictive and malicious, accusing me of everything from immorality to arson, began arriving at my new school district. Most were unsigned but left little doubt as to their authors.

While I no longer live and work in the San Joaquin Valley, a large part of my heart still resides with the children of Earlimart where the mention of my name assures two very different responses. I am told that the Mexican Americans and others in their unhappy station refer to me as "the principal who cared." The growers have placed me in the distinguished company of Cesar Chavez by labeling me a "commie agent."

And what of Earlimart today? No better. The administrator who followed me clings tenaciously to the last vestiges of the preschool and "English as a Second Language" programs. He hangs on, hoping for a unification decree from the state, or the election of some tender, sensitive people to the board, or a miracle, perhaps.

I still drive up Highway 99 occasionally, but the lush green foliage seems to fade away and for me there is but one vision. I see once again six small children picking through the still smoking embers of what was, just the night before, their teeming, rat-infested one-room shack. The older ones are trying to find a few scraps of clothes to wear and a bite of food to eat, for the school bus will soon be there. What a cruel reward awaits these little children so eager to learn.

Their failure is foreordained.

2. P. BOYD MATHER

Tama Indians Fight for Their Own Schools*

HIGH-HANDED CLOSING

Rejecting the Indians' protest, the Bureau of Indian Affairs has closed down the primary school which it had operated since 1938 at the Mesquakie Indian settlement on the Iowa river just west of Tama, Iowa. The 56 first-through-fifth graders have been assigned to South Tama community school centers as out-of-district, tuition-paying pupils. Headstart and kindergarten pupils and students in grades six through 12 are already attending the South Tama schools on that basis.

The Indians raise three primary objections to the closing: (1) They see it as just one more instance of the B.I.A.'s making a decision they think should rest with the tribal council. (2) They say their children have experienced considerable discrimination in the white school system. (3) Though they agree with B.I.A. officials that vast improvement in Indian education is called for, they want their children to be educated in an Indian rather than a white setting.

Unless the B.I.A. reverses its decision, the Indians will apparently choose between compliance and protest through direct action while seeking legal redress through the courts. That a middle ground is not possible became obvious at a meeting of the tribal council with B.I.A. officials on July 19, at which a grave lack of communication was evident. For instance, the B.I.A. officials refused to answer direct questions about whether the bureau's school in the settlement was actually closed. Nine days later Otto Knauth of the *Des Moines Register* reported that a B.I.A. official in Minneapolis had confirmed the closing in a telephone interview, but that "for reasons not immediately apparent" neither tribal leaders nor local B.I.A. officials had been notified.

*P. Boyd Mather, "Tama Indians Fight for Their Own Schools," *The Christian Century*, Vol. LXXXV (October 2, 1968), pp. 1251-52.

In several previous conflicts between bureau officials and Indians the Tamas have conceded to white power. This time many Indians believe they cannot concede without endangering the very fiber of their tribal structure. Chairman Columbus Keahna of the Mesquakie tribal council, the other six council members and the clan leaders are unanimous in opposition to the closing. The Indians consider the council, not the B.I.A., the legal local government of the tribe, and they resent the bypassing of the council on this and many other matters.

SPECIAL BACKGROUND

The Mesquakie settlement occupies an unusual position in Indian affairs. The Mesquakies, a part of the Fox group, are the only tribe still in Iowa among the 17 that once lived here. They are here because in 1856 their leaders returned from Kansas and at great personal sacrifice bought 80 acres of land. Gov. James Grimes served as trustee in that land purchase and sponsored enabling action in the Iowa general assembly. Through other purchases the settlement has grown to 3,000 acres. The population is about 430.

In 1896 the federal department of the interior took over administration of the tribe and, as Knauth wrote in the *Register,* "the Bureau of Indian Affairs has since sought to control tribal affairs as if the settlement were a reservation." Yet the settlement differs from a reservation in that the latter consists of land set aside from the public domain, while Tama land was bought from private owners. That is why the Indians believe the council should control tribal and settlement affairs, why they deeply resent the B.I.A.'s paternalism. (At the July 19 meeting, for instance, government officials called Keahna by his first name, reserving "mister" for white men.) The school closing has added fuel to rumors that the B.I.A. intends to dissolve the settlement, possibly distributing the commonly owned property to individual families.

The tribal council has voted unanimously "never to agree to the complete transfer of all students from the Indian school." Chairman Keahna commented, "It looks like the only way we can apply pressure is by keeping our children out."

DISCRIMINATION

The Mesquakies believe, and they illustrate their belief with many personal impressions and experiences, that they are discriminated against in the white schools. Tom Knight, a VISTA worker at the settlement until mid-August when he was transferred to Montana, offers two illustrations: In one class in which four Indian children were present a white teacher told the pupils that she was "tired of paying taxes so the Indians can live off the fat of the land." Another teacher baited Indian pupils "to get them mad because the only time they will talk about their religion is when they are mad." (Incidentally, Knight was sent to the settlement without the Indians' consent, though he did not know this until he arrived. But he was soon accepted by them, and it was over their objection that he was transferred.)

Whether or not such incidents are verifiable, the Indians clearly believe that how their children fare depends on the lightness or darkness of their skin. "The lighter they are the better they get along," said one grandmother; "the darker, the more trouble they have." In this connection it is interesting to note that the Mesquakies have a deep appreciation of their own redness. I quoted to one young Indian the probably correct assertion of Glenn R. Landbloom of the B.I.A. that it is easier for Indian children to make the adjustment to white society when they are young, and that attending public school will facilitate that adjustment. In reply the young Mesquakie held out his bare arm and said proudly, "I am colored."

The B.I.A. asserts that the South Tama county officials are willing and ready to assume the responsibility of providing quality education for all children of the settlement, and have geared their educational program for the transfer. Everyone agrees that the schools have adequate physical facilities and over-all educational program. The schools do not, however, offer any systematic teaching of Indian history, legends or customs, nor are they likely to teach the Mesquakie language, an educational element the Mesquakies consider essential.

Because the settlement is not part of the South Tama school district, which completely surrounds it, the Indian pupils have no official relationship to the public school board, which makes decisions and sets policy. Moreover, since the government funds last year fell about $8,800 short in paying Indian tuition, one wonders how long the district will be willing to accept the settlement children.

NEED FOR IMPROVEMENT

The one point of agreement between the B.I.A. and the Indians is that the quality of Indian education needs improvement. Points out Don Wanatee, an early alumnus of the bureau school: "It has taken the B.I.A. 70 years to admit what we have known for a long time: they've been giving us an inferior education." The Indians want the present facilities in the settlement developed into a "model school" for Indian education. They are not clear as to all details of what that model should be, but it would certainly be one that would preserve the Indian language and culture while providing a basic education, that would remain federally financed and that would be under tribal control.

The importance of the Mesquakie language to the Tama Indians cannot be overestimated. Mr. Wanatee told me: "If you take away our language, you take away our religion. If you take away our religion, you take away our tribe. The three go together." Mrs. Wilson Brown, one of the mothers, explained: "We don't want our children at 35 or 40 years of age doing what we have seen other Indians doing—scrambling around trying to find out what their language and their religion are, when no one can remember." And she had another observation: "Our situation is similar to that of the Amish: we want our own schools, but we want fully accredited teachers, the best available—which we have never had—so we can get the best education possible."

In seeking to retain Indian identity the Mesquakies follow in the tradition of their great Chief Maminwanika, who was their leader for over 30 years before their return to Iowa. It is written that while he advocated peace with the whites, he steadfastly opposed adoption of the white man's customs, dress or education. Today's Mesquakies do not reject the 20th century, but they do seek to continue the distinctive heritage preserved for them by Maminwanika.

At least twice before in this century the Mesquakies and the B.I.A. have come to a showdown on the education of the children in the settlement. Each time the Mesquakies have won, but they still have not won the war to establish the quality of education they want. Each previous time *part* of the issue has been whether the education was to be "red" or "white." Perhaps that is *the* issue in 1968.

3. CHARLES V. HAMILTON

Now That You've Got Your Administration Building Back, What Do You Do Next?*

A great deal of the recent protest by black college students focuses on the demand to make the courses on their campuses more "relevant" to the needs of a black American society. There is no question in my mind of the intense necessity for changes in the present curriculum in that direction. But it is important to be specific, to spell out as precisely as possible what is meant by "relevant."

First of all, in relation to the black society, designers of new courses should emphasize action as well as academe. I think it is very important to attempt to combine classroom studies with practical, in-field application. When many black students demand "relevant" courses, this means moving out of the ivory tower and into the community. I think this is valid. And its validity stems not only from a desire to satisfy the action oriented nature of many youths today, but precisely because only by redefining the "classroom" can we really get at much of the data. In addition, black Americans are in an urgent stage of development. This means, to me, that education, wherever possible, must be related functionally to particular needs which speak to that urgency.

This is especially important where the college or university has a relatively sizable [and growing] black student body, and where, as in many places, there is an accessible or nearby black community. This would mean, for example, courses in economics that deal specifically with the problems and prospects of development of producer and consumer co-ops and other business ventures in the ghetto. It would mean courses in political science that deal with the problems and prospects of developing viable, independent grass-roots electoral and pressure-group organizations. Given certain political constraints, what are the problems involved in organizing potentially successful representative groups in low socioeconomic black communities? The emphasis would be on *academe for action*, on implementation, on development.

There are precedents for such emphasis. Roosevelt University has had a Jewish studies program for several years. It has language, literature, culture studies and history courses leading to a bachelor's degree.

*Charles V. Hamilton, "Now That You've Got Your Administration Building Back, What Do You Do Next?," *Chicago Tribune Magazine,* June 8, 1969.

It is quite conceivable that a black studies program would prepare students for service careers to the black community. This is what many black students mean when they say they want to "take our skills back to the community." Many students are aware that talk of black power and "community control" must move to the next stage of development of talent to implement the rhetoric. Black economic power is not possible without first the education tools to put such power together.

I believe we should build into our pre-medical, pre-law, and other pre-professional programs courses dealing with the responsibility of these professions for helping in the development of a black society. I might add that many young doctors, dentists, and lawyers already are working this out on their own as they enter these professions. It is about time, I suggest, that the professors caught up with their students.

We should allow for much more work-study arrangements whereby students would be able to go out into the community for a part of their school year and work and study. I would strongly urge that colleges think in terms of setting up storefront branches in the communities. The models are already there in agricultural extension work, and some colleges and universities do this in other fields. I am not advocating some glamorous, dramatic, "let's-go-to-the-people" kind of idolatry of the poor. If what I am suggesting is seen as gimickry to serve as a substitute for the dull, 10-10:50, M. W. F. format, then I have been misunderstood. I am not interested in making the college courses more exciting for the sheer sake of excitement, but more relevant for the sake of a more meaningful education.

In addition, I would say that we should be prepared to rethink our definition of what constitutes a "qualified" instructor. Perhaps the traditional criteria for hiring professors will have to be revised. A Ph.D. with a list of publications behind his name might have to give way to an indigenous activist who has knowledge of the subject not recognized by the established methods of judgment. This is not fatal. It might threaten some professors who have spent years in the library stacks, but modernization always has this element of challenging the old with new elite groupings. Neither should he be overly concerned with "accreditation," simply because the thrust is toward substantially *new* criteria for judgment of excellence, relevancy, and substance. And the accrediting agencies will have to come to terms with this, lest *their* credibility be challenged.

Secondly, it is important to incorporate more material on black Americans into the lower-level introductory courses: history, economics, political science, psychology, sociology, literature. Obviously, much could be done by simply breaking out from the reading lists the professors hand out year after year. Those lists [and the lecture notes] must be revised now. In a real sense, many professors must re-tool. But, there must be the recognition that a substantial portion of lecture material in those innumerable introductory courses is lacking of meaningful reference to black people. And this has led a number of black students to ask the question: an introduction into what?

The introductory courses in American government omit material dealing with the development of independent party organizations such as the Lowndes county [Alabama] Freedom party, or the relatively sucessful efforts of the state-wide Mississippi Freedom Democratic party—both very important political developments among black people. Introductory American Literature courses do not teach the writings of Phyllis Wheatley or Claude McKay.

At the same time, it is possible to develop specialized courses on black history, black literature, black politics, black psychology, etc., at the upper, advanced levels. Clearly, there is enough material to justify individual courses in many of these fields. I would suggest we take care and not move hastily here, precisely because there is indeed a lot to learn. If the college cannot get a "qualified" person to teach these advanced courses, I would be opposed to some of the makeshift efforts I see taking place around the country. Many professors are literally throwing together highly technical courses within two or three weeks.

There is a substantial difference between re-tooling to include some relevant material on black people in an over-all introductory course and preparing a semester-long, specific, advanced course. In political science [the discipline I know best], it is a difference between discussing in an American government introductory course a limited amount of material on black political groups in the section on political parties and pressure groups, and offering a highly specialized course on the politics of black Americans, the forms, styles, and goals of the various groups. The latter course requires much more preparation and knowledge.

This process is followed now with other areas in the discipline. Some political scientists, who are specialists, for example, in constitutional law, also teach general introductory American government courses covering the Presidency, Congress, parties, the judiciary, foreign policy, to name a few. Everyone knows, however, that these professors are "stronger" in constitutional law, and they could hardly be expected to offer specialized courses "overnight."

In the same sense, advanced courses in black studies must not be made the object of "instant expertise." Some colleges have tried to deal with this situation by bringing in guest lecturers thruout the semester to lecture on special topics for which they have a long-developed competency. Brooklyn College followed this procedure in the 1968-69 school year. This could be an answer for the time, while colleges recruit permanent professors.

We should not overlook the fact that many of the existing courses must come under scrutiny themselves. Some professors do not like the idea of tampering with their "pet" courses. Thus, they would prefer that the department create a separate course dealing with a black-oriented subject. But this, to me, is intellectually dishonest. I spoke recently with a professor in a Missouri college who indicated that in his advanced courses on international economic development, it never occurred to him to deal with the economic involvement of private American investments in South Africa—and what that means politically and economically. Indeed, most of the courses around the country are woefully lacking of any reference to America and her lack of significant economic aid to Africa. We who style ourselves professional seekers-after-knowledge have an obligation to raise these kinds of questions in our courses.

It is also important that changes in the courses are necessary not just where there is a black student body, or an adjacent black community. The need is equally great in all-white, suburban-locked colleges. These places must have courses that reinterpret the impact of slavery and oppression on both white and black Americans. White students need to know the history of black Americans as much as black students; white students need to know the poetry of Langston Hughes and Countee Cullen as well as that of Walt Whitman and Carl Sandburg. They need to know the sociopolitical study of W. E. B. DuBois and Charles Johnson as well as those of Max Weber and V. O. Key Jr. They need to examine and understand the impact of Marcus Garvey as well as that of William Jennings Bryan.

My point is that unless these all-white colleges begin to revise their curriculum, they will continue to graduate students into a middle-class mediocrity. They will be mediocre precisely because they will be incomplete in their knowledge of this heterogenous world and puzzled by the pluralistic forces beginning to make their voices heard. While this article deals with curricular changes to meet the needs of a *black* society, those needs cannot be met if we focus only on the black society. That society cannot be understood or helped in a vacuum.

Indeed, I would go further and suggest that many of the problems in the black society begin without question with the ignorance and insensitivity in the *white* society.

Finally, I would strongly propose that each and every college and university in this country establish immediately a form of "curricular-reevaluation mechanism." Yes, unfortunately, *another* faculty committee! Such a group would conduct penetrating research, in-depth examination of courses being offered on their campuses. The goal would be to *advise* professors and departments about ways to make relevant changes, and not to dictate what should be taught. Understandably, many professors need such substantive advice [the example earlier of the international economics course is pertinent here], precisely because they are products themselves of relatively insensitive graduate schools that have shortchanged *them* in *their* education.

We must be careful to guard against the situation whereby a black studies department is set up and then no further attention is paid to the rest of the curriculum. The committee should be composed of knowlegeable black students, faculty in the field, and black consultants in particular fields of expertise. [Such black experts *do* exist around the country. Granted, they are at a premium, but that simply means that these ventures will cost money. We have always known that education was an expensive undertaking!]

The point is that each college should develop some serious, competent, on-going mechanism for reviewing and suggesting changes in its curriculum in regard to matters pertaining to race and race relations. I think this could open up a fruitful area of intellectual discourse. I would suggest that these colleges begin to think in such specific, substantive terms as they devise their lecture series for the next academic year. This would be far more meaningful—academically—than much of what I see happening now, the big campus-wide symposiums on "white racism" or "black power," for example, with outside speakers coming in, talking generally, answering a few questions and leaving.

Why not hold sessions where experts are invited to come to deal with literature being used in specific areas of study, criticize it, suggest innovations, etc.? This is an approach that has not been tried up to now. This would be intellectually stimulating, academically useful, and it would, hopefully, avoid those all-too-frequent mass, emotional sessions of charges and counter-charges.

Many of the demands made by black students call for the creation of "autonomous" black studies departments free to do their own hiring and firing of personnel and selection of courses and materials. This is not as unique or extreme as a first impression might suggest. Many established departments have such powers today. Of course, there should be some representative body in the college to which the department must be responsible. It is hardly likely that the opposite could prevail [that is, no accountability]. Absolute autonomy would amount to the creation of an independent school, and it is hardly possible that a college [which is paying the cost] will agree to that.

One reason for the demand for autonomy by black students is their lack of trust and confidence in the existing administrations and faculties. Students believe the administrators have been and are insensitive to the needs of black people, and that this insensitivity will hamper the development of the program. Because this is in large measure true, a wise administration would go a long way toward giving the new department as much operating room as possible. As these programs are implemented and conducted, quite possibly the alienation will be overcome. And what now appear to be "irresponsible" demands for absolute control could turn into cooperative relationships—or at least into relationships rather similar to the ones existing now between other departments and the administration.

The last point relates to the demand made on some campuses that only black teachers be recruited to teach the "black-oriented" courses. This demand, likewise, sounds at first more extreme [and racist] than it really is. Many black students are saying, in effect, that it is *psychologically* better to be taught black history, black culture, and similar courses by black persons. This psychological dimension must not be overlooked. A simplistic response might assume that the only relevant qualification for a teacher is his knowledge of the subject and his ability to teach the subject, regardless of his race.

In many instances, this might be true. But time and again, many black students say, and sincerely believe, that a nonblack person will bring to the study of black culture and black history an orientation influenced by his own background, and in a comparative vein, I have heard some black students suggest that it would be unthinkable to have an Arab teach a class of Jewish students about Jewish culture and history. They are saying, in other words, that in some areas ability is affected by race.

I suspect there is more merit to the black students' position than a mere rejection out of hand would recognize. In the final analysis, it is probably best not to formalize any rules on this. Several of these kinds of problems will be worked out as the various programs develop. Clearly, many courses cannot be staffed by black teachers, if only because of the shortage of such teachers in different places. The important point is that many of the demands must be seen in a political and psychological context as well as from a purely academic point of view.

This is the sort of situation in which many colleges find themselves today with the demands of black students. And if these colleges would revise their approaches and courses to meet the needs of a black society, they would recognize the *diplomacy* [as well as the academic substance] necessary to get through this period.

V. Self-Affirmation and Expression

In his classic 1903 work, *The Souls of Black Folk*, W. E. B. DuBois captured the dual essence of the minority experience in America. "Between me and the other world," he wrote, "there is ever an unasked question . . . How does it feel to be a problem?" How does it feel to be different, an outsider, a victm of prejudice and brutality? How does it feel to live in a homeland hostile to you? But, he went on, the realities of racism and discrimination are only part of the problem of the minority group member. He faces also a personal, deeper, ultimately more vexing dilemma: existing in a land that "yields him no true self-consciousness, but lets him see himself through the revelation of the other world."

> It is a peculiar sensation, this double consciousness, this sense of always looking at one's self through the eye of others, of measuring one's soul by the tape of a world that looks on in amused contempt and pity. One ever feels his twoness,—an American, a Negro; two souls, two thoughts, two unreconciled strivings; two warring ideals in one dark body, whose dogged strength alone keeps it from being torn asunder.

Other chapters in this book deal with the outward struggle of ethnic minorities to live and survive in America. This chapter is about their struggle to live with themselves.

Long before the advent of Black, Red, and Brown power slogans, minority artists and intellectuals struggled with the inner problems of identity and self-expression. But, as DuBois suggested, few were able to find a satisfactory self-image. The dominant American culture may have appreciated and even assimilated certain elements of minority art and traditions, but it formally stereotyped, altered for white consumption, and trivialized genuine ethnic contributions. There is a saying in the Black community that white Americans have spent their childhood playing Indians, their adolescence dancing to Black and Latin music, and their adult life rejecting all of them.

The inner crisis of identity and self-esteem among ethnic minorities came to a head in the 1960s. It took the form of assertive self-affirmation, which led to a new emphasis on reclaiming and expressing their genuine ethnic heritages. Minority communities erupted with a new burst of creativity. Art institutions proliferated in urban ghettoes and barrios across the nation. In south central Los Angeles alone, the community that had exploded in violence in 1965, suddenly gave birth to the Watts Writers' Workshop, the Watts Summer Festival, Studio Watts, the Performing Arts Society of Los Angeles, and a variety of other literary and artistic enterprises.

For great numbers of minority youths, art and literature became powerful instruments of protest and the means by which they could demonstrate to the world the beauty and significance of their ethnic heritages. And by those means they could prove to their own communities that self-knowledge, creativity, and untrammeled self-expression were essential to the strengthening of ethnic pride.

Yet art in the minority communities was far more than simply protest or group celebration. Indigenous groups, for example, contributed to the development of new theatrical styles. The American Theater of Being, the Free Southern Theater, and El Teatro Campesino are among the best illustrations of that thrust. Moreover, the works of minority artists provided insights not only into the experiences of the disinherited, but also into the universal drama of the human condition.

Ethnic self-affirmation has also had an impact on American religion. The development of a new consciousness has led minorities to question the role, practices, and even the symbolism of Western Christianity. Ethnic minorities now indict the status quo stances of the churches and the racism in Christian theology as well as the stances and racism of other American institutions. Beyond that, minority churchmen have worked to develop theological insights that eliminate dependency on Western culture—to which American Christianity is deeply committed—while remaining true to Christian orthodoxy. This movement has already had a far-reaching impact on established religious institutions.

A. GROUP SELF-IMAGE AND THE DEVELOPMENT OF A NEW CONSCIOUSNESS

Ethnic consciousness and self-affirmation are not unique to post-World War II America. Though suppressed by white society in innumerable subtle and not so subtle ways, members of minority groups have always possessed a strong sense of heritage. Rarely, however, did large numbers proclaim their ethnic pride in one voice (an obvious exception being the militant Universal Negro Improvement Association of Marcus Garvey). This section explores the development of ethnic consciousness since the Second World

War and looks at the struggle of ethnics to reinforce pride in themselves and gain the esteem of others.

In the first selection John Oliver Killens describes the growing willingness among Blacks to affirm that they are not simply white men in black skins, that, as they always knew but felt reluctant to admit, they are culturally different from whites in many ways, and that cultural "difference" should not be mistaken for cultural "deficiency." Blacks, he argues, must shed the traditional image invented for them by Anglo-Saxon society, recognize the true value of their lives, learn pride in their ethnic heritage, and demand the right to live in America as free and equal citizens.

Next Vine Deloria, Jr., discusses the development of militant self-affirmation among Native Americans. In the 1969 seizure of Alcatraz Island he sees a visible, dramatic demonstration of Indian pride combined with a protest against conditions on the reservations and in the cities. Using the example of his own life, beginning as a boy on the Pine Ridge Reservation in South Dakota, he describes the slow, painful realization by Native Americans that their lives could be improved only through their own action and not through white paternalism. Among other things this means returning to traditional tribal methods of government and problem solving and rejecting the advice of white bureaucrats and "Indian experts."

In the third selection Linda Aquilar relates the growing self-consciousness of ethnic women and her belief that in the Mexican-American community Chicanas must struggle as much against the inequities of a *machismo* social ethic as against the inequities of Anglo society. Chicanas thus have a double fight, and until Chicanos recognize this and respond positively, she concludes, Mexican Americans as a group will be deprived of a better future.

1. JOHN OLIVER KILLENS

Explanation of the "Black Psyche"*

When I was a boy in Macon, Ga., one of the greatest compliments a benevolent white man could give a Negro was usually found in the obituary column of the local newspaper: "He was a black man, but he had a white heart." And the burden of every black man was supposedly just a little easier

*John Oliver Killens, "Explanation of the 'Black Psyche,' " *New York Times Magazine*, June 7, 1964. Copyright © 1964 by the New York Times Company. Reprinted by permission.

to bear that day. It was a time when many of us black folk laughed at the antics of Amos 'n' Andy and wept copious tears at a ridiculous movie, very aptly titled "Imitation of Life." Most of us looked at life through the eyes of white America.

The great fictional and filmic masterpieces on the American racial theme usually fell into two categories. One theme dealt with the utter heartbreak of the mulatto, who rejected his black blood and was in turn rejected by his white blood. A variation of this theme was the shattering experience of "passing." The other theme was the "Uncle Tom" or, what I like to call the "Gunga Din," theme. This one also had many variations, but over all there was the image created by that great apologist for colonialism, Rudyard Kipling, of a man who—

> . . . For all 'is dirty 'ide
> 'E was white, clear white, inside
> When 'e went to tend the wounded
> under fire!

With some "additional dialogue" by Hollywood, dear old "white inside" Gunga was a marvelous figment of Western Man's wistful imagination, the personification of his wish fulfillment. Gunga was a water boy for the British regiment and, in the movie, finally blew the bugle against his own people. And how "whiter" inside could a "noble savage" be?

I am waging a quiet little campaign at the moment to substitute the term "Gunga Din" for that much maligned character "Uncle Tom," in designating the contemporary water boys who still blow the bugles for ol' Massa, better known these days as "Mister Charlie." For, although Mrs. Stowe's beloved "Uncle Tom" was indeed an Uncle Tom, as we understand the term today, he, nevertheless, in the final confrontation, chose death rather than blow the bugle against his people.

Variations of the Gunga Din theme were seen in a rash of movie epics like "Gone With the Wind" and "Virginia" and "Kentucky," etc., ad infinitum, ad nauseam, always played magnificently with tongue in check by such stalwarts as Hattie McDaniel and Louise Beavers. In the great emotional scene the black mammy was usually in the big house, weeping and moaning over little pure-white-as-the-driven-snow Missy Anne, who had just sneezed, while mammy's own youn'un was dying of double pneumonia, unattended down in the cabins. All in all, the slaves were presented as carefree and contented in their idyllic degradation. If the black man *really* believed in this romantic version of American slavery, he would have long since wasted away, pining for those good old happy-go-lucky days of bondage.

Last year I did considerable research on that bygone utopian era, and I got a very different picture, slightly less romantic. I found that the slaves were so happy that most of the plantation owners could not afford the astronomical rates of fire insurance. These rapturous slaves were setting fire to the cotton patches , burning down the plantations, every day the good Lord sent them. They organized countless insurrections, killed their masters, poisoned their mistresses, put spiders in the big-house soup. They demonstrated their contentment in most peculiar ways.

I shall never forget an evening I spent in a movie house in Hollywood, watching a closed-circuit television broadcast of the first Patterson-Johansson fight, and the great shame I felt for my white countrymen that night, as they began to smell a possible victory for the white foreigner over the black American. Forgotten entirely was the fact that soft-hearted Floyd Patterson was a fellow-countryman. Color superseded patriotism. As I sat there hearing shouted exhortations like, "Kill the nigger!", I felt that Patterson and I were aliens in a strange and hostile country, and Ingemar was home amongst his people.

In fairness to my countrymen in the closed circuits of America that night, their reactions were not intellectual, not even willful. They were spontaneous, not unlike a conditioned reflex. This ecstasy at the sudden emergence of a new white hope came from the metaphoric guts of them, from their hearts, their souls, their bellies. This was their white insides reacting.

It has been rationalized to me that this incident had no racial implications at all, that these rabid Johansson fans were merely in the Old American tradition of rooting for the underdog. Well, I was also rooting for the underdog, and I knew that, win or lose, the underdog in America was Floyd Patterson, Harry Belafonte, Emmett Till, Rosa Parks, Meredith, Poitier, the black American *me*. The words, "Kill the nigger!" could not possibly have come screaming from my throat, subconsciously, unconsciously or otherwise.

Just as surely as East is East and West is West, there is a "black" psyche in America and there is a "white" one, and the sooner we face up to this social and cultural reality, the sooner the twain shall meet. Our emotional chemistry is different from yours in many instances. Your joy is very often our anger, and your despair our fervent hope. Most of us came here in chains and most of you came here to escape your chains. Your freedom was our slavery, and therein lies the bitter difference in the way we look at life.

You created the myth of the faithful slave, but we know that the "loyal slave" is a contradiction in terms. We understand, though, that the master must always make himself believe in the undying love of his slave. That is why white America put words in the black man's mouth and bade him sing—improbable lyrics like

All de darkeys am a-weepin'
Massa's in de cold, cold ground.

But my great-grandmother told me differently. "We wept all right, honey! Great God Almighty! We cried for joy and shouted hallelujah," when old master got the cold, cold ground that was coming to him.

In order to justify slavery in a courageous new world which was spouting slogans of freedom and equality and brotherhood, the enslavers, through their propagandists, had to create the fiction that the enslaved people were subhuman and undeserving of human rights and sympathies. The first job was to convince the outside world of the inherent inferiority of the enslaved. The second job was to convince the American people. And the third job, which was the cruelest hoax of all, was to convince the slaves themselves that they deserved to be slaves.

The propagandists for American slavery (the creative writers of the time) tackled these tasks with alacrity and a great measure of success, the effects of which still remain with us today, a hundred years after the Emancipation Proclamation, almost 200 years after the Declaration of Independence. Thus, the Negro was invented and the American Revolution thwarted. Knock on any door in Harlem. Ask any black man or woman in Alabama or Mississippi: Was 1776 for real?

Ironically enough, the fathers of our magnificent Revolution, Washington and Jefferson, themselves owned hundreds of human chattels and even though the great Thomas Jefferson made many speeches against the peculiar institution, he was never able to convince himself to the extent of manumitting his own slaves during his own lifetime.

Surely the great irony of the situation did not escape my ancestors back in the days of the Revolution. And now, today, it does not escape their great-great-grandchildren. When we black folk hear one of our white leaders use the phrase, "the free world," even though the same white leader may very well be the Governor of the state of Mississippi or Alabama, or any other state, for that matter, we—as the slaves of Washington and Jefferson must have done—stare at him incredulously and can not believe our ears. And we wonder how this word "freedom" can have such vastly different meanings, such conflicting connotations.

But the time has come for you (white America) and me (black America) to work this thing out once and for all, to examine and evaluate the differences between us and the differences inside of us. Time is swiftly running out, and a new dialogue is indispensable. It is so long overdue it is almost half past midnight.

My fight is not to be a white man in a black skin, but to inject some black blood, some black intelligence into the pallid main stream of American life, culturally, socially, psychologically, philosophically. This is the truer deeper meaning of the Negro revolt, which is not yet a revolution—to get America ready for the middle of the 20th century, which is already magnificently here.

This new epoch has caught our country (yours and mine) napping in a sweet nostalgia of the good old days. Our country slumbers in a world of yesteryears, before Africa and Asia got up off their knees and threw off the black man's burden: the good old days when you threw pennies to the "natives" and there were gunboats in the China Sea and Big Stick Policies and Monroe Doctrines and "Old Coasters" from the U.K. sipped their gin-and-tonics in Accra and Lagos and talked about the "natives," as they basked in their roles of Great White Fathers in that best of all possible worlds.

That world is gone forever, and black and brown men everywhere are glad, deep in their hearts, but most Western men are chagrined, which is the understatement of the century. This is why the world is becoming much too much for Western men, even for most of you liberal Western men, even you radical Western men, whoever you are, and wherever.

But the world is becoming more and more to my liking, to my taste and in my image. It gladdens my heart to see black and brown men and women come with dignity to the United Nations in affirmation of the manhood and the selfhood of the entire human race.

The American Negro, then, is an Anglo-Saxon invention, a role the Anglo-Saxon gentlemen invented for the black man to play in this drama known euphemistically as the American Way of Life. It began as an economic expedient, frankly, because you wanted somebody to work for nothing. It is still that, but now it is much more than that. It has become a way of life within a way of life, socially, economically, psychologically, philosophically.

But now, in the middle of the 20th century, I, the Negro, am refusing to be your "nigrah" any longer. Even some of us "favored," "talented," "unusual" ones are refusing to be your educated, sophisticated, split-leveled "nigrahs" any longer. We refuse to look at ourselves through the eyes of white America.

We are not fighting for the right to be like you. We respect ourselves too much for that. When we fight for freedom, we mean freedom for us to be black, or brown, and you to be white and yet live together in a free and equal society. This is the only way that integration can mean dignity for both of us.

I, for one, am growing weary of those well-meaning white liberals who are forever telling me they don't know what color I am. The very fact that they single me out at the cocktail party and gratuitously make me the beneficiary of their blessed assurances gives the lie to their pronouncements.

My fight is not *for* racial sameness but for racial equality and *against* racial prejudice and discrimination. I work for the day when my people will be free of the racist pressures to be *white like you*; a day when "good hair" and "high yaller" and bleaching cream and hair-straighteners will be obsolete. What a tiresome place America would be if freedom meant we all had to think alike and be the same color and wear the same gray flannel suit!

If relationships are to improve between us Americans, black and white and otherwise, if the country is to be saved, we will have to face up to the fact that differences do exist between us. All men react to life through man-made symbols. Even our symbolic reactions are different from yours. To give a few examples:

In the center of a little Southern town near the border of Mississippi, there is a water tower atop which is a large white cross, illuminated at night with a lovely (awesome to Negroes) neoned brightness. It can be seen for many miles away. To most white Americans who see it for the first time it is a beacon light that symbolizes the Cross upon which Jesus died, and it gives them a warm feeling in the face and shoulders. But the same view puts an angry knot in the black man's belly. To him it symbolizes the very very "Christian" K.K.K.

To the average white man, a courthouse, even in Mississippi, is a place where justice is dispensed. To me, the black man, it is a place where justice is dispensed with.

Even our white hero symbols are different from yours. You give us moody Abraham Lincoln, but many of us prefer John Brown, whom most of you hold in contempt and regard as a fanatic: meaning, of course, that the firm dedication of any white man is *prima facie* evidence of perversion and insanity.

You look upon these times as the Atomic Age, the Space Age, the Cold War era. But I believe that when the history of these times is written, it will not be so important who reached the moon first or who made the largest bomb. I believe the great significance will be that this was the century when most of mankind achieved freedom and human dignity. For me, this is the Freedom Century.

So now it is time for you to understand us, because it is becoming increasingly hazardous for you not to. Dangerous for both of us. As Richard Wright said in his "Twelve Million Black Voices," voices you chose not to heed: "Each day when you see us black folk upon the dusty land of your farms or upon the hard pavement of your city streets, you usually take us for granted and think you know us, but our history is far stranger than you suspect, and we are not what we seem."

The Rev. Ralph Abernathy of Montgomery placed the question humorously when he said that the new Negro of Montgomery had stopped laughing when he wasn't tickled and scratching when he didn't itch.

In a word we are bringing down the curtain on this role you cast us in, and we will no longer be a party to our own degradation. We have become unbelievers, no longer believing in the absolute superiority of the white man's juju. You have never practiced what you preached. Why would we want to be like you? We have caught you in too many lies. You proud defenders of the chastity of womanhood, you champions of racial purity, you are, if I may coin a phrase, "the last of the great miscegenators."

Yes, we are different from you and we are not invisible men, Ralph Ellison notwithstanding. We are the most visible of Americans. We are both Americans and Negroes. Other Americans, for the most part, excepting Puerto Ricans and Mexicans, are just Americans. But we are more than just Americans, not because of our color but because of how America exploited our color. We are different, not because we willed it, but because America set us apart from the rest of the community for special exploitation. And so we are special, with extraspecial insights.

In the summer and fall of 1961 I traveled in a Land Rover 12,000 miles through Africa. I talked to people in the cities, on the farms, in the villages. I talked with workers, farmers, artists, market women, ministers of state, politicians, teachers, and the same question was asked me everywhere I went, with variations: "How can we believe your country's professions of goodwill to us, with whom they have not lived, when they deny human dignity to you who come from us and have lived with them for centuries and helped to build their great civilization?"

It is a question America has to answer to the entire New World of Africa and Asia. The only way we Americans, black and white, can answer this question affirmatively is to make freedom and democracy work *here* and *now*. Just as most Negroes still believe that the ultimate solution for us is in America, I am firmly convinced that the ultimate salvation of America is in the Negro.

The Negro loves America enough to criticize her fundamentally. Most of white America simply can't be bothered. Ironically enough, in the middle of the 20th century, the Negro is the new white hope. To live castrated in a great white harem and yet somehow maintain his black manhood and his humanity—this is the essence of the new man created out of the Negro Invention. History may render the verdict that this was the greatest legacy handed to the New World by the West.

Western man wrote *his* history as if it were the history of the entire human race. I hope that colored men all over the world have watched Western man too long to commit the fatal folly of writing history with a colored pencil. For there is a great wisdom in the old Ghana proverb, which says "No one rules forever on the throne of time."

We black folk have learned many lessons during our sojourn in this place. One of them is the truth of another Ghana proverb that says: "Only a fool points to his heritage with his left hand." We are becoming prouder and prouder of our heritage in America and Africa. And we know the profound difference between pride and arrogance; the difference, if you will, between James Meredith and Ross Barnett, both of Mississippi. . . . Yes, we black people stand ready, eager, willing and able to make our contribution to the culture of the world. Our dialogue will not be protest but *affirmation* of the human dignity of all people everywhere.

I know there are white folk who want America to be the land of the free and the home of the brave, but there are far too few of them, and most of them are seldom brave. And I, too, cherish old John Brown and Garrison and William Moore. Let the winter patriots increase their ranks. Let those who truly love America join the valiant Negro Revolt and save the beloved country.

2. VINE DELORIA, JR.

This Country Was a Lot Better Off When the Indians Were Running It*

On Nov. 9, 1969, a contingent of American Indians, led by Adam Nordwall, a Chippewa from Minnesota, and Richard Oakes, a Mohawk from New York, landed on Alcatraz Island in San Francisco Bay and claimed the 13-acre rock "by right of discovery." The island had been abandoned six and a half years ago, and although there had been various suggestions concerning its disposal nothing had been done to make use of the land. Since there are Federal treaties giving some tribes the right to abandoned Federal property within a tribe's original territory, the Indians of the Bay area felt that they could lay claim to the island.

For nearly a year the United Bay Area Council of American Indians, a confederation of urban Indian organizations, had been talking about submitting a bid for the island to use it as a West Coast Indian cultural center and vocational training headquarters. Then, on Nov. 1, the San Francisco American Indian Center burned down. The center had served an estimated 30,000 Indians in the immediate area and was the focus of activities of the urban Indian community. It became a matter of urgency after that and, as Adam Nordwall said, "it was GO." Another landing, on Nov. 20, by nearly 100 Indians in a swift midnight raid secured the island.

The new inhabitants have made "the Rock" a focal point symbolic of Indian people. Under extreme difficulty they have worked to begin repairing sanitary facilities and buildings. The population has been largely transient, many people have stopped by, looked the situation over for a few days, then gone home, unwilling to put in the tedious work necessary to make the island support a viable community.

The Alcatraz news stories are somewhat shocking to non-Indians. It is

*Vine Deloria, Jr., "This Country Was a Lot Better Off When the Indians Were Running It," *New York Times Magazine*, March 8, 1970. Copyright © 1970 by the New York Times Company. Reprinted by permission.

difficult for most Americans to comprehend that there still exists a living community of nearly one million Indians in this country. For many people, Indians have become a species of movie actor periodically dispatched to the Happy Hunting Grounds by John Wayne on the "Late, Late Show." Yet there are some 315 Indian tribal groups in 26 states still functioning as quasi-sovereign nations under treaty status; they range from the mammoth Navajo tribe of some 132,000 with 16 million acres of land to tiny Mission Creek of California with 15 people and a tiny parcel of property. There are over half a million Indians in the cities alone, with the largest concentrations in San Francisco, Los Angeles, Minneapolis and Chicago.

The take-over of Alcatraz is to many Indian people a demonstration of pride in being Indian and a dignified, yet humorous, protest against current conditions existing on the reservations and in the cities. It is this special pride and dignity, the determination to judge life according to one's own values, and the unconquerable conviction that the tribes will not die that has always characterized Indian people as I have known them.

I was born in Martin, a border town on the Pine Ridge Indian Reservation in South Dakota, in the midst of the Depression. My father was an Indian missionary who served 18 chapels on the eastern half of the reservation. In 1934, when I was 1, the Indian Reorganizaton Act was passed, allowing Indian tribes full rights of self-government for the first time since the late eighteen-sixties.* Ever since those days, when the Sioux had agreed to forsake the life of the hunter for that of the farmer, they had been systematically deprived of any voice in decisions affecting their lives and property. Tribal ceremonies and religious practices were forbidden. The reservation was fully controlled by men in Washington, most of whom had never visited a reservation and felt no urge to do so.

The first years on the reservations were extremely hard for the Sioux. Kept confined behind fences they were almost wholly dependent upon Government rations for their food supply. Many died of hunger and malnutrition. Game was scarce and few were allowed to have weapons for fear of another Indian war. In some years there was practically no food available. Other years rations were withheld until the men agreed to farm the tiny pieces of land each family had been given. In desperation many families were forced to eat stray dogs and cats to keep alive.

By World War I, however, many of the Sioux families had developed prosperous ranches. Then the Government stepped in, sold the Indians'

*See John Collier, "The Indian New Deal," in Ch. IV, section A, above.

cattle for wartime needs, and after the war leased the grazing land to whites, creating wealthy white ranchers and destitute Indian landlords.

With the passage of the Indian Reorganization Act, native ceremonies and practices were given full recognition by Federal authorities. My earliest memories are of trips along dusty roads to Kyle, a small settlement in the heart of the reservation, to attend the dances. Ancient men, veterans of battles even then considered footnotes to the settlement of the West, brought their costumes out of hiding and walked about the grounds gathering the honors they had earned half a century before. They danced as if the intervening 50 years had been a lost weekend from which they had fully recovered. I remember best Dewey Beard, then in his late 80's and a survivor of the Little Big Horn. Even at that late date Dewey was hesitant to speak of the battle for fear of reprisal. There was no doubt, as one watched the people's expressions, that the Sioux had survived their greatest ordeal and were ready to face whatever the future might bring.

In those days the reservation was isolated and unsettled. Dirt roads held the few mail routes together. One could easily get lost in the wild back country as roads turned into cowpaths without so much as a backward glance. Remote settlements such as Buzzard Basin and Cuny Table were nearly inaccessible. In the spring every bridge on the reservation would be washed out with the first rain and would remain out until late summer. But few people cared. Most of the reservation people, traveling by team and wagon, merely forded the creeks and continued their journey, almost contemptuous of the need for roads and bridges.

The most memorable event of my early childhood was visiting Wounded Knee where 200 Sioux, including women and children, were slaughtered in 1890 by troopers of the Seventh Cavalry in what is believed to have been a delayed act of vengeance for Custer's defeat. The people were simply lined up and shot down much as was allegedly done, according to newspaper reports, at Songmy. The wounded were left to die in a three-day Dakota blizzard, and when the soldiers returned to the scene after the storm some were still alive and were saved. The massacre was vividly etched in the minds of many of the older reservation people, but it was difficult to find anyone who wanted to talk about it.

Many times, over the years, my father would point out survivors of the massacre, and people on the reservation always went out of their way to help them. For a long time there was a bill in Congress to pay indemnities to the survivors, but the War Department always insisted that it had been a "battle" to stamp out the Ghost Dance religion among the Sioux. This does not, however, explain bayoneted Indian women and children found miles from the scene of the incident.

Strangely enough, the Depression was good for Indian reservations, particularly for the people at Pine Ridge. Since their lands had been leased to non-Indians by the Bureau of Indian Affairs, they had only a small rent check and the contempt of those who leased their lands to show for their ownership. But the Federal programs devised to solve the national economic crisis were also made available to Indian people, and there was work available for the first time in the history of the reservations.

The Civilian Conservation Corps set up a camp on the reservation and many Indians were hired under the program. In the canyons north of Allen, S. D., a beautiful buffalo pasture was built by the C.C.C., and the whole area was transformed into a recreation wonderland. Indians would come from miles around to see the buffalo and leave with a strange look in their eyes. Many times I stood silently watching while old men talked to the buffalo about the old days. They would conclude by singing a song before respectfully departing, their eyes filled with tears and their minds occupied with the memories of other times and places. It was difficult to determine who was the captive—the buffalo fenced in or the Indian fenced out.

While the rest of America suffered from the temporary deprivation of its luxuries, Indian people had a period of prosperity, as it were. Paychecks were regular. Small cattle herds were started, cars were purchased, new clothes and necessities became available. To a people who had struggled along on $50 cash income per year, the C.C.C. was the greatest program ever to come along. The Sioux had climbed from absolute deprivation to mere poverty, and this was the best time the reservation ever had.

World War II ended this temporary prosperity. The C.C.C. camps were closed; reservation programs were cut to the bone and social services became virtually non-existent; "Victory gardens" were suddenly the style, and people began to be aware that a great war was being waged overseas.

The war dispersed the reservation people as nothing ever had. Every day, it seemed, we would be bidding farewell to families as they headed west to work in the defense plants on the Coast.

A great number of Sioux people went west and many of the Sioux on Alcatraz today are their children and relatives. There may not be as many Sioux in California as there are on the reservations in South Dakota because of the great wartime migration.

Those who stayed on the reservation had the war brought directly to their doorstep when they were notified that their sons had to go across the seas and fight. Busloads of Sioux boys left the reservation for parts unknown. In many cases even the trip to nearby Martin was a new experience for them, let alone training in Texas, California or Colorado. There were always going-away ceremonies conducted by the older people who admonished the boys to uphold the old tribal traditions and not to fear death. It was not death they feared but living with an unknown people in a distant place.

I was always disappointed with the Government's way of handling Indian servicemen. Indians were simply lost in the shuffle of 3 million men in uniform. Many boys came home on furlough and feared to return. They were not cowards in any sense of the word but the loneliness and boredom of stateside duty was crushing their spirits. They spent months without seeing another Indian. If the Government had recruited all-Indian outfits it would have easily solved this problem and also had the best fighting units in the world at its disposal. I often wonder what an all-Sioux or Apache company, painted and singing its songs, would have done to the morale of élite German panzer units.

After the war Indian veterans straggled back to the reservations and tried to pick up their lives. It was very difficult for them to resume a life of poverty after having seen the affluent outside world. Some spent a few days with the old folks and then left again for the big cities. Over the years they have emerged as leaders of the urban Indian movement. Many of their children are the nationalists of today who are adamant about keeping the reservations they have visited only on vacations. Other veterans stayed on the reservations and entered tribal politics.

The reservations radically changed after the war. During the Depression there were about five telephones in Martin. If there was a call for you, the man at the hardware store had to come down to your house and get you to answer it. A couple of years after the war a complete dial system was installed that extended to most of the smaller communities on the reservation. Families that had been hundreds of miles from any form of communication were now only minutes away from a telephone.

Roads were built connecting the major communities of the Pine Ridge country. No longer did it take hours to go from one place to another. With these kinds of roads everyone had to have a car. The team and wagon vanished, except for those families who lived at various "camps" in inaccessible canyons pretty much as their ancestors had. (Today, even they have adopted the automobile for traveling long distances in search of work.)

I left the reservation in 1951 when my family moved to Iowa. I went back only once for an extended stay, in the summer of 1955, while on a furlough, and after that I visited only occasionally during summer vacations. In the meantime, I attended college, served a hitch in the Marines, and went to the seminary. After I graduated from the seminary, I took a job with the United Scholarship Service, a private organization devoted to the college and secondary-school education of American Indian and Mexican students. I had spent my last two years of high school in an Eastern preparatory school and so was probably the only Indian my age who knew what an independent Eastern school was like. As the program developed, we soon had some 30 students placed in Eastern schools.

I insisted that all the students who entered the program be able to qualify for scholarships as students and not simply as Indians. I was pretty sure we could beat the white man at his own educational game, which seemed to me the only way to gain his respect. I was soon to find that this was a dangerous attitude to have. The very people who were supporting the program—non-Indians in the national church establishments—accused me of trying to form a colonialist "élite" by insisting that only kids with strong test scores and academic patterns be sent east to school. They wanted to continue the ancient pattern of soft-hearted paternalism towards Indians. I didn't feel we should cry our way into the school; that sympathy would destroy the students we were trying to help.

In 1964, while attending the annual convention of the National Congress of American Indians, I was elected its executive director. I learned more about life in the N.C.A.I. in three years than I had in the previous 30. Every conceivable problem that could occur in an Indian society was suddenly thrust at me from 315 different directions. I discovered that I was one of the people who were supposed to solve the problems. The only trouble was that Indian people locally and on the national level were being played off one against the other by clever whites who had either ego or income at stake. While there were many feasible solutions, few could be tried without whites with vested interests working night and day to destroy the unity we were seeking on a national basis.

In the mid-nineteen-sixties, the whole generation that had grown up after World War II and had left the reservations during the fifties to get an education was returning to Indian life as "educated Indians." But we soon knew better. Tribal societies had existed for centuries without going outside themselves for education and information. Yet many of us thought that we would be able to improve the traditional tribal methods. We were wrong.

For three years we ran around the conference circuit attending numerous meetings called to "solve" the Indian problems. We listened to and spoke with anthropologists, historians, sociologists, psychologists, economists, educators and missionaries. We worked with many Government agencies and with every conceivable doctrine, idea and program ever created. At the end of this happy round of consultations the reservation people were still plodding along on their own time schedule, doing the things they considered important. They continued to solve their problems their way in spite of the advice given them by "Indian experts."

By 1967 there was a radical change in thinking on the part of many of us. Conferences were proving unproductive. Where non-Indians had been pushed out to make room for Indian people, they had wormed their way back into power and again controlled the major programs serving Indians. The poverty programs, reservation and university technical assistance groups were dominated by whites who had pushed Indian administrators aside.

Reservation people, meanwhile, were making steady progress in spite of the numerous setbacks suffered by the national Indian community. So, in large part, younger Indian leaders who had been playing the field began working at the local level to build community movements from the ground up. By consolidating local organizations into power groups they felt that they would be in a better position to influence national thinking.

Robert Hunter, director of the Nevada Intertribal Council, had already begun to build a strong state organization of tribes and communities. In South Dakota, Gerald One Feather, Frank LaPointe and Ray Briggs formed the American Indian Leadership Conference, which quickly welded the educated young Sioux in that state into a strong regional organization active in nearly every phase of Sioux life. Gerald is now running for the prestigious post of chairman of the Oglala Sioux, the largest Sioux tribe, numbering some 15,000 members. Ernie Stevens, an Oneida from Wisconsin, and Lee Cook, a Chippewa from Minnesota, developed a strong program for economic and community development in Arizona. Just recently Ernie has moved into the post of director of the California Intertribal Council, a statewide organization representing some 130,000 California Indians in cities and on the scattered reservations of that state.

By the fall of 1967, it was apparent that the national Indian scene was collapsing in favor of strong regional organizations, although the major national organizations such as the National Congress of American Indians and the National Indian Youth Council continued to grow. There was yet another factor emerging on the Indian scene: the old-timers of the Depression days had educated a group of younger Indians in the old ways and these people were now becoming a major force in Indian life. Led by Thomas Banyaca of the Hopi, Mad Bear Anderson of the Tuscaroras, Clifton Hill of the Creeks, and Rolling Thunder of the Shoshones, the traditional Indians were forcing the whole Indian community to rethink its understanding of Indian life.

The message of the traditionalists is simple. They demand a return to basic Indian philosophy, establishment of ancient methods of government by open council instead of elected officials, a revival of Indian religions and replacement of white laws with Indian customs; in short a complete return to the ways of the old people. In an age dominated by tribalizing communications media, their message makes a great deal of sense.

But in some areas their thinking is opposed to that of the National Congress of American Indians, which represents officially elected tribal governments organized under the Indian Reorganization Act as Federal corporations. The contemporary problem is therefore one of defining the meaning of "tribe." Is it a traditionally organized band of Indians following customs with medicine men and chiefs dominating the policies of the tribe, or is it a modern corporate structure attempting to compromise at least in part with modern white culture?

The problem has been complicated by private foundations' and Government agencies' funding of Indian programs. In general this process, although it has brought a great amount of money into Indian country, has been one of cooptation. Government agencies must justify their appropriation requests every year and can only take chances on spectacular programs that will serve as showcases of progress. They are not willing to invest the capital funds necessary to build viable self-supporting communities on the reservations because these programs do not have an immediate publicity potential. Thus, the Government agencies are forever committed to conducting conferences to discover that one "key" to Indian life that will give them the edge over their rival agencies in the annual appropriations derby.

Churches and foundations have merely purchased an Indian leader or program that conforms with their ideas of what Indian people should be doing. The large foundations have bought up the well-dressed, handsome "new image" Indian who is comfortable in the big cities but virtually helpless at an Indian meeting. Churches have given money to Indians who have been willing to copy black militant activist tactics, and the more violent and insulting the Indian can be, the more the churches seem to love it. They are wallowing in self-guilt and piety over the lot of the poor, yet funding demagogues of their own choosing to speak for the poor.

I did not run for re-election as executive director of the N.C.A.I. in the fall of 1967, but entered law school at the University of Colorado instead. It was apparent to me that the Indian revolution was well under way and that someone had better get a legal education so that we could have our own legal program for defense of Indian treaty rights. Thanks to a Ford Foundation program, nearly 50 Indians are now in law school, assuring the Indian community of legal talent in the years ahead. Within four years I foresee another radical shift in Indian leadership patterns as the growing local movements are affected by the new Indian lawyers.

There is an increasing scent of victory in the air in Indian country these days. The mood is comparable to the old days of the Depression when the men began to dance once again. As the Indian movement gathers momentum and individual Indians cast their lot with the tribe, it will become apparent that not only will Indians survive the electronic world of Marshall McLuhan, they will thrive in it. At the present time everyone is watching how mainstream America will handle the issues of pollution, poverty, crime and racism when it does not fundamentally understand the issues. Knowing the importance of tribal survival, Indian people are speaking more and more of sovereignty, of the great political technique of the open council, and of the need for gaining the community's consensus on all programs before putting them into effect.

One can watch this same issue emerge in white society as the "Woodstock Nation," the "Blackstone Nation" and the block organizations are developed. This is a full tribalizing process involving a nontribal people, and it is apparent that some people are frightened by it. But it is the kind of social phenomenon upon which Indians feast.

In 1965 I had a long conversation with an old Papago. I was trying to get the tribe to pay its dues to the National Congress of American Indians and I had asked him to speak to the tribal council for me. He said that he would but that the Papagos didn't really need the N.C.A.I. They were like, he told me, the old mountain in the distance. The Spanish had come and dominated them for 300 years and then left. The Mexicans had come and ruled them for a century, but they also left. "The Americans," he said, "have been here only about 80 years. They, too, will vanish, but the Papagos and the mountain will always be here."

This attitude and understanding of life is what American society is searching for.

I wish the Government would give Alcatraz to the Indians now occupying it. They want to create five centers on the island. One center would be for a North American studies program; another would be a spiritual and medical center where Indian religions and medicines would be used and studied. A third center would concentrate on ecological studies based on an Indian view of nature—that man should live *with* the land and not simply *on* it. A job-training center and a museum would also be founded on the island. Certain of these programs would obviously require Federal assistance.

Some people may object to this approach, yet Health, Education and Welfare gave out $10-million last year to non-Indians to study Indians. Not one single dollar went to an Indian scholar or researcher to present the point of view of Indian people. And the studies done by non-Indians added nothing to what was already known about Indians.

Indian people have managed to maintain a viable and cohesive social order in spite of everything the non-Indian society has thrown at them in an effort to break the tribal structure. At the same time, non-Indian society has created a monstrosity of a culture where people starve while the granaries are filled and the sun can never break through the smog.

By making Alcatraz an experimental Indian center operated and planned by Indian people, we would be given a chance to see what we could do toward developing answers to modern social problems. Ancient tribalism can be incorporated with modern technology in an urban setting. Perhaps we would not succeed in the effort, but the Government is spending billions every year and still the situation is rapidly growing worse. It just seems to a lot of Indians that this continent was a lot better off when we were running it.

3. LINDA AQUILAR

Unequal Opportunity and the Chicana*

The traditional role of the Mexican American female, or Chicana, has been that of housewife and mother whose primary purpose in life is to serve and assist her man, the Chicano. This is no longer true. The Chicana has stepped out of the kitchen into the world to become a visable force for change and the elimination of discrimination. Therefore, it is understandable when the general public assumes that the Mexican American woman who has

*Linda Aquilar, "Unequal Opportunity and the Chicana," *Civil Rights Digest*, 5 (spring 1973), pp. 31-33.

become very vocal and assertive is part of the current "Women's Liberation Movement" sweeping the country, or has at least been inspired by its efforts.

Actually, emergence of the Chicana as a strong motivating force within the Spanish-speaking community has been in conjunction with that of the Chicano. For this reason, her struggle cannot be paralleled with the Anglo woman's fight for rights against the Anglo male. Chicanas have fought side by side with their men in the struggle for equal opportunity in all areas of American life. Unfortunately, because the major emphasis has always been on opening doors of opportunity for the Mexican American male, the female in essence . . . fights the battle, but does not share in the spoils.

Much has been written on the problem of lack of equal opportunity for Chicanos in the various areas of employment. Practically no one has ventured to write about employment discrimination directed at Chicanas, not only from Anglo male employers, but potential Chicano employers as well. I say potential because from my experience if she seeks any type of administrative position, a Chicana has a better chance of being employed by an Anglo than by a Chicano.

One can see that part of the reason for this is that the Anglo administrator does not feel that his masculinity is threatened by the Chicana. Rather, he finds it enhanced, if he even vaguely falls for the stereotype of the Mexican American female—Mexican women are said to be for the most part hot blooded, primitives interested only in sexual gratification and grateful for any attention from Anglo males. This image is constantly reinforced by the various media, television, movies and publications. Rare is the film that does not depict the Chicana as a loose, wanton woman.

The Chicano Revolution has brought about great changes in the Mexican American community and family structure. The Mexican American female has taken on some characteristics of what has been described as a *Macho*. She may be very vocal, aggressive, and an effective community organizer. She may prefer to pursue interests outside the home and reject homemaking as the total fulfillment in her life.

This is the new image for some Mexican American females. The docility and submissiveness are evidently dwindling and although the Chicano views her with interest, this interest is not totally absent of fear, wonder and suspicion. Fear, because Mexican American women always have been expected totally to be submissive to males. Wonder, because Chicanas are now demonstrating abilities the Chicano thought them incapable of. Lastly, suspicion, because one is always suspicious of something one does not understand. Chicanas who have grouped together for strength and unity of purpose are, at best, tolerated, more often ostracized and ridiculed by Chicanos.

Women have stepped out of the background into the spotlight as spokesmen at various public meetings. School boards, commissions, and city councils, t name a few, have felt the sting of the verbal slaps from irate Mexican American women. Chicanas have shown themselves to be alert, forceful, and intelligent and they have proved to be a major catalyst in the Chicano community. The aggression on the part of the Chicana towards the Anglo has not only been condoned but encouraged by the Mexican American male. The results have been good. Capable and competent Chicanos have been hired into decent positions of administration by a reluctant Anglo community.

The problem begins. The same forceful Chicana that berated the Anglo looks to the Chicano for employment. She has been forced into a leadership role in the community but finds that with the Chicano employer, the outmoded man/woman relationship that existed in the home has not changed. In the book *A Forgotten American*, Luis Hernandez writes:

> Traditionally all men (Chicanos) are considered to be superior to women (Chicanas), a girl looks forward to the day she will fulfill her role as a woman . . . where her first duty is to serve her husband

As far as the Chicano is concerned, the role of the Chicana has not really changed. It has merely been transferred from the home to the office. If a Chicana seeks employment above clerical help status, her fiercest opposition comes from the Chicano. The reprieve from the kitchen has been temporary, or more realistically, not a reprieve at all, for although a Chicana is encouraged to "stand up" to an Anglo, deference to the Chicano is still mandatory. In his book *Pensamientos*, Elius Carranza states,

> Chicanos are exposed with a little bit of honesty to the big lie that we are all free, we are all equal . . .

Perhaps the time has come for Chicanas to also expose "with a little bit of honesty" the big lie that we are all free, we are all equal. In our own San Jose, California community the number of Spanish surname females employed by the city is 21, out of a work force of 2,575. In a special program, the Emergency Employment Act (EEA), the number employed is 20 out of 288. These numbers do not mean that 41 Chicanas are employed by San Jose City. Some of these women are Anglo females married to Mexican American males. In addition, the majority of these positions are non-supervisory.

Equality in employment for Chicanas is simply not a reality although the Chicano family organization is certainly changing. Chicanas, through divorce, separation, or other factors, are assuming the role of family bread-winner. In these families headed by women two thirds of the incomes in the Los Angeles area alone are below the poverty level.

Most Chicanas work because they have to. Either they must supplement their husband's income or they are the sole support of their families. This is a reality that Chicanos must face. It demands more than a shrugging of shoulders and a mumbling that it's too bad. Along with standing on the speakers platform and demanding relevant education for Chicano youngsters, Chicanos must realize that without adequate housing, decent clothing, and basic food necessities, Chicano youth will continue to fail. Words will not provide for needs, but actions will.

Chicanos must be willing to provide employment opportunities to Chicanas faced with these problems or continue to deal with the situation of children who are too preoccupied with family problems, including a lack of food, to be concerned with something as nebulous to them as education. In an article on the plight of Mexican Americans, Edward Cassavantes writes:

> We also need to constantly stress to the individual Mexican American that he can make it . . . We need only to banish our poverty and our ignorance. If prejudice and discrimination stand in our forward thrust towards those ends, then we will need to take action against that prejudice and discrimination.

What of the competent Chicanas who have little chance of "making it" simply because they are women? What of those who are properly educated and still remain economically poor due to the disparity in wages? This is a more acute problem for Chicanas since, traditionally, they have had less opportunity for furthering their education, while the Anglo female was encouraged to attend college, if only to provide a favorable environment for meeting a husband. Finally, if the prejudice and discrimination are directed at us from our own brothers do we then take action against them? At this time in the "Movimiento" this is hardly conceivable.

Are we to settle for working side by side with men in the fields and the migrant camps? Chicanos must realize that women, too, need an outlet for their creativity, need fulfillment, need to utilize their talents, and most of all need to be able to earn a living to upgrade their lives. Deprive us of a decent living because we are women and you also deprive Chicanos of a better future, for in depriving us you deprive our children, and our children are the future.

B. LITERARY EXPRESSION

An essential means by which a people defines, explains, and celebrates itself is through its art. In America the pressures to conform to white society have often suppressed forthright ethnic artistic expression. In recent years, as minority group members have turned inward in search of themselves and toward the past in search of their authentic heritages, there has been a prolific outpouring of ethnic art. This section examines the historical minority struggle for free literary expression and presents a sampling of poetry that offers ethnic perceptions of life in America.

The first selection, "The Negro Artist and the Racial Mountain," written almost half a century ago by Langston Hughes, stands as an early monument to minority self-affirmation in the arts of twentieth-century America. Having come to terms with his own blackness and certain of the beauty, power, and humanity of Black art, Hughes calls on all Black artists to abandon their "urge to whiteness"—a central problem for all minority artists in America—and to "express their individual dark-skinned selves without fear or shame."

Next is the poem, "what's happening . . . ," by the Chicano poet and teacher Alurista. More than an angry document, more than a manifesto of liberation from the hypocrisy and the self-serving declarations of concern by Anglos, this represents an organic Chicano literary style. A product of two cultures, Alurista shifts between English and Spanish in an interior monologue of rage.

Winston Weathers evokes the poignant memories, symbols, joys, and spiritual reawakening of an Indian people during the brief life of the Osage August Dances. Almost as soon as they "undress from the white world," however, the dances end. The Indians must return to the grey cities and place their ceremonial costumes—and their souls—in the closet for another year.

1. LANGSTON HUGHES

The Negro Artist and the Racial Mountain*

One of the most promising of the young Negro poets said to me once, "I want to be a poet—not a Negro poet," meaning, I believe, "I want to write

*Langston Hughes, "The Negro Artist and the Racial Mountain," *Nation*, 122 (June 23, 1926), pp. 692-94.

like a white poet''; meaning subconsciously, ''I would like to be a white poet''; meaning behind that, ''I would like to be white.'' And I was sorry the young man said that, for no great poet has ever been afraid of being himself. And I doubted then that, with his desire to run away spiritually from his race, this boy would ever be a great poet. But this is the mountain standing in the way of any true Negro art in America—this urge within the race toward whiteness, the desire to pour racial individuality into the mold of American standardization, and to be as little Negro and as much American as possible.

But let us look at the immediate background of this young poet. His family is of what I suppose one would call the Negro middle class: people who are by no means rich yet never uncomfortable nor hungry—smug, contented, respectable folk, members of the Baptist church. The father goes to work every morning. He is a chief steward at a large white club. The mother sometimes does fancy sewing or supervises parties for the rich families of the town. The children go to a mixed school. In the home they read white papers and magazines. And the mother often says ''Don't be like niggers'' when the children are bad. A frequent phrase from the father is, ''Look how well a white man does things.'' And so the word white comes to be unconsciously a symbol of all the virtues. It holds for the chigdren beauty, morality, and money. The whisper of ''I want to be white'' runs silently through their minds. This young poet's home is, I believe, a fairly typical home of the colored middle class. One sees immediately how difficult it would be for an artist born in such a home to interest himself in interpreting the beauty of his own people. He is never taught to see that beauty. He is taught rather not to see it, or if he does, to be ashamed of it when it is not according to Caucasian patterns.

For racial culture the home of a self-styled ''high-class'' Negro has nothing better to offer. Instead there will perhaps be more aping of things white than in a less cultured or less wealthy home. The father is perhaps a doctor, lawyer, landowner, or politician. The mother may be a social worker, or a teacher, or she may do nothing and have a maid. Father is often dark but he has usually married the lightest woman he could find. The family attend a fashionable church where few really colored faces are to be found. And they themselves draw a color line. In the North they go to white theaters and white movies. And in the South they have at least two cars and a house ''like white folks.'' Nordic manners, Nordic faces, Nordic hair, Nordic art, (if any), and an Episcopal heaven. A very high mountain indeed for the would-be racial artist to climb in order to discover himself and his people.

But then there are the low-down folks, the so-called common element, and they are the majority—may the Lord be praised! The people who have their nip of gin on Saturday nights and are not too important to themselves or the community, or too well fed, or too learned to watch the lazy world go round. They live on Seventh Street in Washington or State Street in Chicago and they do not particularly care whether they are like white folks or anybody else. Their joy runs, bang! into ecstasy. Their religion soars to a shout. Work maybe a little today, rest a little tomorrow. Play awhile. Sing awhile. O, let's dance! These common people are not afraid of spirituals, as for a long time their more intellectual brethren were, and jazz is their child. They furnish a wealth of colorful, distinctive material for any artist because they still hold their own individuality in the face of American standardizations. And perhaps these common people will give to the world its truly great Negro artist, the one who is not afraid to be himself. Whereas the better-class Negro would tell the artist what to do, the people at least let him alone when he does appear. And they are not ashamed of him—if they know he exists at all. And they accept what beauty is their own without question.

Certainly there is, for the American Negro artist who can escape the restrictions the more advanced among his own group would put upon him, a great field of unused material ready for his art. Without going outside his race, and even among the better classes with their "white" culture and conscious American manners, but still Negro enough to be different, there is sufficient matter to furnish a black artist with a lifetime of creative work. And when he chooses to touch on the relations between Negroes and whites in this country with their innumerable overtones and undertones, surely, and especially for literature and the drama, there is an inexaustible supply of themes at hand. To these the Negro artist can give his racial individuality, his heritage of rhythm and warmth, and his incongruous humor that so often, as in the Blues, becomes ironic laughter mixed with tears. But let us look again at the mountain.

A prominent Negro clubwoman in Philadelphia paid eleven dollars to hear Raquel Meller sing Andalusian popular songs. But she told me a few weeks before she would not think of going to hear "that woman," Clara Smith, a great black artist, sing Negro folksongs. And many an upper-class Negro church, even now, would not dream of employing a spiritual in its services. The drab melodies in white folks' hymnbooks are much to be preferred. "We want to worship the Lord correctly and quietly. We don't believe in 'shouting.' Let's be dull like the Nordics," they say, in effect.

The road for the serious black artist, then, who would produce a racial art is most certainly rocky and the mountain is high. Until recently he received almost no encouragement for his work from either white or colored people. The fine novels of Chestnutt go out of print with neither race noticing their passing. The quaint charm and humor of Dunbar's dialect verse brought to him, in his day, largely the same kind of encouragement one would give a sideshow freak (A colored man writing poetry! How odd!) or a clown (How amusing!).

The present vogue in things Negro, although it may do as much harm as good for the budding colored artist, has at least done this: it has brought him forcibly to the attention of his own people among whom for so long, unless the other race had noticed him beforehand, he was a prophet with little honor. I understand that Charles Gilpin acted for years in Negro theaters without any special acclaim for his own, but when Broadway gave him eight curtain calls, Negroes, too, began to beat a tin pan in his honor. I know a young colored writer, a manual worker by day, who had been writing well for the colored magazines for some years, but it was not until he recently broke into the white publications and his first book was accepted by a prominent New York publisher that the "best" Negroes in his city took the trouble to discover that he lived there. Then almost immediately they decided to give a grand dinner for him. But the society ladies were careful to whisper to his mother that perhaps she'd better not come. They were not sure she would have an evening gown.

The Negro artist works against an undertow of sharp criticism and misunderstanding from his own group and unintentional bribes from the whites. "O, be respectable, write about nice people, show how good we are," say the Negroes. "Be stereotyped, don't go too far, don't shatter our illusions about you, don't amuse us too seriously. We will pay you," say the whites. Both would have told Jean Toomer not to write "Cane." The colored people did not praise it. The white people did not buy it. Most of the colored people who did read "Cane" hate it. They are afraid of it. Although the critics gave it good reviews the public remained indifferent. Yet (excepting the work of DuBois) "Cane" contains the finest prose written by a Negro in America. And like the singing of Robeson, it is truly racial.

But in spite of the Nordicized Negro intelligentsia and the desires of some white editors we have an honest American Negro literature already with us. Now I await the rise of the Negro theater. Our folk music, having achieved world-wide fame, offers itself to the genius of the great individual American Negro composer who is to come. And within the next decade I expect to see the work of a growing school of colored artists who paint and model the beauty of dark faces and create with new technique the expressions of their own soul-world. And the Negro dancers who will dance like flame and the singers who will continue to carry our songs to all who listen—they will be with us in even greater numbers tomorrow.

Most of my own poems are racial in theme and treatment, derived from the life I know. In many of them I try to grasp and hold some of the meanings and rhythms of jazz. I am sincere as I know how to be in these poems and yet after every reading I answer questions like these from my own people: Do you think Negroes should always write about Negroes? I wish you wouldn't read some of your poems to white folks. How do you find anything interesting in a place like a cabaret? Why do you write about black people? You aren't black. What makes you do so many jazz poems?

But jazz to me is one of the inherent expressions of Negro life in America: the eternal tom-tom beating in the Negro soul—the tom-tom of revolt against weariness in a white world, a world of subway trains, and work, work, work; the tom-tom of joy and laughter, and pain swallowed in a smile. Yet the Philadelphia clubwoman is ashamed to say that her race created it and she does not like me to write about it. The old subconscious "white is best" runs through her mind. Years of study under white teachers, a life-time of white books, pictures, and papers, and white manners, morals, and Puritan standards made her dislike the spirituals. And now she turns up her nose at jazz and all its manifestations—likewise almost everything else distinctly racial. She doesn't care for the Winold Reiss portraits of Negroes because they are "too Negro." She does not want a true picture of herself from anybody. She wants the artist to flatter her, to make the white world believe that all Negroes are as smug and as near white in soul as she wants to be. But, to my mind, it is the duty of the younger Negro artist, if he accepts any duties at all from outsiders, to change through the force of his art that old whispering "I want to be white," hidden in the aspirations of his people, to "Why should I want to be white? I am a Negro—and beautiful!"

So I am ashamed for the black-poet who says, "I want to be a poet, not a Negro poet," as though his own racial world were not as interesting as any other world. I am ashamed, too, for the colored artist who runs from the painting of Negro faces to the painting of sunsets after the manner of the academicians because he fears the strange un-whiteness of his own features. An artist must be free to choose what he does, certainly, but he must also never be afraid to do what he might choose.

Let the blare of Negro jazz bands and the bellowing voice of Bessie Smith singing Blues penetrate the closed ears of the colored near-intellectuals until they listen and perhaps understand. Let Paul Robeson singing Water Boy, and Rudolph Fisher writing about the streets of Harlem and Jean Toomer holding the heart of Georgia in his hands, and Aaron Douglas drawing strange black fantasies cause the smug Negro middle class to catch a glimmer of their own beauty. We younger Negro artists who create now intend to express our individual dark-skinned selves without fear or shame. If white people are pleased we are glad. If they are not, it doesn't matter. We know we are beautiful. And ugly too. The tom-tom cries and the tom-tom laughs. If colored people are pleased we are glad. If they are not, their displeasure doesn't matter either. We build our temples for tomorrow, strong as we know how, and we stand on top of the mountain, free within ourselves.

2. ALURISTA

what's happening . . . *

what's happening . . .
    mr. jones
where is it?
    do you know?
pero nunca te importó
    and now; now
you tell me you care
    do you . . .
        mr. jones?
el águila de nuestro orgullo
    is now settled on the cactus of your apathy
devouring
    the serpent of inhumanities
that crawled viciously in your amérika
"amérika"
blind to the lake of human values
floating emaciated in its ethnocentricity
jose luis peralta, genaro arciago,
macario juan infante, y richard pérez
nosotros!
we care, nos importa mucho!
. . . mr. jones
we know where it's at,
    mr. jones . . .

*Alurista, "what's happening . . . ," reprinted from *floricanto en aztlán* (Los Angeles: Aztlán Publications, Chicano Studies Center, University of California, 1971), Poem 19. Reprinted by permission of Alurista and Aztlán Publications.

we do
    and make happen,
    mr. jones
the happening
    es obra nuestra
we done it; mr. jones
    dig?
dig mr. jones?
    mr. jones!
do you or do you not dig!
    mr. jones wake up!
the apathy of your eyelids
  —it stupefies you
        and you can't see
    can you . . .
    . . . mr. jones?

3. WINSTON WEATHERS

Osage August Dances*

1

Let me undress from the white world
And step from the new closet
Into the old wideness. I hear the drums
Softly and neatly, beckoning me
Into the world of bright color
A feather for the deep lake running
  within me.
And a feather for the sky and earth and
  the soft smoke, ascending.
And a feather for the supple skin over the
  strong limbs in wigwam and body.
And jingling bells in far-away calling.
(A costume for my soul.)

*Winston Weathers, "Osage August Dances," in *Indian and White* (Lincoln, Nebraska, University of Nebraska Press, 1970), pp. 52-61. Reprinted by permission of the University of Nebraska Press.

Let my muscles ripple through my thighs
and lead me strongly
Through the patterns of my people and
my fathers.

2

I hear the drums, neatly besieging
The mind, indigenous,
And the long arm reaches
Beyond our conceptions.
I will take feathers and walk toward the
gathering
Singing and chanting in drum-beating
rhythm.
Sun will shine on me and glisten my color
And I will reflect in bronze adoration
The things of the hillside and things of
the valley
And eagles flying upon the blue sky.
I will come freely into the rainbow
Chanting the spectrum, singing the
sunlight.
Leaving the closet of faded wild-roses.
Walking in silence upon the dry grasses.

And here are the others, the warriors, the
people,

Assembled, addressing, in blankets of
blackness
And eyelids of oldness. Here are the
drummers
Keeping the edges beaten and rounded
Into the centuries, trailing behind us.

3

All through my body the warm blood is
singing

And my feet in soft leather are nervous
 and moving.
Fathers and sons are naked and native.
Loins are tightened like clustered
 persimmons
Frosted in winter with strength and
 fertility.
And warrior faces are painted in scarlet
Bled from the berries on low bushes
 growing.
(Cover our bodies in soft woven clothing
And dance with the bells tinkling
 beside us
And feathers are growing up over our
 faces
And fur-tails are dangling on wrists and
 on ankles.)

The drummers are starting the routinous
 beat.
Lift up our memory, raise up our feet
And into the dust and over the clay
And through the thickness of August's
 hot day
Repeat the soft stomping that echoes
 with age.

4

Let us rotate, circular
About the drums, sacred.
Fathers and sons, bending
Earthward and skyward.

Quickly our glances
Upward and downward,
Swiftly our movements
Sharply and smoothly

We are the panther,

The eagle, flying,
We are the buffalo,
The turkey and deer.

Warriors in strenuous
Gesticulation,
Vivid communion
With vigorous nature.

Louder the drumbeat,
Higher the calling,
Ripple the shrill tongue
Warbled and wavered.

And the dark old ones,
In old animation,
Long hair in dark braids
And old faces darkened.

Let them do tail dances
Slowly toward center.
Then the quick stopping,
And then the quick silence.

5

Inward the warriors,
Outward the women,
Men in gay feathers,
Women in blankets.

Warriors in fervor,
Women in calmness,
All in one rhythm,
All in one dancing.

Nearest the drumbeat
The loud-shouting warriors.
Outward toward nature
The all-silent maidens.

Old squaw and papoose,
The tan-faded feather.
In small step and low step
Marking the dust.

And maidens in doeskin,
Sun-white and moon-white.
Dancing near warriors,
Brave and virgin.

6

Where in the dances are old faces hidden?
John Stink and Bacon Rind and Osage
  chieftains?
Where is Pa-se-to-pah and old Susie
  Blackhawk?
Where is Pawhuska of many years back?
Are they the strange whispers blowing
  among us?
Are they the drum-echoes silent upon us?

Where have our fathers gone dancing
  this summer,
In fields of great hunting and lodges of
  sweetness?

Do they remember their families and
  children
Far in the distance beside the great river,
Then the great prairie, then the low hills?

Our fathers, our chieftains are wakened
  from sleeping,
Moved from their hunting, stirred from
  their peace.
The drummers are beating songs for the
  ancients,
Songs for the living. We are the dancers,

The living, the ancient, the fathers and
sons.

7

August has fallen,
Dances are given,
Tribes are assembled
Of Osage and Ponca.

Feasts are partaken
Of squaw-bread and jerked meat.
Children are playing
With spotted, lean dogs.

Dry leaves are scattered
Under the oak trees,
Winds from the south sun
Rustle and crush them.

How are the warriors
And how are the wars?
Dance for the dead ones
Silent and gone.

Walk in the sunlight,
Dance in its brightness.
Move in the nighttime,
Move in its shadow.

Dance in the moon, three-quarter risen,
Ing-thus-ka dances,
Leading young warriors
Into the patterns.

8

And after the dances, lengthy and stirring,

After the beaters of drums, and
  drum-keepers
Have spoken in silence and not in their
  rhythms,
We shall take feathers down from our hair.

Undo our trappings,
Scented with dancing,
We must go back
Into the closet.

Forsake what is native,
The past is our dream.
A pale shadow haunts us
And falls in our eyes.

Turn to the city
Of colorless towers.
The world is too small
And time must go on.

C. THE ROLE OF RELIGION

Every society would like to capture religion, domesticate it, and put it to work for its own objectives. Where it supports the practices of the dominant majority, religion enjoys the patronage of a grateful society. But where it makes objective judgments and calls people to their neglected moral responsibilities, it creates tension and unrest. American Christianity has played both roles. It has been the weapon of those who have exploited minorities as well as a source of energy for those who have resisted oppression. The selections that follow describe the role of religion and people of religion in the ethnic struggle for justice, self-realization, and freedom in the United States.

In the first selection Martin Luther King, Jr., explains the relevance to Blacks of Christ's command to "love your enemies." Not only is such a commitment necessary for human survival in a nuclear age, he declares, but as the most durable power on earth, love alone can turn enemies into friends. Through the redemptive power of love and the moral authority of religion, he says, Blacks can achieve their dream of freedom and equality in America.

A different view of the role of religion is found in "Black Power and the American Christ." Vincent Harding rejects white Christianity and the white image of the sedate, genteel Christ as having little relevance for Blacks. The real Christ, he says, is not that of white America. The true Christ would repudiate racist oppression, the rape of Africa, and the bombing of innocent Asians; and churches faithful to the real Christ would work actively to prevent and denounce such acts. Blacks, he concludes, must reject the white man's Christ and seek religious reality "more faithful to [their] own experience."

Next we observe an important change occurring within the Roman Catholic church, the attempt of Chicano priests to serve the temporal as well as spiritual needs of Mexican Americans through the creation of PADRES, Padres, Asociados para Derechos Religiosos, Educativos y Sociales (Priests United for Religious, Educational, and Social Rights). In his address at Notre Dame University in April, 1973, Rev. Juan Romero, executive director of PADRES, describes the history and purpose of this organization. Founded in 1969, PADRES is an association of activist Chicano priests "engaged in the front lines of struggle" for a greater Chicano role in church government and committed fully to the cause of La Raza.

Vine Deloria, Jr., discusses the importance of religion in the Indian protest movement. The salvation of the Indian, he explains, lies in the return to traditional forms of tribal government and to traditional religious precepts—veneration of the land and the worship of nature. Christianity is silent, he says, on precisely what matters most in Indian religion, and Christian churches have failed therefore to grasp the essential character of Indian protests. Unable to find a Christian consciousness that comprehends or is willing to act meaningfully on their problems, Native Americans must discover a "universal sense of justice" that rises above the shortcomings of the white man's religion and the hypocrisy of his politics.

1. MARTIN LUTHER KING, JR.

Loving Your Enemies*

Ye have heard that it hath been said, Thou shalt love thy neighbour, and hate thine enemy. But I say unto you, Love your enemies, bless them that curse you, do good to them that hate you, and pray for them which

*Martin Luther King, Jr., "Loving Your Enemies," in *Strength To Love* (New York, Harper & Row, 1963), pp. 34-41. Copyright © 1963 by Martin Luther King, Jr., reprinted by permission of Harper & Row Publishers, Inc.

despitefully use you, and persecute you; that ye may be children of your Father which is in heaven.

Matthew 5:43-35

Probably no admonition of Jesus has been more difficult to follow than the command to "love your enemies." Some men have sincerely felt that its actual practice is not possible. It is easy, they say, to love those who love you, but how can one love those who openly and insidiously seek to defeat you? Others, like the philosopher Nietzsche, contend that Jesus' exhortation to love one's enemies is testimony to the fact that the Christian ethic is designed for the weak and cowardly, and not for the strong and courageous. Jesus, they say, was an impractical idealist.

In spite of these insistent questions and persistent objections, this command of Jesus challenges us with new urgency. Upheaval after upheaval has reminded us that modern man is traveling along a road called hate, in a journey that will bring us to destruction and damnation. Far from being the pious injunction of a Utopian dreamer, the command to love one's enemy is an absolute necessity for our survival. Love even for enemies is the key to the solution of the problems of our world. Jesus is not an impractical idealist; he is the practical realist.

I am certain that Jesus understood the difficulty inherent in the act of loving one's enemies. He never joined the ranks of those who talk glibly about the easiness of the moral life. He realized that every genuine expression of love grows out of a consistent and total surrender to God. So when Jesus said "Love your enemy," he was not unmindful of its stringent qualities. Yet he meant every word of it. Our responsibility as Christians is to discover the meaning of this command and seek passionately to live it out in our daily lives.

I

Let us be practical and ask the question, *How do we love our enemies?*

First, we must develop and maintain the capacity to forgive. He who is devoid of the power to forgive is devoid of the power to love. It is impossible even to begin the act of loving one's enemies without the prior acceptance of the necessity, over and over again, of forgiving those who inflict evil and injury upon us. It is also necessary to realize that the forgiving act must always be initiated by the person who has been wronged, the victim of some great hurt, the recipient of some tortuous injustice, the absorber of some terrible act of oppression. The wrongdoer may request forgiveness. He may come to himself, and, like the prodigal son, move up some dusty road, his heart palpitating with the desire for forgiveness. But only the injured neighbor, the loving father back home, can really pour out the warm waters of forgiveness.

Forgiveness does not mean ignoring what has been done or putting a false label on an evil act. It means, rather, that the evil act no longer remains as a barrier to the relationship. Forgiveness is a catalyst creating the atmosphere necessary for a fresh start and a new beginning. It is the lifting of a burden or the canceling of a debt. The words "I will forgive you, but I'll never forget what you've done" never explain the real nature of forgiveness. Certainly one can never forget, if that means erasing it totally from his mind. But when we forgive, we forget in the sense that the evil deed is no longer a mental block impeding a new relationship. Likewise, we can never say, "I will forgive you, but I won't have anything further to do with you." Forgiveness means reconciliation, a coming together again. Without this, no man can love his enemies. The degree to which we are able to forgive determines the degree to which we are able to love our enemies.

Second, we must recognize that the evil deed of the enemy-neighbor, the thing that hurts, never quite expresses all that he is. An element of goodness may be found even in our worst enemy. Each of us is something of a schizophrenic personality, tragically divided against ourselves. A persistent civil war rages within all of our lives. Something within us causes us to lament with Ovid, the Latin poet, "I see and approve the better things, but follow worse," or to agree with Plato that human personality is like a charioteer having two headstrong horses, each wanting to go in a different direction, or to repeat with the Apostle Paul, "The good that I would I do not: but the evil which I would not, that I do."

This simply means that there is some good in the worst of us and some evil in the best of us. When we discover this, we are less prone to hate our enemies. When we look beneath the surface, beneath the impulsive evil deed, we see within our enemy-neighbor a measure of goodness and know that the viciousness and evilness of his acts are not quite representative of all that he is. We see him in a new light. We recognize that his hate grows out of fear, pride, ignorance, prejudice, and misunderstanding, but in spite of this, we know God's image is ineffably etched in his being. Then we love our enemies by realizing that they are not totally bad and that they are not beyond the reach of God's redemptive love.

Third, we must not seek to defeat or humiliate the enemy but to win his friendship and understanding. At times we are able to humiliate our worst enemy. Inevitably, his weak moments come and we are able to thrust in his side the spear of defeat. But this we must not do. Every word and deed must contribute to an understanding with the enemy and release those vast reservoirs of goodwill which have been blocked by impenetrable walls of hate.

The meaning of love is not to be confused with some sentimental outpouring. Love is something much deeper than emotional bosh. Perhaps the Greek language can clear our confusion at this point. In the Greek New Testament are three words for love. The word *eros* is a sort of aesthetic or romantic love. In the Platonic dialogues *eros* is a yearning of the soul for the realm of the divine. The second word is *philia,* a reciprocal love and the intimate affection and friendship between friends. We love those whom we like, and we love because we are loved. The third word is *agape,* understanding and creative, redemptive goodwill for all men. An overflowing love which seeks nothing in return, *agape* is the love of God operating in the human heart. At this level, we love men not because we like them, nor because their ways appeal to us, nor even because they possess some type of divine spark; we love every man because God loves him. At this level, we love the person who does an evil deed, although we hate the deed that he does.

Now we can see what Jesus meant when he said, "Love your enemies." We should be happy that he did not say, "Like your enemies." It is almost impossible to like some people. "Like" is a sentimental and affectionate word. How can we be affectionate toward a person whose avowed aim is to crush our very being and place innumerable stumbling blocks in our path? How can ae like a person who is threatening our children and bombing our homes? This is impossible. But Jesus recognized that *love* is greater than *like.* When Jesus bids us to love our enemies, he is speaking neither of *eros* nor *philia*; he is speaking of *agape,* understanding and creative, redemptive goodwill for all men. Only by following this way and responding with this type of love are we able to be children of our Father who is in heaven.

II

Let us move now from the practical *how* to the theoretical *why: Why should we love our enemies?* The first reason is fairly obvious. Returning hate for hate multiplies hate, adding deeper darkness to a night already devoid of stars. Darkness cannot drive out darkness; only light can do that. Hate cannot drive out hate; only love can do that. Hate multiplies hate, violence multiplies violence, and toughness multiplies toughness in a descending spiral of destruction. So when Jesus says "Love your enemies," he is setting forth a profound and ultimately inescapable admonition. Have we not come to such an impasse in the modern world that we must love our enemies—or else? The chain reaction of evil—hate begetting hate, wars producing more wars—must be broken, or we shall be plunged into the dark abyss of annihilation.

Another reason why we must love our enemies is that hate scars the soul and distorts the personality. Mindful that hate is an evil and dangerous force, we too often think of what it does to the person hated. This is understandable, for hate brings irreparable damage to its victims. We have seen its ugly consequences in the ignominious deaths brought to six million Jews by a hate-obsessed madman named Hitler, in the unspeakable violence inflicted upon Negroes by bloodthirsty mobs, in the dark horrors of war, and in the terrible indignities and injustices perpetrated against millions of God's children by unconscionable oppressors.

But there is another side which we must never overlook. Hate is just as injurious to the person who hates. Like an unchecked cancer, hate corrodes the personality and eats away its vital unity. Hate destroys a man's sense of values and his objectivity. It causes him to describe the beautiful as ugly and the ugly as beautiful, and to confuse the true with the false and the false with the true.

Dr. E. Franklin Frazier, in an interesting essay entitled "The Pathology of Race Prejudice," included several examples of white persons who were normal, amiable, and congenial in their day-to-day relationships with other white persons, but when they were challenged to think of Negroes as equals or even to discuss the question of racial injustice, they reacted with unbelievable irrationality and an abnormal unbalance. This happens when hate lingers in our minds. Psychiatrists report that many of our inner conflicts, are rooted in hate. They say, "Love or perish." Modern psychology recognizes what Jesus taught centuries ago: hate divides the personality and love in an amazing and inexorable way unites it.

A third reason why we should love our enemies is that love is the only force capable of transforming an enemy into a friend. We never get rid of an enemy by meeting hate with hate; we get rid of an enemy by getting rid of enmity. By its very nature, hate destroys and tears down; by its very nature, love creates and builds up. Love transforms with redemptive power. . . .

We must hasten to say that these are not the ultimate reasons why we should love our enemies. An even more basic reason why we are commanded to love is expressed explicitly in Jesus' words, "Love your enemies . . . *that ye may be children of your Father which is in heaven.*" We are called to this difficult task in order to realize a unique relationship with God. We are potential sons of God. Through love that potentiality becomes actuality. We must love our enemies, because only by loving them can we know God and experience the beauty of his holiness.

The relevance of what I have said to the crisis in race relations should be readily apparent. There will be no permanent solution to the race problem until oppressed men develop the capacity to love their enemies. The darkness of racial injustice will be dispelled only by the light of forgiving love. For more than three centuries American Negroes have been battered by the iron rod of oppression, frustrated by day and bewildered by night by unbearable injustice, and burdened with the ugly weight of discrimination. Forced to live with these shameful conditions, we are tempted to become bitter and to retaliate with a corresponding hate. But if this happens, the new order we seek will be little more than a duplicate of the old order. We must in strength and humility meet hate with love.

Of course, this is not *practical.* Life is a matter of getting even, of hitting back, of dog eat dog. Am I saying that Jesus commands us to love those who hurt and oppress us? Do I sound like most preachers—idealistic and impractical? Maybe in some distant Utopia, you say, that idea will work, but not in the hard, cold world in which we live.

My friends, we have followed the so-called practical way for too long a time now, and it has led inexorably to deeper confusion and chaos. Time is cluttered with the wreckage of communities which surrendered to hatred and violence. For the salvation of our nation and the salvation of mankind, we must follow another way. This does not mean that we abandon our righteous efforts. With every ounce of our energy we must continue to rid this nation of the incubus of segregation. But we shall not in the process relinquish our privilege and our obligation to love. While abhorring segregation, we shall love the segregationist. This is the only way to create the beloved community.

To our most bitter opponents we say: "We shall match your capacity to inflict suffering by our capacity to endure suffering. We shall meet your physical force with soul force. Do to us what you will, and we shall continue to love you. We cannot in all good conscience obey your unjust laws, because nonco-operation with evil is as much a moral obligation as is co-operation with good. Throw us in jail, and we shall still love you. Send your hooded perpetrators of violence into our community at the midnight hour and beat us and leave us half dead, and we shall still love you. But be ye assured that we will wear you down by our capacity to suffer. One day we shall win freedom, but not only for ourselves. We shall so appeal to your heart and conscience that we shall win *you* in the process, and our victory will be a double victory."

Love is the most durable power in the world. This creative force, so beautifully exemplified in the life of our Christ, is the most potent instrument available in mankind's quest for peace and security. Napoleon Bonaparte, the great military genius, looking back over his years of conquest is reported to have said: "Alexander, Ceasar, Charlemagne and I have built great empires. But upon what did they depend? They depended on force. But centuries ago Jesus started an empire that was built on love, and even to this day millions will die for him." Who can doubt the veracity of these words. The great military leaders of the past have gone, and their empires have crumbled and burned to ashes. But the empire of Jesus, built solidly and majestically on the foundation of love, is still growing. It started with a small group of dedicated men, who, through the inspiration of their Lord, were able to shake the hinges from the gates of the Roman Empire, and carry the gospel into all the world. Today the vast earthly kingdom of Christ numbers more than 900,000,000 and covers every land and tribe. Today we hear again the promise of victory:

> Jesus shall reign where'er the sun
> Does his successive journeys run;
> His kingdom stretch from shore to shore,
> Till moon shall wax and wane no more.

Another choir joyously responds:

> In Christ there is no East or West,
>   In Him no South or North,
> But one great Fellowship of Love
>   Throughout the whole wide earth.

Jesus is eternally right. History is replete with the bleached bones of nations that refused to listen to him. May we in the twentieth century hear and follow his words—before it is too late. May we solemnly realize that we shall never be true sons of our heavenly Father until we love our enemies and pray for those who persecute us.

2. VINCENT HARDING

Black Power and the American Christ*

The mood among many social-action-oriented Christians today suggests that it is only a line thin as a razor blade that divides sentimental yearning over the civil rights activities of the past from present bitter recrimination against ''Black Power.'' As is so often the case with reminiscences, the nostalgia may grow more out of a sense of frustration and powerlessness than out of any true appreciation of the meaning of the past. This at least is the impression one gets from those seemingly endless gatherings of old ''true believers'' which usually produce both the nostalgia and the reciminations. Generally the cast of characters at such meetings consists of well dressed, well fed Negroes and whites whose accents almost blend into a single voice as they recall the days ''when we were all together, fighting for the same cause.'' The stories evoke again the heady atmosphere, mixed of smugness and self-sacrifice, that surrounded us in those heroic times when nonviolence was our watchword and integration our heavenly city. One can almost hear the strains of ''our song'' as men and women remember how they solemnly swayed in the aisles and around the charred remains of a church or in the dirty southern jails. Those were the days when Martin Luther King was the true prophet and when we were certain that the civil rights movement was God's message to the churches—and part of our smugness grew out of the fact that *we* knew it while all the rest of God's frozen people were asleep.

A VEIL BETWEEN THEN AND NOW

But as the reminiscences continue a veil seems to descend between then and now. The tellers of the old tales label the veil Black Power, and pronounce ritual curses on Stokely Carmichael and Floyd McKissick and their followers.

The trouble with these meetings is that they are indeed becoming riCual, cultic acts of memory that blind us to creative possibilities. Because that ''veil'' may be a wall, not primarily for separating but for writing on—both sides of it. Or it may be a great sheet ''let down from heaven''; or a curtain before the next act can begin. Most of us appear totally incapable of realizing

*Vincent Harding, ''Black Power and the American Christ,'' *The Christian Century*, January 4, 1967, pp. 10-13. Copyright © 1967 Christian Century Foundation. Reprinted by permission of *The Christian Century.*

that there may be more light in blackness than we have yet begun to glimpse.

Such possibilities should be pondered especially by those of us who combine the terrible privileges of blackness and Christian commitment within a single life. We are driven to see now only what was happening in our warm, genteel days of common black-white struggle, but to grasp clearly what is happening now. We have no choice but to hold Black Power in our black arms and examine it, convinced that Christ is Lord of this too. Anyone who is black and claims to be a part of the company of Christ's people would be derelict if he failed to make such an examination and to proclaim with fear and trembling and intimations of great joy what he has discovered.

Perhaps the first and central discovery is also the most obvious: there is a strong and causative link between Black Power and American Christianity. Indeed one may say with confidence that whatever its other sources, the ideology of blackness surely grows out of the deep ambivalence of American Negroes to the Christ we have encountered here. This ambivalence is not new. It was ours from the beginning. For we first met the American Christ on slave ships. We heard his name sung in hymns of praise while we died in our thousands, chained in stinking holds beneath the decks, locked in with terror and disease and sad memories of our families and homes. When we leaped from the decks to be seized by sharks we saw his name carved on the ship's solid sides. When our women were raped in the cabins they must have noticed the great and holy books on the shelves. Our introduction to this Christ was not propitious. And the horrors continued on America's soil. So all through the nation's history many black men have rejected this Christ—indeed the miracle is that so many accepted him. In past times our disdain often had to be stifled and sullen, our anger silent and self-destructive. But now we speak out. Our anger is no longer silent; it has leaped onto the public stage, and demands to be seen and dealt with—a far more healthy state of affairs for all concerned.

If the American Christ and his followers have indeed helped to mold the Black Power movement, then might it not be that the God whom many of us insist on keeping alive is not only alive but just? May he not be attempting to break through to us with at least as much urgency as we once sensed at the height of the good old "We Shall Overcome" days? Perhaps he is writing on the wall, saying that we Christians, black and white, must choose between death with the American Christ and life with the Suffering Servant of God. Who dares deny that God may have chosen once again the black sufferers for a new assault on the hard shell of indifference and fear that encases so many Americans?

If these things are difficult to believe perhaps we need to look more closely both at the American Christ and the black movement he has helped to create. From the outset, almost everywhere we blacks have met him in this land, this Christ was painted white and pink, blond and blue-eyed—and not only in white churches but in black churches as well. Millions of black children had the picture of this pseudo-Nazarene burned into their memory. The books, the windows, the paintings, the filmstrips all affirmed the same message—a message of shame. This Christ shamed us by his pigmentation, so obviously not our own. He condemned us for our blackness, for our flat noses, for our kinky hair, for our power, our strange power of expressing emotion in singing and shouting and dancing. He was sedate, so genteel, so white. And as soon as we were able many of us tried to like him.

GLAD TO BE BLACK

For a growing edge of bold young black people all that is past. They fling out their declaration: "No white Christ shall shame us again. We are glad to be black. We rejoice in the darkness of our skin, we celebrate the natural texture of our hair, we extol the rhythm and vigor of our songs and shouts and dances. And if your American Christ doesn't like that, you know what you can do with him." That is Black Power: a repudiation of the American culture-religion that helped to create it and a quest for a religious reality more faithful to our own experience.

These young people say to America: "We know your Christ and his attitude toward Africa. We remember how his white missionaries warned against Africa's darkness and heathenism, against its savagery and naked jungle heart. We are tired of all that. This Africa that you love and hate, but mostly fear—this is our homeland. We saw you exchange your Bibles for our land. We watched you pass out tracts and take in gold. We heard you teach hymns to get our diamonds, and you control them still. If this is what your Christ taught you, he is sharp, baby, he is shrewd; but he's no savior of ours. We affirm our homeland and its great black past, a past that was filled with wonder before your white scourge came. You can keep your Christ. We'll take our home." That is Black Power: a search for roots in a land that has denied us both a past and a future. And the American Christ who has blessed the denial earns nothing but scorn.

The advocates of Black Power know this Christ well. They see his people running breathlessly, cursing silently, exiting double-time from the cities with all their suffering people. They see this white throng fleeing before the strangled movement of the blacks out of the ghettos, leaving their stained-glass mausoleums behind them. This very exodus of the Christians from the places where the weak and powerless live has been one of the primary motivating forces of Black Power.

The seekers of Black Power, seeing their poorest, most miserable people deserted by the white American Christians, have come to stand with the forlorn in these very places of abandonment. Now they speak of Black Unity, and the old Christian buildings are filled with Negroes young and old studying African history. The new leaders in the ghettos tell them: "Whites now talk about joining forces, but who has ever wanted to join forces with you? They only want to use you—especially those white American Christian liars. They love you in theory only. They love only your middle class incarnations. But they are afraid of you—you who are black and poor and filled with rage and despair. They talk about 'progress' for the Negro, but they don't mean *you.*"

These young people whose names we old "true believers" intone in our nightly litanies of frustrated wrath have listened with the perception born of alienation to white Christians speaking to Negroes of "our people and your people, our churches and your churches, our community and your community, our schools and your schools." And they hear this hypocrisy crowned with the next words from bleeding Christian hearts: "Of course some of your most spiritual (and quiet) people may come to our churches, and your wealthiest (and cleanest) people may move into our communities, and your brightest children may come to our schools. But never forget: we expect regular hymns of gratitude for our condescension. Always remember that they are still ours and not yours—people and communities and schools and churches." And as an afterthought: "But of course we all love the same Christ."

SENSITIZED BY APPREHENSION

To this the angry children of Malcolm X shout fiercely: "To hell with you and your Christ! If you cannot live where we live, if your children cannot grow where we grow, if you cannot suffer what we suffer, if you cannot learn what we learn, we have no use for you or your cringing Christ. If we must come to where you are to find quality and life, then this nation is no good and integration is irrelevant."

Then Black Power leaders turn to the people of the ghettos. "Let us use the separateness that the white Christians have imposed upon us," they say to the black brothers. "Let us together find our own dignity and our own power, so that one day we may stand and face even those who have rejected us, no longer begging to be accepted into their dying world, but showing them a world transformed, a world where we have shaped our own destiny. We shall build communities of our own, where men are truly brothers and goods are really shared. The American Christ is a Christ of separation and selfishness and relentless competition for an empty hole. We want no part of him."

Let there be no mistake. These evangels of a new movement are not deaf. They hear all the American words. They listen when good Christians ask: "Why should we pay our taxes to support those lazy deadbeats, those winos, those A.D.C. whores? Our money doesn't belong to them. Our money . . . our money . . ." Sensitized by long years of apprehension, the blacks need only look into the mirror to know who those "deadbeats" and "winos" are and what the "A.D.C. whores" look like. At the same time they wonder why the same white Christians sing no sad songs about tax rebates for General Motors' investments in South Africa's apartheid, and why they raise no complaints about the tax money given to farmers for planting nothing.

Groveling No More

They open that American family magazine the *Saturday Evening Post* and find an enlightened northern editor saying to rebellious blacks that all whites are Mississippians at heart. He adds: "We will do our best, in a half-hearted way, to correct old wrongs. [Our] hand may be extended grudgingly and patronizingly, but anyone who rejects that hand rejects his own best interests." To those who live in the realm of Black Consciousness this snarling voice is the voice of the people of the American Christ. Out of their anguished indignation the black rebels reply: "We reject your limp, bloodied hand and your half-hearted help. We shall use our own black hands and lives to build power. We shall love our own people. We shall lead them to a new justice, based on the kind of power that America respects—not nonviolence and forgiveness, but votes and mony and violent retaliation. We shall beg no more. You shall define our best interests no longer. Take your Mississippi hand and your Cicero Christ and may both of them be damned." That is Black Power.

As black men they have long seen into the heart of American darkness. They have no patriotic illusions about this nation's benevolent intentions toward the oppressed nonwhite people of the world, no matter how often the name and compassion of divinity are invoked. With eyes cleared by pain they discern the arrogance beneath the pious protestations. The American Christ leads the Hiroshima-bound bomber, blesses the marines on their way to another in the long series of Latin American invasions, and blasphemously calls it peace when America destroys an entire Asian peninsula. And as black men they know from their own hard experience that these things can happen because this nation, led by an elder of the church, is determined to have its way in the world at any cost—to others. How often have the white-robed elders led the mob thirsting for the black man's blood!

Black people are not fooled by the churchly vestments of humility. They hear arrogant white pastors loudly counting dollars and members, and committees smugly announcing the cost of their new modern churches—hollow tombs for Christ. They hear the voices: "Negroes, oh Negroes, you must be humble, like Christ. You must be patient and long-suffering. Negroes, don't push so hard. Look at all we've given you so far." And the voices trail off: "Negroes, dear Negroes, remember our Lord taught how good it is to be meek and lowly." And then a whisper: "Cause if you don't, niggers, if you don't, we'll crush you."

So the Black Power advocates sanely shout, "Go to hell, you whited sepulchers, hypocrites. All you want is to cripple our will and prolong our agony, and you use your white Christ to do it." To the black people they say: "Don't grovel, don't scrape. Whether you are 1 per cent or 50 per cent or 100 per cent black, you are men, and you must affirm this in the face of all the pious threats. You must proclaim your manhood just as the white Christians do—in arrogance, in strength and in power. But the arrogance must be black, and the strength must be black, and black must be the color of our power."

CHRISTIAN BLASPHEMERS

Then comes the sharpest of all moments of truth, when Christian voices are raised in hostility and fear, directing their missionary chorus to the young men drained of hope by the ghetto. "Black boys," they say, "rampaging, screaming, laughing black boys, you must love—like Christ and Doctor King. Black boys, please drop your firebombs. Violence never solved anything. You must love your enemeies—if they're white and American and represent law and order. You must love them for your rotting houses and for your warped education. You must love them for your nonexistent jobs. Above all, you must love them for their riot guns, their billy clubs, their hatred and their white, white skin."

It would be terrifying enough if the voices stopped on that emasculating note. But they go on: "Just the same, black boys, if the enemies have been properly certified as such by our Christian leaders, and if they're poor and brown and 10,000 miles away, you must hate them. You must scream and rampage and kill them, black boys. Pick up the firebombs and char them good. We have no civilian jobs for you, of course, but we have guns and medals, and you must kill those gooks—even if some of them do resemble the image reflected in the night-black pool of your tears."

What can a nation expect in response to such vicious words? It gets the truth—far more than it deserves. For the black men reply: "Hypocrites, white hypocrites, you only want to save your skin and your piled-up treasure from the just envy-anger of your former slaves, your present serfs and your future victims. In the name of this Christ you deny our past, demand our present and promise us no future save that of black mercenaries in your assaults upon the world's dark and desperate poor."

Their rage cries out: "Give us no pink, two-faced Jesus who counsels love for you and flaming death for the children of Vietnam. Give us no blood-sucking savior who condemns brick-throwing rioters and praises dive-bombing killers. That Christ stinks. We want no black men to follow in *his* steps. Stop forcing our poor black boys into your legions of shame. We will not go."

"If we must fight," they say, "let it be on the streets where we have been humiliated. If we must burn down houses, let them be the homes and stores of our exploiters. If we must kill, let it be the fat, pious white Christians who guard their lawns and their daughters while engineering slow death for us. If we must die, let it be for a real cause, the cause of black men's freedom as black men define it. And may all the white elders die well in the causes they defend." This is Black Power—the response to the American Christ.

Unbelievable words? If any Christian dare call them blasphemous, let him remember that the speakers make no claims about Christ or God. Only we Christians—black and white—do that. If the just creator-father God is indeed alive, and if Jesus of Nazareth was his Christ, then we Christians are blasphemers. We are the ones who take his name in vain. We are the ones who follow the phony American Christ and in our every act declare our betrayal of the resurrected Lord.

If judgment stands sure it is not for Stokely Carmichael alone but for all of us. It is we Christians who made the universal Christ into an American mascot, a puppet blessing every mad American act, from the extermination of the original possessors of this land to the massacre of the Vietnamese on their own soil—even, perhaps, to the bombing of the Chinese mainland in the name of peace.

If judgment stands sure it is not primarily upon SNCC that it will fall, but upon those who have kidnaped the compassionate Jesus—the Jesus who shared all he had, even his life, with the poor—and made him into a profit-oriented, individualistic, pietistic cat who belongs to his now narrowly defined kind and begrudges the poor their humiliating subsistence budgets. These Christians are the ones who have taken away our Lord and buried him in a place unknown.

We shall not escape by way of nostalgia or recrimination. For if he whom we call the Christ is indeed the Suffering Servant of God and man, what excuse can there be for those who have turned him into a crossless puppet, running away from suffering with his flaxen locks flapping in the wind?

If God is yet alive we cannot afford time to reminisce about the good old days of the civil rights movement when everybody knew the words of the songs. The time of singing may be past. It may be that America must now stand under profound and damning judgment for having turned the redeeming lover of all men into a white, middle class burner of children and destroyer of the revolutions of the oppressed.

CHANCE FOR REDEMPTION

This may be God's message for the church—through Black Power. It is a message for all who claim to love the Lord of the church. If this reading is accurate, our tears over the demise of the civil rights movement may really be tears over the smashing of an image we created or the withdrawal of a sign we were no longer heeding. Therefore if we weep, let it not be for the sins of SNCC and CORE but for our own unfaithfulness and for our country's blasphemy. And let us begin to pray that time may be granted us to turn from blond dolls to the living, revolutionary Lord who proclaimed that the first shall be last and the last, first.

If this message can break the grip of self-pity and nostalgia on us, the power of blackness may yet become the power of light and resurrection for us all. Has it not been said that God moves in mysterious ways his wonders to perform? I can conceive of nothing more wonderful and mysterious than that the blackness of my captive people should become a gift of light for this undeserving nation—even a source of hope for a world that lives daily under the threat of white America's arrogant and bloody power. Is that too much to hope for? Or is the time for hoping now past? We may soon discover whether we have been watching a wall or a curtain—or both.

3. FR. JUAN ROMERO

Chicano Liberation and the Church*

BRIEF HISTORY *(overview of P.A.D.R.E.S.)*

Many of our Chicano priests all over the country were feeling the same pressures, and asking the same questions. Some had arrived at conclusions: the church is *not* responding effectively to the needs of our people, pastorally, nor is she truly a servant of the poor.

They were concerned that the church they love, and are a part of, was assimilating some of the racist attitudes of the dominant society (Anglo) in regards to the Mexican Americans. This deep concern brought men from all over the Southwest in February of 1970 to Tucson. At this meeting P.A.D.R.E.S. emerged as *a national Chicano priest's group.* Its members were hard hitting activists, engaged in the front lines of struggle and their concerns were for a more effective service of La Raza through a greater share in leadership roles at every level within the church. They called for Chicano bishops, and talked about a mobile team ministry which would more effectively serve the pastoral needs of the Spanish-speaking.

We are small in number. There are only a few over two hundred Mexican American priests in a Catholic population which is one-fourth Hispanic. Blacks have as many or perhaps more . . . priests than we do, in spite of the fact they constitute only 2% of the Catholic population. Hands down, the Protestant church (whose Latino population is only about 8% of the total Spanish-surnamed people in this country) has many more clergymen—between 5 to 800!!!

In spite of our small number, praise God! there have been some significant things happening in the church of the W.S.A. because of P.A.D.R.E.S.

1) An aroused consciousness of the presence and special pastoral needs of the Latino.

*From the address "Chicano Liberation and the Church," given by Father Juan Romero, Executive Director of P.A.D.R.E.S., at the MECHA Conference, April 12, 1973, Notre Dame University. Reprinted by permission of Father Juan Romero.

2) One Chicano bishop—ordained four months after P.A.D.R.E.S. first national meeting.

3) Special training to some priests, sisters, and laity in theology of liberation and pedagogy of conscientizacion. . . .

4) Effort made to spread . . . the process through the *leadership development workshops. . . .*

5) The founding of the M.A.C.C. . . .

6) Support of fraternal help to las Hermanas

7) To advocate within institutions for structural changes. . . .

8) Working to implement *encuentro conclusions*!

Our Common Task

Implication: You are Chicano (at least at heart). You are Christian: *baptized.*

Both of us, all of us are called to work for and towards an authentic liberation y *hacia una liberación total y autentica.* This will be a true Chicano power, not to oppress as new dominators others, but to *serve* and *upbuild* a *new people,*

LA RAZA COSMICA

This is a process, at times very painful, and always long. It will not be completed now, nor maybe not even very soon. It will not be done through the clichés of empty rhetoric, *but by a true emptying of self for the people* and *their upbuilding*!!!

This is accomplished by the dynamic of *reflection and action*, ongoing, and mutually enriching. Reflection-action. One without the other becomes distorted.

I wish to suggest to you the need for a *prayerful* reflection—an authentic prayer which rises out of concrete *engagement en los hechos*—signs of the times.

Implication:

In spite of your ethnic background, and your hope and willingness to "identify" con el pueblo del barrio, you are part of a sophisticated elite.

In grades 1 to 8, while there are no anglo drop-outs, and only 1.2% of the blacks drop out in that level, *almost 14%* of the Mexican American kids beginning elementary school *"drop out"* by the time they reach the 8th grade. Push outs! Push outs!

In high school years, 15% of the anglos drop out, 36% of the blacks and

ABOUT HALF 47% of the Mexican Americans who begin high school graduate (53%), 27% of the blacks graduate from high school, and only *16% of* Mexican Americans! You're being Chicano in college (or university) makes you rare, and in a private (Catholic) university—even *rarer.*

> In a sense, then, you can never be truly poor all the way. You have been enriched by your education which can never be taken from you. You are among that 16% of the Mexican American population that is emerging while 85% are the victims of many forms of institutionalized violence in this country. They are the *"THIRD WORLD WITHIN THE FIRST WORLD."*

One of my fears is that some of you may join "the main stream of American life," fully assimilating its culture and values, and thus become so alienated from your roots of the problems of La Raza. I am not advocating that you live a life style of St. Francis or Dorothy Day, but a spirit of poverty is crucial for you, I feel. This means a spiritual emptying of self and spiritual identification with our oppressed brothers. Only in this spirit can you be helpful in any kind of authentic liberation.

"Men liberate each other in unity and communion." (Paulo Freire). Many of you, I'm sure, know middle class Chicanos created by O.E.O. programs, and who have become fund grabbers and ego trippers, totally accepting and living by the materialistic, individualistic, anti-values of the dominant society.

You are called to be an agent of a full and authentic *liberación de la Raza.* You can and must do it, not in isolation but *en equipo,* in community.

Padres, las Hermanas, Bishop Flores are nothing, and just spinning wheels without support de la Base, people power that is organized to upbuild and serve. We are called to serve, and desire to help our people "get it together!"

You have power *now* which you can use to upbuild and serve, and will have other and different opportunities to do it later. Some of the things you can be involved in towards an authentic liberation of La Raza are the following:

> NOW - 1. Be and keep in contact with other groups like yours, especially those on Catholic campuses. You have a special contribution to make for the organizing of La Raza. I heard Rosalio Muñoz recently bemoan the fact that almost nobody is organizing in the Chicano community these days. PRIORITIES—Comunidades (ecclesiales) de Base, etc. - 2. Study and research through a process of analysis and synthesis los hechos y effectos de la realidad chicana. This anthropological analysis will yield the prob-

lematic of *tal Pedro Chicano*, man in the concrete. Only then can there be relevant response by the various institutions in this country.
3. Once having discovered more deeply the Chicano culture which is emerging, communicate and share that discovery with the various institutions (educational, church, government) so they can better appreciate and respect that reality. There are true values en la cultura chicana which must be affirmed.
4. Focus on the church—it is yours, and must respond pastorally to the real needs.

Later:

After leaving Notre Dame, I hope you will continue in the direction of some of the above suggestions. However, the field will be much wider *for your being part of a movement for effective change* towards a total liberacion—government, education, and the church. . . .

1. Yours could be a needed service for the equal justice in the courts of law *as a Chicano attorney.*
2. The political impotency of our people has been demonstrated often. It's causes are many but high among them is the systematic ways which are used to keep 'those people' powerless—even when they are in a minority. Gerrymandering political districts does this effectively. Politicians in tune with the realities? and dedicated to change some of the oppressive systems are needed. There is at present no Chicano voice in the senate or congress on a national level. (Jose Bernal of San Antonio was defeated in the last election!)
3. You heard, a moment ago, some statistics on the *Chicano educatonal scene.* There has been some improvement in recent years, but we still have a long way to go. Helping to instill the positive self-image, and to develop the habit of *critical thinking* . . . is a very worthwhile and important way to spend a life for authentic liberation.
4. The whole social field of jobs and housing always need committed people who can bring a true and Christian value system to patterns which tend to be so individualistic and materialistic; changing those patterns is a Christian task which is yours, and it will not be a comfortable job.
5. Just as Chicanos all over the land were getting the message that the schools and government and financial systems were supposed to benefit and serve their needs, they began to reclaim those institutions and became an effective part of them. Some, it is true, were corrupted by the systems.

The church is yours; you are the church's, You are the church!

Go back, reclaim it, help it to become truly relevant
To the lives of all Chicanos! by:
a) Active and interested laymen,
b) Some of you—*priests & bishops!*
"impose hands"—(call upon spirit)

Conclusion

You are Chicanos and you are Christians. As such, you are called to be pedagogues of an authentic and total liberation of our people. The Easter freedom from the bonds and weights of structural and institutional slavery and oppression will come only through and after the tough struggle of the process of liberation. Men, all people, liberate each other in unity and communion, unity and communion. As an emerging people, La Raza Nueva, we are steadily on the way to the fullness of freedom from sin and every oppression. You have the tremendous challenge to give truth and new dimension to the often rhetorical and empty cry *"Chicano power!" It can be, should be, and you can make it be*—a shibboleth—a clarion call to a true liberation wherein el pueblo Chicano is subject of its own destiny, and enjoying and carrying out a power not to oppress, but to serve and build up.

¡VIVA LA RAZA NUEVA!
¡VIVA LA RAZA COSMICA! QUE VIVA!!!

4. VINE DELORIA, JR.

The Theological Dimension of the Indian Protest Movement*

Church groups in America have been severely buffeted in recent years because of their support of social causes. Their participation in the civil rights movement of the '60s was important in itself and proved sustaining when the outlook was bleak. Indeed, it was perhaps the church's involvement in concerns of this kind that provided a bridge across the contrarieties of the '60s so that the entire decade turned out to be one that fostered a concentrated drive for improvement and reform and the inculcation of a deeper sense of justice in the American people.

Part of the ideology which sustained this drive grew out of the Christian

*Vine Deloria, Jr., "The Theological Dimension of the Indian Protest Movement," *The Christian Century,* September 21, 1973, pp. 912-14. Copyright © 1973 Christian Century Foundation. Reprinted by permission of *The Christian Century.*

teaching of the brotherhood of man. Translated into the politics of integration under law, this concept swept the American psyche clean of the cobwebs of two centuries. But the shift from the ideological defense of integration to the launching of power movements by the racial minorities caught many people unawares. Hence there developed a furious backlash against church involvement in social issues. For the power movements stressed the group rather than individuals, and church people by and large could not apprehend within the Christian context the need for group identity felt by the various distinct minorities in the American mass.

On their part, the power movements themselves failed to develop a proper ideology. In North America, when the group or community becomes all-important (as it has in recent years), Western notions of democratic leavening are somewhat beside the point. What is needed is a truly native ideology—that is, the tribal ideology of the American Indian.

Attaching themselves to the power movements when these were at their zenith, the Indians were welcomed into the revolutionary changes which the civil rights movement had failed to engender. The possibilities of protest on a group basis were first discerned in the Poor People's March of 1968. This of course represented a negative value in that all its participants lacked economic power. Solving the problem of poverty would have required a more or less immediate redistribution of wealth, and the political and economic changes such a program would have involved posed a threat to white America. But though its results were meager, the Poor People's March did suggest that the group could wield positive power. Hence Indians were accepted by non-Indians primarily because they were seen adding leverage in the pursuit of power.

I

It was in the following year, 1969, that Indians emerged in the media. The capture of Alcatraz provided a symbolic center for the Indian protest, but the message of Alcatraz failed utterly. Basically, Alcatraz raised the question of land, first in the political and property sense of ownership and second in the larger sense of the relationship of land to communities and, ultimately, to religious understanding. The result of Alcatraz was hardly comforting to Indians. They never received title to the island. White society simply evaded the whole problem by harking back to the days of Sitting Bull and Chief Joseph. People were damn sorry about the depredations of the past, but they could not recognize the depredations of the present because they could not go beyond the first step of the land question. The Christian religion had little to say concerning land and nature: it was an otherworldly religion which boasted that it was in the world but not of it. Failing to understand the Indians' relationship to the land, non-Indians saw Alcatraz as nothing more than a symbolic defiance of the federal government—in which nearly everyone had lost faith anyway. Thus they responded to the Indian protest by allowing Indians to have their day in the media sun. Oceans of pitying tears flowed down, but no waters of righteousness. The mood of white society seemed to be one of sadistic fairness: we have hurt them; now we must let them hurt us.

No wonder the Indian activists went wild. Between 1969 and early 1972, they took over piece after piece of federal surplus property, declaring that they had rights to it under the 1868 Sioux treaty. Invariably, charges of disturbing the peace and inciting to riot were lodged against them, though eventually they were able to negotiate amnesty on these. Their movement was at once exciting and boring. Would they one of these days uncover a piece of property that the federal government might give them? Yet watching another group of Indians on the evening news claiming another abandoned federal lighthouse grew wearying. In their own minds, the Indians' escalation of their demands and the increasing violence of their protest recalled the days of Indian glory. To the white society, the protest was novel because of its intensity.

II

The turning point came in 1972, when one of the Indian activists happened to read the 1868 Sioux treaty. There was the text in black and white. It said nothing about returning Alcatraz or the lighthouse in Milwaukee, but it did promise that the United States would protect the tribal form of government. To many Indians, this meant that the reservation governments which had been created in 1934 as quasi-modern corporations were contrary to Indian tradition. In the light of this discovery the activists began to talk with the old men of the tribes, and from them learned a new understanding of life. Hitherto they had believed that Indian identity depended on establishing a preferential pecking order in relationships with federal bureaucrats. Now, taught by the elders, many activists concluded that their own salvation and their people's lay in a return to the old ways, the old religion and the old political structure. Meanwhile, the failure of the reservation governments to minister to the needs of their people had induced a mood of frustration which, by the fall of 1972, turned into desperation. So when the organizers of the Trail of Broken Treaties arrived to recruit followers for the march on

Washington, many Indians broke with the traditional rule of silence and joined the protest.

The ensuing occupation and destruction of the Bureau of Indian Affairs headquarters in Washington was completely misinterpreted by Indians and non-Indians alike. Many Indians saw it as a way of paying the white society in its own coin. They were entitled to doing a little demolition, they felt. But Washington officials—particularly those closest to the seats of power—said the destruction was the work of hoodlum urban Indians who were angry over the federal government's recently announced decision to refuse aid to off-reservation Indians. The fact is that this decision was taken in defiance of the Snyder Act of 1920.

III

The most important result of the Trail of Broken Treaties was the 20-point program its participants drew up. Listing the Indians' grievances and suggestions for remedying them, this document was perhaps the most detailed ever presented to the U.S. government by an Indian group. Its proposals—insofar as they touched on the nature of the federal relationship—were designed to return Indian communities step by step to the status they had held in the 1870s. One point dealt with the institution of a new land policy reflecting the basic theology that the older tribal men had preserved. Federal officials could not fathom a program based on the assumption that tribal religious ideas were valid. Apparently they refused to consider the nature of the proposed changes and the fact that these would place additional responsiblities on the Indians. In January, after a Task Force had allegedly reviewed them, the 20 points were rejected by the federal government.

The people who had traveled the Trail of Broken Treaties felt betrayed. Many of them vowed to go on protesting. Toward the end of February a series of events on the Pine Ridge Sioux Reservation produced the Wounded Knee occupation. A grasping tribal chairman who used his tribal police as a personal bully squad, a force of federal marshals bewildered by not knowing which group of Indians would be shooting at them the next day, a White House staff that both welcomed Wounded Knee as a distraction from the then developing Watergate scandal and deplored it as further evidence of the bankruptcy of the Nixon domestic policies—all combined to make the 72-day occupation one of the more entertaining incidents of the winter television season.

Fundamentally, the Wounded Knee issue was a moral one involving the Fort Laramie Treaty of 1868, which forbids the taking of any Sioux land without the approval of three-fourths of the adult males of the tribe concerned. In effect the Indians were asking the United States why it refused to live up to its own laws. A hard question which allowed no quibbling. When it signed the treaty, the United States surely anticipated that whites would want the Black Hills some day. Therefore it could not pretend that events had now created a situation so desperate as to require overriding the promises made in the treaty. To have given an adequate answer at Wounded Knee, the federal government would have had to admit that it is and always has been made up of pathological liars. But by definition whites and Christians, the civilized peoples of the world, do not lie.

IV

Who knows whither the Indian movement is going? As we de-escalate from Wounded Knee and face the prospect of political trials, the religious dimensions of Indian protest become plain. On the one hand the Indian theology demands that the sacred places of the earth be discerned and communities of whole human beings be allowed to live on them. On the other hand the Indian protesters are intent on demonstrating that the white man's religion and his government are hollow, without honor and without substance. Experienced Indians regard this desire to show up the bankruptcy of the whites' values as suicidal. Of course practically every Indian is convinced that the white man is corrupt at the core, but many Indians reject attempts to demonstrate as much because—and they point to Vietnam and to the massacres of the 1800s—they believe that the white man will kill his opposition rather than win it over by example or reasoning. There was Ghost Dancing at Wounded Knee in 1890 and also in 1973, but in neither case did it stop the marshals' bullets.

A nation that has long conceived of political protest and social movement in theological terms must come to a new religious understanding of man in his community before it undertakes any more actions. For where such understanding is lacking, appeals to man's kinder and higher instincts are useless. The dilemma of the Indian today is: How call upon a more universal sense of justice than the world can presently sustain or fulfill?

VI. The Emergence of a New Militancy

To look deeply into nearly every minority community in America is to discover growing numbers of individuals expecting and demanding more out of life. This mood of dissatisfaction, especially strong among the young, is reflected in the social, political, and economic militancy of minorities in recent years. The selections in this chapter describe the dimensions of contemporary minority activism and examine the continuing debate in minority communities over goals and tactics.

Minority activism is not new in America, but widespread, well-organized, broadly coordinated civil rights movements are products of this century. On a national scale the twentieth-century struggle for equal rights began among Blacks with W.E.B. DuBois' Niagara Movement (1905) and the organization that soon absorbed it, the National Association for the Advancement of Colored People (1910). For Chicanos in the Southwest the Alianza Hispano Americana—which had begun in Tucson in 1894 to provide insurance and funeral benefits for Chicanos—led in the struggle for equal political rights, as did such later groups as La Orden de Hijos de America (1921) and the League of United Latin-American Citizens (1929). Among Native Americans, the All Pueblo Council waged a successful campaign during the twenties to retain tribal lands against white encroachments and in doing so won national attention and support.

Through the efforts of these organizations and such others as the National Urban League (1911), A. Philip Randolph's Brotherhood of Sleeping Car Porters and Maids (1925), and El Congreso de Pueblos de Habla Español (Congress of Spanish-Speaking People, 1938), some progress was made, especially in the fight for equal rights under the law and in employment practices. New Deal programs were administered more equally among whites and nonwhites; in 1941 President Roosevelt established the Fair Employment Practices Commission benefiting all ethnic minorities, and in 1944 the Supreme Court outlawed the exclusion of Blacks from primary elections in the Texas Democratic Party. Chicanos also began to win important antisegregation battles in the Southwest, and with the creation of the National Congress of American Indians in 1944, Native Americans became organized for the first time on a truly national scale.

Yet the pervasiveness of individual and institutional racism nullified many legal victories. During World War II discrimination in defense industries was common. Whites walked off the job en masse at Detroit auto factories to protest the promotion of Blacks. Race riots broke out in Beaumont, Texas, New York, Los Angeles, Mobile, and Detroit. Native Americans returned from the war expecting to share in the fruits of victory—freedom, equality, and opportunity—and instead met bitter disappointment. Evidence of white intransigence was widespread and helped encourage minorities to organize; NAACP membership rolls alone increased from just over 100,000 before the war to 500,000 in the late forties.

The movement for equal rights accelerated after the war and produced notable successes. In a series of stunning legal victories engineered principally by the NAACP, discriminatory practices were prohibited in housing, public transportation, and the use of public recreational facilities. The greatest victory came in 1954 with the Supreme Court's school desegregation ruling in *Brown* v. *The Board of Education.* At the same time other minority organizations were active. The Congress of Racial Equality (CORE) tested Southern compliance with court decisions, the Community Service Organization helped to register thousands of Chicano voters in the late forties and early fifties, the American GI Forum fought for the rights of Chicano veterans against discriminatory job and housing practices, the National Congress of American Indians pressed forward in its campaign in behalf of Native American interests.

In 1955 Martin Luther King, Jr., a young Baptist minister in Montgomery, Alabama, began his equal rights campaign in the South by applying the philosophy of nonviolent resistance and appealing to the moral conscience of the nation. Under his leadership the pace of integration quickened and nonviolence became a veritable sacred code of protest. Other minority groups soon began to apply the techniques of peaceful "creative disorder" to their own situations. Chicano agricultural labor organizer César Chávez and leaders of other minority communities allied with King in an effort to create a broad populist coalition of the disinherited, but cooperation succumbed to the diversity of needs and to group self-interest.

There soon appeared minority dissidents who denounced the progress of the civil rights movement of the early 1960s as "too little, too late." For them the only clear beneficiaries had been those Southern rural Blacks who had won the vote and token school desegregation. Few tangible benefits had been produced for Blacks, Chicanos, and Native Americans in the North and West. There, patterns of discrimination in jobs and housing had undergone little change; and for Southern Blacks in areas where white vigilantism was strong, the fruits of the civil rights struggle were uncertain. To the more militant civil rights activists it appeared that the white power structure was unwilling to yield to peaceful and just demands for change and that white Americans had neither the will nor the desire to respond to the needs of minorities. The assassination of three leaders in the fight for equality—President John F. Kennedy, Martin Luther King, Jr., and Robert F. Kennedy—served to confirm their beliefs.

While the majority of minority-group members continued to work within the system for justice and equality, such minority leaders as Stokely Carmichael, Robert Browne, Rodolfo "Corky" Gonzales, and Vine Deloria, Jr., spoke increasingly of other goals, calling for ethnic power and a new kind of pluralism. They insisted on political, economic, and cultural independence from whites. The Student Nonviolent Coordinating Committee (SNCC), which helped spearhead the Southern civil rights drive in the early sixties, adopted a militant "Black Power" program, advised whites to work in their own communities while Blacks worked on the needs of their communities, and called for Black political action independent of established political parties. Yet only a relatively few minority leaders urged the abandonment of nonviolent tactics. Those who did rejected the idea that meaningful, peaceful change was possible in America. Groups like the Black Panther Party, and the Brown Berets, pledged to adopt the strategy of physical resistance when necessary for their own survival and lauded it as a tactic compatible with the American tradition.

In the late sixties and early seventies the most militant groups received the greatest public attention. Between 1965 and 1968 full-scale rebellion erupted in major cities from coast to coast. In 1967 Chicanos in New Mexico physically claimed land as having been stolen from their ancestors, and in 1973 leaders of the American Indian Movement seized control of Wounded Knee, South Dakota. Destruction of property and armed resistance dramatized minority problems and produced a few positive changes. But prolonged confrontations with federal, state, and local authorities usually ended with the exile, imprisonment, or death of those leaders labeled as "too radical"—as with Eldridge Cleaver, Robert F. Williams, Reies López Tijerina, "Rap" Brown, and Fred Hampton. Moreover, rioting—which sometimes brought increased job opportunities—also brought considerable destruction to already substandard neighborhoods, causing thousands of small businesses to close for good and leaving behind gutted housing projects and empty, charred family dwellings.

Recognizing the limits of confrontation, some of the more activist minority spokespeople, most notably Black Panther Bobby Seale in Oakland and Imamu Amiri Baraka (formerly playwright LeRoi Jones) in Newark, have currently turned to the political battlefield and stressed "ballots not bullets" as the most viable means of changing the socioeconomic structure of minority communities.

In illustrating the various approaches of minorities to social problems in the post-World War II period, the selections in this chapter also illustrate a fundamental fact of American minority-majority relations—as long as the aspirations of the ethnic underclasses for freedom, justice, and equality remain frustrated, the minority struggle will remain a powerful, and sometimes strident, feature of American life.

A. The Debate over Goals

Ideally a pluralistic society allows for cultural diversity, mutual interaction, the sharing of pride in heritages, equal rights, equal opportunities, and maximum self-fulfillment. America has traditionally thought of itself in this manner. Pluralism in America, however, has been hierarchical rather than egalitarian. Anglo-Americans have established their own cultural values as normative while regarding the standards and practices of other groups as deviant, comical, and inferior. Pointing to the failure of American pluralism, minorities have debated whether they should continue to try to assimilate, integrate, accommodate, separate, or attempt some combination. This is not a new subject of debate among minorities, but never before has it engaged so many members of minority communities and inspired such heated argument. The selections below illustrate the ways in which minority groups have defined their goals and have attempted to produce a truly pluralistic America.

The exchange between Robert Browne and Bayard Rustin in "Separation or Integration: Which Way for America" is an example of the debate over goals in the various minority communities. Browne argued in the 1960s that integration was not only unattainable but undesirable and potentially harmful to Blacks. He defined integration as assimilation and assimilation as the loss of racial identity, concluding that the answer was Black separation or at least control of their own neighborhoods and school systems. Rustin argues that separatist talk has historically been most common during times of extreme frustration for Blacks, and that now, as always, separation is unrealistic. The way for Blacks to get ahead in America, he says, is for them to participate as fully as possible in the political process instead of separating from it.

César Chávez's "Plan of Delano" describes the goals of Chicano farm workers. Founded as the National Farm Workers Association in 1962, the United Farm Workers Union believes that only through unity and a vigorous program of social reform can farm workers compel growers to end an agricultural system characterized by "starvation wages, contractors, day-hauls, forced migration, sickness, illiteracy, filthy labor camps, and subhuman living conditions." As Chávez makes clear, farm workers do not want charity. They want a better life—for themselves and for all farm workers whatever their ethnic backgrounds—and believe they can gain it only through a strong union committed to a peaceful "revolution" in the fields.

The third selection—highly controversial in the Indian community and among liberal whites and civil rights activists—is William Whitworth's interview with Kahn-Tinenta Horn, a young Mohawk Indian woman. By emphasizing the cultural and racial uniqueness of Indians, eschewing association with the civil rights movement, and calling on Indians to "straighten out," Kahn-Tinenta Horn has antagonized people across the spectrum of Native American activism. Yet in doing so she has illuminated two fundamental and enduring goals of many American Indians: to win back Indian land and wealth from the United States government and to restore as much as possible of ancient tribal ways—the deep sense of community, the customs, the ceremonies, and the autonomy that alone can make it all possible.

1. ROBERT S. BROWNE AND BAYARD RUSTIN

Separatism or Integration: Which Way for America*

ROBERT S. BROWNE: A CASE FOR SEPARATION

There is a growing ambivalence in the Negro community which is creating a great deal of confusion both within the black community itself, and within those segments of the white community that are attempting to relate to the blacks. It arises from the question of whether the American Negro is a cultural group, significantly distinct from the majority culture in ways that are ethnically rather than socio-economically based.

If one believes the answer to this is yes, then one is likely to favor emphasizing the cultural distinctiveness and to be vigorously opposed to any

*Robert S. Browne and Bayard Rustin, *Separatism or Integration: Which Way for America* (New York, A. Philip Randolph Fund, 1968), pp. 7-18. Reprinted by permission of Robert S. Browne and Bayard Rustin.

efforts to minimize or to submerge the differences. If, on the other hand, one believes that there are no cultural differences between the blacks and the whites or that the differences are minimal and transitory, then one is likely to resist the placing of great emphasis on the differences and to favor accentuating the similarities.

These two currents in the black community are symbolized, and perhaps over-simplified, by the factional labels of separatists and integrationists.

The separatist would argue that the Negro's foremost grievance is not solvable by giving him access to more gadgets, although this is certainly a part of the solution, but that his greatest thirst is in the realm of the spirit—that he must be provided an opportunity to reclaim his own group individuality and to have that individuality recognized as having equal validity with the other major cultural groups of the world.

The integrationist would argue that what the Negro wants, principally, is exactly what the whites want—that is, that the Negro wants "in" American society, and that operationally this means providing the Negro with employment, income, housing, and education comparable to that of the whites. This having been achieved, the other aspects of the Negro's problem of inferiority will disappear.

The origins of this ideological dichotomy are easily identified. The physical characteristics that distinguish blacks from whites are obvious enough; and the long history of slavery, supplemented by the post-emancipation pattern of exclusion of the blacks from so many facets of American society, are equally undeniable. Whether observable behavioral differences between the mass of the blacks and the white majority are more properly attributable to this special history of the black man in America or are better viewed as expressions of racial differences in life style is an arguable proposition.

What is not arguable, however, is the fact that at the time of the slave trade the blacks arrived in America with a cultural background and a life style that was quite distinct from that of the whites. Although there was perhaps as much diversity amongst those Africans from widely scattered portions of the continent as there was amongst the European settlers, the differences between the two racial groups was unquestionably far greater, as attested by the different roles which they were to play in the society. . . .

To many observers, the separatist appears to be romantic and even reactionary. On the other hand, his viewpoint strikes an harmonious chord with mankind's most fundamental instinct—the instinct for survival. With so powerful a stimulus, and with the oppressive tendencies congenitally present in the larger white society, one almost could have predicted the emergence of the burgeoning movement toward black separatism. Millions of black parents have been confronted with the poignant agony of raising black, kinky-haired children in a society where the standard of beauty is a milk-white skin and long, straight hair. To convince a black child that she is beautiful when every channel of value formation in the society is telling her the opposite is a heart-rending and well-nigh impossible task. It is a challenge that confronts all Negroes, irrespective of their social and economic class, but the difficulty of dealing with it is likely to vary directly with the degree to which the family leads an integrated existence. A black child in a predominantly black school may realize that she doesn't look like the pictures in the books, magazines, and TV advertisements, but at least she looks like her schoolmates and neighbors. The black child in a predominantly white school and neighborhood lacks even this basis for identification. . . .

BLACK POWER, BLACK CONSCIOUSNESS, AND AMERICAN SOCIETY

Black Power may not be the ideal slogan to describe this new self-image that the black American is developing, for to guilt-ridden whites the slogan conjures up violence, anarchy, and revenge. To frustrated blacks, however, it symbolizes unity and a newly found pride in the blackness with which the Creator endowed us and which we realize must always be our mark of identification. Heretofore this blackness has been a stigma, a curse with which we were born. Black Power means that henceforth this curse will be a badge of pride rather than of scorn. It marks the end of an era in which black men devoted themselves to pathetic attempts to be white men and inaugurates an era in which black people will set their own standards of beauty, conduct, and accomplishment.

Is this new black consciousness in irreconcilable conflict with the larger American society?

In a sense, the heart of the American cultural problem always has been the need to harmonize the inherent contradiction between racial (or national) identity and integration into the melting pot which was America. In the century since the Civil War, the society has made little effort to find a means to afford the black minority a sense of racial pride and independence while at the same time accepting it as a full participant in the larger society.

Now that the implications of that failure are becoming apparent, the black community seems to be saying "Forget it! We'll solve our own problems." Integration, which never had a high priority among the black masses, now is being written off by them as not only unattainable but as actually harmful—

driving a wedge between those black masses and the so-called Negro elite.

To these developments has been added the momentous realization by many of the 'integrated' Negroes that, in the United States, full integration can only mean full assimilation—a loss of racial identity. This sobering prospect has caused many a black integrationist to pause and reflect, even as have his similarly challenged Jewish counterparts. . . .

THE BLACK NATIONALISTS

If one were to inquire as to who the principal spokesmen for the new black nationalism or for separatism are, one would discover that the movement is essentially locally based rather than nationally organized. In the San Francisco Bay Area, the Black Panther Party is well known as a leader in the tactics of winning recognition for the black community. Their tactic is *via* a separate political party for black people, a format which I suspect we will hear a great deal more of in the future. The work of the Black Muslims is well known, and perhaps more national in scope than that of any other black nationalist group. Out of Detroit there is the Malcolm X Society, led by attorney Milton Henry, whose members reject their United States citizenship and are claiming five southern states for the creation of a new Black Republic. Another major leader in Detroit is the Rev. Albert Cleage, who is developing a considerable following for his preachings of black dignity and who has also experimented with a black political party, thus far without success.

The black students at white colleges are one highly articulate group seeking for some national organizational form. A growing number of black educators are also groping toward some sort of nationally coordinated body to lend strength to their local efforts for developing educational systems better tailored to the needs of the black child. Under the name of Association of Afro-American Educators, they recently held a national conference in Chicago which was attended by several hundred public school teachers and college and community workers.

This is not to say that every black teacher or parent-teacher group that favors community control of schools is necessarily sympathetic to black separatism. Nevertheless, the general thrust of the move toward decentralized control over public schools, at least in the larger urban areas, derives from an abandoning of the idea of integration in the schools and a decision to bring to the ghetto the best and most suitable education that can be obtained. . . .

BAYARD RUSTIN: TOWARD INTEGRATION AS A GOAL

Dr. Browne dealt with the concept of separation in psychological rather than sociological terms. The proposition that separation may be the best solution of America's racial problems has been recurrent in American Negro history. Let us look at the syndrome that has given rise to it.

Separation, in one form or another, has been proposed and widely discussed among American Negroes in three different periods. Each time, it was put forward in response to an identical combination of economic and social factors that induced despair among Negroes. The syndrome consists of three elements: great expectations, followed by dashed hopes, followed by despair and discussion of separation.

POST-CIVIL WAR SEPARATISM

The first serious suggestion that Negroes should separate came in the aftermath of the Civil War. During that war many Negroes had not only been strongly in favor of freedom but had fought for the Union. It was a period of tremendous expectations. Great numbers of Negroes left the farms and followed the Union Army as General Sherman marched across Georgia to the sea; they believed that when he got to the sea they would be not only free but also given land—"forty acres and a mule." However, the compromise of 1876 and the withdrawal of the Union Army from the South dashed those expectation.Instead of forty acres and a mule all they got was a new form of slavery. . . .

POST-WORLD WAR I SEPARATISM

The second period of frustration and the call for separation came after World War I. During that war, 300,000 Negro troops went to France—not for the reason Mr. Wilson thought he was sending them, but because they felt that if they fought for their country they would be able to return and say: "We have fought and fought well. Now give us at home what we fought for abroad. . . ."

The war having created great expectations, and the conditions following the war having shattered them, a really great movement for separation ensued—a much more significant movement than the current one. Marcus Garvey organized over 2,000,000 Negroes, four times the number the NAACP has ever organized, to pay dues to buy ships to return to Africa.

PRESENT-DAY SEPARATISM

Today, we are experiencing the familiar syndrome again. The Civil Rights Acts of 1964 and 1965 and the Supreme Court decisions all led people seriously to believe that progress was forthcoming, as they believed the day Martin Luther King said, "I have a dream." What made the March on Washington in 1963 great was the fact that it was the culmination of a period of great hope and anticipation.

But what has happened since? The ghettoes are fuller than they have ever been, with 500,000 people moving into them each year and only some 40,000 moving out. They are the same old Bedford-Stuyvesant, Harlem, Detroit, and Watts, only they are much bigger, with more rats, more roaches, and more despair. There are more Negro youngsters in segregated schoolrooms than there were in 1954—not all due to segregation or discrimination, perhaps, but a fact. The number of youngsters who have fallen back in their reading, writing, and arithmetic since 1954 has increased, not decreased, and unemployment for Negro young women is up to 35, 40, and 50 percent in the ghettoes. For young men in the ghettoes, it is up to 20 percent, and this is a conservative figure. For family men, the unemployment is twice that of whites. Having built up hopes, and suffered the despair which followed, we are again in a period where separation is being discussed.

A FRUSTRATION REACTION

I maintain that, in all three periods, the turn to separation has been a frustration reaction to objective political, social, and economic circumstances. I believe that it is fully justified, for it would be the most egregious wishful thinking to suppose that people can be subjected to deep frustration and yet not act in a frustrated manner. But however justified and inevitable the frustration, it is totally unrealistic to divert the attention of young Negroes at this time either to the idea of a separate state in the United States, or to going back to Africa, or to setting up a black capitalism (as Mr. Nixon and CORE are now advocating), or to talk about any other possibility of economic separation, when those Negroes who are well off are the 2,000,000 Negroes who are integrated into a trade union movement of this country.

This is not to belittle in any way the desirability of fostering a sense of ethnic unity or racial pride among Negroes or relationships to other black people around the world. This is all to the good, but the ability to do this in a healthy rather than a frustrated way will depend upon the economic viability of the Negro community, the degree to which it can participate in the democratic process here rather than separate from it, and the degree to which it accepts methods of struggle that are productive. . . .

2. CÉSAR CHÁVEZ

The Plan of Delano*

All things have a reason, an idea and a plan. Here then is the plan for our movement—a plan for the liberation of the farm workers of the United States of North America, affiliated with the unique and true union of farm workers, the United Farm Workers, AFL-CIO, seeking social justice in farm labor with those reforms that they believe necessary for their well-being as workers.

We, the undersigned, gathered in Pilgrimage to every agricultural area of the United States, make penance for all the needs of Farm Workers. As free and sovereign men and women, we do solemnly declare before the civilized world which judges our actions, and before the nation where we work, the proposition we have formulated to end the injustice that oppresses us.

We are conscious of the historical significance of our Pilgrimage. It is clearly evident that our path travels through a valley of tears well-known to all farm workers, because in all valleys the way of the farm worker has been one of sacrifice for generations. Our sweat and our blood have fallen on this land to make other men rich. This Pilgrimage is a witness to the suffering we have seen for generations.

The penance we accept symbolizes the suffering we shall have in order to bring justice to all farm workers throughout the land. The Pilgrimage we make symbolizes the long historical road we have traveled until now, and the long road we have yet to travel, with much penance in order to bring about the Revolution we need, and for which we present the propositions in the following plan:

1) This is the beginning of a social movement in fact and not in pronouncements. We seek our basic, God-given rights as human beings. Because we

*César Chávez, "The Plan of Delano." Reprinted by permission of the United Farm Workers, AFL-CIO.

have suffered, and are not afraid to suffer in order to survive, we are ready to give up everything—even our lives—in our struggle for social justice. We shall do it without violence because it is our destiny. To the growers and to all those who oppose us, we say the words of Benito Juarez, "Respect for another's rights is the meaning of peace."

2) We seek the support of all political groups and the protection by the government which is also our government, in our struggle. For too many years we have been treated like the lowest of the low. Our wages and working conditions have been determined from above, because irresponsible legislators who could have helped us, have supported the argument that the plight of the farm worker was a "special case." They saw the obvious effects of an unjust system, starvation wages, contractors, day-hauls, forced migration, sickness, illiteracy, filthy labor camps and sub-human living conditions, and acted as if they were irremediable. The farm worker has been abandoned to his own fate—without representation, without power—subject to the mercy and the caprice of the grower. We are tired of words, of betrayals, of indifference. To the politicians we say that the years are gone when the farm worker said nothing and did nothing to help himself. But now we have new faith. Through our strong will, our movement is changing these conditions. Due to our movement, farm worker leaders are developing who are faithful to the ideals and the propositions of the farm workers. They shall represent us. WE SHALL BE HEARD.

3) We seek and have the support of the Church in what we do. Our movement is non-sectarian. Our movement includes all religions. We are all brothers and sisters, sons and daughters of the same God; that is why we say to all men and women of good will, in the words of Pope Leo XIII, "Everyone's first duty is to protect the workers from the greed of speculators who use human beings as instruments to provide themselves with money. It is neither just nor human to oppress men with excessive work to the point where their minds become enfeebled and their bodies worn out." GOD SHALL NOT ABANDON US.

4) We are suffering. We have suffered, and we are not afraid to suffer in order to win our cause. We have suffered unnumbered ills and crimes in the name of the Law of the Land. Our men, women and children have suffered not only the basic brutality of stoop labor, and the most obvious injustices of the system; they have also suffered the desperation of knowing that the system caters to the greed of callous men and not to our needs. Now we will suffer for the purpose of ending the poverty, the misery, and the injustice, with the hope that our children will not be exploited as we have been. They

have imposed hunger on us, and now we hunger for justice. We draw our strength from the very despair in which we have been forced to live. WE SHALL ENDURE.

5) We shall unite. We have learned the meaning of unity. We know, from other unions, the reasons why workers organize. The strength of the poor is also in unity. We know that the poverty of the farm worker in California is the same as that of all farm workers across the country—the Mexicans, Filipinos, Blacks and poor whites; the Puerto Ricans, the Japanese, the Indians, the Portuguese and the Arabs—in short, all the races that comprise the oppressed minorities of the United States.

Most of us farm workers in this Pilgrimage, work in California. But the triumph of our cause depends on the organization of all farm workers in the nation. Many of us have been fooled by the growers and contractors by their empty promises and lies, which they have used to get wealthier at our expenses. These dishonest acts are just some of the cynical jokes that jab at our impotence. This is why we must join with the true union of farm workers. UNITED WE SHALL STAND.

6) We shall strike; we shall organize boycotts; we shall demonstrate, and have political crmpaigns. We shall pursue the revolution we have proposed. We are sons and daughters of the farm worker's revolution, a revolution of the poor seeking bread and justice. Our revolution wull not be armed, but we want the existing order of agri-business to dissolve; we want a new social order for the farm workers in the fields. We are poor; we are humble and our only choice is to strike in those ranches where we are not treated with the respect we deserve as working men and women; where our rights as free and sovereign men and women are not recognized. We do not want the paternalism of the grower. We do not want the contractor. We do not want charity at the price of our dignity. We want to be equal with all the working men and women in the nation. We want a just wage, better working conditions, a decent future for our children. To those who oppose us, be they growers, contractors, scabs, police, politicians, or speculators, we say that we are going to continue struggling until we win or die. WE SHALL OVERCOME.

Across the San Joaquin Valley, across California, across the entire nation, wherever there are injustices against men and women who work in the fields—there you will see our flags—with the black eagle with the white and red background, flying. Our movement is spreading like flames across a dry plain. Our Pilgrimage is the match that will light our cause for all farm workers to see what is happening here so that they may do as we have done. The time has come for the liberation of the poor farm worker.

History is on our side. We support all farm worker strikes. We support the boycott as our most powerful non-violent weapon. We must work hard so that this can become a truly great movement. Long live the cause of the farm workers!
SI SE PUEDE!

3. WILLIAM WHITWORTH

Speaks with Sharp Tongue*

One of the prettiest and most disconcerting figures on the college lecture circuit these days is Kahn-Tineta Horn, a young Mohawk Indian woman who once was successful as an actress and model and now is prominent among North America's Indian activists. Student audiences often find Miss Horn's rhetoric unsettling, perhaps because it won't fit comfortably into any of the familiar pigeonholes on the left or the right. In a typical speech, Miss Horn may annoy conservatives and centrists with her description of white society as confused, insecure, misguided, power-hungry, and murderously aggressive. Before the leftists in the audience can say "Right on!," Miss Horn is telling them that they are insincere, destructive, misinformed, naïve, and unable to distinguish a slogan from an idea. Liberals who want to help out are dismissed as "bleeding hearts and do-gooders," and advised to stay away from Indians. Blacks, if they are mentioned at all, receive the same advice. Given enough time, Miss Horn will go on to hurt the feelings of numerous other groups, including integrationists, egalitarians, pot-smokers, junkies, the dairy industry, newspaper reporters, believers in universal education, sexist men, advocates of women's liberation, prudes, and the Indians themselves. We aren't qualified to assign a place in the spectrum of Indian opinion to Miss Horn's views, but Richard La Course, of the American Indian Press Association, in Washington, says that most of them are shared by most Indian activists.

Miss Horn lives a few miles from Montreal, on the Caughnawaga Reservation—the home of a group of Mohawk Indians who have become famous in the United States as steelworkers, because of their seemingly innate ability to work with ease at great heights. Miss Horn is studying law at McGill University, and in her spare time she wages a one-woman campaign

*William Whitworth, "Speaks with Sharp Tongue," *The New Yorker* (May 27, 1972), pp. 28-31. Copyright © 1972 The New Yorker Magazine, Inc. Reprinted by permission.

to obtain legal aid for Indians, as individuals and as a group. When she was in town the other day to meet with some steelworkers, we invited her to lunch.

"People are upset by what I say because they don't like to have their old, comfortable assumptions challenged," Miss Horn told us. "Even people who mean well think that the Indian is asking for a handout, and that they, in their superiority and generosity, are going to give him a few crumbs. They say, 'We want to help. What can we do?' And I say, 'The best thing you can do is stay away from us. Don't help us.' White people feel they are their brothers' keepers, and they're going to help you even if it kills you. For example, Ralph Nader was up in Montreal recently making some statements about the James Bay project, in northern Quebec. This is a big hydro project that could displace about ten thousand Indians who live near it. Now, we're making a study of this, and we're going to be making our moves. And what happens? Mr. Nader comes up there—a foreigner, a white man, someone who doesn't know anything about Indians—and starts making a big splash in the papers and on television, with all kinds of statements about the project. This was very, very destructive to us. It makes it look as though Mr. Nader is our leader and we can't come up with a decent leader of our own. It makes us look stupid, with a white man leading us again. Besides that, we had moves that we were planning to make in negotiations with the government, and Mr. Nader has come up and absolutely destroyed everything. This is the kind of do-gooder, bleeding-heart white person that I'm trying to keep away from Indians."

We asked what Miss Horn thought about Jane Fonda's efforts on behalf of Indians, and ducked. *"Jane Fonda!"* Miss Horn almost shouted. "The sooner she never mentions Indians again the better. She led the Indians into Fort Lawton, and when the television and newspaper people came around and started interviewing her, she was protesting Vietnam. She forgot which crusade she was on. She's done *so* much harm to Indians. She makes us look ridiculous. Do we need a white woman to lead us? She's just exploiting us. If she really wants to help, why doesn't she give money for legal aid and stay in the background, as a lot of sincere white people do? Not her. She has to be in the forefront. She degrades Indians and makes white people lose respect for us. What makes it even worse is that she's a leftist. No good can come of Indians' associating with any organization or person that is leftist or Socialist or Communist. Because our treaties are with the Establishment, and whatever we can get that belongs to us we can get only from the Establishment. We are existing only by the good will of the white people, who could wipe us out any time they felt like it. If the white man wanted to, he could pass some legislation and get rid of our Indian rights, our Indian lands, and our Indian status as a separate nation. I don't think we will accomplish anything by antagonizing the white man. I think we have to do things that will gain us more respect. I don't think marching up and down in front of some building, carrying signs, is going to gain us much respect.

"A lot of the Indian organizations have fallen by the wayside because of interference by bleeding-heart white people," Miss Horn went on. "These white people come in there and divert the Indians from what they're supposed to be doing. They want to start up some protests, take children out of school, occupy the Bureau of Indian Affairs offices, and things like that—things that are very damaging to Indians. In one case, some Indians were thrown out of a hotel and some more Indians were not allowed to register there. Well, some bleeding hearts pushed the Indians and said they ought to take the case to court, on the basis of the Bill of Rights. I advised the Indians not to go into court, because I knew about those Indians. There were about nineteen of them in the room, and they made a mess of the room, and they were drunk, and they were having, you know, like a three-day party. The hotel was trying to throw them out. So the Indians went into court, and what do you think came out in the court? *The bad behavior of Indians.* That's what they got for their trouble—bad publicity. Oh, I was so *ashamed* when I read the reports, because I knew they were true. We don't need that kind of thing. It makes people hate Indians even more than they already do."

"Do you think people hate Indians?" we asked.

"*Sure* they do," Miss Horn said. "Why shouldn't they? You think they should love us for doing things like that—what they did in that hotel? Go to a city like Winnipeg, where about five per cent of the population is Indian. The Indians are on welfare, they're derelicts, they're always in jail. Go to magistrate court Monday morning and there's one Indian after another—drinking and fighting, drinking and fighting. Thirty-nine killings in that area, and all but six involving Indians. So there is a certain amount of bad feeling there. Can you blame the whites?"

"Well, who *is* to blame?" we asked.

"Liquor, in the killings," Miss Horn said. "Plus no development on the reserves, so that the Indians are migrating to the cities."

"Who's to blame for what happens to them in the cities?"

"Both sides. You may think you love Indians, until you get involved with them. If you knew them, you might not like them. They're an awfully difficult bunch of people. Very complicated, very difficult, very hard to understand, very unpredictable."

"Isn't it a clash of cultures?" we asked.

"That goes without saying," Miss Horn replied. "Both sides are to blame. For existing, for being born. Liquor is really a big problem—the easy availability of liquor. Liquor was controlled until a few years ago, and there were few killings among Indians. Now, as far as the clash between the two cultures goes—the Indians are being asked to be white people, and they can't be. They can't be two people at once. They're trying to strip the Indian of his identity. The Indian is different. He can't make it in the white society. If the Indian can't have his ancient feeling of community, if he can't 'go on the warpath'—that is, do work that suits him—if he can't go through the old rituals that signify to him that he has become a man, then he is emasculated. He's a caged animal. That's why he has so much trouble in the city. So a crucial problem is the lack of development of the Indian environment. This is ultimately the responsibility of the government, of the white people. Because the white people have the money, and it's our money. That's why we let you people live here. For the rent you pay on the continent."

Miss Horn holds the unfashionable view that there are inborn differences between the races, and that to ignore them is dangerous for Indians. This conviction underlies her hostility to higher education for Indians, to efforts to integrate Indians into white society, and to Indian involvement in the civil-rights movement.

"I want there to be a recognition that Indians are mentally and physically and culturally different," Miss Horn told us. "Everyone goes around saying that everybody is the same. This is a kind of propaganda pitch. Especially in the higher levels of education, they like to say that if everybody's brought up in the same environment they're going to turn out the same. That's like saying, 'Let's bring down a team of little Eskimo basketball players and raise them in Harlem, and maybe someday they'll beat the Harlem Globetrotters.' This outlook has been very destructive to Indians. I can give numerous examples of Indians brought up right here in the city, and they're still Indians and they still feel Indian, and they don't know why they're so confused.

"To cite just one basic physical difference between Indians and other people, our reaction to milk is not the same as that of white people. Milk has some kind of gluey substance in it that requires a certain enzyme for its assimilation, and that enzyme is missing in Indians. This stuff coats the inside of your throat, the respiratory area, the intestines, the arteries around the heart, and it's very bad for you. I think this is why we've had a high infant-mortality rate. I haven't been able to get the Indian Health Service to stop sending milk to Indians, and they wonder why Indians are so sick. We've never had cows in all our history.

"Now, why are our people so good at working on the high steel? They're like mountain goats up there. I'm convinced that it's an inherited ability of some sort. And this brings me to education. In order to function as a good steelworker, you have to have very good reflexes, of course, and you can't really think about what you're doing. It has to do with getting messages to your muscles from a certain part of your brain—the lower part, which controls your reflexes. Something happens to you if you get too much education. I guess the electric charges go into the other part of your brain. I don't know. But for some reason your reflexes aren't as good after you start getting more education. That's why my brother had to quit working on high steel. He fell once, and he knew he was going to kill himself—as our father did—so he quit. Virtually all of the Indian steelworkers who have fallen in the past thirty years have been men who were improving their education. This is why I'm opposing the establishment of a high school in Caughnawaga. I think most Indians shouldn't go past about the seventh grade. Right now, we have about ninety-five-per-cent employment on our reserve. The men do a certain kind of work—it suits them, it appeals to them, they make good money, they look after their families. They bring about four hundred thousand dollars a week in wages into the reserve. If they get a better education, they can't work on high steel and there are no other jobs for them, so they end up unemployed. So if we're concerned about Indians' being employed and being self-sufficient, then education is a drawback."

We asked Miss Horn if her theories about education applied to all Indians or just to those in Caughnawaga.

"Well, I'm talking principally about Caughnawaga," Miss Horn replied. "But I think most Indians shouldn't get the same education that white people get. Some of us have to get an education. We need professional people—doctors and lawyers. But not all Indians should have this education. We had fifty Indian students at McGill this year, and it was pretty sad to see what happened to some of them. We need some way to find out which Indians can go to college and not be ruined by it and degenerate the way these kids did. They're ruined for life. They can't even go back up North without infecting the communities they came from."

"Infecting them with what?"

"The diseases they picked up down in white society. The fashionable confusions, the drugs, the venereal diseases, the white values that they're taking back up there and confusing the Indians with. Those Indians up there are doing very well the way they are. They're very unconfused, they're looking after their families, they're leading a happy life. And these kids go back up there and say, 'Look here, why are you so happy? You shouldn't be happy.' I think that at a certain age Indians should be given aptitude tests and guided into the kinds of skills they need so that they can go to work. They're no good at office work. They aren't good at working in mines. They're good at operating machinery, at flying, at operating tourist camps, and at being guides."

We asked Miss Horn why she advised Indians not to coöperate with blacks in the civil-rights movement.

"I say this because our problems are very different from those of the Negroes," Miss Horn said. "The Negroes want integration, and that doesn't work for Indians. They use tactics—demonstrations, marches, and so on—that aren't productive for us. Besides that, it confuses the issue for us to be involved with them. It creates the impression that we're full-fledged citizens, which we aren't, and that we're just another minority group, which we aren't. We're a separate people, with special rights guaranteed by the laws of this country. People get very upset when I compare the history of the Indians with that of the Negroes. I always say that Negroes have been very well treated here. They started out as less than a million, and now there are twenty-two million of them. Indians, on the other hand, have dwindled to about a tenth of what they were. There was a policy of genocide against them—*real* genocide, with millions of murders. But people don't look at it that way. It's as though you had a field containing five hundred horses and five hundred cows, and you came back twenty years later and there were five thousand horses and three cows, and everybody said, 'Isn't it awful how those horses have been treated?' I was speaking at a university not long ago, and a bunch of Black Panthers came there and were very insistent about their idea that Indians should form a group like the Black Panthers. And I thought, How silly! We're less than one percent of the population. We don't represent any kind of threat, either in buying power or political power. And here they were, saying that we had to have a group like the Black Panthers. I really thought they were kidding. I said, 'What are we gonna call ourselves? The Pink Panthers?' And they got so mad! They didn't have any sense of humor about it."

We asked Miss Horn to tell us a little about her legal-aid efforts in behalf of Indians.

"I'm mainly interested in Constitutional law," she said. "I'm hoping that after I get my law degree I'll be taking on a few Constitutional cases—anything concerning treaties and land rights. For now, well, I was involved in getting white people off the Caughnawaga Reservation. Squatters.

According to law, they're not supposed to be there, but the federal government wouldn't take them off. I had a test case against my sister, who had married a white man, and I got them off."

"How did she like that?" we asked.

"She didn't like it," Miss Horn replied. "She'll never speak to me again. But—law before love. I'm also concerned with Indians who get into trouble with the law. Murders. Ever since a case we had in the Northwest Territories in the late sixties, there's much more leniency in giving liquor to Indians. As a result, Indians make up about fifty per cent of the jail population in parts of western Canada. I would like for it to be very hard for Indians to get liquor. They just go berserk on it, and the next day they don't even remember what happened. I go up to the Kingston, Ontario, Penitentiary and talk to the women, and they're all in there for manslaughter or murder. And every one of them committed the crime under the influence of liquor. I haven't come across a single exception. It's a very sad situation."

B. NONVIOLENT REFORM

Nonviolence in America, even when preached by the clergy and avowed pacifists, rarely means submissiveness or passivity. Rather, it embodies an activist commitment to social reform involving forms of protest ranging from peaceful candlelight vigils and orderly marches to acts of "civil disobedience." Because of its emphasis on peaceful change, its implicit faith in democratic processes, and its heavy religious and moral appeal, nonviolence as an instrument of protest has been a powerful force in minority communities. This section examines the philosophy of nonviolence and illustrates a variety of nonviolent approaches adopted by minorities seeking justice and equality in America.

In the first selection Rev. Martin Luther King, Jr., discusses the philosophy of nonviolence and the deep personal commitment that form of protest requires. Nonviolence, he asserts, may be "physically passive," but it is "active spiritually. It is not passive nonresistance to evil, it is active nonviolent resistance to evil." Central to King's philosophy is love for one's fellow man (*agape*), belief that the act of suffering carries with it powerful redemptive energies from which men draw knowledge and are transformed, and the conviction that in the end victory will be won and justice will triumph.

Antonio Camejo illustrates the potential for nonviolent change through Chicano political organization. He describes how Chicanos in Texas have begun to win political control of local communities by means of La Raza Unida Party. In some towns Chicanos constitute more than eighty-five percent of the population but possess none of the political power commonly enjoyed by population majorities. In Crystal City the mayor, city council, and school board before 1969 were either Anglos or *vendidos*, "coconuts (brown on the outside, white on the inside)—Chicanos who think like gringos." However, out of a 1969 school walkout—begun as a protest against an inadequate, unresponsive, and Anglo-dominated educational system—La Raza Unida Party arose. A voter registration campaign was started, a popular slate of Chicanos ran for the school board, and the old board was defeated. For the first time Chicanos in Crystal City controlled their own school board, from the springboard of that victory launched successful drives to win their own city council and city hall as well, and generated the La Raza Unida political movement, which has spread throughout the country.

The third selection is W. Hedgepeth's brief, poetic description of the 1969 Indian seizure of Alcatraz Island, which he sees as an act of nonviolent protest. The occupation of Alcatraz, he says, was not only an affirmation of an emerging "pan-Indian consciousness," but also a "long overdue adoption of Negro Civil Rights tactics." By this deed young Native Americans proclaimed their commitment to nonviolent, activist pursuit of their goals. As Hedgepeth makes clear, however, this daring act was largely misunderstood by federal authorities and by many in the white community.

1. MARTIN LUTHER KING, JR.

Pilgrimage to Nonviolence*

Since the philosophy of nonviolence played such a positive role in the Montgomery Movement, it may be wise to turn to a brief discussion of some basic aspects of this philosophy.

First, it must be emphasized that nonviolent resistance is not a method for cowards; it does resist. If one uses this method because he is afraid or merely because he lacks the instruments of violence, he is not truly nonviolent. This is why Gandhi often said that if cowardice is the only alternative to violence, it is better to fight. He made this statement conscious of the fact that there is

*Martin Luther King, Jr., "Pilgrimage to Nonviolence," in *Stride Toward Freedom: The Montgomery Story.* Copyright © 1958 by Martin Luther King, Jr. Reprinted by permission of Harper & Row, Publishers, Inc.

always another alternative: no individual or group need submit to any wrong, nor need they use violence to right the wrong; there is the way of nonviolent resistance. This is ultimately the way of the strong man. It is not a method of stagnant passivity. The phrase "passive resistance" often gives the false impression that this is a sort of "do-nothing method" in which the resister quietly and passively accepts evil. But nothing is further from the truth. For while the nonviolent resister is passive in the sense that he is not physically aggressive toward his opponent, his mind and emotions are always active, constantly seeking to persuade his opponent that he is wrong. The method is passive physically, but strongly active spiritually. It is not passive non-resistance to evil, it is active nonviolent resistance to evil.

A *second basic fact* that characterizes nonviolence is that it does not seek to defeat or humiliate the opponent, but to win his friendship and understanding. The nonviolent resister must often express his protest through noncoöperation or boycotts, but he realizes that these are not ends themselves; they are merely means to awaken a sense of moral shame in the opponent. The end is redemption and reconciliation. The aftermath of nonviolence is the creation of the beloved community, while the aftermath of violence is tragic bitterness.

A *third characteristic* of this method is that the attack is directed against forces of evil rather than against persons who happen to be doing the evil. It is evil that the nonviolent resister seeks to defeat, not the persons victimized by evil. If he is opposing racial injustice, the nonviolent resister has the vision to see that the basic tension is not between races. As I like to say to the people in Montgomery: "The tension in this city is not between white people and Negro people. The tension is, at bottom, between justice and injustice, between the forces of light and the forces of darkness. And if there is a victory, it will be a victory not merely for fifty thousand Negroes, but a victory for justice and the forces of light. We are out to defeat injustice and not white persons who may be unjust."

A *fourth point that characterizes* nonviolent resistance is a willingness to accept suffering without retaliation, to accept blows from the opponent without striking back. "Rivers of blood may have to flow before we gain our freedom, but it must be our blood," Gandhi said to his countrymen. The nonviolent resister is willing to accept violence if necessary, but never to inflict it. He does not seek to dodge jail. If going to jail is necessary, he enters it "as a bridegroom enters the bride's chamber."

One may well ask: "What is the nonviolent resister's justification for this ordeal to which he invites men, for this mass political application of the ancient doctrine of turning the other cheek?" The answer is found in the realization that unearned suffering is redemptive. Suffering, the nonviolent resister realizes, has tremendous educational and transforming possibilities. "Things of fundamental importance to people are not secured by reason alone, but have to be purchased with their suffering," said Gandhi. He continues: "Suffering is infinitely more powerful than the law of the jungle for converting the opponent and opening his ears which are otherwise shut to the voice of reason."

A *fifth point concerning nonviolent resistance* is that it avoids not only external physical violence but also internal violence of spirit. The nonviolent resister not only refuses to shoot his opponent but he also refuses to hate him. At the center of nonviolence stands the principle of love. The nonviolent resister would contend that in the struggle for human dignity, the oppressed people of the world must not succumb to the temptation of becoming bitter or indulging in hate campaigns. To retaliate in kind would do nothing but intensify the existence of hate in the universe. Along the way of life, someone must have sense enough and morality enough to cut off the chain of hate. This can only be done by projecting the ethic of love to the center of our lives.

In speaking of love at this point, we are not referring to some sentimental or affectionate emotion. It would be nonsense to urge men to love their oppressors in an affectionate sense. Love in this connection means understanding, redemptive good will. Here the Greek language comes to our aid. There are three words for love in the Greek New Testament. First, there is *eros.* In Platonic philosophy *eros* meant the yearning of the soul for the realm of the divine. It has come now to mean a sort of aesthetic or romantic love. Second, there is *philia* which means intimate affection between personal friends. *Philia* denotes a sort of reciprocal love; the person loves because he is loved. When we speak of loving those who oppose us, we refer to neither *eros* nor *philia;* we speak of a love which is expressed in the Greek word *agape. Agape* means understanding, redeeming good will for all men. It is an overflowing love which is purely spontaneous, unmotivated, groundless, and creative. It is not set in motion by any quality or function of its object. It is the love of God operating in the human heart.

Agape is disinterested love. It is a love in which the individual seeks not his own good, but the good of his neighbor (I Cor. 10:24). *Agape* does not begin by discriminating between worthy and unworthy people, or any qualities people possess. It begins by loving others *for their sakes.* It is an entirely "neighbor-regarding concern for others," which discovers the neighbor in every man it meets. Therefore, *agape* makes no distinction between friend and enemy; it is directed toward both. If one loves an individual merely on account of his friendliness, he loves him for the sake of the benefits to be gained from the friendship, rather than for the friend's own sake. Consequently, the best way to assure oneself that Love is disinterested is to have love for the enemy-neighbor from whom you can expect no good in return, but only hostility and persecution.

Another basic point about *agape* is that it springs from the *need* of the other person—his need for belonging to the best in the human family. The Samaritan who helped the Jew on the Jericho Road was "good" because he responded to the human need that he was presented with. God's love is eternal and fails not because man needs his love. St. Paul assures us that the loving act of redemption was done "while we were yet sinners"—that is, at the point of our greatest need for love. Since the white man's personality is greatly distorted by segregation, and his soul is greatly scarred, he needs the love of the Negro. The Negro must love the white man, because the white man needs his love to remove his tensions, insecurities, and fears.

Agape is not a weak, passive love. It is love in action. *Agape* is love seeking to preserve and create community. It is insistence on community even when one seeks to break it. *Agape* is a willingness to sacrifice in the interest of mutuality. *Agape* is a willingness to go to any length to restore community. It doesn't stop at the first mile, but it goes the second mile to restore community. It is a willingness to forgive, not seven times, but seventy times seven to restore community. The cross is the eternal expression of the length to which God will go in order to restore broken community. The resurrection is a symbol of God's triumph over all the forces that seek to block community. The Holy Spirit is the continuing community creating reality that moves through history. He who works against community is working against the whole of creation. Therefore, if I respond to hate with a reciprocal hate I do nothing but intensify the cleavage in broken community. I can only close the gap in broken community by meeting hate with love. If I meet hate with hate, I become depersonalized, because creation is so designed that my personality can only be fulfilled in the context of community. Booker T. Washington was right: "Let no man pull you so low as to make you hate him." When he pulls you that low he brings you to the point of working against community; he drags you to the point of defying creation, and thereby becoming depersonalized.

In the final analysis, *agape* means a recognition of the fact that all life is interrelated. All humanity is involved in a single process, and all men are brothers. To the degree that I harm my brother, no matter what he is doing to me, to that extent I am harming myself. For example, white men often refuse federal aid to education in order to avoid giving the Negro his rights; but because all men are brothers they cannot deny Negro children without harming their own. Why is this? Because men are brothers. If you harm me, you harm yourself.

Love, *agape*, is the only cement that can hold this broken community together. When I am commanded to love, I am commanded to restore community, to resist injustice, and to meet the needs of my brothers.

A *sixth basic fact* about nonviolent resistance is that it is based on the conviction that the universe is on the side of justice. Consequently, the believer in nonviolence has deep faith in the future. This faith is another reason why the nonviolent resister can accept suffering without retaliation. For he knows that in his struggle for justice he has cosmic companionship. It is true that there are devout believers in nonviolence who find it difficult to believe in a personal God. But even these persons believe in the existence of some creative force that works for universal wholeness. Whether we call it an unconscious process, an impersonal Brahman, or a Personal Being of matchless power and infinite love, there is a creative force in this universe that works to bring the disconnected aspects of reality into a harmonious whole.

2. ANTONIO CAMEJO

A Report From Aztlán: Texas Chicanos Forge Own Political Power*

The formation of La Raza Unida Party, an independent Chicano political party, has raised the Chicano struggle for self-determination to a higher level.

On April 4, 1970, the slate of La Raza Unida Party swept the school board elections in Crystal City, Texas, defeating the candidates of the Democratic Party. Although the elections were officially "non-partisan" the party affiliations were known to all.

Jose Angel Gutierrez, 25 a founder and former state chairman of the Mexican American Youth Organization (MAYO), headed a slate of three Chicanos. Elected with Gutierrez were Arturo Gonzales, 21, a gas station attendant, and Miguel Perez, 31, operator of a Chicano dance hall.

Defeated were two Democratic *vendidos* [sellouts], Luz Arcos, 61, a

*Antonio Camejo, "A Report from Aztlán: Texas Chicanos Forge Own Political Power," in *La Raza Unida Party in Texas* (New York, Pathfinder Press, 1970), pp. 3-8. Reprinted by permission of Pathfinder Press, inc.

county employee, and Rafael Tovar, 54, a supervisor in the local Delmonte packing plant. Also defeated was rancher E. W. Ritchie, Jr., 46, who in desperation began claiming he was "half Mexican."

On April 7, 1970, La Raza Unida candidates again swept to victory in the city council elections in three cities. In Carrizo Springs, Company D headquarters of the Texas Rangers, Rufino Cabello was elected first Chicano mayor in the city's history. In Cotulla, Raza Unida candidate Alfredo Zamora was elected mayor. In both cities, an additional Raza Unida councilman was elected. In Crystal City two Raza Unida councilmen were elected to the five-member city council, which for several years has been half Chicano.

The racist anglo ruling class in Crystal City (or gringos as they are referred to in Texas) pretty much gave up trying to run their own people for the city council there eight years ago. Their tactic has been to run *vendidos,* or coconuts (brown on the outside, white on the inside)—Chicanos who think like gringos. That is why the city council was composed of four Mexican-Americans and only one gringo.

How did it come about that in these elections young militant Chicanos were able to defeat the gringo and *vendido* candidates of the Democratic Party who were backed up by the ranchers and the other monied interests?

To understand this we must look at the city of Cristal, as the Chicanos there refer to Crystal City. Cristal is 85 percent Chicano and 15 percent gringo, with a small number of anglos friendly to La Raza Unida Party. The people there are primarily migrant laborers who must follow the harvest north into Colorado, North Dakota, Minnesota and Wisconsin each spring, work for miserable wages throughout the summer and return home in the fall.

In many cases, families are forced to put all their possessions into hock to raise enough money for the trip to the beet fields. The small amount of money they bring back barely gives them enough to get out of hock and survive the winter months.

Median family income in Zavala County where Cristal is located, is $1,754 per year. The median educational level is 2.3 grades, which is lower than some impoverished Latin American nations. All the agricultural land is owned by gringos, 95 percent of the businesses in the city are also owned by gringos.

In 1962 an attempt was made to give the *mexicano* in Cristal some political representation. PASO (Political Association of Spanish-speaking Organizations) got some Mexican-American Democrats together and ran them for office against the gringo incumbents. Inrthe 1963 elections they rucceeded in throwing out the gringo mayor of some 38 years in Cristal, as well as creating the all-Chicano city council. They also had successes in other counties.

PASO, which had not built up any kind of an independent mass movement, became frightened by the unexpected victory. It abandoned the candidates, eventually losing almost all posts within four years. PASO today is the Texas version of the California Mexican-American Political Association (MAPA)—vote getters for the Democratic Party.

But in 1970 something new was added to the picture. La Raza Unida Party came out of a mass movement which developed as a result of the school walkouts in Cristal. Secondly, unlike PASO, La Raza Unida Party does not view itself as simply an electoral coalition to elect candidates, but as a political party in the full sense of the word—participating in strikes, boycotts of gringo-owned businesses, and the fight for community control of the schools.

In the spring of 1969, Cristal students raised a series of demands for improvement of the schools. The school board and the administration, however, succeeded in intimidating the students into capitulation.

The resentments and desire for change were not dissipated, however, and remained under the surface until December when again the Chicano students rallied around demands calling for bilingual education, participation in federal programs, such as a lunch program, better physical plant conditions, Chicano counselors, scholarships, the right to bring whatever literature they wanted into the schools, and an end to racist practices in selection of cheer leaders.

The result was one of the best organized and most successful school walkouts in Texas, and probably in the Southwest. Approximately 1,700 out of 2,300 students in grades one through 12 walked out, virtually closing all the schools in the city.

During the Christmas holidays, teachers came from surrounding areas, Chicano restaurants and beer halls closed and turned over their facilities for classroom space, and workers used their trucks for buses to transport students to a Chicano freedom school.

Many of the students who at first were not very political quickly began seeing things in their true light. The assistant principal of the high school, a Chicano, was mayor of the city. But it wasn't until they saw his reactionary role during the strike that they made the connection that he was also a *vendido* Chicano. Likewise with the Chicano teacher who also served on the city council. Thus, the real basis for the independent campaign of La Raza Unida Party came out of the desire of the parents and students to throw out the existing racist school board and city council.

But the involvement of the Chicano community quickly went beyond the issue of the schools. Students who were fired from their jobs in local stores for participating in mass marches and rallies were quickly backed up by the entire community which proceeded to boycott those stores.

But they didn't stop there. They contacted the parent company and applied for their own franchises to compete with the gringo stores. This resulted in the opening up of community-controlled Chicano businesses. Much of the financing for La Raza Unida Party and other community projects has come out of these small businesses.

Furthermore, to show their attitude toward Chicano *vendidos,* they boycotted the cleaners owned by the *vendido* Chicano school board member.

For about a week, the community went to the gringo cleaners in town to drive home the point that they would not tolerate one Chicano exploiting another. They then proceeded to set up a community cleaners. As result of these actions no more students were fired from their jobs.

Students put a coat of brown paint on the statue of Popeye, symbol of the spinach industry, that stands in front of City Hall. After two and a half months (17 actual school days) the school board capitulated.

This would have been a resounding victory in itself. But the Chicano community was not about to let up on its initiative. The high school students, together with the adults, mounted a voter registration campaign which put La Raza Unida Party on the ballot in three counties and netted an almost 100 percent registration among *mexicanos.*

This was a first in the history of Texas and without doubt in all of Aztlan. Maximum voter registration had varied from 15 to 30 percent, as is the case throughout Texas. The power of this burgeoning movement rightly frightened the local ruling class (100 percent gringo) who desperately tried to hinder the party legally.

Pablo Puente, Raza Unida candidate for city council, was ruled off the ballot in Cristal on the basis of a municipal law requiring candidates to own property. But they succeeded in having the law ruled unconstitutional in the federal courts. Puente was placed on the ballot and subsequently won the election along with Ventura Gonzales, Jr.

La Raza Unida Party also succeeded in forcing the Civil Rights Commission to come to Cristal to observe the elections so that the ranchers and agri businessmen could not blatantly intimidate people with threats of violence, loss of job for voting, or tamper with the ballots.

The real significance of the electoral victory for the Chicano community in Cristal was apparent at a board of education meeting I attended May 11. The meeting was held in the high school cafeteria, which was packed to overflowing with at least 250 people, predominantly Chicano.

While the board had previously consisted of five gringos and two Chicanos, it now consisted of three Raza Unida Party members, three gringos, and a Chicano who decided to move to the left, giving La Raza Unida Party a majority.

Jose Angel Gutierrez, new president of the board by a 4-3 vote, called the meeting to order.

Among the points discussed were the following: The school district would build houses for school employees, but rent would be based on a percentage of the individual's salary. From now on the school buses had to patronize all gas stations equally, including the Chicano gas stations, such as the one where board member Arturo Gonzales works (previously all business had gone to anglo-owned service stations). Employment of personnel for school maintenance must reflect the composition of the community which is 85 percent Chicano.

On all controversial points such as the denial of contracts for the fall to two racist teachers, the vote was four Chicanos, *si*, three gringos, *no*.

The most controversial point, however, was reflected in the minutes of a special meeting of the school board held on April 27. At this meeting Gutierrez suggested that Cristal accept transfers from the Uvalde School District. The motion itself was routine and harmless enough—on the surface. It touched off a heated fight and a lawsuit.

Uvalde is a town similar to Cristal about 40 miles to the north. It had been the scene of a militant strike by Chicano students around 14 demands such as: the right of teachers to be politically active without intimidation (Jorge Garcia, candidate of La Raza Unida Party for county judge, was fired from his teaching job); bilingual education; Chicano studies; more Chicano teachers; the right to bring any literature into the schools; revision of racist text books; and amnesty for striking students upon returning to school.

As in Cristal last December, the Uvalde school board refused to accept the demands of the students and used every means of intimidation, such as arrests, and denial of graduation to seniors, in an attempt to break the walkout.

The students in Uvalde, many of them MAYO activists, turned to Cristal for aid. Attorney Jesus Gamez, now the official attorney of both the Cristal school board and the city council, represented the students before the Uvalde board.

But aid was even more direct. Gutierrez held that if Uvalde wouldn't graduate the striking seniors, then Cristal High School would. The vote: four Chicanos, si, three gringos, no.

The defeated minority on the board then took the board of education to court. Jesus Gamez as the attorney for the board successfully won the case in court, and at the May 11 meeting, Gutierrez matter-of-factly presented the superintendent, a gringo at least twice his age, with a bill for $2,500 for services rendered by Attorney Gamez and told him "See that it's taken care of."

The complete defeat and humiliation of the gringo board members evoked a very apparent manifestation of pride and elation in the Chicano audience.

Toward the end of the board meeting, Armando Trevino, brother of walkout leader Mario Trevino, pointed out to the board that in a school that was 85 percent Chicano, 20 out of the 25 chosen for the National Honor Society were anglos. (The five Mexican-Americans were considered vendidos by the Chicano students.)

One anglo teacher denied that there had been any discrimination, that it was only because more Chicanos "weren't qualified." Armando Trevino replied, "This happened when I was in school, and it is still happening that qualified students are not elected by teachers . . . I would like the school board to look into it."

One of the gringo board members, typically, objected to discussing this point because it wasn't on the agenda. But this was a new school board now, a Chicano school board. Gutierrez quickly responded: "If there is any problem that any one student or parent has we will always incorporate it into the agenda."

He then added, "This board is not going to stand for any kind of discrimination. And any time an allegation of this nature is made we are going to look into it." A committee headed up by Gutierrez was formed on the spot to investigate the charge.

One could not help but be overcome by what was occurring in that room in South Texas. For the first time, the majority of the people, the Chicano people, were running the schools and beginning to mete out justice to racist teachers and administrators. The Chicano community was being heard before its own school board, rather than being insulted by a gringo board representing a tiny minority.

This reality has already resulted in important gains for the entire Chicano community. By a simple motion of the Chicano board, for example, free breakfast is now provided for every child in every school.

Gutierrez aims to improve the schools and make the education there relevant to Chicanos and thus cut down the 71 percent dropout rate.

The Chicano community has been faced with difficult problems from the beginning of this endeavor. Over thirty anglo faculty members, including some administrators, have resigned from the schools because of the victory of La Raza Unida Party and the actions taken by the board. In spite of this, the school board is moving ahead. Since the candidates of La Raza Unida Party assumed office on April 15, 1970 the following programs have been instituted in the Crystal City Independent School District:

1. Complete bi-lingual education from kindergarten through third grade.

2. A free breakfast and lunch program for every student in every school

3. Banning of the use of the culturally biased I.Q. tests and English Proficiency tests.

4. The use of relevant texts in the classroom, even though they are not "state approved," which relate the true contributions made to society by Chicanos. *El Espejo*, an anthology of Chicano writings, will be used as a high school English book, and Stan Steiner's *La Raza* will be a high school reader, as only two examples.

5. Student records have been declared *completely* confidential. Crystal City High School is the first secondary school in the United States which will no longer provide the Selective Service Board with any information. This is a reflection of the growing anti-war feelings of Chicanos who suffer one of the highest death rates in Vietnam. Crystal City suffered one of the first casualties when U.S. troops invaded Cambodia and Laos this past May.

All the changes in the schools would be too numerous to list here. Chicanos are being hired to fill vacancies at all levels from teachers, counselors, band director, to vice principals and principals. Even the school song has been changed to "Jalisco." Bi-cultural education (Chicano studies) will now become a reality in Crystal City. For the first time in its history Cristal has the possibility of providing real education for Chicano youth and adults alike.

The City Council in Cristal has also been taking action to improve the living conditions of the *mexicano.* The jurisdiction for law enforcement by the State police and the Texas Rangers has been revoked by the council. This will seriously hinder the ability of these two racist "law and order" outfits to harass the people of Crystal City within their own city limits. The all Chicano city police force is now required to undergo a community involvement training program headed up by La Raza Unida Party.

A 20 year contract of municipal tax exemption and services for the DelMonte Corporation was voided when La Raza Unida Party learned that the former city councilman who signed the contract had been under salary from DelMonte at the time. This will result in increased revenues for the city. Also recently, the Department of Housing and Urban Development granted $25,000 to the city for the formulation of a comprehensive city plan. Thus Chicanos will be in the position of determining priorities for city improvement. At present at least one-third of the Chicano community has no sewage service or paved streets. Also, when citizens now appear before the city council to ask for action on these and other problems they will find official business conducted in both Spanish and English, so that they may use their native tongue. Likewise in school board meetings.

If La Raza Unida Party is victorious in the county elections in November, a lawsuit may well follow which could bring in tax revenues to the predominantly Chicano counties. This is a result of the revelation that the oil companies in Texas have been cheating on taxes by digging wells and then capping them. As long as they are capped, they don't pay taxes. But they have received lucrative loans from banks on the basis of the value of the wells. It is easy to understand why the ruling powers in Texas are worried about the turn of events.

At almost every meeting of the school board since the elections, anglo lawyers, from as far away as Dallas and Houston, have been present in the hope of catching La Raza Unida board members on something. But the Chicano community is standing firm. An oppressed people have gotten a little taste of freedom and they are not about to let that go without a fight.

Rather than being intimidated, the new Chicano party is projecting an ambitious organizing drive which could see the party on the ballot in 26 South Texas counties by 1972.

As the result of an open nominating convention of La Raza Unida Party May 2, the gringo power structure (i.e., the Democratic Party) will face some 40 Chicano candidates in the Nov. 3 elections. La Raza Unida is running a full slate of candidates in the counties of Zavala, La Salle, Dimmit and Hidalgo for all county offices.

The giant step that has been taken in South Texas is an example of what can be done throughout Aztlan. There are scores of cities in Aztlan where the Chicano is a majority. But even in cities where the Chicano makes up only 10 or 20 percent of the population, significant gains can be made by breaking politically from the two capitalist parties. The fight for community control can be a dynamic force if properly led by an independent Chicano political party.

What is needed, however, is to *mobilize* people into action around such demands as community control of the schools in the Chicano community.

What is needed are Raza Unida parties everywhere throughout Aztlan. Such a party will have to continually struggle against those who want to channel every movement for social change into support of the gringo ruling class through the Democratic Party, on the one hand, and those ultra-leftists who consider electoral activity "meaningless" and therefore give a free hand to capitalist politicians in keeping the Chicano and Latino communities under illusions and "under control."

The success of La Raza Unida Party in South Texas should be an inspiration to create two, three, many Cristals. As Gutierrez pointed out on May 4, 1970: "Aztlan has begun, in the southwest part of Texas."

3. W. HEDGEPETH

Alcatraz: The Indian Uprising That Worked*

The island upjuts like a squat wart smothered in the mist of San Francisco Bay, calling attention to itself at relentless intervals with the ghastly bray of a foghorn—which must surely have sharpened the anguish of inmates up until the prison was abandoned seven years ago. But today, between the gaspings of the horn, come fresh sounds: the scuttle of children tossing Frisbees. Or snatches of rock music.

*W. Hedgepeth, "Alcatraz: The Indian Uprising That Worked," *Look* Magazine (June 2, 1970), pp. 44-45. Reprinted by permission of the Cowles Syndicate.

Or sporadic eerie
blendings of tribal
chants. Just before
Thanksgiving, a militant,
mostly collegiate Indian
band landed and laid
claim to this ugly clump
of crumbling buildings.
They found Alcatraz
had no running water;
no public facilities;
no game to hunt
or land to farm. Why,
it's like a reservation.
Like Home. It'll do us
just fine, thank you,
they said. And so they
stayed. Since 1887,
Indian acreage has
shrunk from 138 million
to 55 million today,
and probably to even
less tomorrow. By
nabbing this site, smiles
John, a 23-year-old
Sioux, "We've just
reversed the process."
Though the Great Spirit
would be hard put to
love Alcatraz, there
exists here a sense of
something exalted and
superbly primeval. The
walls are scrawled with
tribal hieroglyphics and
signs like, "THIS LAND
IS MY LAND," and
"CUSTER HAD IT
COMING." Scents of
victory fill the air. "It's

the best thing that's happened for Indian unity since Little Bighorn,'' exults an Apache, one of the 70 tribes represented. ''It's our Statue of Liberty,'' claims a Comanche. Whatever they call it, this invasion amounts to THE symbolic act of Indian awareness. The long-overdue adoption of Negro civil rights tactics. The beginning of the warpath! These Red Nationalists now want title to the island, to erect an educational-cultural center as well as to renew old customs, seek new rites, galvanize hard core pan-Indian consciousness, and turn the lighthouse into a huge totem pole. The Feds—finding it awkward to deal with Indians as real people—offered to make the place a park and hire a few of the Indians as forest rangers. The Indians replied by threatening to draw up their own deed ''by right of discovery''—the basis for Anglo claims to one-time Indian lands. John and I climb to the roof of the cellblock building. It is morning, and the baleful horn is wailing away. "Because of all the brainwashing," he says, "whites don't realize that Indians are very nonviolent, a very civilized people who believe you always take care of your own. Basic to all our religions is that you respect your brother's dreams." A sailboat in the bay begins veering toward the island. "Whites wouldn't have much trouble getting us off here. We're unarmed. And besides," he shrugs, "we believe it would be wise of us to make them look foolish." The sailboat is now passing just off the east bank. Five fat bottomed yachtsmen—who've apparently been partying all night—gape and point at the prison and all erupt with great guffaws when one of them, draped around the mast, puts his hand to his mouth, like Hollywood's idea of an

Injun Brave, and belts
out a loud: "WOO-
WOO-WOO-WOO-
WOO. . . ."

C. LIBERATION BY WHATEVER MEANS NECESSARY

Even before the assassination of Martin Luther King, Jr., in 1968—which Eldridge Cleaver called a requiem for nonviolence—the philosophy of passive resistance had begun to lose adherents in minority communities. Despite attempts at peaceful coercion and the faith-inspired efforts of nonviolent reformers, poverty, frustration, and discrimination remained the lot of most Blacks, Chicanos, and Native Americans. Some minority leaders lost patience with nonviolent efforts to reform a society they believed was committed to inertia at best and, at worst, to institutionalized repression of minority appeals for change. To some degree the tactics of nonviolence were replaced by the tactics of "self-defense" and a more aggressive affirmation of the potential of violence. Youthful, militant spokespeople vowed to defend themselves and their communities against police violence and political repression and pledged to seize their objectives by force if necessary. However, while the rhetoric of violence became the informal language of public rallies and declarations, armed confrontation was more often a slogan than a program, never appealing to large segments of minority communities. As the selections below indicate, however, there was an increase in aggressive activities in ghettos, barrios, and reservations across the nation.

Robert F. Williams—who in 1957 led the Black community of Monroe, North Carolina, in armed resistance against Ku Klux Klan assaults and who became a fugitive from state and federal authorities and an exile in Cuba—makes a compelling argument for militant self-defense tactics. Armed Blacks have not been the ones who introduced violence to America; it has long existed there, he asserts, and is at the heart of all racist systems. It is utter hypocrisy, therefore, for whites to preach pacifism to Blacks, who for three hundred years have been victimized by racist violence. While he does not reject the tactics of passive resistance, believing that Blacks must be flexible in their methods, Williams believes that they must arm and respond in kind to white assaults against them, their families, and their property. In this way, he concludes, "with violence working both ways constituted law will be more inclined to keep the peace."

Joseph L. Love, discusses the revolutionary efforts of the Alianza Federal de las Mercedes (Alliance of Free City States) to seize most of central and northern New Mexico and establish the independent Republic of Chama. Led by charismatic Reies López Tijerina, committed to the return of lands they claim rightfully belong to the native Hispano population, and impelled by deep religious convictions, the Alianza symbolizes militant Chicano liberation. Love explains how the movement grew out of the frustrations common among all "poor, dark-skinned and disaffected Americans," but emphasizes what he feels are differences between the rural, "peasant," millenarian Alianza movement and the urban, industrial Black revolts in Watts, Newark, and Detroit.

In the third selection Roy Bongartz examines the activism of Mad Bear, the indomitable upstate New York Tuscarora Indian. Determined to assert Indian sovereignty over tribal lands, to compel complete observance of Indian treaties from federal and state government, and to preserve Indian customs and identity against encroaching white society, Mad Bear has employed a variety of tactics, ranging from simply and delightfully outwitting white lawmen to aggressively driving them from Indian lands. Bongartz also describes the problems faced by the "new Indian." Differences over tactics between older tribal leaders and young activists have produced tensions and divisions in Indian communities; but through the efforts of people like Mad Bear, he concludes, the hopes for genuine Indian liberation have been revitalized.

1. ROBERT F. WILLIAMS

Self-Defense: An American Tradition*

The stranglehold of oppression cannot be loosened by a plea to the oppressor's conscience. Social change in something as fundamental as racist oppression involves violence. You cannot have progress here without violence and upheaval, because it's struggle for survival for one and a struggle for liberation for the other. Always the powers in command are ruthless and unmerciful in defending their position and their privileges. This is not an abstract rule to be meditated upon by Americans. This is a truth that was revealed at the birth of America, and has continued to be revealed many

*From Robert F. Williams, *Negroes with Guns.* Reprinted by permission of Third World Press, Chicago, Illinois.

times in our history. The principle of self-defense is an American tradition that began at Lexington and Concord. . . .

Why do the white liberals ask us to be non-violent? We are not the aggressors; we have been victimized for over 300 years! Yet nobody spends money to go into the South and ask the racists to be martyrs or pacifists. But they always come to the downtrodden Negroes, who are already oppressed and too submissive as a group, and they ask them not to fight back. There seems to be a pattern of some sort of strange coincidence of interest when whites preach a special doctrine to Negroes. Like the choice of theology when the plantation-owners saw to the Christianization of the slaves. Instead of the doctrines which produced the rugged aggressively independent and justice-seeking spirit that we associate with Colonial America as the New England Conscience, the slaves were indoctrinated in the most submissive "trust-your-master" pie-in-the-sky after-you-die form of Christianity.

It is because our militancy is growing that they spend hundreds of thousands of dollars to convert us into pacifists. Because our militancy is growing they come to us out of fear.

Of course, the respectable Negro leadership are the most outspoken exponents of non-violence. But if these people, especially the ministers, are such pure pacifists, why is it that so few, if any, criticize the war preparations of this country? Why is it that so few speak out against the Bomb? Isn't that the sort of preaching one expects and *hears* from sincere pacifists? The responsible Negro leadership is pacifist in so far as its one interest is that we do not fight white racists; that we do not "provoke" or enrage them. They constantly tell us that if we resort to violent self-defense we will be exterminated. They are not stopping violence—they are only stopping defensive violence against white racists out of a fear of extermination.

This fear of extermination is a myth which we've exposed in Monroe. We did this because we came to have an active understanding of the racist system and we grasped the relationship between violence and racism. The existence of violence is at the very heart of a racist system. The Afro-American militant is a "militant" because he defends himself, his family, his home, and his dignity. He does not *introduce* violence into a racist social system—the violence is already there, and has always been there. It is precisely this unchallenged violence that allows a racist social system to perpetuate itself. When people say that they are oppsed to Negroes "resorting to violence" what they really mean is that they are opposed to Negroes defending themselves and challenging the exclusive monopoly of violence practiced by white racists. We have shown in Monroe that with violence working *both ways* constituted law will be more inclined to keep the peace. . . .

2. JOSEPH L. LOVE

La Raza: Mexican Americans in Rebellion*

In early June, 1967 a group of Spanish-speaking Americans who call themselves the *Alianza Federal de Mercedes* (Federal Alliance of Land Grants) and claim that they are the legal and rightful owners of millions of acres of land in Central and Northern New Mexico, revolted against the governments of the United States of America, the State of New Mexico, and Rio Arriba (Up River) County, formally proclaiming the Republic of Rio Chama in that area.

On June 5 an armed band of forty or more *Aliancistas* attacked the Tierra Amarilla courthouse, released 11 of their members being held prisoner, and wounded a deputy sheriff and the jailer. They held the sheriff down on the floor with a rifle butt on his neck, searched for the District Attorney (who wasn't there) and for an hour and a half controlled the village (population 500). They took several hostages (later released when the getaway car stuck in the mud).

Despite some of the melodramatic and occasionally comic opera aspects of the affair, both the members of the *Alianza* and the local and state authorities take it very seriously. This is not the first time the Aliancistas have violated federal and state law, attempting to appropriate government property (in October, 1966, for instance, their militants tried to take over Kit Carson National Forest, and to expel the rangers found there as trespassers); nor is it the only time their activities have resulted in violence. In this case the state government reacted frantically, sending in armored tanks, 300 National Guardsmen and 200 state police. They rounded up dozens of Spanish-speaking persons, including many women and children, and held them in a detention camp, surrounded with guns and soldiers, for 48 hours. The raiders got away, but in several days all of them—including their fiery leader, former Pentecostal preacher Reies López Tijerina—were captured.

It has become common to associate these actions of the Alianza with other riots or revolts by poor, dark-skinned and disaffected Americans—with Watts, Newark and Detroit. Tijerina himself helps reinforce this impression by occasionally meeting with, and using the rhetoric of, some leaders of the black urban revolt. The fact is, however, that the Alianza movement is really a unique example in the United States of a "primitive revolt" as defined by

*Joseph L. Love, "La Raza: Mexican Americans in Rebellion," *TRANS-action*, Vol. VI (February, 1969), pp. 35-41.

Eric Hobsbawm, a kind almost always associated with developing nations, rather than advanced industrialized countries—and which includes such diverse phenomena as peasant anarchism, banditry, and millenarianism (the belief that divine justice and retribution is on the side of the rebels and that the millenium is at hand). The attack on the courthouse, in fact, had more in common with the millenarian Sioux Ghost Dance cult of 1889-91 than with Watts.

As the Aliancistas see it, they are not violating any legitimate law. The territory around Rio Arriba belongs to them. They demand the return of lands—primarily common lands—taken from *Hispano* communities, most of which were founded in the Spanish colonial era. Their authority is the famous *Recopilación de leyes de los Reinos de Indias* (*Compilation of Laws of the Kingdoms of the Indies,* generally shortened to *The Laws of the Indies*) by which the Crown of Castile governed its New World possessions. They claim that according to these laws common lands were inalienable—could not be taken away. Since most of such lands were in existence when the Treaty of Guadalupe Hidalgo was signed in 1848—and since in that treaty the United States government pledged itself to respect property rights established under Mexican rule—the Alianza insists that those land grants remain valid. The members speak primarily of common lands, rather than individual heirs, and define the towns in question as "closed corporations, with membership restricted to the descendants and heirs of the founding fathers and mothers"—that is, themselves.

The Alianza's interpretations of law and history are, of course, selective, and tend to ignore inconvenient facts and other interpretations. It claims that *The Laws of the Indies* were not abrogated when "Mexico invaded and occupied New Mexico," nor when the United States did the same in 1846. The Aliancistas are the early settlers, the legitimate heirs.

THE MAXIMUM LEADER

The Alianza and its actions cannot really be understood without knowledge of its background and its leader. First, the people from whom it draws its members and its strength—the Mexican-American minority in the US—and specifically New Mexico; second, the rapid economic changes throughout the area since World War II that have so greatly affected their lives; and last but surely not least the dynamism, determination and charisma of Reies Tijerina, without whom the movement would probably never have arisen.

In the 1960 census Mexican-Americans, though they made up only 2.3 percent of the population of the United States, constituted 12 percent of the population of Texas, New Mexico, Arizona, Colorado and California—almost three and a half million persons.

Generally they are a submerged minority that have only lately begun to articulate their demands. They formed "Viva dennedy" committees in 1960; since then three Mexican-American Congressmen have gone to the House, and New Mexico's Joseph Montoya sits in the Senate. The end of the *bracero* program in 1964 opened the way to a successful unionization drive among agricultural workers; and the celebrated "Huelga" strike in Delano, California in 1965 was a symptom of and stimulus to the new awakening. The federal and state poverty programs, and the example of the Negro revolt, have also undoubtedly had their effects.

New Mexico is a distinctive area of Latin culture. It was the last state in the Southwest to be overwhelmed by Anglo-American civilization, and is the only one with two official languages. The Mexican-American population has been traditionally located along the Rio Grande and its tributaries, and extends into southern Colorado.

Until recent years, the Mexican Americans of New Mexico have been isolated from other members of *la raza* (the Mexican-American "race"). Texas and California have more than 80 percent of the Mexican-American population of the Southwest, yet most of these crossed over from Mexico after 1900, or descended from persons who did. But, the New Mexican *Hispanos* (the local name) have resided there for many generations, and some strains go back to the seventeenth century (Santa Fe was founded in 1609). Moreover, large numbers of English-speaking Americans only began to compete seriously for rural property in the 1880's, and appropriation continued into the 1920's.

In the 1960 census New Mexico had a higher percentage of "native born of native parents" than any other Southwestern state (87.4 percent). The mobility of Hispano males between 1955 and 1960 (defined in terms of changing residence) was lower in New Mexico than elsewhere. In 1960 New Mexico had the highest percentage of rural non-farm inhabitants with Spanish surnames.

In absolute numbers New Mexico's Anglo population was for many years roughly in balance with the Hispano. It is now surging ahead as a result of the economic boom which began with the atomic testing program of World War II. In no other Southwestern state was the disparity between the growth of Anglo and Latin populations greater from 1950 to 1960 than in New Mexico, where the former increased by 59.1 percent and the latter by a mere 8.1 percent. Yet in spite of this, New Mexico in 1960 still had a greater proportion of Mexican-Americans than any other state: about two-sevenths of its inhabitants had Spanish surnames, compared to one-seventh of Texans, and one-eleventh of Californians.

The job situation for the Hispanos of New Mexico has also worsened more rapidly than in other states. In 1950 male Mexican-Americans had a greater percentage of jobless in California, Colorado, and Arizona than in New Mexico; but ten years later the Hispanos of New Mexico had the dubious distinction of leading the list.

As some observers have noted, in certain ways New Mexico resembles Quebec: Both are centers of Latin culture founded in the seventeenth century, and both are subject to an increasing degree of Anglo domination. And like the Quebeckers, the New Mexicans have their fringe-group separatists—the *Alianza Federal de Mercedes.*

The Alianza was born in 1963, partly to combat the alienation and isolation of the Hispanos, but specifically to reclaim lands taken from the Spanish-speaking population since 1848. In colonial New Mexico (1598-1821), Spanish officials made land grants of indeterminate size to both individuals and to communities as commons, and the latter were respected through the era of Mexican rule (1821-1848). When Anglo-Americans began to enter New Mexico in significant numbers in the 1880's, they found it possible to wrest lands from the native inhabitants through the legal and financial devices of land taxes, mortgages, and litigation over disputed titles. By 1930, through legal and extralegal means, the Anglos had taken over most of the farming and ranching land in the state, and the state and federal governments appropriated much of the common lands that had previously belonged to the incorporated towns and villages. The Spanish-speaking population ultimately lost 1.7 million acres of community lands and two million acres in private holdings. The Hispanos sporadically reacted to this process by forming secret societies and vigilante groups; but at most this constituted harassment rather than effective resistance.

The Alianza now demands the return of these lands.

Yet in all probability, the Alianza would not exist but for the efforts of a single man, a leader who devotes his life to his cause, and inspires his followers to do likewise. Reies López Tijerina is a man of rare charisma who is most in his element when haranguing a large crowd. Of average height, he seems to have great physical strength as he grasps a microphone with one sinewy arm and gesticulates artfully and furiously with the other. He sometimes shouts violently as he asks rhetorical questions of his audience in Spanish—the language he uses by preference—and gets "Sí!" and "No!" bellowed back in appropriate cadences. The author witnessed a Tijerina performance last fall on the steps of the state capitol in Austin, Texas, where the Alianza leader told a group of Mexican-American Labor Day marchers he supported their demand for a state minimum wage of $1.25 an hour, but did so "with shame." Why should Mexican-Americans in Texas ask so little of the Anglos, whose government had repeatedly broken the Treaty of Guadalupe Hidalgo?

Reies Tijerina uses a demagogic style before a crowd, but he holds the tenets of his faith with unshakeable conviction: "It's something in me that must come out," Tijerina proclaims. His followers regard him with awe. He is "Caudillo" (leader) of the Alianza, but disclaims any desire to be dictator. He points out that a Supreme Council has ultimate control—though he, clearly, makes the decisions. It seems obvious that no one could step into his shoes, nor has anyone been groomed to do so. In any event Tijerina has no doubt that his followers require strong and able leadership. He justifies this by arguing that the Hispanos are a "young" race. They were "born," he explains, by virtue of a royal decree in 1514 allowing Spaniards to marry Indians; the term "Hispano" or "Spanish American" therefore can generally be equated with "mestizo." This young race is still learning, painfully, how to defend itself and requires strong direction. It is not an ancient and clever people like the Jews, he says.

Recognizing the diverse historical experiences of Texas, New Mexico, and California, the Caudillo realizes that his constituency for the foreseeable future will be limited to New Mexico. He does believe, however, that the land grants to Mexican-Americans in California can still be identified and claimed like those of New Mexico.

It is no coincidence that Tijerina's style and language recall Pentecostal protestantism. He has been a minister in the Assembly of God, and was an itinerant revival preacher for many years to Mexican-Americans throughout the Southwest.

But, unlike the vast majority of his followers, he was not born in New Mexico but in Texas ("A prophet is not without honor save in his own country"). One of seven children of a migrant farm family, once so desperate that they were reduced to eating field rats, he picked crops and preached in Illinois and Michigan as well as in Texas and Arizona. He did not settle in New Mexico until 1960; and, with his five brothers, formed the Alianza three years later.

The quasi-religious fervor of Tijerina has strongly shaped the aspirations and style of the Alianza. However, there is greater emphasis on Old Testament justice than New Testament love. *Justicia* is a word frequently on the Caudillo's lips.

The Alianza now claims to have 30,000 dues-paying members paying at least $2.00 per month. A scholar guesses that 10,000 may be closer to the true figure. It seems clear that Tijerina's computation includes sympathizers or at least persons who have only occasionally contributed funds.

As with some sectors of the American Negro movement, the Alianza's programs began with an emphasis on litigation; and when that failed, frustration and a disposition toward violence emerged.

In April 1966 the "President and Founder" of the Alianza journeyed to Spain in order to gather materials on the registration of New Mexican land grants in the colonial era; from such documents he hoped to generate a strong legal case to present in federal courts.

In July Tijerina presented a petition to the Governor of New Mexico, Jack Campbell, and stated, "We do not demand anything. We just want a full investigation of the issue." Yet Governor Campbell would do little more than receive Tijerina and hear him out.

In January 1967, the Caudillo, one of his brothers, and a self-styled legal expert in the Alianza named Gerry Noll made a trip to Washington, D.C., where they "limited" their claims to 500,000 acres in the Kit Carson National Forest and to an area around the city of Albuquerque. He only obtained a brief hearing with a State Department attorney and a sympathetic interview with New Mexico's Senator Montoya.

In 1966 the Alianza had already begun to give up hope of legal redress. The Supreme Council of the Alianza "passed a resolution of non-confidence in the Courts of the State of New Mexico and of the United States of America" because of "corruption" and "low standards of knowledge of law."

ALIANCISTAS PROCLAIM INDEPENDENT REPUBLIC

On October 22, 1966 the Aliancistas proclaimed the existence of the Republic of San Joaquín del Río de Chama (in Rio Arriba County) with Tijerina as "city attorney" (*procurador*) of the community; they simultaneously attempted to take over Kit Carson Forest, which covers most of the county. They arrested U.S. Forest Rangers for trespassing, decided to print hunting and fishing licenses, and commandeered government vehicles. The rebels were quickly dispersed by local authorities, and Tijerina and four lieutenants were charged on counts of assault, converting government property to private use, and conspiracy.

Demonstrations and protest meetings continued. On January 15, 1967 the Alianza declared it would seek redress in the United Nations if the U.S. Congress failed to act. On April 17 several hundred Aliancistas paraded before the State House in Santa Fe, and Reies Tijerina, out on bond, delivered an ominous message: "We will . . . issue to the public and the federal government and the world the last human legal notice exposing the truth. . . .The government is being warned and advised if anybody is found trespassing on these land grants they will be arrested and punished. . . ."

At the beginning of June the District Attorney of Santa Fe, Alfonso Sánchez, expressed concern about the "communist philosophy" of the Alianza and alleged that Aliancistas were amassing "machine guns, M-1 rifles, and 15,000 rounds" of ammunition. Eleven members of the Alianza were promptly arrested and jailed in Tierra Amarilla, an Alianza stronghold and the seat of Rio Arriba County.

The reaction was swift and violent: On June 5, as noted, the Aliancistas launched their revolt and attacked the Tierra Amarilla courthouse. This time, when caught, the Caudillo and his principal aides were charged with kidnapping, three counts of conspiracy to commit murder, and bombing a public building (the courthouse). Despite the gravity of the charges, Tijerina and some of his men were released on bond after six weeks in prison. The failure of the attack by no means dampened the spirits of the Aliancistas.

In the months following, Tijerina traveled throughout the Southwest to gain backing. He found it, both in radical organizations of Mexican-Americans and Negroes, and in some Mexican-American associations with more traditional reformist leadership.

On October 15, Tijerina was in Los Angeles, linking his cause to the peace movement at an anti-war rally. Labeling the United States' involvement in Vietnam "the most criminal in the history of mankind," he contacted radical Negro and Mexican-American groups in the Los Angeles area. One week later, at a convention of the Alianza de Mercedes on October 21, Tijerina announced that a "Treaty of Peace, Harmony, and Mutual Assistance" had been contracted between his organization and SNCC, CORE, and the Black Panthers. The Caudillo also obtained statements of support from the Crusade for Justice, a Mexican-American organization of slumdwellers in Denver, and from MAPA, an important Mexican-American political group in California.

While gathering support from non-Anglo groups outside New Mexico in the here and now, Tijerina and his deputies have not discouraged the movement's latent tendencies towards millenarianism* and belief in special divine favor back home on the Upper Rio Grande. During the raid at Tierra

*Nancie González was the first to note millenarian tendencies in the Alianza.

Amarilla, several Aliancistas witnessed the appearance of a double rainbow, a sure sign of God's grace. According to others, the Caudillo is the prophet of Montezuma who will miraculously return in the imminent future to punish the Anglos for their appropriation of Hispano lands.

Another legend has it that a leader will come "from the east" and expel the foreigners who took the Mexican-Americans' lands. (Tijerina fits, since Texas is east of New Mexico.)

In the *"Corrido de Rio Arriba,"* which appeared shortly after the June raid, the balladeer told his audience that when bullets started flying

"Las mujeres y los niños iban corriendo y llorando,
Y en este instante pensamos Que el mundo se iba acabando."
("Women and children ran about in tears
And at that moment we thought the world was coming to an end.")

Although the "free city-states" which Tijerina hopes to erect are of this world, they clearly represent a sort of secular paradise, a recaptured golden age, somewhat along the lines prescribed in *The Laws of the Indies.* The inhabitants will be able to do any work they please, explains the Caudillo; but most will be herdsmen using the common lands *(ejidos)* of the pueblos. Tijerina himself will simply become City Attorney of the Republic of Chama.

If "la raza" is specially favored and will come into its millenium, why is it suffering so now? This is explained as the result of a "fall from grace" which occurred after the Anglo-American invasion of New Mexico in 1846 and the collusion of certain Hispanos with the alien conquerors. An allegorical mural at Alianza headquarters tells the story: A sacred temple in the center of the mural represents paradise entwined by a serpent, which also clutches three figures symbolizing the oppressed races—the Negro, the Indian, and the Hispano. The snake personifies the "Santa Fe Ring"—the Anglo and upper-class Hispano politicians who appropriated the poor Hispanos' lands in the 1880's and later. Figures on the right side, representing the People, begin to emerge from the Darkness and a reptile-devouring secretary bird, personifying Justice, arrives to attack the snake. At the top of the canvas is a rainbow (a symbol of God's blessing) and the phrase "Justicia." Just below this emblem is the City of Justice, which will once more be reconstituted on earth.

Yet there is a sinister element in the apocalypse which must precede the millenium: Anglos must be driven out. And Hispanos will be judged by whether they aided, stood aside from, or hindered the cause. Those who hindered will be treated harshly.

Gerry Noll, the Caudillo's lieutenant, has proclaimed as part of the Alianza creed:

> . . . KNOW YE that We have exclusive and supreme jurisdiction within [New Mexico] over all persons and property situated therein. . . ."
> We cannot afford to permit the present status quo to be maintained without actually destroying Our independence and autonomy. Consequently, We must take measures calculated to curtail the activities of any aggressors with the utmost dispatch . . . We shall enter troops into these territories to restore Our authority . . . woe to him who obeys the orders of the aggressor, for he shall be punished without mercy. . . .
> THEREFORE KNOW YE that We shall commence to liberate Our kingdoms, realms, and dominions . . . We shall not take any prisoners of war, but shall take only war criminals and traitors and try [them] by a military tribunal and execute them.

At Tijerina's direction, the October 1967 convention of the Alianza unanimously set forth a weird dynastic claim: Gerry Noll was henceforth transformed into "Don Barne Quinto Cesar, King-Emperor of the Indies," the legitimate descendant of Ferdinand VII of Spain.

DYING IS PART OF A KING'S DAY'S WORK

In November Tijerina, "Don Barne," and several other Aliancistas stood trial for the charges stemming from the invasion of Kit Carson Forest in 1966. During the trial it was revealed that Noll's real name was Gerald Wayne Barnes, convicted of bank robbery in 1945, grand larceny in 1949, forgery in 1953, and third-degree assault in 1963. Found guilty, Noll and Tijerina were sentenced to three and two years respectively. At the trial Don Barne declared, "I am willing to die for my country and for my people. This is part of my job as king and all in a day's work." When sentenced in mid-December he retorted to the court, "It is I who make the laws—not the United States of America."

While waiting trial on the multiple charges of the June '67 raid and appealing against the decision in the first case, Tijerina and his co-defendants were once more released on bond. On January 3, 1968, again in Tierra Amarilla, Deputy Sheriff Eulogio Salazar was kidnapped and beaten to death. Governor David Cargo, Campbell's successor, immediately revoked the bonds. Protests rapidly poured into the Governor's office from SNCC, MAPA, and other organizations, and a short time later Tijerina was out on bail again. . . .

Tijerina had hoped to run for governor in the November 1968 elections, but the New Mexico Supreme Court disallowed his candidacy in October because of his conviction the previous year. Meanwhile the second (Tierra Amarilla) trial took place, during which Tijerina dramatically dismissed his lawyers and conducted his own defense. In mid-December his self-confidence was justified by his acquittal of kidnapping and two lesser counts. Other charges against him and nine other defendants had yet to come before the courts at the end of 1968.

But the real historical and sociological meaning of the Alianza cannot be solely understood in terms of its current embroilments or recent history in New Mexico. Most of the literature on the movement, so far, has dealt with the spectacular, bizarre, or violent elements involved; but the roots of primitive revolt go far back.

Since the enclosure movement began in Europe in the twelfth century, there have been scores of peasant revolts. Many sought the restoration of common lands taken by nobles and gentry.

In medieval Spain, many villages owned herds and land in common, and a number of these arrangements survived as late as the Spanish Civil War. These towns had once enjoyed special legal sanctions called *fueros,* by which they could themselves decide whether or not to enforce royal decrees and pay taxes.

One historian has written that "The village communities spontaneously developed an extensive system of municipal services, to the point of their sometimes reaching an advanced stage of communism." A scheme was proposed in 1631 to "nationalize all pasturage and establish each peasant with sufficient head of sheep and cattle to support him." In 1633 the Crown tried to implement this project by regulating tenancy and fixing rents in perpetuity, making leases irrevocable and hereditary, and setting up regulation commissions. Though the plan failed, the demands of shepherds for adequate grazing land were part of the Hispanic tradition to which Tijerina appeals and went to Spain to study.

One student of Mexican-American culture, anthropologist Nancie González, writes that ". . . Virtually all contemporary accounts by social scientists comment upon the people's stated preference for this occupation. . . ." This preference explains why in Tijerina's Utopia the common lands are so highly valued. The Chama region, where the Tierra Amarilla revolt broke out, was principally a sheep-grazing area until after the Second World War.

What has occurred in New Mexico has been a breakdown of the traditional society, the ripping of the fabric of Hispano culture. In 1950, 41 percent of the Spanish-surname population in the state lived in urban areas; but by 1960, 61 percent did. Many of those moving to the cities (especially to Albuquerque) were ill prepared for their new way of life. In 1956 one investigator found that 834 out of 981 women in Albuquerque who received Aid to Dependent Children had Spanish surnames.

While the number of Anglo-Americans rapidly increased in New Mexico after World war II, the Mexican-American populations was almost static, the high birth rate being offset by emigration to California. Consequently by 1960 the Anglo population in the state constituted almost two-thirds of the whole.

The legal structures of a modern capitalist society had by the late 1930's wrecked the traditional land-tenure patterns of the Upper Rio Grande. In 1940 Dr. George Sanchez reported that in Taos County "65 percent of the private lands represent land grants which have been subdivided or otherwise lost to the communities and families to which they were originally assigned. Of the original nine *mercedes* in Taos County, four were community grants and five were lands granted to individuals. . . . This cornerstone of Taos' economy has been destroyed by taxation and by uncontrolled exploitation." Furthermore, "Commercial livestock operators have acquired [the Hispano's] land grants and compete with him for grazing leases and permits on public lands. Exorbitant fees, taxes, and forced sales have crowded him out of his former grazing domain."

For a time the full impact of these changes were softened by the booming war and atomic energy economy in New Mexico, and by the fact that the National Forest Service seems to have acted as a surrogate patrón for the Hispano shepherd. Until drought in the 1960's forced a cutback, the Hispano could still obtain the use of federal lands for pasturing his livestock.

Rio Arriba County was one of the areas least affected by the state's economic growth. In 1960 it had the highest percentage of rural non-farm populations of all New Mexico's counties (91.3 percent). It ranked high in native-born inhabitants, and low in the percentage of migrants. It had the third lowest median education and the fifth lowest median family income. In Rio Arriba and the other northern counties where the Spanish-speaking population predominates, the average per capita income in 1967 was less than $1,000, compared to the state average of $2,310 and the national average of $2,940. Furthermore, according to Governor Cargo, "11,000 of 23,000 residents of Rio Arriba County are on welfare rolls." The 1960 census showed that county with the state's highest rate of unemployment—15.1 percent—almost three times the state average.

GOVERNMENT CONTROLS GRAZING LANDS

But it is not only unemployment that makes the residents of Rio Arriba dependent on federal and state largesse—72.1 percent of all land still available for grazing is owned by the US government in Kit Carson Forest. And what the government grants, it can, and sometimes does, also refuse.

The disintegration of the traditional Hispano community seems well underway, and Tijerina articulates widely-shared feelings that his people do not want to assimilate into Anglo culture. He also rejects relief as demoralizing to its recipients, stating again and again, "We will no longer take powdered milk in exchange for justice." Recent increases in welfare assistance may actually have aggravated the situation by raising the Hispanos' hopes for greater improvement.

Reaction to social disintegration can take many forms, and the Hispanic religious tradition—plus Tijerina's own background as a Pentecostal preacher—have helped channel it into millenarianism. In the 1930's a religious group called the Allelujahs, an Hispano version of the Holy Rollers, became popular, and before it faded out as many as half the people of some northern New Mexico communities had joined, taking part in religious services in which "Passages from the Revelation of St. John are favorite texts [according to a 1937 report], and lead to frenzies of religious ecstasy." The Allelujah experience has helped prepare the ground. So perhaps have the *Penitentes*, a lay brotherhood of Hispano mystics and self-flagellants that traces its origins back to the colonial era.

When the Alianza failed to obtain redress through the courts, the hope for and belief in extra-legal and supernatural means of relief—natural enough in the presence of the charismatic and fiery Tijerina—became exacerbated. When the National Forest Service recently cut back the use of grazing lands because of drought, the Hispanos were the hardest hit—and Tijerina was at hand to transform frustration into action. The frequency of millenarianism when belief in and identity with the dominant society are lost has been well documented in sociological literature. The Alianza constitutes an almost classic case.

Yet there is a "modern" dimension to the Alianza, and this is a direct outgrowth of its appearance in an industrial society with rapid transcontinental communications and ever-vigilant news media. The Alianza fits the requirements of a "primitive rebellion" or "revitalization movement," but its links with urban radical and reformist groups outside New Mexico show its potential for evolving into something more modern. Thus there are two distinct dimensions of the movement—the "primitive," rural, grassroots constituency on the tributaries of the upper Rio Grande; and the "modern," urban, nationally-connected leadership in Albuquerque. The "visible" media-oriented sector is modern, but the "invisible" millenarian sector is not.

Tijerina's primary concern is still regaining lost community lands, as his action at the Poor People's March showed. The hunger for community lands—the *ejidos*—remains the basis for the "real" movement, despite manifestos of solidarity with the Black Panthers and denunciations of the war in Vietnam.

The ignorance of government officials of the basic nature of the movement is almost monumental. They tend to explain the Alianza away by easy, modern clichés. Some find in the references to common lands the spore of modern communism.

At the November 1967 trial, the prosecuting attorney declared, "This is not a social problem we're trying. This is a criminal problem." Even some sympathetic observers have used singularly inappropriate terms. Tom Wicker of the *New York Times* and Congressman Joseph Resnick, chairman of the House Agriculture Subcommittee on Rural Development, have both referred to Rio Arriba County as a "rural Watts."

But Rio Arriba has little in common with Watts. The majority of Aliancistas, the rural grassroots, are not industrial proletarians but primitive rebels—peasants reacting and striking back in millenarian fashion against the modernization that is tearing their society apart.

3. ROY BONGARTZ

The New Indian*

A massive brown man sits at a table in the doorway of a small cinder-block garage, writing a letter in a bold, florid hand: "Dear Mr. President." It is a modest setting indeed for a leader about to set up a new American nation. At the sight of a visitor, he bounces to his feet, and reaches out a welcoming hand, a broad grin on the wide, heavy-featured face with the slashing scar on one check. This is the indomitable Mad Bear, main arrow of a new movement to find a true American Indian identity.

*Roy Bongartz, "The New Indian," *Esquire*(August, 1970), pp. 107-9, 125-26. Copyright © 1970 by Roy Bongartz. First published in *Esquire* magazine. Reprinted by permission of Cyrilly Abels, literary agent.

The key word is: Unite. The fact that Indians, routed and demoralized by the white man, have never before joined together in any sort of continent-wide alliance doesn't worry Mad Bear a bit. All over the U.S. and Canada he spreads word of an Indian rebirth: as the white man destroys his own world with guns and garbage, the Indians will inherit the land once again. The sympathetic nationalist revolutionaries in India, in South Africa, in Aden, in Brazil, in Cuba, in Yugoslavia, in Taiwan, in Japan have been amazed to hear this forty-two-year-old, 284-pound Tuscarora merchant seaman, while on shore visits in port cities, assure them that the traditional solidarity of the Iroquois Confederacy—the Six Nations of New York State and eastern Canada—is reaching out, someday to become fifty or a hundred Indian nations in one.

Last summer he organized a caravan of Indians from some sixty tribes that barnstormed through Iroquois reservations like a traveling circus, encouraging the locals to see a wide, bright future for themselves and their distant brothers, in spite of the fact that the outside world still insists there cannot be *real* Indians in the East anymore. All day, in the traditional longhouses, in an atmosphere heavy with emotion, they poured out their hearts to one another, arguing about Red Power and their No. 1 problem, the White Man; with a rare exception, non-Indians, especially government "spies," were kept out. Mad Bear, a prophet honored "save in his own country," is not a chief of his own Tuscarora nation, but he says this just gives him more freedom to act, and he wears the deer antlers of a chief anyway. In any case, he is the acknowledged leader of tradition-minded Iroquois who hope their way of life may survive, and elsewhere his influence is growing fast; Western Indians accept the leadership of the Iroquois (Onondaga, Mohawk, Seneca, Oneida, Cayuga, and Tuscarora), with their advanced political organization and written constitution. Mad Bear, articulate and sparkling with imagination and humor, is able to deal with the white man on his own terms, yet he remains sensitive to the central peacefulness of the Indian mind, which, despite his rambunctious nature, he shares.

This goal of a separate, unified Indian nation has come out of hundreds of battles to defend Indian rights, mostly involving land grabs; the Indian is fast realizing that with those last remaining bits of real estate goes his identity. In the past two decades, Mad Bear has been in an awful lot of these fights. In 1957 he helped the Mohawks fight the New York State income tax on the grounds of Indian sovereignty by leading some four hundred Indians from the St. Regis reservations into court at Massena, and tearing up summonses issued to Indians for tax refusal. When a trooper tried to arrest him for contempt, Indian women shoved the lawman out of the courtroom and knocked him down a flight of stairs, then made off safely with Mad Bear, to meet later at the longhouse for a ceremonial burning of the tattered summonses.

Then, in 1958, back at home on the Tuscarora reservation outside Niagara Falls, there came a greater threat. Without consulting the Indians, Robert Moses, chairman of the Power Authority of the State of New York, had condemned 1383 Indian acres for a reservoir in a $705,000,000 power project. Says Mad Bear, "The land is your mother. You cannot sell your mother." Indians blocked surveyors' transits and deflated their car tires. When they returned the next day, escorted by over a hundred state troopers and sheriff's deputies, some two hundred Indians fought them. Women scratched, and children as young as four years tackled the invaders. Mad Bear, with another, was jailed for unlawful assembly; released the next day, they kept up the resistance. Guns were fired over surveyors' heads; kids threw firecrackers at them. An eighty-three-year-old woman shoved a marshal into a creek. The Authority tapped Indian leaders' telephones; the Indians promptly switched to the Tuscarora language. The Authority sent out false news for television that the Indians had given up, but nobody believed it. When bulldozing began, Mad Bear called thirty Indian operators off the job. "We have no more time for stalling and debate," said Moses, and made a final offer of $3,000,000 to the one hundred seventy-five Indians involved. The not very rich Indians knew perfectly well that this was Moses' final offer, and they turned it down. And in the new ruling in early 1959, the Federal Power Commission said the Indians could not be compelled to sell. At the time, the Buffalo *Courier-Express* commented that "Mad Bear, more than anyone else, was responsible for the tribe's decision."

A month later, Mad Bear was up at the Six Nations Reserve in Brantford, Ontario, fomenting a week-long revolution in which the traditionalists captured and occupied the Council House—a one-story government and administration center built something like an old-fashioned schoolhouse—that had been seized by Mounties in 1924 and turned over to government-appointed Indians who were working toward assimilation of all Indians into the general population. The rebels ousted the "official" Iroquois and rounded up, arrested, and disarmed a dozen Mounties—Mad Bear had issued "I.P." ("Iroquois Patrol") armbands to a number of young insurgents. Mad Bear likes to follow a certain protocol, so had warned Ellen Fairclough, the Canadian commissioner for Indian affairs, beforehand of the coming attack; according to the press, she had laughed and told them to go ahead, that she would keep order anyway. Seven tractable Mounties were released on their promise to get off the Indian land, and were given back their guns at the border. Five defiant ones were kept half a day in a damp basement awaiting a hearing before the chiefs upstairs; then they were let go, too. Mad Bear and his junta held out for a week. Then at three o'clock one morning some fifty armed Mounties surrounded the Council House with fifteen cars, cleared out the rebels, and clubbed and jailed three of the Indian patrol. More stimulated than dismayed by this defeat, Mad Bear went home. (Mad Bear operates as freely in Canada as he does at home in the U. S.; since Iroquois lands extend to both sides of the border, he's in his own territory in either country, and has the treaty of 1784 to prove it.)

Fired up, Mad Bear next joined Indians from all over the U. S. in a march on the Bureau of Indian Affairs in Washington protesting a termination bill that was to do away with reservations. (Several tribes were "dumped" this way before the law was changed; now Canada is threatening the same move, which traditional Indians plainly call genocide because it does away with tribal rolls, with Indian identity altogether.) With a posse of some three hundred Indians, Mad Bear tried to make a citizen's arrest on the Indian Commissioner, but officials cleverly reminded them that they had been denying their citizenship, thus making a "citizen's" arrest doubtful. So the Indians got a cooperative retired U. S. Army general to try to make the arrest for them, but they failed. "The commissioner hid under his desk," says Mad Bear. Picket lines surrounded the Bureau, and when one Indian, Chief Ray Johnson, of Canby, California, dropped dead of a heart attack, Mad Bear saw a rare opportunity for bringing public sympathy to the Indian cause. Johnson's body was paraded in a U-Haul trailer with a sign reading: "Administrative Murder." Bureau officials told the Indians they couldn't drive around with a body like that, and offered to handle funeral arrangements, but the Indians refused, and Mad Bear found a cut-rate Negro undertaker who would embalm Johnson's body for sixty dollars. When this was done, the Bureau offered to fly the body back to California, agreeing to take along Johnson's wife and his four dogs as well—officials were anxious to see the last of Chief Johnson. Instead of accepting the offer, Indians formed a twelve-car caravan to drive the chief across the country, ignoring warnings that transporting a corpse was illegal. They set off, Mad Bear among them, and he says, "Nobody wanted to stop us; in fact, most towns gave us a police escort to get rid of us as fast as they could." Police in an Oklahoma town met the Indians at the city limits with box lunches ready for them so they would have no excuse to stop on their way through, but they made headlines all the way across the country anyway.

In order to punish the government for denying these Washington protests, all the Indians had to do was to let the *prophecy* do its work: There were to be many gates closed to America. Mad Bear says the Iroquois little people, who up to a dozen years ago had extended their spiritual protection to U. S. leaders, withdrew it, with the result that Nixon was attacked in Venezuela, Eisenhower had to cancel a trip to Japan, and a long spate of attacks on American embassies and libraries began. This prophecy is an elusive, unwritten, changeable series of predictions and explanations of world events by myth that the Iroquois recite every ten years in a special longhouse ceremony that takes from sunrise to noon of exactly four days to complete; it is due again next summer. Some Hopi prophecies seem to agree with those of the Eastern Indians, but since they are all kept orally only, they cannot be frozen into a single version. Yet Mad Bear and the other Indians refer to "the prophecy" in the same taken-for-granted way they talk about a supply of bread and corn ordered for the summer caravan's kitchen tent. One part of it now says that the white man will soon blow himself off the face of the earth.

When Mad Bear accompanied some Florida Indians to Cuba, hoping for moral support from Fidel Castro and Che Guevara, they were grandly received in public ceremonies, but Castro later went at the Indians statistically, wanting to know the exact percentage of the U. S. population they represented. Returning rather empty-handed from Cuba, Mad Bear was threatened by Miami immigration officials with loss of citizenship for overstaying his travel permit to Cuba, but he denied that they could touch his Iroquois nationality and refused to be interrogated about his Cuba trip. Two F.B.I. agents followed him home on the plane and tried to grill him in the two-hundred-year-old log cabin, built by a French trapper, he was then living in—its chimney has since crumbled and Mad Bear has moved into a new one-car garage down the road. Mad Bear ordered the G-men off the reservation, but they claimed they could go anywhere within the continental limits of the U.S. Mad Bear showed them a treaty signed by George Washington specifying that U. S. Territory ended at the Tuscarora border, and one G-man said, "They told me you were a fanatic, and now I really believe it." Mad Bear brandished his .40-.22 combination rifle; the G-men were armed, too, but a number of other Indians, also with guns, circling the cabin outside, finally persuaded the F.B.I. to retreat, and they never came back.

The Thomas E. Dewey Thruway was another challenge. When, during the Revolution, George Washington asked the Six Nations to leave off demanding tolls of guns and blankets from his impoverished troops moving through Iroquois lands, they agreed on condition that the U.S. guarantee forever a free right-of-way for Indians along the main pathway between

Albany and Black Rock (now Buffalo). Mad Bear found out that this agreement had since been put into New York State law, so one day in 1960, when he and five other Indians were driving east to visit the Onondaga reservation, they refused to pay any toll at the Syracuse exit. They wouldn't sign a bill for unpaid toll, either, and showed a hundred-dollar bill to prove they were solvent. For two hours the toll taker put in a lot of telephone calls until finally the state attorney general sent word to the tollbooth that the Indians could pass without payment until a legal study could be made. For eight months the Indians drove free on the toll road; then the state withdrew the special status on the ground that the Thruway had not been foreseen by the original treaty makers. Mad Bear intends to try refusing the toll again one of these days.

A hint as to why Mad Bear is not always universally admired by his fellow Indians may be seen in his scheme to sabotage the annual Tuscarora dance festival that brought out thousands of admission-paying non-Indians and made certain Tuscaroras a good deal of money. To Mad Bear it was phony un-Iroquois dancing, with all kinds of flamboyant Western feathered headdresses, done by Indians hired from Ontario; there wasn't a Tuscarora in the bunch. Mad Bear telephoned the dancers to tell them it was immoral and un-Indian to take money for dancing and to pretend to be local Tuscaroras, and asked them to cancel their appearance. When he warms up to an issue of Indian tradition, Mad Bear can be persuasive, and the dancers agreed not to show up, leaving the festival with five scheduled performances and no performers—noneeof the Tuscaroras knew any dances. Mad Bear to the rescue: he had, waiting in the wings, some sixty members of the Wanka Tanka dance troupe from Buffalo—just great, except that these enthusiasts of Indian dancing are all whites. As they came onstage in the outdoor arena, Mad Bear jumped up and grabbed the microphone, shouting, "Shame on you Indians! We should all bury our heads, that we have to hire whites to dance for us!" His message got through, and soon afterward Indian parents were sending their children to lessons in traditional Tuscamora dancing that Mad Bear organized in the reservation school on Sundays, starting just as nearby church bells rang.

A certain Niagara Falls judge has also been treated to a sample of Mad Bear's wiles. After Mad Bear got a summons from a game warden for illegally catching a sturgeon (Indians claim exemption from restrictions on hunting and fishing on their own lands), before the case came up he invited the judge to a picnic. The Indians brought on the fresh sturgeon and began eating it with gusto until the judge asked for a taste. They gladly gave him a plateful and then took his picture, his mouth full of sturgeon, with a grinning Mad Bear right beside him. Then Mad Bear showed him the summons. The case was dropped. . . .

For some years, since he took part in the Council revolution, Mad Bear has had standing against him a deportation order from Canada, but he regularly ignores it. Recently, however, on a trip to Canada to get brother Iroquois to agree to the hiring of an Egyptian lawyer to represent the Indians before the United Nations, Canadian officials lowered a gate in front of his car and tried to question him. He smashed through the gate and went on his way. Returning home a few days later, U.S. border officials, generally more willing than the Canadians to admit to Indian rights of unmolested passage across the line, told him that the Canadians had asked them to stop him. "They're sore because you broke their gate," they said. Mad Bear cheerfully suggested they send him a bill for the damage, and drove on. "If I get one I'll just send it on to the Indian Bureau," he says. . . .

Other border trouble had broken out last winter on the international bridge at Cornwall, Ontario, when Canadian customs began charging duty on goods that Mohawks were taking from one part of their reservation, which is in New York State, to another part, which is in Canada. The Indians assert that this is a direct violation of the Jay Treaty; Canadians say that the treaty was between the U. S. and England and does not concern them. Indians blocked the bridge with stalled cars; forty Mohawks were arrested and dragged off. That night a bullet tore into the customs house and bounced lightly off an officer. Tension kept up through the summer; one night, Indians sneaked past an armed guard into the customs house, which is on Indian land, and turned on the water in an upstairs bathroom. The resulting flood ruined the ceilings. Thus the arrival at the bridge of a caravan of some hundred Indian cars—including Mad Bear's, being pushed—one day last August was not designed to calm the jittery nerves of Canadian police and border agents, especially when the Indians all demanded to be let over the bridge without paying the dollar toll (they were). A good number of the cars had Western license plates, and all sported bumper stickers: I SUPPORT THE NORTH AMERICAN INDIAN UNITY CARAVAN, IF UR INDIAN UR IN, WE REMEMBER THE WOUNDED KNEE MASSACRE, or CUSTER DIED FOR YOUR SINS. But there were no incidents.

Besides his skirmishes with the Canadians and with Robert Moses' surveyors, Mad Bear has been put under house arrest in Capetown after publicly advising black South Africans to burn their identity cards, and he was arrested in Taiwan for associating with "recalcitrant" aboriginals and for photographing graves of Taiwan-for-the-Taiwanese activists executed by the government. But except where a roadblock or tollgate may have to suffer, Mad Bear follows a basic philosophy of nonviolence which is central to Indian philosophy. All his protests are marked by a certain sense of wit combined with impeccable logic and an extremely stubborn, if passive, resistance. "Getting arrested is not important." Mad Bear is fascinated by any new way of advertising Indian independence; when a Passamaquoddy Indian in the caravan told how ninety members of his tribe had formed a human barrier across highway U.S. 1 in Maine in July, and charged travelers a dollar per car to pass, Mad Bear's eyes sparkled with admiration. "Hey, maybe we ought to try that." he exclaimed.

Among Mohawks especially in the East and with many young Western Indians the tenet of nonviolence has hard going; they want action. Many young Mohawks are workers in high steel, building skyscrapers and bridges all over the U.S. and Canada. They are well-paid, and proud, and they feel like using their strength on Indian grievances. In this Mad Bear showed himself as a bridge between young and old, between brash activists and stolid chiefs who like to give weeks of meditation on any question. This difference—it never came to an actual split—came up once with the pretty twenty-six-year-old Indian-rights campaigner Kahn-Tineta Horn, a Mohawk known for her fiery speeches in colleges from coast to coast. Facing trial on a concealed-weapons charge in the bridge blockade, she demanded help from the chiefs, who, she said, had let her down. "I'm all alone! I don't want to go to jail!" she said loudly. Mad Bear assured her that she was not alone, and then Seneca Chief Beeman Logan told her rather severely, "A chief does not give a reply in fifteen minutes!" It transpired that the girl had spurned the legal counsel hired by the other Indians and had gone off on her own, but with great tact Mad Bear brought the two sides (the girl and her brother Taio Tekane Horn, another activist, both feeling a bit abandoned and unloved by their elders; and the chiefs, feeling they were being pushed too fast by loud, ungrateful youngsters) slowly together. The young brother and sister agreed to meet with the chiefs before the trial and to accept their advice; in return, the chiefs promised to provide plenty of moral support in person at the trial. (Fifty Indians did show up in the Cornwall Court, ready to carry Kahn-Tineta off by force, at her trial a week later, but she was acquitted.)

The differing approaches were apparent, too, in a debate on the wording of a statement to government leaders, including Prime Minister Trudeau (Smart Snake). Protesting unemployment, loss of children to religious schools, alcoholism as a result of Indian disgust with white society, and police brutality, the suggested wording was that unless conditions changed the Indians "feared a violent reaction against law-enforcement agents." Strong protests against the word "violent" came—this was not the Indian way. Then a stocky young woman in a buckskin dress, an Ojibway from Upper Slave Lake in Alberta named Rose Ojek, cried out in an emotional burst, "The violence is here already! Changing the word won't stop it. There are young Indians in Alberta who are going to burn the schools and the churches. They're not criminals in their hearts, but one of them says he's going to get a huge Caterpillar tractor and go to High Prairie and bulldoze the liquor store, pretend he's drunk. The police arrest them when they get drunk; a girl was arrested for that, and when her brother tried to touch her hand, that she was reaching out of the police car, they arrested him, too, and he got *six months*! I can't stand it when I hear of talking peace!" The Indians crowded along the benches in the Council House muttered the approving, "Huh!" And again Mad Bear brought about the amazing Indian unanimity that followed every disagreement: this time, he said, Indians must not be too timid to use a word; it was not a threat of violence, but only a warning, and anyway, "It's only a word in the white man's language—what are you worried about?"

As chairman, Mad Bear also led stormy sessions on the question of letting government-employed Indians into the Council House. So that the Indians could express themselves freely, all non-Indians, with the exception of a magazine writer, had already been excluded from most of the meetings. When an Indian couple known to be employed by the Canadian government showed up and asked to be admitted, the local chief—this happened on the Maniwaki Reserve, north of Ottawa—refused them, and sent them away. But at the meeting he was having second thoughts. Shouldn't *any* Indian be received here as a brother? This was a *unity* convention. "No!" shouted Taio Tekane Horn. Glaring, he clenched his teeth angrily. "They're spies, traitors, and they deserve to be put to death." But the others wanted unity. The peaceful atmosphere they had built here could only be a help to Indians who had strayed from the path. Mad Bear thought that mixing with the traditional-minded Indians would be good for the soul of any lost brother, and thus it was decided that the convention should welcome any Indian who might like to come in. The Indians also decided to impeach Secretary of the Interior Walter Hickel for "his high-handed, inconsiderate and illegal theft of native Alaskan, Eskimo and Indian tribal lands," and to denounce the South Dakota death sentence upon a twenty-one-year-old Rosebud Sioux named Thomas White Hawk. They want to issue identity cards to all North American Indians who want one, as soon as a properly "Indian-looking" design can be made, so as to take the business of saying who is and who is not an Indian away from white men's governments. As a further token of unity, tribal delegates would in the future go from various areas to join in local demonstrations involving Indians. And the unity caravan will ride again: next year to Oklahoma and Alberta.

After a dinner of traditional corn soup and roast beaver with beans baked in sand, the Indians straggle off toward a blazing campfire, where soon the dancing begins to last all night—the stomp dance, the rabbit dance, the welcome dance, the duck dance. A trio of tireless young Mohawks pounds on drums and sings a hoarse, sharp, and haunting accompaniment from out of a lost and distant time. In the shadows along the edge of the field, where cars and tents line the way, Mad Bear sits talking to friends. Shadows from the horns of his headdress bob in the firelight against a canvas wall as he relates some of the prophecy; the white man's money will soon be worthless; his society is crumbling. "We don't want to be a part of it," he says. "We don't want to have to hate the black man." But the Indians don't want the help of black activists, either—"We have our own power," says Mad Bear. The roguish delight he'd shown in recounting his many forays against the enemies of traditional Indians now becomes subdued as he speaks of the perishable Indian identity, the Indians' most precious possession, that still survives amid the blithe ignorance of the white man, who assumes the Indian must want to become white too. The Indians' hardest job is to fight the indifference all around him, the idea that he is cute and amusing, his story a fit subject only for children, or worse, the belief that he does not exist at all. Boxed in by white men's religion no less based on articles of faith than are the longhouse legends, he sees his myths and spirits derided. But the longhouse faith is growing fast; where only a dozen Indians showed up for a ceremony five years ago, now all the benches are full. They're leaving the white society's edges. . . .